The Class

CONNECTED YOUTH AND DIGITAL FUTURES

This series explores young people's day-to-day lives and futures. The volumes consider changes at the intersection of civil and political reform, transformations in employment and education, and the growing presence of digital technologies in all aspects of social, cultural, and political life. The John D. and Catherine T. MacArthur Foundation's Digital Media and Learning (DML) Initiative has supported two research networks that have helped launch this series: the Youth and Participatory Politics Research Network and the Connected Learning Research Network. The DML Initiative and the DML Hub at the University of California, Irvine, also support production and open access for this series.

connectedyouth.nyupress.org

By Any Media Necessary: The New Youth Activism
Henry Jenkins, Sangita Shresthova, Liana Gamber-Thompson,
Neta Kligler-Vilenchik, and Arely Zimmerman

The Class: Living and Learning in the Digital Age
Sonia Livingstone and Julian Sefton-Green

The Class

Living and Learning in the Digital Age

Sonia Livingstone and Julian Sefton-Green

NEW YORK UNIVERSITY PRESS

New York

NEW YORK UNIVERSITY PRESS
New York
www.nyupress.org

References to internet websites (URLs) were accurate at the time of writing. Neither the author nor New York University Press is responsible for URLs that may have expired or changed since the manuscript was prepared.

ISBN: 978-1-4798-8457-5 (hardback)
ISBN: 978-1-4798-2424-3 (paperback)

For Library of Congress Cataloging-in-Publication data, please contact the Library of Congress.

New York University Press books are printed on acid-free paper, and their binding materials are chosen for strength and durability. We strive to use environmentally responsible suppliers and materials to the greatest extent possible in publishing our books.

Manufactured in the United States of America

10 9 8 7 6 5 4 3 2 1

Also available as an ebook

Contents

Figures and Tables

Acknowledgments

We first acknowledge the generosity and openness of the class of 13-year-olds and their families who let us into their lives during 2011–2012; this book may not make them famous, but we hope they like it should they choose to read it. We also warmly thank the school and the teachers who accommodated our research so helpfully, despite not knowing what we might say about them. We wish we could thank them by name, but we cannot as the school and the class could then be identified.

We also want to thank the many colleagues who have read drafts, debated ideas, and had their brains picked over the past few years. These include Hans-Christian Arnseth, Shakuntala Banaji, Alicia Blum-Ross, Georgina Born, David Buckingham, Lynn Schofield Clark, John Coleman, Ola Erstad, Pete Fraser, Oystein Gilje, Jenny Grahame, Glynda Hull, Henry Jenkins, Ken Jones, Koen Leurs, Andres Lombana-Bermudez, Danny Miller, Helen Nixon, Ricarose Roque, Stuart Poyntz, Jennifer Rowsell, Michael Simmons, Joseph Tobin, and many others—including the anonymous reviewers for New York University Press.

The project was conceived and nurtured as part of the Connected Learning Research Network, led by Mizuko Ito; we have benefited greatly from collaborating with Dalton Conley, Kris Gutiérrez, Heather Horst, Ben Kirschner, Mizuko Ito, Vera Michalchik, Bill Penuel, Kylie Peppler, Jean Rhodes, Katie Salen, Juliet Schor, S. Craig Watkins, and Amanda Wortman and with Connie Yowell from the MacArthur Foundation.

As we conducted the fieldwork, we made many calls—variously interesting or tedious—on our able research assistants Adnan Muhammad, Svenja Ottovordemgentschenfelde, Yinhan Wang, and Rafal Zaborowski; we thank them too, as well as Dawn Rushden, who edited the final manuscript for us.

Sonia was fortunate to spend several months with the Social Media Collective at Microsoft's New England Research and Development Center, where she discussed *The Class* with Nancy Baym, Kate Crawford, danah boyd, Megan Finn, Mary Gray, Jessa Lingel, and Kate Miltner. She was, at the same time, a faculty associate at the Berkman Center for Internet and Society, thanks to an invitation from Urs Gasser. There she joined the book-writing group with Judith Donath, Rey Junco, Doc Searls, and Sara Watson and benefited from conversations with these and many others at the center. She is also grateful to the Department of Media and Communications at LSE for both accommodating her fieldwork commitments and then allowing her extended absence while writing this book. The book group she formed on her return from Cambridge stimulated the rethinking and rewriting that got the book finished: warm thanks to Bart Cammaerts, Lilie Chouliaraki, Ellen Helsper, Peter Lunt, and Shani Orgad.

Julian would like to thank friends and colleagues who invited presentations and seminars on aspects of the work as it unfolded—many embryonic ideas from those sessions have now found their way into this book. Especial thanks to Imanol Aguirre, Jim Albright, Sara Bragg, Barbara Comber, Anna Craft, Michael Dezuanni, Keri Facer, Samuel Leong, Meaghan Morris, Greg Noble, Megan Watkins, Rupert Wegerif, and their colleagues and students. Thanks also to Jen Teitle, who edited a special issue of the *Bankstreet Occasional Papers*, where some early ideas from several chapters were published.

We have written this book with an eye to the interests and concerns of parents, teachers, and others responsible for young people's learning and welfare. We have tried to make it readable; but it is also an academic text, and so we have tried to find a style that can address a range of audiences. We want this book to provide an informed basis for policy and hope that its analysis can help teachers, parents, and others to navigate the difficult challenges of what it means to grow up today.

This book has taken up a good four years of our lives. Among other things, we have learned a good deal from working with each other. This book is a genuine and equal collaboration; we have shared and pored over every phrase and note, resulting in almost countless iterations of every chapter. Collaboration often requires some adjustment, and we both feel that each other's skill, expertise, and knowledge has extended and challenged the other and that this book has taken us to a point we could not have reached separately.

Nevertheless, writing is largely a solitary activity, and we both have more personal thanks. Sonia is hugely grateful to her family, who endlessly discussed the project as it unfolded, read more drafts than they could have ever wished, and put up with her absence while she stared at her computer for months on end: Harry Hutchinson, Anna Livingstone, Angela Livingstone, Joe Livingstone, Rodney Livingstone, and especially, Peter Lunt. Julian no doubt bored Alison and Sam Vydulinska even more than usual but appreciated Sam's lovingly sarcastic "how was school today?" during the daily grind and still believes that this book can offer some answer to the fatalistic critique—"it's school, what do you expect?"

* * *

Formally, we note that this book is based on a research project supported by the John D. & Catherine T. MacArthur Foundation under Prime Award no. 10-97572-000-USP and the Regents of the University of California. Any opinions, findings, and conclusions or recommendations expressed in this publication are those of the authors and do not necessarily reflect the views of the John D. & Catherine T. MacArthur Foundation or the Regents of the University of California.

Introduction

An Invitation to Meet the Class

We first met the class at the end of a sunny afternoon in July in the quiet of a London suburb. We found ourselves addressing a blur of teenage faces turned expectantly toward us. We explained that we wanted to find out how they lived their lives at school, at home, and online, about their friendships and their learning. We quickly got a conversation going. Who, we asked, used Facebook, and who had a mobile phone? Most hands shot up, although Toby made a point of saying no to Facebook. Some faces were animated, some were blank, and the students began nudging and whispering to each other, as curious about us as we were about them.

All seemed willing to participate, and we were relieved, one crucial hurdle passed. For although Catherine, their class teacher, was enthusiastic about our project, the headteacher (school principal) had been particularly skeptical, and we had no idea yet what the parents would say. Most important, we had yet to gain the class's trust, and we could not know in advance how the project would unfold.

On that day, all the young people looked alike in their school uniform, and although we had interrupted their lives in full flow, we had no idea of their histories of friendship or hostility, achievement or struggle. Gradually, they became better known to us over the year we spent with them, so that now it is difficult for us to return to that first meeting, knowing the young people as well as we do now. But then, as we met those 28 young people for the first time, we naturally searched for ways to identify them. The most obvious was gender, although typically for a London classroom, the ethnic and racial diversity also caught our eyes (see the appendix). The boys and girls sat in same-sex pairs with boys outnumbering girls almost two to one. It was obvious that some pairs were closer to each other than others.

Among the girls, Megan and Adriana muttered to each other at the back of the room as we were being introduced to the class; both were discreetly made up, with earrings and nail varnish. One girl, Lydia, sat by herself and seemed withdrawn from the others. She was pushing at the boundaries of the school-uniform regulations with visible makeup and socks pulled high over her knees—something the teacher had already commented on. Sara and Giselle appeared good friends—sitting under the teacher's nose and exuding confidence. Another ethnically diverse pair of girls, Alice and Jenna, did not seem at all close to each other, but we later discovered they were great friends, unlike as it turned out Sara and Giselle. Dilruba and Salma sat amicably together, while Abby—a larger young woman than her peers—seemed rather dazed.

Two boys stood out for us instantly because of the way they were marked by the adults. Aiden, a small, quiet, dark-skinned boy, had a classroom assistant with him, having had trouble at his previous school. Toby had somewhat wild hair and turned out to be registered with special educational needs; although he answered our questions directly and politely, he did not seem to integrate or talk with other members of the class. Three boys sought to engage with us one to one. Sergei, taller and more physically mature than his peers, spoke to us in a likable and engaged, if rather formal, way. Sedat caught our eye quickly and wanted to ask us lots of questions. He constantly put his hand up to seek reassurance about the simplest of tasks, and already we could see how he tended to annoy those around him. Nick, a polite and light-skinned mixed-race boy whose grandmother had replied very positively to our initial letter about the project, seemed popular with everyone.

The rest of the boys were a bit of a blur. Many were quiet, shy, and clearly nervous about meeting us. Yusuf, a giant of a child, sat with Hakim. Both boys flushed when spoken to and muttered back to us in monosyllabic replies. The same was true of Mark and Joel, both of whom seemed quiet and serious. Two of the boys, Dominic and Sebastian, had fashionably spiky hair, were well turned out, and spoke with middle-class accents. They were chatting with Jamie, a Chinese-looking taller boy, who was always talking with his peers but reserved with us. Large and self-conscious, Shane grinned rather vacantly at us. He sat next to Fessehaye (Fesse), a dark-skinned and lively character who seemed a bit dazed as he replied to us and who was the butt of jokes from several teachers; he appeared to have a bit of a reputation—we were not sure for what—but it all felt very friendly. A small, very self-composed boy, Max, seemed not to have any close friends. A fringe fell over his eyes, but his eyes followed us; and he was evidently very curious about us, replying to questions precisely, in middle-class tones. Adam, tousled haired and sleepy looking, seemed to typify those adolescent boys who do not want to get out of bed; and Gideon was quiet and focused.

We return to these characters often as our book unfolds. We realize that it is difficult for readers to recall each of them from these quick sketches, just as it was for us at the start. There is a list with everybody named in the appendix. We realize, too, that our sketches are full of personal, often superficial assumptions about social class, ethnicity, and all the other cultural indicators that we as "natives" pick up on, just as teachers do when faced with a new class. But this is part of the point: our book unpacks the first impressions on which much of social life is based, to reveal the deeper patterns, influences, and relationships.

This knowledge is the researchers' privilege. After all, teachers know little of the students out of at school, and some do not know them well in school either; so first impressions, even stereotypes, may have lasting effects. Then, a child known so well to his or her parents can appear very different at school, and it became important to our research method to note the different personae that the young people projected, or were known by, in different settings. By mapping continuities and disjunctures in our experiences of the class across settings, we hoped to grasp the connections and disconnections that mattered to them and those around them. How are their lives shaped by themselves and others? What opportunities and constraints do they face, growing up in these early years of the 21st century?

What This Book Is About

This book is about a class of 13- to 14-year-olds at an ordinary urban secondary school in London, England, over the school year 2011–2012.[1] It is a tricky age, difficult for parents and teachers and for the young people themselves. What do young people want, how do they see the world, and how do they find a path through the opportunities and constraints they face? Much depends on them, but it also matters how they are supported or undermined; and this, in turn, depends on a society that is itself changing, often questioning what it can or should offer young people. Increasing social inequality, along with historical processes of globalization and individualization, give rise to considerable uncertainties about the future, and frequently the media report crises of confidence in the family, contested visions of educational goals, and a host of anxieties about norms and values. To throw some light on the many competing claims about youth today, this book asks, What matters to them? How do they approach life at home and school? Is it really a matter of "all change" in the so-called digital age? What vision of the future do they think their parents and teachers are preparing them for?

After outlining our project to people, it becomes apparent that the very notion of "the class" has a curious fascination, implying a seemingly closed, intense, yet fragile world.[2] Fueling this fascination are the plentiful fictional portraits of school life in our culture. Perhaps their appeal is that they invite us to remember—or reimagine—the intensely felt, bounded world of childhood. Indeed, part of our contention is that much of children's lives are relatively inaccessible to the adults around them—their teachers know little of their home lives; their parents know little of their life at school. We wanted to understand the ways in which young people build their own meaningful worlds, how these intersect with those of others, and how they imagine their future.

The study of one class provided a useful means of doing this, and we should take a moment to explain the notion of "a class" in relation to the British school system. As is common, although not universal, the class we studied was one of eight in a year group of 250 at a large secondary school of some 1,500 11- to 18-year-olds. We use the term "year" where the US would use the term "grade" to describe a level and year of schooling. Having arrived at the school aged 11 and been assigned to "their" class,[3] the students had spent the first year often together in their lessons, being divided by aptitude for a few subjects. Now in Year 9 (or Grade 8 as it would be in the US), they were divided for all of their subject lessons depending on aptitude or simply to mix them with others in the year group. But a key continuity with previous years was that every day began and ended with "tutor time," 15 minutes in which they assembled in "their" classroom with Catherine to prepare for or review the day as "a class."[4]

In exploring the lives of these young people within and beyond the bounds of the class and the school, this book offers a rich portrait of the young people's everyday lives. Most simply, we wanted to get beyond the many fearful claims circulating among adults about today's youth—that they are so immersed in the online world that they cannot concentrate on learning, that they neglect family life, that they disrespect their parents and teachers, even that they no longer establish their own values or sustain a sense of privacy. These claims—often crystallized in adult dismay over young people's enthusiastic use of digital technologies—matter because they make parents worried about their children and teachers critical of their students, leading them to restrict opportunities that could otherwise be fruitful for the young people.

We include "in the digital age" in the subtitle of our book not because we believe the world has been radically transformed by the advent of ubiquitous digital networks[5] but to address the prominent public and policy discussions linking digital media and young people. "The digital" focuses public attention on the complex changes of late modernity opening up opportunities and stimulating critique and debate about what it mean to be young and to grow up. Some of the ways in which digitally networked, convergent technologies have entered people's ordinary lives may facilitate socially progressive change—supporting youth participation and creative and learning opportunities and providing resources designed for disadvantaged groups. At the same time, there is reason to fear that those same technologies are, with perhaps greater force, being actively reinvented by powerful elites to ensure that political and commercial logics dominate. However, in drawing attention to technologies in this way, we emphasize that they gain their meaning through particular practices and contexts of design and use.[6]

But it is not just digital technologies that make for change between the present and previous generations—many other changes have shaped the possibilities for and influences on young people in recent decades, and these changes have been more thoroughly researched and theorized, as we discuss in chapter 1. The school was situated in a London suburb, and as we shall show, living on the edges of a multicultural world city shaped the young people's experiences too. So while their lives were often intensely local, we wanted to understand how such experiences might make sense within a framework of grand claims about the increasingly globalized, individualized, and consumerist society in the counties of the global North. In such analyses, people have become detached from their traditional roots in social class, ethnicity, or neighborhood. While this potentially frees them to construct their own identities, make their own choices, and forge their own direction in life, a growing body of research shows that this is far from liberating. Increasingly, individuals must bear the risks of managing their lives under conditions of reduced support or security and increasing complexity and uncertainty. As educational and economic opportunities, jobs for life, supportive communities, welfare consensus, and trust in institutions are all in one way or another undermined, the prospects for young people seem bleak.

Some people respond to these pressures by adopting a stance of *competitive individualism*, on the grounds that if life is becoming more uncertain and safety nets are withdrawn, it is better to try as hard as possible to win these diminishing rewards. Education represents a prime resource in this competition, as do the diverse and unequal economic and cultural resources provided by families and communities. Such a response is associated with our current phase of neoliberal capitalism,[7] and critics argue that such behaviors are precisely the response that the state desires.

Yet our research with the class leads us to identify a further stance enacted by some of their families. We call it *conservatism* with a small *c*, to distinguish it from any political party. This is the view that the seemingly inexorable process of change can be slowed or stalled by bolstering the authority of established institutions such as family, school, community, and church and endorsing their traditional values. This stance draws on a language of fairness and civility, as we shall show; yet the outcomes can be far from fair.

Neither of these two stances dispels any pessimism toward the future—hence our interest in a third, more progressive stance, based on the capabilities and potentialities of network *connections*, especially those that aim to foster new and collaborative forms of community, creativity, and civic participation. "Connection"—a buzzword heavily cited in government statements, advertisements, and public policy rhetoric—currently has a particular appeal. In this discourse, connection is good, and disconnection is bad. Schools reach out to parents, education policy embeds schools in their locale, youth workers link up community sites, and parents join groups to support their children's play, sports, and after-school clubs. Many public and private hopes center on the possibility that digital networked technologies in particular can engender positive connections for the benefit of youth and society.

Yet here, too, research into how young people actually live their lives can help tease out the rhetoric surrounding such hopes. While some observers hold that digital networks render life more superficial, fast paced, and inattentive, others worry that commercial (rather than public) interests are increasingly driving living and learning in the digital age.[8] It is society's embrace of digital networks that extends the power of commerce into once-public processes of learning, knowledge production, and civic participation.

These commercially owned networks are becoming ever more important in once-private processes of identity, personal relationships, and pleasure as well as being implicated in state surveillance, and this is why, in this book, we pay attention to the concept of identity. Identity, it is argued, has taken on a different kind of burden under the stress of individualization. This could be said for everyone living in the relatively affluent, multicultural, highly modernized countries of the global North. But exploration of different aspects of identity and their intersections is particularly absorbing for young teenagers. We worked with the class for over a year and came to conceptualize their identities as simultaneously situated and relational. By saying that identities are situated, we mean that they are not just expressed in but also constituted through what happens in particular places—usually home, school, and community. For young people, these are all contexts heavily shaped by parents, teachers, and the wider structures of society. But as we shall see, young people are keen to seek out "in between" places, whether visible or hidden, sanctioned or transgressive, to retain a measure of autonomy—for example, by taking their time over the walk home from school, hanging out on Facebook, or putting a "no entry" sign on their bedroom door. By saying that identities are relational, we mean that young people's identities are developed and performed through social interaction—especially with family, teachers, and peers. People figure out who they are through their relationships with others—and these relationships may be demanding or complacent, constructive or problematic.

Many aspects of identity are at play in this book—family identity, learner identity, peer identity, cultural and ethnic identities, urban identity as Londoners, digital identity—all these must be contextualized within the different spheres and relationships that make up young people's lives. In late modernity, scholars have talked of "the project of the self" or of "self-making," which helped us focus on how teenagers, as much if not more than everyone else, are reflexive about this process.[9] Significantly, for young people in the early 21st century, never have so many visions been offered—of who they could be, what they could achieve, what they might want. Thirteen- to 14-year-olds are situated between dependence and independence, their ambiguous and often difficult social positioning being particularly interesting. Indeed, this in itself gives us some difficulty in referring to them in this book, since they no longer wish to be called children; "adolescents" seemed to us too clinical; "teenagers" or "kids" seemed too patronizing; thus we settled for the neutral term "young people." Of course, to their parents they are still children, and to their teachers they are students.

Our Approach

Since our study is of a school class, we began our investigation with the school, an institution that plays a defining role in young people's lives. We soon realized that how they made sense of their classroom experiences and school life was largely unaffected by the fierce discursive struggle going on above their heads among governments, pedagogues, technologists, and pundits seeking to redefine the purposes and practices of education in the digital, networked age. But school had, nonetheless, been reshaped by these struggles in ways that mattered for the students, making their school experience in some ways continuous with that of their parents but in other ways very different.

As we go on to consider, home and family occupies another important part of the picture, and here, too, there are lively public debates about transformations in childhood. These were evident in the teachers' speculations about students' home lives—since they rarely gained the direct insight into the home that we were able to. Debates about childhood and family life were also visible in the parents' anxieties (more so than in their children's accounts)—often surfacing in their fraught reflections on managing the influx of digital devices into the home. For young people, the peer group is the third and crucial element. In some ways, this was the hardest for us to observe directly; yet it was the sphere of life that the young people were most keen to tell us about as they got to know us. Here we try to capture the range of their relationships, from personal friendships through to the largely civil relations among members of the class, their wide and diverse digital social networks, and, for many in the class, family connections with their country of origin as well as connections within various diasporas. Each of these spheres—or increasingly, networks—of school, home, and peer groups is now substantially mediated by mobile and online technologies; yet as we found, the forms taken by these mediating processes were sometimes surprising, working both to connect and to disconnect in complex ways.

Around these three intersecting spheres, we can draw the wider circle of community and culture, shaped by urban, regional, and ethnic influences and crosscut by social class. Beyond this is the wider society, a world that the young people know partly through the news, film, television, and social media and partly through living cheek by jowl with others from all walks of life. To grasp as much of this as we could, we observed the class, both as individuals and as a group, interact during and around lessons, and we visited their homes and families, joined in some out-of-school activities, and peeked into their digital worlds. The first impressions with which we opened this chapter set up a host of possibilities to be explored as the research progressed. For instance, we could see instantly that the class was diverse in terms of ethnicity, but we did not yet know what the markers of either ethnicity or, indeed, social class (beyond how we picked up spoken accents) might mean for the individuals, the school, or the families we were to meet later on. We could also see straight away that some young people were seen as a source of trouble, like Lydia and perhaps Sedat; some young people had a reputation for being a joker, like Fesse, although most appeared to be good, compliant students, notably, Sara, Giselle, Dom, and Sebastian. Differentiating the rest was difficult, and working out what kind of identity they possessed for themselves, for their peers, parents, and teachers occupied us for some time.

As explained in chapter 1, we grounded our analysis in the detailed descriptions of the texture of the experiences and the various economic, social, and cultural resources that members of the class could draw on—the houses they lived in, the bedrooms they had to themselves or had to share, or the kinds of technology bought for them by their parents.

We also listened to the many expectations, hopes, and anxieties that intertwined and held them and those around them, shaping their trajectories. These details seemed to ground the young people's experiences of living and learning in the digital age, while also challenging some of our readings of the data we collected. We therefore went back and forth between data and interpretation and between fieldwork and writing. Yet we have tried to keep our analytic narrative fairly light and accessible, presenting the fieldwork in ways that provoke and unsettle the customary discourses around education and family and sometimes inviting multiple readings precisely because what it means to live and learn in the digital age can be thought about from so many perspectives.[10] We imagine that some readers of this book might be interested in the stories from the class from different perspectives: as students, teachers, parents, policy makers, or, of course, fellow scholars.[11]

We have enjoyed the challenge of conveying the range of perspectives, the variety of personal histories, and the diversity of social experiences that we witnessed.[12] By following the young people at school, into their homes, and around their neighborhood, we have prioritized the links and contrasts among the different social worlds that this group of young people inhabited and yet shared with each other. We were especially stimulated to do this since few studies based in schools include any mention of children's lives at home. Equally, most studies of life at home rarely follow children outside it, tending toward a portrayal of the home as a rather closed world. We could continue: research on informal learning settings is often poorly related to research on learning in school; and research on engagement with digital networks tends to focus on online interactions only, struggling to show how online and offline interactions are linked. There are, of course, significant exceptions, and several of these inspired us, as we discuss during the chapters that follow. But the task of pursuing the actual and potential connections and disconnections across places in young people's lives—where they themselves were often the link—became both a major challenge and a major theme of this book.

To bring the views of these young people alive, we invite you to engage with the class as you might with characters in a novel. Unfortunately, however, we are not fiction writers: we are not going to make up dialogue, we cannot offer you an omniscient narrator's point of view to tell you what everyone is really thinking, and doubtless our writing style lacks elegance. But we prefer not to follow the sociological convention whereby research subjects are categorized primarily in demographic terms—their gender or ethnicity, for example, although these and, especially, social class emerge as important themes at various points. Instead, we borrow from the literary tradition that introduces the dramatis personae through their roles in the action (and you can find details about all of them in the appendix). We have also tried to learn from the tradition of ethnographic writing[13] so as to depict young people's experiences of living and learning in the digital age in cities in the global North a decade or so into the 21st century.[14]

Overview of the Book

This book aims to answer abstract historical and sociological questions with the everyday experiences of our class. Our premise is that the young people's experiences simultaneously ground and yet are illuminated by wider debates about how young people themselves interpret and negotiate their pathways across the times and places that shape their lives. It does so at a particularly interesting point in late modernity, in which the contrary forces of socio-technological innovation and the reproduction of traditional structures (the school, the family, social class) threaten to pull young people in different directions.

Chapter 1 frames our inquiry in terms of theory. Curiously, our central concepts of connection and disconnection—which we see used everywhere in academic, policy, commercial, and public discourses—have been remarkably little theorized. Their value connotations are clear enough and rarely challenged, but why is it good to connect, whether the connections link people, places, or ideas? Our starting point is that meaning itself is generated through connection. Identities are relationally constituted. Learning extends across sites and experiences. Today, more than ever before, the networks of connection that enmesh us seem both unlimited and increasingly flexible. Yet, arguably, the claims of the network society—underpinned by digital transformations, open to both emancipation and exploitation—are overstated: identities are not infinitely flexible, institutions impose boundaries, privilege reproduces itself, and cultures are rooted in tradition even as they open up to new routes and flows. To interrogate and critique the significance of connection and disconnection for today's youth, chapter 1 builds a framework for understanding both the shifting interrelations among identity, knowledge, and power in a digitally networked age and the forces of social reproduction that sustain continuities with previous times. As we discuss, we find the analysis of individualization and the risk society helpful in capturing the dilemmas and tensions that young people experience and that adult society projects on them and structures for them. However, we acknowledge the critiques of these theories, especially insofar as they appear to overstate individual agency, undervalue historical continuities, or celebrate the emancipatory potential of late modernity even as, simultaneously, they foretell a gloomy vision of our future.

Chapter 2 explains our research process. At the outset, we envisaged young people's lives in terms of a Venn diagram, with three more or less interconnected circles, representing school, home, and peers. To understand just how these circles within circles work in the lives of 21st-century children, we mapped these three domains onto the three terms of the school year, resulting in a sequential research design that occupied us from the summer before the fieldwork year until the autumn term following it. Thus, we began in the classroom, then followed the students home, and lastly explored their connections with friends and peers, extended family, or other activities in a range of places both online and offline. In each place, we were as much interested in the intersections—for example, how home was talked about in school—as we were in the places themselves. Primarily, our method sought to recognize young people's agency and voice, although the strong influences and constraints they faced demanded that we also attend to the views of their parents and teachers as well as of the wider society, not least because these also found their expression in what the young people said to us. Thus, we began to think more of education and family as the two dominant institutions within and sometimes against which young people negotiated their present and future possibilities. On this view, friendships—pursued online and face-to-face, including in the in-between places in and around their home and locale[15]—allowed for the exploration and enjoyment of alternative modes of connection and disconnection. We bring the main steps of our research methods to life by reflecting on a typical "day in the life" and "year in the life" of the class, leaving the methodological details to the appendix. This allows us to introduce the important themes in the young people's lives and, therefore, for the empirical chapters that follow.

We begin, however, with a social network analysis of the class, using this as a heuristic to unpack the reconfiguration of young people's social, learning, and online networks in the digitally networked age. Social network analysis is currently popular for offering insights into the "big data" produced by social network activity or other large-scale records of interactions and transactions. But here we draw on the long tradition of sociological inquiry into small and relatively bounded networks such as our class. People create and re-create patterns of sociality—of inclusion and exclusion, connection and disconnection—through their everyday routines of meeting and greeting, giving and receiving. The network is, therefore, a way of grasping how the ordinary practices of daily life shape more or less durable structures, structures that in turn pose both opportunities and constraints to daily life. Chapter 3 constructs a "whole-class network," finding that through the young people's own practices of mutual connection or disconnection they have sorted themselves into some relatively stable groupings that fit their personalities and interests, on the one hand, and yet are strongly differentiated in terms of gender, ethnicity, and socioeconomic status, on the other. But when we explore each class member's "ego network," his or her position within the class turns out to be significant only for some and superficial for many. More important, it turns out, are structures of friendship and family.

While young people's experiences of life at home or school are greatly influenced by parents and teachers, they have rather more control over their friendships. It is thus no surprise that teenagers experiment with different aspects of their identity, trying out possible selves and finding ways to build relationships under the radar of the adult gaze, the subject of chapter 4. Although such activities give rise to considerable public anxiety about young people's values and practices, especially in relation to digital networking, we found the young people to be rather cautious and sensible in building their friendships. They prioritized face-to-face communication as a still manageable and private means of connecting with others, and despite having many contacts on social networking sites, those whom they called "friends" comprised a handful of people well known to them and trusted by them. This is not to say that digital communication played no role in their lives—far from it. But rather than a simple online/offline boundary, the young people were exploring ways of relating to others in different social situations, each of which spanned the online and offline in particular ways, depending both on the nature of particular online platforms and on the interests or motivations of the young people.

Since the sites or places of young people's experiences have far from been overtaken by the flows of their experiences within networks, in chapter 5 we examine the texture of experience in the contemporary classroom, a place where children and young people spend many long hours and yet that few parents see. Classrooms vary, of course, although the dimensions of difference can be articulated. At Victoria Forest School (henceforth VFS), located in the cosmopolitan suburbs of London, a typical class encompassed wide variation in socioeconomic status and ethnicity and, therefore, in parental aspirations and resources as well as cultural values and traditions. Our fieldwork revealed an overriding concern for maintaining social order—to enable both effective learning of the curriculum and also, more subtly, learning what has been called "the hidden curriculum." We analyze this in terms of the demands of civility—how students are required to fit in and get along with each other, at least superficially, although as we also show, these normative demands are nowadays far from "hidden." Is this a matter of democratic, even cosmopolitan, ideals of an open and tolerant community? Or is it a way of ensuring conformity to white middle-class norms among a diverse population? Mass media were used by teachers—and tolerated by students—for offering a shared worldview, a set of popular culture resources and reference points that supports rather than disrupts the norms of civility that are considered paramount for sustaining a broadly positive, if undemanding, school experience. The chapter also examines how peer-to-peer relationships are valued by young people within the more authoritarian constraints of the school and how these were used in negotiating more authentic ways of being in school.

In chapter 6, we take a close look at something that surprised us. The classroom in VFS in 2011–2012, as in many other UK schools, was heavily framed by the measurement system implemented in support of the government-mandated national curriculum. The result was a discursive and practical focus on "levels"—with learning managed through a rigorous regime of quantification and standardization that extended across all subjects, even including out-of-school activities. As with the emphasis on civility, the focus on levels also served to bound the classroom as an inwardly focused space that impeded flexible flows of learning across home, school, and elsewhere, distancing parents and constraining teachers. Beyond the surprise of uncovering so endemic a language of learning, what surprised us even more was that the students, parents, and teachers all preferred to embrace levels rather than risk more diverse, creative, or networked visions of learning.

One of the most striking experiences for us was going home with the young people we had only met at school, the subject of chapter 7. Having formed our accounts of their learning and social identities in one setting, we had to revise our views of many of them when we saw them again at home—with their family, by themselves in their bedrooms, when they went online. As already foreshadowed by the network analysis, home and family was in many ways a more fundamental source of values and sustenance, but it was also a place of emotion. The media—both mass and networked—were heavily implicated in the domestic setting of values, emotions, and identities. Families sought to overcome the perceived threat the media posed to family boundaries by seeking, instead, to use the media as a source of shared understanding, a convivial experience of family solidarity that served further, however, to distance home from school. The array of disconnects that we uncovered between home and school—both chosen and inadvertent—was itself problematic for some young people, and yet these were sufficiently commonplace for us to begin also to wonder about those for whom home and school offered consistent and compatible experiences.

The next two chapters, 8 and 9, examine the opportunities for learning outside school that were made available, pursued, and rejected by members of the class. Here we particularly focus on the ways that families from different kinds of social backgrounds—traditional middle-class, more bohemian, and highly educated families, along with desperately aspirational parents, especially those who had experienced some of the tragedies of enforced migration, as well as those who live their lives embedded in community practices far away from the classrooms of London—provided for, encouraged, and defined learning for their offspring. In chapter 8, we pay particular attention to forms of cultural capital, which is the kind of knowledge and expectations that stem from parental education and, of course, wealth. We describe how different homes construct opportunities for learning physically (how they arrange rooms and resources, especially technology), socially (how they establish habits and rhythms), and conceptually (how they see the purpose and nature of learning). The chapter concludes by setting these descriptions in the context of lively debates about whether and how digital media can be expected to overcome the more fundamental challenges faced by education in the risk society and by problematizing what connections between home and school mean in practice.

Chapter 9 examines more closely how social capital is created and enacted, by exploring six examples of music making out of school. Examining informal music making allowed us to see how ways of learning that are developed in school may or may not be carried across into cultural activities outside school, demonstrating both connections and disconnections in discipline and habit. While two of our young people, Megan and Adriana, became fed up with being made to do music by their parents, we sat in with Max as he pursued classical piano, and we contrast this with the more progressive pedagogy of Giselle's music making across keyboard, vocals, guitar, and technology, paying particular attention to the ways that these two informal "classrooms" differ from or show continuity with the teacher-student relationships and attitudes toward school-based learning described in chapter 6. Our third pair of musicians tells a story of music making as entirely self-taught, on the one hand, and embedded in the Turkish community, on the other. Not only do both cases shed further light on these questions of pedagogy and connections with school, but they also challenge ideas of cultural capital being a solely middle-class property. Diverse forms of cultural capital help to nuance the distinctions evident in the class—both in terms of young people's music learning and, looking back to the previous chapter, in terms of how parents try to equip the home so as to support school learning.

Our final empirical chapter shifts the frame from connections across the places of young people's lives to connections or disconnections over time. We inquire into the pathways set out for the class by their school and homes, the trajectories they follow in practice, and the factors that facilitate or block them. While our observations permitted an analysis that spans the fieldwork year, our interviews with the young people looked backward and forward over a longer timescale. By the age of 14, many of the young people were reflexively self-aware of the pathways and possibilities that faced them, and they were coming to terms with rather more mundane futures than the popular hyperbole of the digital age would suggest. Moreover, in this chapter, as in other longitudinal sociological and social psychological studies, the effects of social reproduction were clear. Here we struggle to reconcile an optimistic recognition of the possibilities still open to our class of young people with the body of research on the lack of social mobility in Western societies that suggests a more predetermined future for many of them.

Stepping back from the close analysis of young people's sense making and self-making, our final chapter develops these normative concerns, to ask what can be said about the prospects for connected living and learning in the digital age. Our portrait of young people's lives is in many senses a heartening one—they are generally sensible, thoughtful, and optimistic; doing reasonably well at school; largely happy at home; and having fun with friends. Encouragingly, we find rather little evidence of the competitive individualism that critics of neoliberalism fear, although we do show how the school especially seeks to instill competition into school life. We find more evidence of an adherence to conservative structures and comfortable pleasures. Is this, inadvertently, sacrificing the potential for radical alternatives that could undermine the seeming straitjacket of social reproduction, reconfigure pedagogic possibilities, and open up more diverse connections and pathways to opportunity?

Answers to such questions cannot be securely answered by the study of one class over one year, however detailed. But if we position our study within the wider analysis of social change, we are pessimistic in the face of continued lack of sustained social mobility or democratic educational reform, along with evidence of increasing labor-market uncertainty and commodification of both public institutions and the private practices of daily life. What we came to see in our fieldwork as the everyday yet apparently minor experiences of missed opportunities and broken pathways can, on this larger view, be interpreted as the routine reproduction of the boundaries between home and school. We could, and often did, bemoan these instances, hoping that tentative expressions of interest would be supported or that new shoots of possibility would flourish. But in the end, we had to ask ourselves why this happened so rarely, since for most of our class, the promises of progressivist educational and societal reformers, newly invigorated by the digital optimists, remained just that, promising visions too little instantiated in practice to be a reality for most young people. Over and again, our fieldwork pointed up the entrenched anxieties about the risks of inappropriate or uncontrolled connection. And over and again, further exploration revealed the strong institutional and commercial interests at stake in reproducing traditional conceptions of school and home. Reimagining young people's futures not only is a larger social project but also remains a challenge for individuals and their families. At this scale, everything is too risky, and thus most young people find a safer pathway somewhere between the competitive individualism invited by commerce and the state and the conservative embrace of familiar values and expectations that, for many, home and community offers.

Goodbye to the Class

Some 15 months after first meeting the class, we found ourselves back in tutor time asking for a final interview with everyone, at home or school, as they chose. It was the right thing to do—they appreciated something to mark the end of the project, and we gained some very thoughtful interviews in which the students relished the chance to be reflective, looking backward over the year and forward to their future. We could also follow up on puzzles or incomplete information revealed so far. Yet the young people were already changing, now in Year 10, with much to say on how learning was more serious or how interests they had had in Year 9 were now over. Faced with so many changes, we felt as if we should either continue forever or leave now.

When conducted at home, these final interviews also gave us a chance to thank parents. Over and again, our fieldwork notes record the sense of a warm reunion on our visiting homes for the last time, after the summer break. Several parents asked what we had found out, and we promised to write and tell them (which we did). The young people showed themselves impatient for a book (about them!) to appear and were disappointed to hear of the glacial pace of academic writing and publication. Foolishly perhaps, in our goodbye to the whole class, we entered into a discussion about what the book should be called. We offered the usual mouthful of academic keywords, only to be firmly overridden by Megan, who confidently called out that it should be called "The Class," of course. So it is.

1

Living and Learning in the Digital Age

Why is it interesting to examine the interconnected lives of a class of 13-year-olds now? How can we explore what matters about their lives—with what concepts and what questions? Public debate asks anxious and judgmental questions about whether families are "broken" or schools are "failing" or young people have lost their "moral compass." These questions typically focus on society's values, practices, and institutions in changing times and are often framed by (inevitable) uncertainties about the future. Such questions may resonate with young people and, more especially, those who provide for them and worry about their future. For the past twenty years, the rhetoric of "the digital age" has loudly claimed that the recent and rapid take-up of digital, online, and networked technologies is fundamentally reshaping homes, schools, and communities.[1] This rhetoric claims that society must find a way to prepare its youth for jobs that have not yet been invented and to live in ways—more digital, more connected—that the adults responsible for them cannot imagine.[2]

Yet there is a substantial disconnect between the public anxieties swirling around young people's everyday experiences, persistently claiming dramatic change, and a sense of continuity with the past. This disconnect is evident to those who live or work with young people and who are often skeptical of the extreme emotions and oversimplified views expressed in discourses about youth. But this "noise" also conceals important questions. These ask less about the "state of youth" or "where society is going" but instead puzzle over the present in relation to the past. What has really changed between, say, the childhoods of today's parents or grandparents and those of children growing up now? What aspects of change or continuity really matter, and over what timescale should changes be gauged?

This perspective pays more attention to what it feels like to be young now compared with previous generations, investigating the texture of home, school, or leisure experiences in order to reach a judgment about what might have been lost or gained. These questions help to put "the digital" in its place, asking just what difference it makes or whether it is too soon to tell. Importantly, the answers tend to position children's own agency in constructing their identities and environments as part and parcel of the more fundamental historical changes of modernity occurring over recent centuries, rather than young people being subject to radical transformation in a matter of a few years.[3]

In this chapter, we develop a framework that sets out our main concepts, unpacks the debates we hope to contribute to, and refines the questions that guided our fieldwork with the class. In terms of structure, we will organize the framework loosely around the three core spheres of young people's lifeworld[4] presented in the introduction, namely, home, school, and peer group. In terms of analysis and evidence, we focus on what is changing, including but going considerably beyond changes in digital technology.

Understanding Change in Modern Society

Even when considering childhood over the past half century in the world's wealthier countries, academics, commentators, and policy advisers have oscillated between claims of continuity and radical change. The case for "all change" draws a contrast between now and then, with "the past" often being only vaguely, even nostalgically, sketched. It sees key changes only in terms of how recent they seem and emphasizes that children know more about the digitally networked world than their parents do; that public and private spheres are now blurred, with people blurting out their intimate lives in public; that commerce is stretching its tentacles into our private spaces and innermost thoughts; and that while people used to be more confident about how they "fitted into" society—in terms of social class, nationality, and ethnicity—now nothing can be taken for granted.[5]

Yet social historians observe that the postwar period exhibited an unusual degree of social stability across Europe and North America, defined by a broad consensus over the legitimacy of the nuclear family, the firm, the public sphere, regulated markets, and the nation-state as the basic building blocks of society.[6] Not only do we now tend to judge the political, socioeconomic, and cultural upheavals of recent years by reference to this period, but since it encompassed the childhood of both today's parents and grandparents, it makes for a shared vision across the generations. Of course, even during this postwar period, much was in flux, radically accelerated by the neoliberal economic restructuring begun in the 1980s.

Theories of late modernity are helpful in framing questions that avoid this polarization between "all change" and "no change," in that they address a complex balance of continuity and change over the past half century (or longer).[7] In these theories, change is understood through a set of "sensitising concepts."[8] These focus on broad historical shifts regarding "individualization" and the "risk society" as well as some more specific concepts with particular relevance to our project—"the democratization of the family" and "the pedagogicization of everyday life" as ways of thinking about the changing family and school, and "the project of the self" as a way of rethinking identity as a task to be performed.

Scott Lash characterizes the post-Enlightenment period in terms of "simple" modernity—industrial societies striving for rational principles of growth and efficient exploitation of resources, prioritizing progress in knowledge and concentration of power for avowedly democratic purposes.[9] Within this period, the individual came to embody the values of the society—self-serving but amenable to education, with rights to be protected and duties to perform.[10] The 19th and 20th centuries saw increasing organization of both economy and society, a growing underpinning of welfare provision, and substantial trust in the key institutions of the state. With much fanfare, Western societies from the 1960s onward (roughly, "late modernity") tore apart any consensus regarding the relation of the individual to society, with neoliberals advocating individual freedoms over the state management of communal goods and with radicals challenging postwar conventions of class and race, gender and sexuality, and political and cultural difference.

But these political debates can also be read as the latest manifestation of more fundamental shifts in the sources of power: from a centralized state to dispersed institutions of governance; from the heartlands of an industrialized economy to the impermanent (although still concentrated) networks and flows of an information economy; and from the primacy of the nation-state to new tensions between the global, regional, and local. The consequence, it is claimed, is a permanent sense of instability, even crisis—in relation to the economy, the family, education, religion, political representation, and the natural environment. This is accompanied by a pervasive sense of personal insecurity and a disturbing lack of trust in the institutions tasked with fixing these problems.[11] Meanwhile, the media, yet another set of institutions that have simultaneously consolidated and yet also dispersed their power through ever more channels and platforms, are increasingly implicated in how we make sense of our world.[12]

The Everyday Experience of Living in Late Modernity

Theories of late modernity paint a vivid picture of large-scale social change. More than ever before, people are charged with charting their own course through life and taking responsibility for their own risks to a degree that contrasts markedly with previous eras, when they would have been "held" by social convention and tradition. In trying to cope with the many harmful consequences of modernity itself, they are beset by unprecedented levels of uncertainty—incomplete knowledge, conflicting experts, complex decisions, precarious alliances, complicit institutions, too little time, Yet socio-technological developments offer enticing prospects to resolve many of these difficulties, appearing to offer solutions to long-standing problems and greater life choices as well of more personal pleasures than ever before.

Ulrich Beck suggests that society is both fascinated by and ambivalent about socio-technological change. Modernity, he says, "has become the threat and the promise of emancipation from the threat that it creates itself."[13] Lash adds, "reflective judgement is always a question of uncertainty, of risk, but it also leaves the door open much more to innovation."[14] We are building new models of family life, enjoying new tastes and lifestyles, designing new pathways to civic engagement. Yet we worry ever more about the value of these changes, whether we are doing the right thing, and whether too much of value is being lost along the way. As a result, we are absorbed in ever more complex calculations of risk and preoccupied by the effort to manage it.

However, it is further claimed, people are exhausted by this task, with more information to gather, complex decisions to make, difficult priorities to weigh up. In reflexive modernity, everyone is inundated with knowledge about the society they live in—receiving a plethora of advice, guidance, commentary, and popular social science that demand they reflect on their lives and make informed choices. To cope with these choices, people are expected to research the possibilities, consult wisely, and make rational decisions—about work, welfare, lifestyle, finances, contracts, and relationships. This chimes with many parents' woes—how to manage the "choice" of school for their child, to ensure they are eating the "right" food, whether they "should" read more books or watch less television, how much sleep they "need." There is plenty of advice out there to guide them, yet as information mounts, so too does complexity, while taken-for-granted assumptions unravel and certainty declines.

Significantly, individuals cannot afford to be passive, because the stable institutions and traditional communities that once provided for their welfare are in retreat, withdrawing lifetime guarantees and safety nets. As they withdraw, individuals have to take on the responsibility for managing their own uncertain futures. While individuals enjoy some new freedoms, choice itself has become burdensome—both in the process of choosing and also in its consequences, as the cost of mistakes falls on individuals too. What was once given is now seen as choice; to marry or not, to have children or not, to live in one country or another—there is no way to avoid such choices. As Zygmunt Bauman puts it, "Modernity replaces determinism of social standing with compulsive and obligatory self-determination."[15] To make the point crystal clear, he cautions, "Let there be no mistake: now, as before, individualization is a fate, not a choice."[16] In facing our fate—the necessity to choose and to bear the full consequences—we are on our own,[17] since traditional networks of support are no longer reliable or ever present.

Paradoxically, then, greater choice may not mean greater scope for personal autonomy. Certainly individualization is not imagined simply as a celebration of agency. Indeed, societal institutions are working harder to anticipate and control individual actions, rendering behavior predictable and steering it in particular directions so as to mitigate the collective costs of individual failings. Ulrich Beck and Elisabeth Beck-Gernsheim translate the concept of *Individualisierung* as "institutionalised individualism," their point being that the state (along with the many regulatory, supervisory, and public/private organizations to which the state has dispersed its power) builds into its operations a host of assumptions about what individuals should know and do and what they need or may deserve:

> On the one hand, individualization means the disintegration of previously existing social forms—for example, the increasing fragility of such categories as class and social status, gender roles, family, neighbourhood etc. . . . [On the other hand,] new demands, controls and constraints are being imposed on individuals. . . . The density of regulations informing modern society is well known. . . . It is a work of art of labyrinthine complexity, which accompanies us literally from the cradle to the grave.[18]

In short, the complexity of today's society renders the individual self-*in*sufficient—almost the inverse of the "self-sufficient individual" celebrated by neoliberal positions that call for more choice and fewer regulations on either individuals or markets. Thus, "you may and you must lead your own independent life, outside the old bonds of family, tribe, religion, origins and class; and you must do this within the new guidelines and rules which the state, the job market, the bureaucracy etc. lay down."[19]

Take the simple example of so-called school choice in metropolitan areas. There used to be little question where children went to school. Working-class families sent their children to the local school, and privileged families paid for their children's education. In the UK, with the postwar introduction of state "grammar" schools, an element of selection through testing was introduced. But with the expansion of the middle classes and the advent of the policy of "parental choice," parents supposedly could choose the school that best suited their child—more or less academic, more sporty or scientific, larger or smaller, and so on. A once-predictable interaction between educational provision and the behavior of individuals according to the dictates of social class has become far more complex. Parents must choose among schools on the basis of imperfect information about school characteristics and uncertain entry calculations. But not all get their choice, leading to a host of complaints, appeals, and workarounds—moving house to be near a "good" school or manipulating entry requirements by tutoring for tests or pretending a religious affiliation, all of which have unintended consequences of their own. While many parents worry, feel inadequate, or try to play the system, schools and local authorities struggle to predict yearly intakes, with over- and undersubscribed schools causing problems for budgets and planning; thus, they try ever harder to direct parental decisions by rejigging catchment criteria or redesigning parental information.[20]

The trend, then, is for institutions to promise choice to the public, then to try to shape how they will respond and then build expectations of how people will behave into their operations. Institutions issue more guidance, dispersing their discursive and regulatory demands into every aspect of our lives and imposing penalties if we fail to act as expected. "The yawning gap between the right of self-assertion and the capacity to control the social settings which render such self-assertion feasible or unrealistic seems to be the main contradiction of the 'second modernity.'"[21] As Beck and Beck-Gernsheim put it, the result is that people try all the harder, with escalating anxiety: "In order to survive the rat race, one has to become active, inventive and resourceful, to develop ideas of one's own, to be faster, nimbler and more creative—not just on one occasion, but constantly, day after day. Individuals become actors, builders, jugglers, stage managers of their own biographies and identities and also of their social links and networks."[22]

Or must they? While the theory is beguiling, it is not without its criticisms. Two of the most prominent are that, first, the many claims made by these theorists are untested or do not address the evidence that contradicts them. Second, the evidence actually points to a major theoretical problem, namely, the continued importance of the processes of social reproduction that sustain traditional structures of power and inequality. In the following sections, we consider both the theory and its criticisms as they apply to children and young people in their three primary spheres of home, school, and peer cultures.

Home and Family

Crucial changes to home and family have affected children's and young people's lives over recent decades.[23] Substantial demographic and social shifts have resulted in greater diversity in what constitutes family, strongly shaped by the increased participation of women in the workplace, control over their fertility, and the changed status of marriage.[24] The changing ethnic and religious composition of the British population has remixed cultural norms and practices in relation to family life.[25] Teenagers are staying on longer at school, taking more exams, more likely to enter higher education, and leaving home at an ever-older age as a result of the collapse in the youth labor market.[26] Social psychologists talk of the extension of adolescence or even of a new life stage—"emerging adulthood"—pinpointing new concerns over what happens during that period and how young people manage the transition to independence.[27] As Stephanie Coontz has observed, "In some ways, childhood has actually been prolonged, if it is measured by dependence on parents and segregation from adult activities. What many young people have lost are clear paths for gaining experience doing responsible, socially necessary work, either in or out of the home, and for moving away from parental supervision without losing contact with adults."[28]

These large-scale social changes have implications for the private life of families. The design of the postwar home centered on public and family spaces (the formal parlor, the busy backstage kitchen, cold bedrooms never used by day). The design of the 21st-century home, by contrast, centers on the multifunctional family room and the individualized bedroom (notwithstanding that many children share). The postwar home was a place for men and children's leisure and women's work. Today's home fuses work and leisure, study and entertainment, for everyone, although women's domestic labor has not lessened. It is simultaneously a hub for interconnections that extend beyond it, even overseas, and a private sanctuary for intimacy, comfort, and escape. At the same time, "home" and "family" are no longer as neatly overlapping as they were just a few decades ago, with some children living in divided families and/or extended families and so sharing more than one home, and some children lacking a secure home of any kind. Many social statistics take the "household" as their unit of analysis and focus of policy planning, this bearing an uneasy relation to both "home" and "family."[29]

The effects of changing living standards, educational opportunities, and employment prospects fall unevenly on families, depending on social class and other forms of advantage or disadvantage.[30] Sociologists point to long-term trends of increasing income inequality and social stratification, including the emergence of an entrenched underclass that disproportionally includes children.[31] In Britain, for instance, one in six children lives in a home where no parent is employed,[32] while some 10% are deemed to live in poverty.[33] The future even for the once-comfortable middle classes is increasingly uncertain.[34] But for people from disadvantaged backgrounds especially at a time of austerity, the routes to independent adulthood are ever more difficult.[35]

Indeed, the UK government's recent horizon-scanning report on young people's social attitudes documents growing insecurity among young people:[36] the expected returns on their now-considerable investment in higher education are not materializing; they are disproportionately affected by unemployment, low pay, housing shortages, and insecure work.[37] As predicted by the individualization thesis, young people are becoming more focused on prestige, personal success, stimulation, and hedonism and less interested in religion, conformity, security, and universalism.[38] This makes them more liberal in some ways—more tolerant toward homosexuality, for instance, and less racially prejudiced—but also more disengaged from civil and civic participation.[39]

Strikingly, today's young people belong to the first generation since the Second World War that does not believe they will enjoy a better life than their parents,[40] although they expect better opportunities for education, travel, and living longer than their parents. They think it will be harder for them to find a good job, buy a home, and afford a reasonable standard of living.[41] There is growing evidence from qualitative research in the US that parents are even more anxious than their children are.[42] In an ethnographic portrait of family life among the American middle-classes, Elinor Ochs and Tamar Kremer-Sadlik (2013) portray a high, even pathological level of guilt, frustration, ambivalence, and stress experienced by many parents, caught in a bind between the increased time pressures of a dual-career, high-earning, insecure, long-hours culture and the unchanging traditions of normative family life centered on time together, shared pleasures, and mutual support. They paint a depressing picture of mothers especially, working hard to manage work and home and struggling to communicate with their children after school and work, while fathers, even when home, do so little domestic work that their presence may not even be noticed. What exists in middle-class America today may also exist in the mixed London suburb where the class lived—or it may be coming tomorrow if it is not here already, as the theories of late modernity predict.[43]

However, trend data suggest that parents are spending more time than in previous decades caring for their children, although this goes hand in hand with increased parental monitoring and supervision (see Gardner et al., 2012). Ann Hagell, Stephen Peck, et al. (2012) finesse this point by claiming that young people spend more quality time with their parents than in the 1970s, although they eat together less often. Also interesting is that contrary to certain popular prejudices, the greatest increases in parental discipline and encouragement are found in poorer rather than wealthier homes; possibly, parents are responding to the growing difficulties and pressures experienced by children (Gardner et al., 2012).

So the evidence suggests that young people's lives at home are broadly positive, even though they worry more than earlier generations did about the future—about what results they will get at school, whether there will be jobs, their parents' finances, their popularity at school, their attractiveness, or being bullied.[44] Ann Hagell and Sharon Witherspoon concluded from a wide-ranging national literature review that "any simple view that the lives of today's adolescents are more 'stressful' than those of their counterparts of 30 years ago would be hard to substantiate."[45] We wonder, then, if young people's worries about the future are founded in genuinely unsettling social changes or, instead, a reflection of the anxious discourses that surround them. The theory of late modernity is itself torn between stressing the problems of increased risks and also identifying some opportunities, noting that those who live in today's ever more anxious, highly regulated, and ultimately unequal society nonetheless feel themselves to be agents fashioning their identities and life course with unprecedented degrees of freedom.

On the basis of our review, we are left with a series of questions for our fieldwork. What is it like growing up an increasingly individualized society? How do young people perceive and respond to the demands made of them by their families and community? Are their lives still strongly shaped by their gender, social class, and ethnicity? Do social changes, including the advent of digitally mediated activities and networks, bring more (or different) risks or opportunities?

The Changing Role of Education in Late Modernity

Although the terms "learning," "education," and "school" are often used interchangeably, they are conceptually distinct. In this book, we particularly draw on socio-cultural perspectives within educational research, as they emphasize that school constitutes a culturally and context specific set of arrangements, norms, and expectations that are central to but not necessarily defining of what it means to be educated.[46] This approach complements and even displaces accounts of learning as cognitive— purely a matter of individual understanding or memory, as something that only happens inside people's heads—by recognizing that schools are social and cultural institutions. This perspective emphasizes how curricular knowledge and disciplinary processes, social conventions, and traditions all work to organize and accredit learning. These processes are, furthermore, culturally and historically dependent on societies' visions of the purposes of education, and these in turn have been the subject of contested and seemingly continuous political reforms.[47] Education, then, refers more broadly to how societies manage and organize knowledge and behavior and how a range of institutional and everyday practices, including but not limited to schools, implements such values. Learning is usually understood at the level of the individual, often emphasizing the learner's agency, perspective, knowledge, and experience.

All three concepts are, moreover, much contested. We would point to debates over whether children learn better in school or out of school; or whether schools should prioritize common or personalized and individualized modes of learning (or whether such concepts even exist); or whether the purpose of education is to fit children for their future as conceived by the state or, instead, to encourage them to think creatively or critique the status quo. Particular concern currently centers on the commodification (or instrumentalization) of education. By this, we mean that access to education is provided and valued primarily for its instrumental economic benefits—to the individual and to the economy[48]—although other benefits to well-being may also be recognized.[49] This excludes the many alternative or critical visions of education that emphasize the value of education for humanistic and liberal purposes, as periodically advocated passionately by progressivists and educational reformers.[50] For instance, the Germanic concept of *Bildung* conceptualizes learning not in terms of gaining discrete bits or even bodies of knowledge or skill but as a total and holistic integration with the development of the self so as to enable people to act as full members of the wider community.[51] But such abstract values are difficult to measure in standardized outcomes (examination scores, school rankings, or the competitive PISA tables produced by the OECD) and so find little favor in mainstream Western education policies.[52] Yet as Andy Furlong and Fred Cartmel write, instrumental approaches "may help create an illusion of equality whilst masking the persistence of old inequalities,"[53] since in practice, exciting new opportunities cannot be taken up equally if their promise centers on individual competitiveness.

While discourses of education encompass a range of purposes, some more idealistic than others, the practices of managing schools and assessing students favor individual competition.[54] Schooling is also under increasing pressure to meet the uncertain demands of the risk society. So, on the one hand, schools are disciplinary organizations burdened with increased expectation to establish social order and produce "good citizens." On the other, since the modern worker is now not necessarily valued for his or her unswerving obedience and compliance, as in the days of the mass industrial factory, schools are expected to foster the initiative, flexible thinking, and assertiveness required by the contemporary and future workplace.[55] With a recognition of the new pressures on individuals to succeed in the risk society, much attention has been paid to how education now strives not to impose control but rather to facilitate self-control, supporting individual processes of self-regulation as part of a regime of power that works through internalized forms of self-motivation.[56] Additionally and controversially, schools are losing their status as the sole route to success, since in addition to formal qualifications, young people must now demonstrate a capacity and willingness to engage in diverse forms of learning throughout their life.[57]

As with the other demands on individuals in late modernity, these shifts suggest both opportunities and risks, and navigating these outcomes brings—for the theorists of late modernity, new forms of anxiety and individualized risk and, for theorists of social reproduction, more intense forms of social inequality. Nonetheless, as we approached our fieldwork, we were struck by the lack of close attention to young people's voices and experiences in these debates. So our fieldwork will ask, What does being educated mean for young people, their families, and their teachers in an individualized risk society. What learner identities do they take up and sustain? What do families see as the point of education, and what do they want from schools? Are they creating connections—across people, sites, or interests—that enable particular visions of learning? And how do they respond to the intense competition around school attainment and performance?

Peer Cultures On- and Offline

Young teenagers often seem to their parents to be absorbed in life with their friends, in their bedrooms, online, or inside the world created by their headphones. There is no simple term for this "place" as there is for family and school, yet we see it as sufficiently coherent to be discussed as a third sphere in our analysis. It is where young people "hang out," an escape from the strictures of home and school. This may mean navigating some personal distance from that same peer culture, seeking a way of "being oneself" together with yet also distinct from peers. We include here the places where young people feel "private," for as we shall see in chapter 4, these may be shared with peers on- and offline while being kept away from parental or public scrutiny. Drawing on the work of Erving Goffman, John Thompson holds that "the private consists of those territories of the self, which include the environment of the self and information about the self, over which the individual seeks to exercise control and to restrict access by others."[58] In other words, the private need not be solitary or hidden. Rather, we explore the idea that what these various peer/private places offer is the opportunity to negotiate space for self-making that evades the often-dominating influences of home and school.

As sociologists of childhood have shown, children and young people find most opportunity to exercise their agency in the interstices of adult-managed timetables and spaces.[59] William Corsaro emphasizes how children view the world through the lens of meanings created within their friendships and peer culture. In this analysis, the so-called new sociologists of childhood integrate theories of late modernity with the political effort to recognize children's rights and hear children's voices by seeing children as people in the present rather than always viewing them—as parents and teachers tend to do—through the lens of who they might or should become.[60] This includes recognizing the places and activities—both self and peer focused—that children strive to keep "under the radar" of adult supervision. In other words, it is precisely the point that there is no agreed term for our third sphere in this book, for this is the interstitial place in between recognized and approved (i.e., adult-managed) places.

A recent study of primary-school playground culture documented children's reworking of television, computer games, films, and comics in their free play—in the stories they told and the games they played with each other together—resulting in a child-centered culture from which children gain value and recognition.[61] Such work draws on a now-established tradition of identifying how young people imbue places with meanings important to themselves and under the radar of adults— bedrooms become places for self-making or the street an opportunity for meeting friends.[62] Cultural geographers have supported the new sociology of childhood in showing how people transform places into symbolic resources by investing them with meanings; this in turn influences the role that places play in situating people as social actors within wider networks, as we explore in chapters 3 and 4.[63]

While social scientists have studied "adolescence," "youth," and "peer culture" ever since the recognition (or emergence) of these very phenomena 50 years or so ago,[64] in just the past decade, one particular activity has seemingly rewritten the norms and practices of teenage communication, being adopted with astonishing rapidity by the vast majority of young people—the use of online social networking sites. From about 2005 onward, it has been implausible to examine young people's friendships and peer networks without recognizing their sudden absorption in sites such as Facebook, MySpace, Twitter, Tumblr, and more.[65]

It does appear, however, that the more offline spaces are controlled, the more young people turn to online spaces and networks to conduct their identity work and to experiment with relationships, thereby also altering (or "remediating")[66] how their relationships are enacted offline.[67] In such spaces, children and young people can be reflexive in their identity work—or what Jerome Bruner calls their "self-making"; like adults, they talk themselves into being, as it were, by drawing on the genres, tools, and narratives available to them.[68] Jeffrey Arnett adds that, while the available "authorized" narratives of the self from parents and school are often moralistic and teleological, young people themselves prefer to control the resources that inform their self-biography, and so they turn to the media[69] or, as danah boyd argues in relation to social media, to the collective conversation among peers online.[70]

Whether, as popularly claimed, the advent of online social networking makes for a transformation in the nature of friendship itself or merely a new site for the exercise of familiar practices was a guiding question for us in this book. Thus, we ask, what is distinctive about the texture of young people's self-making and social relationships, compared with previous generations? How do young people make sense of and negotiate ideas of self-making, for the present and as they anticipate the future? Are young people affected by concerns about surveillance, and what does it mean to be private at the age of 13? Are their activities, preoccupations, and aspirations familiar or new, and are they facilitated or constrained by home and school, on- and offline?

Identity: Being and Becoming

As each young person moves among the three spheres of daily life (and others), they themselves are the crucial link among the roles, meanings, and potentials that characterize each sphere. As the structures and practices underpinning each sphere change over the decades, so do the resources and constraints that shape the processes of identity formation and identification. Much current theory thus assumes fluidity and change, emphasizing the complexity of "who people are to each other."[71] As Zygmunt Bauman puts it, " 'Individualization' consists in transforming human 'identity' from a 'given' into a 'task' " since rather than inheriting fixed identities based on employment or social roles, people now have to work at making themselves simultaneously distinct from and yet connected to each other.[72]

How, then, do children and young people create a sense of themselves at home, school, and with their friends. What ways of being and participating do the institutions of family and school offer them? For us, identity is constituted through discourse[73]—for example, through talk about the self by individuals and by those around them, including at the level of wider cultural pronouncements on certain categories of people (girls, musicians, students, "digital natives," etc.). Since discourses vary across contexts, identities, too, are expressed in different, though overlapping, ways. In part, individuals cannot control this—they are defined by others, and they "give off" meanings that they may not have intended.[74] But people also actively undertake "identity work"—enacting who we are to each other, coconstructing our own and other identities according to particular desires or interests.

Much of young people's identity work is necessarily tactical, given the power of adults to determine the main structures within which they live.[75] Young people may evade, circumvent, or even resist the ways that parents and teachers manage the spaces and timetables of their everyday lives, but they rarely assert a more strategic authority over their own lives. By contrast, schools are arguably inflexible or unresponsive places, from young people's point of view. They are as much concerned with the maintenance of social order and the production of social selves as with the overt purpose of teaching and learning.[76] Critics have examined how certain social transactions and disciplinary practices are used to ensure social-class-based reproduction where academic "failure" is as much a desired outcome of the system as "success" in a world that needs a stratified labor force.[77] Empirical analyses have revealed how forms of discipline and control at school work to produce particular kinds of class-based identities (for example, how working-class boys "learn to labour"[78] or how girls took up new opportunities in the burgeoning service industries as labor markets changed in the early 21st century[79]).

Thus, a "being" perspective—which we want to recognize—cannot entirely evade one of "becoming." In this book, we document various disciplinary practices at school—for example, how and where young people sit, when they can talk, what they wear, and how they are punished—which are intertwined with the discourses that explain how learning is valued and by whom and for what ends.[80] In short, communication and social relationships in school are not innocent; they embed hidden and implicit values and rewards in order to mold and direct preferred social values and identities.[81] A similar case may be made regarding the home and family life, for although families vary, how domestic life is ordered, valued, and explained, especially by adults, is often the most significant influence on children's social development.[82]

In *Inventing Adulthoods*, Sheila Henderson et al. showed how the constraints and expectations of family and neighborhood similarly shape the trajectory from adolescence to adult independence.[83] Their point is not that social structures are simply determining in a mechanistic way, because not all young people straightforwardly reproduce the circumstances they were born into. Rather, they argue that what matters is how young people come to understand themselves and their potential—through processes of meaning making, self-efficacy, and validation from others.[84] "Inventing adulthoods" appears to allow individuals choice while, in practice, closely managing "the process through which the appearance of choice and control is created."[85] Nonetheless, a measure of flexibility in late modernity means that, rather than simply reproducing the norms and behaviors of previous generations, "old forms of inequality such as class, gender and race are being remade in new ways"[86]—a process we were able to observe in the class.

Social Change or Social Reproduction

In the face of widespread and indeed increasing social and economic equality across the world,[87] the persistence of social class and the power of social reproduction to keep the socially advantaged and disadvantaged distinct is much debated among late modern theorists. For Anthony Giddens, in "post-traditional" society, the established norms of gender, generation, and social class are being rewritten: people can no longer fall back on what people of their gender or generation or social class have always done—nor do they want to.[88] Thus, he coined the phrase "the project of the self" (see also Beck and Beck-Gernsheim's "choice biography" or "do-it-yourself biography") to capture the efforts devoted to creating and sustaining a desirable and plausible identity.[89] The array of potential resources for building such an identity is expanded by global media cultures, allowing for possibilities far beyond those directly encountered in daily life.[90]

But, as critics have observed, these claims make too little reference to a sound evidence base, and where there is evidence, it suggests a far slower and less linear process of social change.[91] At the heart of this debate is the continued social reproduction of social class. Contrary to some misinterpretations of Beck, Giddens, et al. as overly celebrating agency and choice, there is agreement on all sides that the unevenness of the resources that individuals can call on only increases socioeconomic and other inequalities.[92] But for Beck and Beck-Gernsheim, "social inequality is on the rise precisely because of the spread of individualization," so we must now recognize "the non-class character of individualized inequalities."[93] Their point is that while inequality is still with us, the "processes of individualization deprive class distinctions of their social identity," resulting in the "individualization of social risks."[94]

Indeed, there does seem to be evidence that it is class-consciousness that is fading, thereby undermining the potential for collective political resistance.[95] Although people still use the labels "middle" and "working" class, the meaning of these terms is changing: the traditional mapping of working and middle class onto left and right wings of the political spectrum or onto labor and management or even onto poor and wealthy is less secure. And these terms no longer predict simple differences in educational and financial resources; instead they seem to refer to a looser notion of social status (or, perhaps, "perceived" social class), encompassing forms of cultural knowledge, social capital, and a host of practices—ways of speaking, dressing, or behaving; knowledge of how institutions work; and so on. Some sociologists argue that the population can still be meaningfully segmented into distinct groupings but that new groupings are emerging, no longer defined in traditional terms.[96] Others argue for the intensification of control mechanisms that perpetuate the social reproduction of advantage and disadvantage and extend the power of institutions ever further into private life.[97]

For instance, in the postwar efforts toward social reconstruction in the 20th century, many progressives hoped that education would enable people to escape hardship and poverty, for their own benefit and also for the wider benefit of society. Yet social mobility—the chance for young people to improve on the material conditions of their parents—has ground to a halt in recent decades, and developed countries can no longer promise future generations increased prosperity or quality of life.[98] Schools' strongest critics hold that they exert "symbolic violence" by employing pedagogic processes that work deliberately to exclude whole swaths of the population so that, as we noted earlier, the idea of individual failure is in some ways part of the wider function of schools to differentiate among people to sort them for a stratified labor market.[99] As Basil Bernstein has shown, the ways in which education "re-contextualises" knowledge works to ensure success for young people from middle-class homes compared with those who are less privileged; thus, education serves as a key instrument of the social reproduction of inequality, notwithstanding that it professes "fairness."[100]

Related arguments have been made regarding processes of social reproduction at home, attuned to the ways in which ordinary or tacit knowledge has become grist to the mill of disciplinary processes, evaluated according to formal and arcane modes of expression, as leisure becomes "curricularised."[101] This has implications for the different ways that families with different economic and cultural capital work to sustain social distinctions.[102] Privileged parents act competitively to get their children "ahead" in what has been termed hyperparenting or the "offensive" sociality of the new middle class (and the "defensive" sociality of the disadvantaged).[103] For example, Annette Lareau's in-depth study of 12 families shows how the rigorous schedule of adult-organized out-of-school enrichment activities ("concerted cultivation"), practiced by middle-class families, breeds a cumulative sense of entitlement in their children that helps them get ahead in institutionalized settings such as the school.[104]

There is no easy resolution to this tension between the case for social change and the one for social reproduction.[105] One question is how far postwar stability has changed, with social class hierarchies less in evidence and more flexible pathways opening up to ever more varied opportunities. We take this as an empirical question to explore in this book. But, as an important rationale for our approach, we note that both theories of individualization and analyses of social reproduction agree that the problems of social inequality are becoming more, not less, acute, and thus finding ways to account for social processes is even more important.

Conclusions: From Theory to Research

> For the total texture is what we begin and end with. There is no Archimedean point outside it whence we can survey the whole and pronounce upon it.
> —Isaiah Berlin[106]

This book is simultaneously wide ranging and tightly focused. We examine the lives of one class of schoolchildren to understand where, when, and how they live, learn, socialize, and dream. Our theories and methods are designed to capture the "total texture" of their lives, insofar as we are able. But we conducted this analysis to investigate the larger changes that preoccupy our times, offering our portrait of the class as an empirical study with which to test claims about young people's social life, the meaning of the education they experience, and the nature of the networks in which they are embedded. As Isaiah Berlin wisely cautioned, we must beware of assuming an all-seeing eye from which we can pronounce definitively on young people's lives and social change. Thus, this chapter has laid out the framework of concepts and questions that we used in our fieldwork.

In general, we are convinced by the growing weight of discussion and evidence suggesting that individualization has become a dominant feature of late modernity. Through this and related processes, people are facing an ever more uncertain and risky future, while also becoming detached from the established norms by which, traditionally, they have brought up their children. Digital technologies are far from the only sources of change in an otherwise stable society. Many vital dimensions of childhood are changing: established values are being challenged, and traditions are being reinvented, shaking people's confidence in the future and leading them to redouble their efforts to control the risks it threatens. For today's young people, the possibilities for work, travel, relationships, identity, and lifestyle are more varied than ever. But at the same time, they face growing uncertainty and insecurity that, combined with deepening social and economic inequality, means they may never benefit from the exciting opportunities that seem to beckon.

The growth of social and economic inequality suggests that traditional political settlements have become inadequate to the challenge of social injustice and economic inequalities. Indeed, questions about socialization, identity, and learning have become ever more urgent, as schools, homes, and communities, as well as the state, attempt to plan for a seemingly rapidly changing future. Given the importance of these larger contexts, we have not endorsed the fashion for all things digital, as this can distract society from addressing the root causes of childhood poverty and exclusion, the lack of jobs, or insufficient investment in education. The structure of this book thus places the digital inside the texture of everyday life, enabling us to see it as an interlinking element in our understanding of how and why the families of the class and the young people themselves "chose" to live their lives in the ways they did.

In the introduction, we observed that, faced with a strong sense of change, people may instead cling all the more to the structures and practices they are familiar with—making them what we called "conservative with a small *c*"; we also suggested that various kinds of network connections were the hallmark of living and learning in a large cosmopolitan city like London. This chapter has reviewed some of the social, institutional, and identity changes that might motivate this conservatism and that explain how forms of connection might be furthered or impeded. To progress these ideas further, we now turn to the fieldwork.

2

A Year of Fieldwork

Progress Day: Exploring Connections

An illuminating moment in our fieldwork took place a few weeks into the first term. On "Progress Day," parents met the class teacher to review their child's progress and to set targets for the year. This complemented the practice of sending home termly written reports; the annual evening in which parents met subject teachers in a lively and complicated carousel in the school hall; and ad hoc year-group meetings to learn of upcoming decisions (for example, selecting subjects for end-of-school qualifications). For Progress Day, each student was expected to bring one or both parents for a ten-minute appointment. The conversation was highly structured. Catherine, the class teacher, sat across a table from the family, and each student was asked to review his or her previous year's self-assessment, while Catherine commented on the student's grades. She then pressed the students on their participation in school life, encouraging extracurricular activities and calling on them to find ways to "shine," to "realize their potential," and to make the school proud. Depending on the circumstances, the interview might conclude with other general comments about the student's enthusiasm, engagement, or, where relevant, disciplinary issues. These rapid-fire interviews were not always straightforward, making for a demanding and at times emotional day for Catherine and for some of the families—and a fascinating day for us.

Being present meant we could meet the parents face-to-face in order to get permission to visit the students at home, to convince them of our integrity and the value of our project. Throughout the day, we sat at the back of the classroom, and Catherine introduced us as each set of parents entered the room so that, once her interview with them was over, they could come to us to ask any questions. We reminded them of the letter we had sent them earlier in the summer, explained our methods in more detail, clarifying in particular how we would ensure anonymity and confidentiality for all participants.[1]

Second, this was an opportunity to witness an important day in the life of the school. Indeed, the interviews could be seen as revealing how "school" was performed for the families. Progress Day also brought out some of the challenges faced by students, teachers, and parents as they all tried to make sense of the school experience from their personal perspectives. This alerted us to the value of listening carefully, not only to what students, teachers, and parents each had to say but also to how each imagined the others—what each thought was important to the others and where he or she anticipated misconceptions or problems.

The review of academic attainment generated some confusion as parents sought to understand how their child was doing in terms of the national curriculum's system of levels. A student's progress in each subject was graded four times over (minimum acceptable grade, maximum anticipated grade, norm-based predicted grade, and actually achieved grade) on a scale from 3e to 8a (where 8 is higher than 3 but *a* is higher than *e*). While a number of parents nodded vaguely as they were told of their child's grades, one mother—recently arrived from eastern Europe—was persistent in trying to understand the meaning of the grading system and its implications for the different system used for formal examinations at age 16. She especially wanted to grasp why her child was not top for each subject, and after some time trying and failing to explain, Catherine had to call in the director of studies for Year 9 to explain the process.

From this tense and increasingly irritable conversation, we learned that the system was complex, if not arcane, to many parents. Equally interesting was how clear the system was to teachers and students, as illustrated by the following exchange between Catherine and Dilruba:

CATHERINE: Your commitment has been excellent this year. Let's make that a target. How would you like to go into Year 10?
DILRUBA: I'd like to reach my minimum targets.

While it seemed the students were at ease with such talk, the conversations held across the day revealed diverse responses from parents. Many appeared to trust the school's management of learning, but some made it clear that they had strong goals of their own that might conflict with the school or, we later discovered, might be pursued independently. Several middle-class parents were frustrated at how difficult the system made it for them to discover their child's ranking within the class, and they persisted in trying to find this out by asking Catherine about policies for setting (sorting by ability) or assessment criteria or what might count to allow further progress.

In the small amount of time for parents to raise individual issues, we saw a painful exchange between Catherine and Alice's mother, concerned that the school had failed to recognize her daughter's dyslexia. For the mother, this not only explained her daughter's uneven grades but also pointed up the need for the school, rather than the girl, to try harder. Catherine listened politely and took the opportunity to generalize about teacher-student interactions and the school's policy regarding special educational needs. We saw a similarly polite yet blank response when the parents of some of the bilingual children (Adam, Adriana) urged the school to enter them for an extra examination in their first language (German, Spanish, etc.). Shane's mother had a difficult discussion about her son's poor behavior, and again the head of Year 9 was called in to support Catherine. This mother was so fired up about perceived injustices and the way that the school dealt with her that, when she came over to talk to us, we were seen as honest brokers to whom she might express her criticisms.

A few families challenged our preconceptions. A whispered conversation between Abby, her father (a much older parent than the others), and Catherine hinted at past difficulties. Quiet Joel had parents with hippie clothes and dreadlocked hair, suggesting a home life little recognized by the school. Lydia—whom we had already witnessed in several disciplinary contretemps—was the only child not to turn up at all. Such observations alerted us to family experiences that we might need to discover. Indeed, the entire fieldwork experience was one of catching threads that led in multiple directions, comparing our experiences as we went along, so as to formulate further questions for future encounters.

Different issues arose in relation to the students who turned up at the meeting without a parent in tow. Yusuf's mother did not speak English, and his father was at work. Fesse and Jenna were each accompanied by older sisters tasked with reporting back to non-English-speaking parents. Hakim and Sedat brought their non-English-speaking mothers with them and acted as interpreters for Catherine. But even when parents were native speakers, their confusion about the school's systems meant that the student's voice was often prominent in these interviews, since the young people understood the system and thus played a mediating role between parent and teacher.[2]

Power relations shifted when the interviews turned to extracurricular activities. We were struck by the young people's reluctance to discuss these, sometimes dutifully participating, sometimes mutely resistant or hoping to get away with easy promises. Far from encouraging youth-led interests, what seemed to be at stake was resisting a certain kind of school-sanctioned behavior. This alerted us to the young people's strong desire to keep some time for themselves, especially when faced with their teachers' and parents' apparently insatiable call on them to do ever more. We could see how spontaneously mentioned interests were seized on, potentially grist to the mill of individual achievement.

However, the exceptions were also interesting—Sedat's expertise in playing the *saz*,[3] which we found out about later, was not acknowledged, so he appeared as a boy with no outside interests; and indeed, as we return to in chapter 9, it was mainly the young people from middle-class homes who were asked about musical accomplishments. The interviews ended with the students being called on to set their own targets for the year ahead, and we observed some confident, middle-class students enjoying the opportunity, neatly deflecting the demand to achieve even more. By contrast, Shane, from a much poorer family, focused on football (that is, "soccer" in the US; we call it "football" in this book, as did the class). These were the kinds of observations that opened up for us the subtle workings of social stratification at school, while also raising questions in our minds about young people's potential to negotiate the path ahead.

An Ethnographic Approach

Progress Day illustrated some key themes of this book: the different perspectives of student, teacher, and parent on the value of formal and informal learning; differential power relations, shaped by socioeconomic status; and possible connections and disconnections between home and school, especially in relation to the young person's identity. We have already seen, in chapter 1, how such themes are important in conceptualizing young people's lives in what has been called the age of individualization or the risk society. We pursue these themes across the chapters that follow.

But Progress Day was just one day. In this chapter, we go back to the start of our fieldwork to set the scene for these and other encounters. We explain how we entered the lives of members of the class, what we did, and how we learned what we did about living and learning in the digital age. Our chosen method for *The Class* is an ethnographic case study of young people's lives.[4] We set out to immerse ourselves in the lives of the young people over an extended period of time, also acknowledging the views of their parents and teachers and the wider context of all their lives. In the past few decades, ethnographic research has been undertaken by social scientists working "at home," in their own cultures, adapting the long-standing tradition among anthropologists of studying "other" cultures.[5] The idea is to uncover the significant patterns immanent within the taken-for-granted nature of people's ordinary practices. This means talking to people in order to get insight into how they explain and interpret their actions but also observing their actions in context, recognizing that talk and action may not match. We were particularly interested in how talk may be more performative than descriptive; in other words, talk can impact on and create social contexts.[6]

Our fieldwork encompassed school, home, and "peer spaces" (in the neighborhood, online, and in the interstices of other, more regulated spaces such as the child's bedroom at home).[7] Building on an imagined Venn diagram of these spheres, we explored how everyday practices might interconnect these spaces in particular ways and with particular consequences.[8] In a digital age, researching connections means exploring the online as well as the offline lives of participants.[9] But overall, none of the places we studied were far apart, as children do not travel far in their daily lives; they walk, catch a bus, or are shuttled around by parents, and apart from occasional trips, they live within a geographic span of a few miles. Thus, the project was also, as in more traditional ethnographic studies, strongly located in one neighborhood.

But before researching a class in all its depth or breadth, we had to find one willing to work with us. On the basis of available government statistics, we approached a mixed community school with no particularly distinctive features and of average size (see the appendix).[10] A personal connection to one of the assistant headteachers helped us get access to the school we selected. Gaining entry took some months, however. We had to gain approval from the headteacher and governing body, to get enhanced certificates from the Criminal Records Bureau (Child Protection), and to meet the requirements of our university's Research Ethics Committee.

Each of these required us to clarify our research processes, to anticipate problems, and to think through some "what if" scenarios. To develop these, we discussed the project with the class teacher (Catherine), the head of Year 9, the deputy head of school who was responsible for child welfare, and the assistant headteacher, our primary "gatekeeper." After all of this, we reached that summer's afternoon described in the introduction when we first met the class. Even having met them, we still had to obtain written permission from each member of the class and his or her parents, doing this initially for the research based at school and then again for the research at home.

Throughout the project, we elaborated our research methods, staying responsive to the opportunities or restrictions that the fieldwork itself brought up. In particular, we sought to capitalize on our complementary expertise as researchers and to pay attention to what the other found surprising. Sonia has spent much of her career with families at home, seeking to understand their media lives and exploring the dynamics of gender and generation in the home. She has been especially interested in children's construction of private spaces for the imagination or identity, including their bedrooms and, more recently, on the internet. Julian has spent much of his career with students and teachers at school, exploring the conditions by which media use at school and elsewhere could enable creativity and knowledge by connecting formal and informal spaces or otherwise sidestepping the constraints of the formal curriculum. This meant that for Sonia, the contemporary classroom was an unfamiliar place, and she felt very visible, even when sitting at the back of the room. For Julian, the classroom was a familiar place of work, so keeping out of the action did not come naturally.[11] We both had to figure out how to comport ourselves—for example, whether to line up for lunch with the students or jump to the head of the line with the teachers. The students also had to solve this problem: as Julian observed, at school they called him Sir, but in the park, it was Julian.

So what was the school like? Victoria Forest School (VFS) had around 1,400 students aged 11 plus, including the sixth form (students aged 17 to 18), and an above-average proportion of students with special educational needs. Nonetheless, the school was achieving above-average academic results.[12] The school was located in a leafy Edwardian suburb some eight miles from the center of London, a journey that many residents might make only rarely. As with other London neighborhoods, there was a range of local shops, access to a public park, and good transport links. The streets in the neighborhood were not dangerous, although they were not risk-free—especially with regard to petty theft—and it was common for young people to walk short distances or to take buses to nearby larger shopping centers. However, VFS's students came from both prosperous and deprived areas. Despite the affluence of the streets immediately surrounding the school, it was just a ten-minute walk from a train line and major road dividing rich and poor.[13] Large areas of social housing and private rental accommodation fell within the school catchment area, and most of the students lived within two or three miles of the school in one direction or another, with roughly half on either side of "the tracks" (see the appendix for an account of the UK education system and its relation to socioeconomic status, race, and ethnicity).

The school also included an above-average proportion of students for whom English was not their first language or who came from a wide range of minority ethnic backgrounds. As we were led to explore in chapter 5, where we consider the classroom as a civil space, it seemed noteworthy to have a child from a million-pound home sitting next to a child from a refugee family, with seemingly little notice being taken of this fact. It also seemed noteworthy that no single ethnicity dominated and that many young people were hard to categorize in simple ethnic or racial terms, having instead hybrid identities reflecting the complexity of contemporary British society.[14] As we explain in the appendix, given these and other complexities, we refer to the members of the class as living in wealthier or poorer households rather than, simply, "middle class" or "working class" (or any other simple labels that we could assign unproblematically). Indeed, the shifting relations among social class, cultural capital, and ethnicity became a substantive theme throughout the book.

The school told us that the class they assigned to us was broadly typical, but without some of the "trouble makers" for whom our presence could prove intrusive. It had rather more boys than girls,[15] and its exact composition fluctuated over the year—one boy was "excluded," a new boy arrived early in the first term, and another girl joined later in the year. Thus, over the year, also taking into account the numbers who consented to the different fieldwork phases, the number of our project participants fluctuated between 25 and 28.

A Day in the Life—At School

We joined the class on the first day of the students' third year at VFS. They were 13 turning 14 years old in the year we spent with them. Any secondary school is a busy place, especially at the start of the year, with corridors full of pushing noisy children and hassled teachers, classrooms loud with scraping chairs and a tide of instructions, and a melee of conversation, shouting, and ball games in the playground. We sat with the students or were silent at the back of the classroom, observing members of the class across all their different subjects as well as lunch breaks, the computer room, homework club, the library, the playground, the teachers' staff room, and so on. We ate in the student canteen, observed the notices banning use of mobile phones, and generally tried to get the feel of life at school.

We used a smart pen for observations in school—usefully, the students loved this: they knew it recorded sound, but it looked like a regular pen for handwritten notes; and it also seemed less obtrusive than an audio recorder from the teacher's point of view. We began simply, listening out for what the young people wished to tell us, along with any talk of learning, interests, or expertise and any use of or mention of digital or other media at school. We observed the style of interaction between teacher and student, noting the kinds of tasks students were given and their approach to completing them. We paid particular attention to how life at school might connect with the student's life at home and elsewhere, recognizing that these connections may be more imagined than actual. We also formally interviewed all the young people over the term, individually or in pairs, mainly during breaks and lunch hours.

Getting to the school ourselves, we were often caught up in the tidal flow of young people converging on an otherwise quiet suburban spot, with the occasional anxious face of a teacher trying to prevent them from overwhelming local residents. The playground seemed at first to rock with the mass of uniformed bodies,[16] but we began to discern various groupings within this larger constellation. When it was time for registration—announced by an air-raid howl wailing across the neighborhood—teachers positioned themselves strategically at entrances and on the staircases to impose their authority and to calm down the pupils. It seemed to us that students were generally positive in and around the school, responding to such forms of control with good-humored banter. They did not seem to mind having to line up outside each classroom before being allowed entry, with the teacher standing at the door to his or her room, greeting each individual, and checking that he or she looked and behaved correctly. At any point, as the teachers walked around the school, we saw them admonishing students and maintaining order in the crowded corridors and playground.

We knew, of course, that the school day began with the effort to arrive on time—even to go to bed early enough the night before. Day after day, we saw Fessehaye (Fesse) turn up late, seemingly surprised that he had to pay for this by staying after school in detention. He told us he played Xbox or watched television late at night and first thing in the morning, often oversleeping or losing track of the time. Other students seemed more in control of the transition from what we came to see as the relative freedom of home to the controlled world of school. Salma told us with pleasure that she always walked to school with the same group of friends and that they texted each other to synchronize meeting up and walking in together.

The class spent the first and last 15 minutes of each day together in tutor time for registration. While this was often more informal than lesson times, it depended on Catherine—if she wanted total silence, she got it, and chat was only allowed when explicitly sanctioned. Often we saw a quiet passive resistance that teachers seemingly ignored. Reading a novel on Tuesday mornings was often a case in point—while some of the students read with evident pleasure, most went through the motions, easily distracted and rarely making much progress. Lydia fiddled with her hair most of the time, while Max—whom we later discovered to be a keen reader at home—stared blankly out the window.

Students' attention in class was generally focused on the teacher at the front of the room, including the smart board.[17] Teachers varied in how much they used small-group work, although all used assigned seating plans, and students varied in their skill in muttering quietly or in getting away with a bit of cheeky chat with friends or even teachers. However, much of the classroom interaction was between a designated student and the teacher, in a set question-and-answer format, rather than in collaborative or other kinds of free-flowing work. Group work in Science or Design and Technology almost always offered the opportunity for carefully controlled social talk under the teacher's radar.

A few days into the term, we also met the teachers in their collective induction meeting—another sea of expectant, if politely skeptical, faces. The headteacher reminded us that he thought the whole idea "mad," but he was relaxed, seemingly no longer worried about our impact on school life. It did not take long before the other teachers welcomed us in the staff room or stopped us in the corridor to chat about the project or to tell us something about the school. No doubt it helped that Julian had been a teacher, that we came from a high-status university, and that we seemed friendly. The school was anticipating a government quality inspection,[18] which had everyone in a state of high anxiety, notwithstanding the headteacher's motivational cheerleading in the twice-weekly staff meetings.

Some teachers needed reassurance that we were there to observe students rather than to criticize them; some students needed to see that we would not "tell tales." Occasionally, we supported the teacher or guided a student, but mostly we watched, writing down all we could. And while we sought to prioritize the young people's experiences, hearing also from their teachers (and, later, their parents) added to our understanding. Our field notes are full of observations about classroom life, capturing the mix of experiences that made up any student's day. We were struck early on by the incessant mention of achievement levels (as discussed in chapter 6). We were also particularly surprised to discover the young people's commitment to their teachers' incessant focus on assessment, leading us to reflect on the interests at stake in sustaining so individualistic a discourse of learning.

We followed the students as they moved through a variety of lessons each day, each lasting an hour, with gaps for a morning break and 45 minutes for lunch. Being released from a classroom into the more liminal space of the corridor was always an interesting experience, allowing for the release of personal talk that had been bottled up during each teaching period. We saw quick flirtations, harsh and nasty words being exchanged, or just boisterous chatter as we followed the students around. Sedat often caught up with his Turkish-speaking friends at these moments, for example. But corridors and staircases quickly became jammed in the transition between classrooms, and teachers added to the hubbub by shouting instructions and trying to keep order. The bathrooms were not popular spaces; they, too, were slightly unfriendly, and although the bathrooms were not directly supervised, few students seemed to congregate there.

Lunchtime and after-school activities had to be fitted in, along with eating lunch itself, which for Year 9 students had to be done on the premises. The canteen, used by most students, offered thumbprint identification technology so that parents could top up the payment or monitor their child's food intake. As the canteen was not large enough to seat the whole school, students spent much of their lunchtime lining up rather than in relaxed socializing, although we did see groups from the class, with others, chatting together over lunch. Shane liked to put his arm around the girls, but we saw little sexualized behavior. Students were sent out of the main buildings at break and lunchtimes.

We attended a range of after-school clubs, finding them more relaxed—even the astronomy class to gain an extra GCSE, for which Sara had been selected. Here, and occasionally in the banter between staff and students in the playground or even in some lessons, there was a leavening of the otherwise rather austere formal relations that dominated the day. For example, rehearsals for the school play were characterized by considerable informality and intimacy—joking or irreverence between student and teacher, flirtatiousness among a number of the students—marking a strong contrast to behavior in school hours. Such contrasts in the learning experience gave us pause for thought. In relation to the play (a popular musical), it seemed that the reward on offer was intrinsic—with mastery and expertise evident to all—although the final performance was also motivating. The learning identity on offer in these rehearsals was different too: rather than disciplined bodies, the chorus was encouraged to be exuberant, the young people were to be sexy, and the stars were to shine.

The final act in the daily school routine[19] was the journey home—often the last opportunity for the students to spend time together face-to-face, so there was a tendency to stretch out the time. We often saw young people hanging around the local shops a little away from the school. Such moments felt relaxed, although teachers sometimes patrolled the park, and the community police officers had accounts of violence or theft on the streets. These moments also illustrate the importance of being open to what the young people wanted to tell us about: listening to them talk about time spent away from school alerted to us to the value of in-between spaces for them, characterized by a very different pace, mood, and sense of agency to that of the often demanding rhythms of the school day. As Giselle explained, it was "a slow journey" on purpose—to free themselves from the demands of school life.[20] It was also peer time; Megan and Gideon told us that, should they find themselves walking home alone, they would pretend to be calling friends "for cover" so as not to look like "a loner." When with friends, Abby told us, "we'll, like, go shopping or just, like, go out to the park or something or just, like, just go do anything really that we feel like doing." Transcribed, she sounds inarticulate, but her point is important—that this time was not determined by others, especially teachers or parents.[21] And there seemed to be an unwritten rule that so long as they got home before their parents did, no questions were asked about where they had been. Since both home and school turned out to strongly define the young people's activities and identities, recognizing when they felt more in control—in corridors at school, bedrooms at home, or with peers on- or offline—was important in grasping how they navigated the pressures on them (see chapter 4).

A Day in the Life—At Home

The feel of the project changed after Christmas as we left behind the busy world of the school, with its injunctions to behave and succeed, and immersed ourselves in the cluttered but quieter world of the home. As we saw even on Progress Day, the parents ranged between mildly positive and very interested in our project. We were welcomed into the homes of all but two members of the class, although of course we had to reassure and account for ourselves with each family. The sheer diversity of household arrangements, styles, and provision struck us immediately, after our immersion in the singular world of school. Some homes were very wealthy, others poor. Some were formal, with tidy front rooms and inaccessible private spaces, while others had a sense of informality, with doors left open and people interrupting or chatting in our presence. In some, other members of the family came to check us out; in others, they kept their distance. We drank a lot of tea, asked a lot of questions, admired pets, poked about as much as felt comfortable, and explained our project as often as asked.[22]

Most, but not all, of the young people seemed at ease at home, although, as we have noted, many would delay reaching home and would even be glad to find what Megan called a "free house" (in other words, a house with no parents present), where they could gather with friends. Once home, they appeared relatively free to lie around and relax. Indeed, "relaxing" was a word they used a lot, referring both to the release from the exhausting discipline of school and to the ability to control their actions, even if this meant being bored or just getting something to eat and watching television—still the most frequent leisure activity. All the girls told us they changed out of their school uniforms first thing once back home, again symbolizing the shift from a public or official school identity to a private one.

Our visits home had to be fitted in around homework, after-school activities, family commitments, and a social life, and these often proved tricky to arrange. For example, Jamie went to tennis practice and Sebastian to drama. Jenna and Yusuf were regular attendees at mosque school, and Yusuf also had a two-hour science class at a local cultural center (see chapter 8). Fitting everything in was a challenge to the young people too, and several—especially some of the boys—seemed tired on reaching home. We could see that finding time for homework somehow meant returning to the demands and control of school—hence their tactics of procrastination or resistance. Keeping Facebook on while doing homework or alternating between homework and chatting to friends while playing computer games seemed to put the young person back in charge.

While triangulating observations and interviews permitted us to gain a deeper insight into the patterns of the young people's lives at home, it took us quite a while to feel confident about the various family dynamics. We had to build up our portraits from informal observations as well as several interviews with the young people, their parents, and some siblings (see chapter 7 on family life). Talking to the young people at home would often cast a different light on what was said at school. At school, for instance, Megan and Adriana, interviewed together, bragged about how they never did any homework. But we were puzzled, knowing that their grades were good, and we rarely saw them in detention. Visiting them at home, however, showed us when and how some homework did get done, allowing us a fuller picture from different information sources. This not only revealed "the truth," as it were, about doing homework but also the girls' desire to act "cool" at school, something that shaped their orientation to most lessons as well as in the informal spaces in between.

In this phase of the research, we listened out for the role that digital media played in the young people's domestic lives.[23] We could not observe the entire day at home, of course, but we learned that, for many of the young people, time at home involved considerable media use—marking the start and end of the day, filling in time, accompanying other activities, all connecting the young people with their friends and peer culture. As one of our short in-class surveys revealed, all had a computer or laptop and internet access at home, although the latter did not always work. Lydia and her best friend were typical in turning their phones on—and not letting go of them—from the minute they left the school gates to when they fell asleep at night. Giselle "organized" her friends via social media, checking Facebook and Tumblr on getting home after school, before becoming absorbed in Minecraft.[24] Dom checked Twitter first thing in the morning to see "what everyone was saying last night."[25] Abby appreciated the effect of music early in the morning, saying that this made her feel happy and more awake. From such snippets, we began to frame the detailed case studies that we explore in this book: Why was Dom an early adopter of Twitter? What did music mean? How could we interpret Giselle's absorption in Minecraft or several of the boys' love of Xbox?

The semistructured nature of the after-school period seemed magnified at weekends and holidays, with rules on time spent on television or games relaxed and bedtimes later (see chapter 7).[26] For some, this meant freedom to engage even more with screen media of one kind or another, but Shane spoke for many in relishing these opportunities: "Yes, I'm always out . . . [with] more of a social life now." Social media were relegated to the status of filler. As Shane further explained, "Facebook, because, like, that's, like, you know, when, like, you're bored at home and you're checking things to do—like, say, if I wanted to play football on the weekends, I'd like to talk to people and watch people, so that's what I really do." Conversations such as these contrasted strongly with the popular discourses of digitally obsessed youth that surrounded us—and the young people themselves—throughout the year. With expressions of urgent concern from parents, teachers, journalists, and policy makers about a generation supposedly lost in the digital world echoing in our ears, we would enter one home or another to find the teenagers itching to hang out with their friends face-to-face or telling us that social networking sites were becoming boring and that they would rather watch television with their family downstairs.[27]

We learned that weekends and holidays did not just allow time to see friends or play computer games, but—even more important—they were valued as time under the control of the young people themselves. This was not always easy for the young people to explain, and we had to listen carefully to grasp their experience of agency. In the following exchange between Megan and Adriana, they define the key features of a weekend:

MEGAN: It's not actually that different to [a weekday]. . . .
ADRIANA: Yes, it is.
MEGAN: No, it's not, except I wake up earlier, and I see the people who I choose to see, because in lessons, it's, like, you're still, like, talking and stuff.
ADRIANA: No, but it is much different because you're—you've got, like, a motive or something.
MEGAN: Yes, you have something that I will do.

They were trying to explain that agency lies not in what you do but in the fact that you decide to do it. That is what makes weekends "just kind of not at school," as Max expressed it. Or as Shane said, "I've just got my own time [on weekends]. I can do whatever I want really." And getting together face-to-face always trumped media use, although "letting" the young people become more independent occasioned anxieties among their parents.[28] We saw some evident gendering—the girls tended to talk of shopping, the boys of playing football or computer games—but we were also alert to the exceptions: Abby turned out to be a good football player; Giselle loved computer games.

A Year in the Life of the Class

Just as each day plays out to its own beat, the school year has its rhythms too. Teachers and students started the year full of good intentions, with lots of talk about targets and aspirations, establishing goodwill and long-term ambitions. Most students had not seen each other over the summer holidays, and they cautiously reestablished (or ended) friendships or alliances. As students felt out the disciplinary tone of unfamiliar teachers, the first few weeks of the new term were conducted carefully, although we saw some strange testing by some—Megan putting her feet on her desk, for instance. Gradually, this was replaced by the constant hum of conversation as the quiet of anticipation blurred into the everyday of routine. Tiredness set in at the end of each week and before holidays; tempers frayed, and the high hopes and lofty rhetoric of achievement faded from classroom talk as everybody focused on meeting weekly targets, completing homework, or preparing for tests.

Often in morning registration, Catherine would remind the students of the array of extracurricular activities on offer, encouraging the students to go along and try things out, checking if they had gone as promised—a message reiterated to every parent on Progress Day, as we saw earlier. But she seemed increasingly dismayed at how hard it seemed to motivate them to join in, although, as we reflected, this could have been precisely because participation was so closely monitored, rewarded, and desired by teachers and parents (see chapter 8). And over time, northern European gloomy mornings and gray evenings added to the general weariness as winter approached. We spent less time in the school through the spring and summer as our focus turned to the home. In any case, teacher workloads changed with the approach of summer, with more focus on preparing the older students for public (national) examinations and less concern with Year 9, this being often seen as part of an internationally recognized "middle-school" problem[29]—neither absorbed in the task of acclimatizing students to secondary school nor focused on the exams that "really count."

Significantly, in Year 9, students and parents had to make some key decisions about academic direction—arts or sciences, languages, or practical subjects—beginning the narrowing of options toward the concentration on just three or four subjects by the age of 16–18. Following the parent-teacher meetings in the autumn term and the Progress Day meetings with Catherine, the spring term saw an "options meeting" for the whole year group, setting out the educational pathways ahead. By the summer term, key choices had been made, amid some anxiety on the part of the students.[30] We examine how the students progressed during the year and how they began to envisage possible futures in chapter 10.

Other developments could be accommodated within the fieldwork year. At the start of the year, the students received a series of invitations to participate—in the school play (a popular musical), in an all-year fund-raiser to go on a "World Challenge" (see the conclusion), in a series of sporting opportunities, and in making a film of life at school, *A Life in the Day of VFS*.[31] It was a distinctive feature of our research design that we could follow some of these over time. For example, we watched as several students from the class initially auditioned for the school play at the start of the year, although only Max and Dilruba followed through. And while some of the young people enjoyed filming *A Life in the Day*, the task of controlling them came to dominate the activity—from preventing Fesse from filming a teacher he thought terrible to not letting the students edit the resulting footage—because it would be too time-consuming and because it risked the final product showing the school in a less-than-ideal light. Unsurprisingly, Adam—whose teacher and parents had pushed him to participate once he expressed a mild interest in photography during Progress Day—complained that the whole thing had become "boring."[32]

These kinds of experiences illustrated something that we observed over and again during the year: how the promises and invitations made at the start of the year fall by the wayside due to lack of time, resources, or, apparently, "student interest." Strikingly, we saw no instances of the converse; over the course of one year in the lives of our class, we saw several interests lapse, but no one developed an interest they had not already had before. Most striking were the blocked or opaque pathways between formal (in-school) and informal (at-home) learning, as we explore particularly in chapter 9 in relation to music learning.

By the early summer, we had completed our fieldwork in class and in homes and had moved into the third phase: a more intensive and detailed exploration of extracurricular and peer-based activities. Travel plans in the summer holidays meant that families found it harder to make time for us, although when we could visit, the time we spent with the young people was often the most relaxed.[33] Having become familiar with the class after spending a year together, the following autumn we decided to do a formal exit interview with each member of the class—inviting them to look back over the year, to reflect on the experience of the project, and to anticipate the next phase of their lives—we were welcomed back into their lives with enthusiasm. By this time, the young people were strongly focused on studying for public exams or on their (now) more intense social and personal lives. What the year had meant to them and what, in retrospect, seemed to have helped or hindered their progress is examined in chapter 10.[34]

Conclusions

In this chapter, we have offered an ethnographic portrait of a day and a year in the life of the class, with two linked purposes in mind. In terms of research methodology, our aim was to demonstrate the main features of our approach to the young people's lives, making clear our own role along with the methodological decisions we made about the research. As readers will vary in their familiarity with the English state school system, the nature of British multiculturalism, or the character of London, further information is provided in the appendix. Demographic and other information about the young people themselves can also be found there.[35] Knowing our dramatis personae should, we hope, permit you to follow their paths through a year in their lives and, thus, through the course of this book.

The second purpose of this chapter was to show how the main themes that occupy the rest of the book emerged from our research. Thus, we have signaled which particular themes will be addressed in each of the chapters to follow, while also acknowledging that they are all interconnected in the young people's everyday lives. What do we mean by saying that the book's themes emerged? In some instances, our theoretical framework or prior expectations (as discussed in chapter 1) defined the themes we wished to pursue. In other instances, we were surprised or intrigued by what we encountered during the research itself, and this led to more in-depth exploration in the chapters that follow. Yet this is too neat a distinction. We had begun our research with the intention of exploring the connections among the practices and places of children's social, digital, and learning lives. Thus, we designed a study focused on school and home, while being prepared to encompass such other places of importance to the young people. Just what we would find at home or school and what any of these places might mean to the young people was far from obvious at the outset, so while we had decided where to start looking, where we ended up and what we saw along the way all emerged over the year of fieldwork and, indeed, in the months of analysis and writing that came after.

In particular, until the fieldwork had progressed sufficiently for us to have accompanied the young people across these different places, talking to them and observing them all the while, we were not fully sensitized to the ways in which young people, parents, and teachers understood or misunderstood each other. So, having observed how teachers referred to parents and home, when we went home with the young people, we listened carefully to how school and teaching was discussed by parents. We were intrigued by the sense that students' life outside school is, to their teachers, elusive, shadowy, and adversely dominated by media. Seemingly, the students materialize at the start of the school day and disappear on leaving the school grounds into a mysterious mix of family customs, homework, hobbies, friendships, television viewing, and Facebook use. All this seemed as vague yet worrying to the teachers as, we learned later, was the life of the school to parents, who tended to see their children disappear each morning to live out a day in which "nothing much happens."

Meanwhile, we became increasingly curious about the young people for whom the places or spheres of life were neatly connected; Dominic and Sara became our two key instances, young people whose identities seemed harmoniously coherent whether at home or at school and, in Dom's case particularly, across differing social worlds. For others, however, it was the disconnections between home, school, and peer group that were most interesting, as well as the young people's strategies—as often digital or online as well as offline—to manage these discordances or disconnections especially when it came to presenting themselves across these contexts. While at first we suspected that this self-management could be a matter of social class, with Dom's and Sara's confidence and achievement seeming to ease their paths in comparison to those who found life at home or school more difficult, our understanding of social class became more nuanced as we grappled with the many complexities and contingencies of economic, cultural, and ethnic differentiation among children's lives in late modernity. What these mean for the social reproduction of relative advantage or disadvantage in the long run, and what economic and cultural capital mean for young people's learner and social identities and experiences in the here and now, became a theme of the book.

The question of the "digital age" also runs across all the chapters. Given the widespread public and policy claims about the supposed differences that the digital makes, we could hardly approach this dimension of the research naively. Therefore we sought deliberately to put these often hyperbolic claims to one side, especially when observing and questioning the young people, although occasionally we referred to these claims deliberately as a means of provoking teachers or parents to think about the role of digital media. Only thus could we have found, as our portrait of a day and a year in the lives of the class already shows, that the digital is simultaneously endemic and mundane, neither all determining nor irrelevant.[36] We began to question in what ways, if at all, living and learning is being reshaped in the digital age, in comparison to which previous forms of mediation, and over what timescale.

Thus, in terms of theory in chapter 1 and here in terms of methods, this book asks, what, if anything, is distinctive about the texture of young people's lives today, and what identities are they forming? What does being educated mean for young people, their families, and their teachers in an individualized risk society? And what are the demands, resources, and institutional practices that facilitate or constrain young people's agency as they seek to determine their future trajectory and life changes? We develop our answers through eight themed empirical chapters that follow. In chapter 3, we meet the class again, now using the lens of social network analysis so as to map their connections and disconnections in the digital age.

3

Networks and Social Worlds

A key challenge we set ourselves in this book was to understand the relations and interconnections among members of the class. In the introduction and chapter 1, we noted that "networks" and "connectedness" are terms often used in initiatives and visions aiming to improve education, quality of social life, and future life chances, by fostering flexible, extensive, and sometimes unanticipated or creative links among people and across places and spheres of knowledge and activity.[1]

In this chapter, we explore how interconnected the members of our class were, in what ways, and what such connections meant to the individuals concerned. In the process, we also explore how their lives make connections across the places of school, home, and elsewhere. Then, in the era of Facebook, we wanted to explore what the idea of online connections means to these young people. We mapped their relationships within and beyond the class, asking what they mean for the members and whether online networks reinforce prior connections or create new ones. We also examined how the social worlds of family or community intersected with school-based networks.

Starting with "the class," this chapter maps the nature and scope of the young people's social networks to understand what patterns emerge and why. The metaphor of the network allows us to recognize the provisional and shifting nature of the ways that people live their lives, focusing on the communicative flows among people and the interconnections or disconnections that result. By prioritizing links over nodes, the network metaphor offers an alternative to research focused either on particular places (such as the small social worlds of home or school or neighborhood) or on particular individuals. Mapping the networks within and beyond the class also allows us to see the class not as a mere aggregate of individuals or a collection of girls and boys or wealthy and poor children but as a mesh of interconnections.

This approach allows us to question claims that the network has become the "dominant cultural logic" of our time. Kazys Varnelis speaks for many contemporary scholars in arguing that, "although subtle, this shift in society is real and radical. During the space of a decade, the network has become the dominant cultural logic."[2] Yet the existence of (nondigital) social networks is as old as society itself.[3] And perhaps even the network metaphor has its limits as a way of explaining relationships, as it is not obvious how it can be squared with the importance of gender, social class, ethnicity, and locale, all of which play a crucial role in young people's lives.[4]

Within and Beyond the Class

In some respects, "the class" is a meaningful unit; in other respects, it is a figure of convenience. Having spent several years together, although frequently split into other classes for teaching with at least half of the year group at VFS, the class had developed a set of shared narratives and ways of being confortable with each other. More widely, the year group—with eight parallel classes—was also important, the source of many friendships for the most of the young people.

Relations within the class varied considerably. Some were fairly superficial—a way of getting on with life at school. Others represented strong friendships that extended beyond the school. Most were in a state of flux, waxing and waning over a matter of months or years. The very notion of the class was more important for some young people than others, and although they had learned to get along with each other, we soon realized that for most of them, the center of gravity of their social worlds lay outside the class. Having had a somewhat troubled start in the school, Gideon talked about the class as a kind of safe haven, a place of familiar faces rather than deep friendships: "Everyone, they might not hang out with each other at break or something, but they will know each other, and they would, like, meet up and talk or something." For a few of the boys, the class is where friends were to be found; indeed, it was this proximity that enabled friendships to be made easily. But much of the friendliness we witnessed in the class, particularly the comfortable pairing of girls sitting together in tutor time, turned out to have little wider significance.

So what were the intersecting relations within and beyond the class? Beyond being placed in the same class, even seated together by teachers, what connections do the young people themselves create? And how do learning, social, and digital networks connect? Using the tools of social network analysis,[5] we constructed a series of networks by asking the students nine questions about their relations with each of their classmates in and beyond the life of the school (see the appendix). The whole-class network, shown in figure 3.1, is based on the combined answers to eight of these questions—here we had to omit the question of whom they were Facebook friends with, precisely because everyone who was on Facebook was "friends" with everyone else.[6]

As may be seen in the figure, the network is centered on a strongly reciprocal core of boys (Fesse, Jamie, Gideon, Dom, Sebastian, Nick, Shane, and Adam), linked to a tightly bonded pair of girls, Adriana and Megan, who, although always seated together in the class, were beginning to separate outside it.

Two girls, Sara and Giselle, labeled "gifted and talented" by the school, sat at the front of the class. Their relationship seemed on first impressions to be important; but the network shows that they had few connections to others in the class, and even their pairing turned out to be a matter of convenience. Over time, they were beginning to grow apart—as Sara explained, "we're more school friends than, like, outside"—but they remained collegial. Neither wished to be in the core group, both valuing distinctive status—Sara described herself as "geeky," while Giselle defined herself as "arty" from the outset. Such "clever" girls, perhaps, were challenging to the heavily male class centered on a lively world of football and computer games (see later in this chapter).

A group of mainly minority ethnic boys, although from diverse cultural backgrounds, formed a distinct subgroup in the class network, with Mark, Yusuf, Hakim, and Sedat all symmetrically bonded. Joel, a white boy who seemed a rather withdrawn outsider, was included in the group.

The group of girls at the other edge of the network were also all from diverse minority ethnic groups; but their interconnections were rather loose, and they and their mutual friendships were far from homogeneous.[7] As we discuss in chapter 5, the other young people were wary of Lydia, who seemed to engage in unpleasant and difficult interpersonal conflict. She was unable to develop relationships with both teachers and peers and lived a rather fragile life in and out of school.

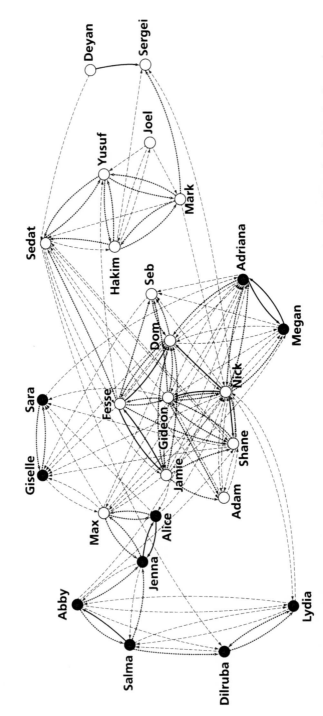

Figure 3.1. The class as a social network. Note: Paler nodes represent boys, darker nodes girls. Also, the darker the lines, the more intense or frequent the connections between people.

Last but perhaps most interesting in terms of what structures a class may enable, Max, Alice, and Jenna formed a clique, in the language of social network analysis, being a fully connected cluster. Yet they were notably heterogeneous—a middle-class white boy living between separated parents, one girl from a happy and confident family, and another girl of East African origin from a much poorer family. Unlike several of the groupings, the clique was stronger outside the school than inside. We often observed the two girls sitting together in class, but at the end of the day, Max would quietly join them at the school gates, as the three crossed the road to hang out at Alice's somewhat bohemian, warmly accommodating home.

Beyond the generally well-behaved and fair-minded unity of "the class," the network diagram shows that the young people's relations beyond the school followed gender, ethnic, and socioeconomic lines, notwithstanding the democratic ambitions of the school, with its seating plan designed to mix them up, and the constant exhortation to act together "as a class" (see chapter 5).[8] No doubt the school did not expect the class members to act in concert outside its walls, but we picked up from teachers the hope that its norms of civility and fairness would carry over into the rest of the young people's lives or, at least, that friendships might be more interest based, not necessarily reproducing conventional social distinctions. The football team was the most obvious enactment of this more democratic ideal, with its mixture of boys from different backgrounds.

It is easy to read the whole-class network as reproducing the types of relationship we see in wider British society. Apart from the clique and the "gifted and talented" girls, the core group included all the middle-class (higher socioeconomic status) young people and most of the white ones. However, Shane, Nick, and Fessehaye are important exceptions to this, as is Adam, a white middle-class boy who was less intensely connected to this group. Interestingly, too, while the core group connected boys and girls and was itself ethnically diverse, the groupings of boys and girls from minority ethnic groups on either side of the network were not themselves interconnected. Nor was there much connection between the middle-class white girls and the minority ethnic girls from poorer backgrounds—although an interest in sports and computer gaming created weak links among the boys across class and ethnic lines.

Sara, a "gifted and talented" middle-class mixed-race girl, was connected with the white middle-class girls and boys rather than the poorer girls from minority ethnic groups.

Explaining the Network

While the patterns in the whole-class network might not have surprised its members, they struggled to account for their seeming reproduction of gender, ethnic, and socioeconomic divides because, as we examine further in chapter 5, the school (and the wider society) stressed inclusion. The young people themselves generally endorsed the idea that all should be equal, treated according to their individual merits rather than their demographic background. We asked middle-class Megan, one of the popular girls in the core group, to explain whom she was friends with. Her answer was highly coded, a matter of who lived where and which school they went to:

> INTERVIEWER: Are you saying that you sort of hang out more with—
> are these more middle-class schools?
> MEGAN: Not really, like, a lot of my friends are—I don't know. Well,
> okay, most people I hang out with, like, I'm not really friends with—
> this sounds bad—any poor people. But that's not because I'm not
> friends with people who are poor. It's just that just happens to be who
> I'm friends with.

We thought this comment suggested a commitment to holding on to these social distinctions, but Megan did not welcome our pushing her on this point. But there is no confident ascription here of herself or others to one or another social class status, and the same was the case when we asked about the importance of ethnicity. Indeed, when we next asked whether the mix of backgrounds at the school was problematic, Megan was glad to explicate the democratic vision of the whole class: "No, I don't really think that's an issue, like, because we all go to the same school, so we're not that different. . . . It's not like we're going to have fights: 'You're not as rich as me. I don't like you.' So I don't think it matters. I think it's good because you can always meet someone who's, like, different to you." Shane, whose family was not well-off, was more willing to have a go at explaining how social class divides the students: "In our year, we've got the posh people. There's the people that play pat ball, football, and the people that chat about rubbish."

Shane had no trouble naming "the posh people" but found it hard to explain why they merited such a label: "They're not posh, but we just call them posh, I don't know why." Although it may not have been obvious from his initial classification, Shane was not keen on those who "play pat ball,"[9] preferring those who play football or "chat about rubbish." He qualified this by saying, "Not chat about rubbish but, like, the people, like, always having a laugh—so me, Nick, Gideon." Along with Fesse, these boys are less culturally or economically privileged than the middle-class boys in the core group, but they have all found a way of rubbing along together, a mode of connection founded on mutual interests in football and computer games, along with a readiness for jokey banter.

Shane anchored his account with an analysis also of those on the edge: "Sedat just hangs out with the pat ball people, but he don't play it. Max, he's just kind of everything. He will never hang around with me—he's not my cup of tea—but I think he's posh. . . . And then we've got Giselle: she's the same as like Sergei and everyone"—by which he refers to Giselle's and Sergei's status as semioutsiders. From what we observed, he was not far wrong: those who were ready to "have a laugh" could find their way toward the center of the network irrespective of socioeconomic status, while those who cultivated an outsider status, for whatever reason, were not comfortably in the center, even if they were middle class (Giselle, Max, and to some extent Sebastian).[10]

Varieties of Connection

While being together in the class is valued by the school as deliberately "democratic," and while everyone was civil at school and "friends" on Facebook, not all forms of association were so open. For out-of-school activities of importance to them, the young people sought to manage inclusion and exclusion carefully. To be sure, the students had been dealt certain cards: the composition of individuals in this class, the locale they live in, the expectations of their family. The school, as is common, draws its catchment across an area bifurcated by major road and rail links that divide richer and poorer families. Yet in principle they have considerable freedom in how they play these cards: whom they hang out with, ask for homework help from, share intimacies with.

The whole-class network was constructed from the 26 young people's answers to eight questions. When we generated networks for each of these separately, the overall groupings discussed earlier held up fairly well. For instance, asked "Who do you hang out with?" the core group remained densely connected, but the girls on the edge split up, naming others beyond the class. The other boys, however, remained more connected via football or computer games. Indeed, the network based on doing out-of-school activities was particularly the preserve of the boys, being heavily sports related.

The network was similar for the question "Who is a close friend?" although in relation to this question, the girls on the edge were fairly strongly interconnected. To those who suspect boys mainly hang out in groups, the network belies this, as the core group of boys and those on the periphery variously claimed close friendships with each other.[11] But this age group seemed not to rely on even those whom they called their close friends when they needed help or advice; instead, as we learned from the individual interviews, young people turned to parents, older siblings, or just one or two other friends for this.

Asking for help with homework revealed the densest network of all (apart from being Facebook friends). The class held strongly together through its shared school tasks rather than as an autonomous social or interest-led unit. But the homework network nonetheless resembled that based on sociability (hanging out, doing after-school activities, etc.). In other words, the young people tended to ask questions about their friends' homework rather than asking those who may be best able to answer them.[12] This is fine if your friends know the answers but may disadvantage those who are less sociable or those whose friends do not know the answers. The notable exception was the "gifted and talented" girls, who were, in the homework network only, among the most densely interconnected, presumably because they would be the most useful. Even so, it was the core group (most of whom were middle class) that turned to them for homework help.

Did these networks also exist online? The question "Who do you chat with by text, Facebook, BBM, or MSN?" revealed that the core group had the liveliest digital connections.[13] The clique was equally well connected online, and so, too, were the girls on the periphery of the class network. The "gifted and talented" girls, by contrast, appeared cut off from the class, as did the boys on the periphery of the network.[14] The boys at the edge were less connected to each other online than offline.

In the digital age, we might expect an offline network also to exist online, and in the case of the class, it did.[15] Within the class, almost everyone had a Facebook link to everyone else, and this mirrored their patterns of face-to-face communication. Since, as Megan put it, "everyone" is on Facebook, the result is both an inclusive and a diverse site of social interaction. For instance, Lydia, a rather sad outsider at school, could chat on Facebook with others in the class and also, for escape, with "different sorts of people," while also maintaining multiple Twitter accounts with different names for interactions that were invisible to her classmates. But being "constantly connected"[16] or "always on"[17] should not be seen as more significant than it is. Simply keeping Facebook open and occasionally posting a "What's up" comment ensured mutual availability with low commitment—more like leaving the door open or a light on than announcing a desire for deep interaction at all times. As Fesse said, "It's sort of on like randomly." Dom agreed: "I usually go on it to see what's happening. I don't really chat to people because it's kind of—I can't really be arsed."[18]

The network interconnecting members of the class—the structure of the grouping of "the class"—was just one of several other networks that enmeshed the students' lives with those of others. To identify these other networks, we asked each student to draw his or her "ego network."[19] As for the whole-class networks, this exercise was undertaken in private at home. On a blank page, each young person wrote his or her name in the center and put the names of people important to them all around. We prompted with similar questions to those asked in the whole-class network, following up as appropriate. The answers helped us to understand how the seemingly equivalent links in the network had very different qualities. We examine three groupings in more depth in the following sections.

The Core Group

The closest bonding in the class stemmed from the boys' activity-based groupings—mainly playing football and computer games both at school and on the weekends, with others from the class, the year group, and other schools. By contrast, the girls tended to pair up. As Adriana explained, "There's me and Megan , . . . Salma and Abby, Giselle and Sara, Lydia and . . . And then the boys are together." The boys did not disagree with this analysis: "Boys don't really have close friends. Like, it's girls that have close friends. Boys kind of all go together," Gideon told us. Yet, as noted earlier, in the boys' private answers to the social network task, they did claim close friendships, so hanging out as a group seems more a matter of performing masculinity. Furthermore, Adriana did not mean her analysis in a derogatory way. As she explained, "Apart from Megan, the only person I talk to is the boys." Megan agreed, although she was keen to subdivide the boys into those who, at the age of 13, could speak to girls and those who could not.

In the whole-class network, the boys at the center were all highly social and good at sustaining links with others. Online, too, the core grouping was still central—Dom went on Facebook most days; his wall was full of interaction with others in the core group, along with jokey rude comments, funny pictures, and news about sports. Nick was among the most flirtatious of the boys (his profile showed him posing with a girlfriend and making sexual jokes).

In some ways, the core group comprised an aggregate of previously constructed pairs or small group bonds developed via proximity in the neighborhood (see later in this chapter). Jamie lived near and was friends with Dom. Dom, Nick, Shane, and Fesse were bound together through playing football, the first two in an out-of-school club and all four of them at break times and for the school team. While Sebastian had considerable interpersonal strengths and was comfortable talking with girls and clearly enjoyed jokey banter, we did not see Adam engaging so obviously in this milieu, and his place in this network surprised us slightly—most likely his enthusiasm for computer games, shared by most of the boys, was key to the explanation. All the members of this group, bar Adam, were often seen as part of an even larger peer group that seemed mainly to revolve around the football team—we saw them congregating at the same spot in the playground and often hanging around by the local shops after school.

Connections through computer gaming is complicated by incompatible console systems. Sony PlayStation 3 and Xbox users can only enter the same game world with others playing the same system. For this reason, Nick had ensured that his Xbox friendship group overlapped between his virtual game friends and the real people who were important to him. As we recorded in our field notes,

> He showed me his live friend community, and this has very strong crossover with his real-world, and especially school-based friendship groupings. He is thus only likely to buy and play games, which allow him to interact within this community. We spent a lot of time talking about how he would chat with his friends and also the relationship between gameplay and in school talk. There is a very clear sense how shared gaming experiences provide the material for real-life talk. He also talked about how he hypothesises the minds, attitudes and pleasures of his virtual opponents/collaborators. This part of the discussion was very interesting as he clearly projects frustrations, competitiveness and pleasures onto his friends.

Adam, perhaps the keenest gamer in the class (see chapters 7 and 8), struggled to sustain such an overlap, as his classmates lacked the expertise he shared with those with whom he met up online, some of whom he knew from his previous school. So, with purely online "friends," the in-game conversation is much more interesting because, Adam said, you can "talk about the game while you're playing it"; but "there wouldn't really be anything [else] to talk about, like, between us because nothing would have happened except for playing games with them." Paradoxically, the very fact that his in-game friends knew nothing about the rest of his life made him feel free: "Well, you can be more confident, because they don't know who—in a way they don't really know who you really are. . . . You could just let yourself out to them. . . . You can just act with them however you want because they don't really know." We explore further the ways that online networks extend the possibilities for identity and expression in chapter 4. What this section has shown is that it took focused social effort to sustain a position in the large "core" group. What can be expressed among the popular group is highly restricted, so being in the center is at once conformist (acknowledging contributions, accepting those who are a little different from oneself, keeping up a level of chat and friendliness) and edgy (making rude jokes, flirting, sharing political links, or swearing excessively). Since the class had more boys than girls, this central position was anchored around football and computer games. There was also a lot of critical talk about the school—unfair rules, annoying teachers, acts of minor resistance—that perhaps communicated social confidence as much as irritation with school. In other classes, matters might be different, but whatever the social "glue," fitting in requires effort and a certain kind of social know-how.[20]

The Clique

The friendship clique of Max, Alice, and Jenna seemed anomalous in terms of gender, class, and ethnicity, and we were able to investigate this on one of the many occasions when they hung out in Alice's house: "Everyone just comes to my house. Like, I have never been to Max's house, and I, like, rarely go to Jenna's house. We just come to my house." What emerged from this Sunday afternoon in the summer holidays, helped by a generous order of pizza and soda, was an understanding of how the clique has created its own small social world, full of wit and critical observation, closely shared between them, and shutting out where each of them comes from. Max rather uncomfortably split his time between his mother's and father's houses; Alice had a strong sense of being second to her "practically perfect" older sister and high-achieving parents; and Jenna lived in an overcrowded house with three sisters to a tiny bedroom and a mother she found it difficult to communicate with sleeping in the living room.[21]

The afternoon developed a life of its own when the clique began to discuss its shared love of *Harry Potter* and *The Hunger Games*. As true fans, they had lined up to get the books first, read them over and over, seen the films, read the online commentary, and played the computer game:

ALICE: Yes, we all read *The Hunger Games* series.
MAX: Yes, but we read it first, before it was mainstream.
ALICE: Yes, we read it, like . . .
MAX: Before all the hipsters came and stole it.
INTERVIEWER: Okay.
ALICE: We read it, like, before it came out.
INTERVIEWER: And before the film, basically.

ALICE: Yes, way before the film.

MAX: Way before the film.

As we waited for the pizza, they compared the school houses in *Harry Potter*. Having stated several times that Hufflepuff is the house for "losers," Alice revealed that this was where the online game Pottermore had put her. Max was in Ravenclaw, for "the clever people"; Jenna was in Slytherin, which is "cool."[22] The next excitement was for Pottermore to classify the researcher (in this case, Sonia), who, to Alice's delight, was put in Hufflepuff. This social situation offered a seemingly typical opportunity to display shared knowledge and to assert membership of the group as a true fan. They keenly drew on their knowledge of J. K. Rowling's commentary on her own books, along with a careful reading of the texts, for example, debating their interpretations to work out whether Dumbledore had killed Grindelvald.

Their social world—participated in by many young people globally[23]— was clearly revealed as we discussed how the books' young heroes saved themselves and others from a threatening world or as we indulged in imaginative play: Could Harry and Hermione fall in love? Is Dumbledore gay? Beyond the proud display of fan expertise and the fun of unpicking the plots, there was a lot of talk about emotions: films that made them cry, fighting with their siblings, angry family arguments. We felt, too, that Max and Jenna enjoyed the busy domestic scene at Alice's house—noisy, messy, yet loving; full of photos, shared meals, and lively talk. Alice described how everyone in her family took turns cooking, leading Max to comment, "You're so lucky because I don't get a turn to cook ever. . . . My parents never let me in the kitchen." However, when we visited his house, Max had just made biscuits with his mother, and they talked about making cakes too; so his comment suggests a certain amount of positioning himself as an outsider. Jenna added that they got a lot of take-out food in her house.

Facebook revealed yet further connections and disconnections. On Facebook, the clique took their profile names from *The Hunger Games*, while a number of their friends appear to study at Hogwarts School.[24] Their online chat with each other echoed the rude repartee of face-to-face interaction among the friends at home, rarely visible at school or to anybody else. But their Facebook profiles also conformed to the norm whereby the two girls, but not Max, could be seen to be friends. Moreover, while Max displayed his fan preferences in his profile, Alice's participation in the clique was hidden online; instead, she represented herself as a fun-loving girl from a happy family who looks after little children and has plenty of friends (even though that identity contrasted with her persona at school). By contrast, Max and Jenna showed little or nothing of family life on their profiles, constructing Facebook as a peer-only domain. This reflects a threefold contrast between the presentation of self at school, at home, and online, which each of the three clique members managed differently. At school, Max frequently seemed bored or withdrawn, sassing his teachers or gazing out the window, unlike in the clique, and we never saw Jenna displaying as much knowledge or enthusiasm at school as she did when discussing Harry Potter in the clique. Yet the clique was hidden from conventional displays of friendship especially on Facebook, as we explore in more detail in chapter 4. In short, these three young people's intense social world together, while not positively disguised, is not especially visible either in social interactions at school or online—for in different ways, these are both kinds of public spaces, and the clique came alive when alone together in a unique configuration of friendship and mutual interest.[25]

The Networks of Migration

Every child in the class was linked to networks that had little connection to life at school, and these came primarily through his or her family. But for those from minority ethnic backgrounds (which in themselves varied considerably; see the appendix), these linkages were not merely to cousins or grandparents or friends of the family but to more far-flung relatives, even to a distinct culture very different from that on offer at school.[26]

Mark was a quiet, serious boy at school, always ready to put his hand up, who achieved good grades and was the class representative on the school council. He was not on Facebook at the beginning of the year we spent with the young people, although he harbored ambitions of being more involved in football at school. He drew a smallish ego network of school friends and immediate family, also including the young people

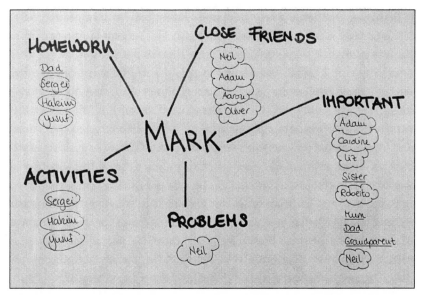

Figure 3.2. Mark's ego network. Key: Name in bubble = member of the class; name in box = other pupils of the school; underlined name = family member; name in cloud = someone from out of school / the neighborhood.

who lived in his block of flats—with whom he played football in the nearby park and computer games at home—and, especially, the two families who had emigrated from the same East African country about the same time as his family and with whom his parents got together every second weekend.

Sedat and his family socialized exclusively with other migrant Turkish families; he spent time out of school with people he called cousins and at school with those who spoke Turkish. He went boxing with other Turkish boys who lived locally and also with extended cousins who seemed to travel over to his house to go to the local club, which was also run by young Turkish men. When we went to his house, his mother seemed to be feeding another young Turkish boy from school in what we took to be an extended form of community-based care. His experiences at a *saz* school (see chapter 9) and his meeting of the people there were completely facilitated by his family. Indeed, for Sedat and Hakim, their membership in the Turkish community made the class seem a secondary form of social organization in their lives.

Language mattered a lot. Sedat and Hakim had both migrated to the UK and very much operated with English as a second language: Turkish was spoken at home. Indeed, all the Turkish boys at the school were operating with English as a second language—unlike many of the other young people from other migrant backgrounds who were more strictly bilingual.[27] Not only did this more restricted use of English impact adversely on their academic performance,[28] but it also ensured that social and interpersonal relationships revolved around Turkish-speaking experiences. Sedat particularly used Turkish in and around the school as a way of creating solidarity and excluding others from his peer group, even drawing a young Turkish-speaking teacher into his repartee. Whereas we saw few relationships that crossed age boundaries for most members of the class, the Turkish boys were much more connected through their membership in this community rather than the narrow boundaries imposed by age-defined membership in the class or the year group.

The friendship among Hakim, Yusuf, Mark, and Sedat seemed unaffected by the fact that Mark and Hakim were not on Facebook (or other electronic media except occasional texts). Being friends for them seemed to be largely a matter of being in the same class, anchored by the fact that Hakim, Yusuf, and Mark also walked to school together, keeping each other company on the journey to the more middle-class neighborhood where the school is located.

The nature of migration patterns and the sheer variety of migrant communities in the locale meant that the young people's sense of belonging to out-of-school networks varied in form and significance. The Turkish community we have just described frequently moved backward and forward between the UK and "home," also encompassing, in Sedat's case, family members who had moved to Germany. Sedat spoke very positively about the small town, with its rural economy, where his grandparents lived and saw his future as much in Turkey as in the UK. However, for Mark and Yusuf, whose families had escaped conflict, "home" was now clearly the UK, and while their families held on to pre-immigration forms of social behavior, the young people saw this more as a background rather than the future. A third group of young people still moved between the country of origin and the UK, emphasizing family connections but not necessarily current peer points of reference. Salma saw her relatives in Pakistan over the summer, and her mother subsequently arranged Skype calls for them to stay in touch; but, she said, "it was better when you were there though." Yusuf's mother used Skype to connect with relatives who were now in Canada, and he, too, visited them over the holiday period.

Fesse, likewise, had been back to East Africa to see relatives over the summer, as had Jenna. However, for these young people, at least at this age, there was a sense of mediating two parallel social worlds, rather than, as in Sedat's case, integrating them. For Deyan, who had recently arrived in the UK, Facebook was in his home language (Sedat's was in both English and Turkish) and thus seemed to keep open connections beyond the social world of the school.

Several of the middle-class students had parents from other European countries, and they seemed to find the maintenance of two parallel social networks hard work. Adam talked about being bored staying with his grandparents back in Germany, although he was proud of his ability to speak German. Adriana, who had a strong circle of people in school, had learned to cope with having to spend a lot of time with relatives in Spain but talked of it being difficult to sustain the same depth of relationships all the time—hence her rather wistful descriptions of spending time cooking with her grandmother back in Madrid.

But neither Adriana nor Adam used networked technologies to stay in touch with family abroad. Indeed, often this role was left to mothers. Deyan's mother used Skype daily to contact her family abroad, back home in Bulgaria, and Jamie's mother, coming from New Zealand, maintained a "family Facebook": "so we put things on, pictures and things like that so we can post to each other and we can see it within the family."[29] Many of these families also subscribed to television services from "home," which were often playing when we went to visit. Nick kept Skype open for his grandmother, suggesting the potential of connected copresence likely to be more common in the future.[30]

Home, Family, and Locale

Much has been said about members of the "digital generation" being so focused on their peer group as to neglect their family, but this was not the case for the class. Generally, the ego networks were filled with friends from school and family almost in equal measure. Figure 3.3

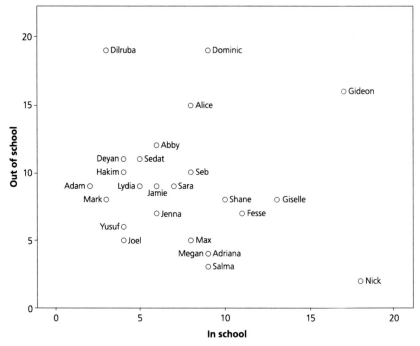

Figure 3.3. Scatterplot of the numbers of in-school and out-of-school contacts that each class member included in his or her ego network.

offers a simple overview of the ego networks, showing the approximate number of people that each class member identified as important to him or her from within the school and from outside it. The numbers should be taken as just a guide,[31] but even so, the patterns are revealing.

First, some members of the class have more populated ego networks than others do: Gideon identified the most people in his; Joel and Yusuf had the fewest. Second, we can see that Dilruba's ego network was strongly focused on family and friends from out of school, while Nick's was strongly focused on people in school. Then we see a spread, rather than any generalized pattern or clear groupings with a balance of in- and out-of-school contacts. Further, at least in this small dataset, we cannot discern any obvious patterns by gender, socioeconomic status, or ethnicity, which suggests that "important" people are a matter of personal choice transcending such conventional social boundaries.

If we were to look more closely into the class members' out-of-school contacts, we would find further differences in the balance between family and other people, whether children or adults. But for all the young people, family was a primary and defining social resource, as we explore further in chapters 7 and 8. To be sure, family life had its problems, and even the meaning of "family" varied: for some, this meant the nuclear family, while for others, the extended family was also significant. Sara's ego network showed a relatively small social world divided into her nuclear family and her close friends, with online connections among the friends but not the family. Adriana—who liked to play the bad girl at school—drew a reassuring daisy-like image, with herself in the center, surrounded by her family and friends all mixed together. Jenna named her three sisters as her close friends in addition to members of the clique and a few others. Virtually all the young people named members of their close family as somebody they would turn to if they had a problem.[32]

In public discussions about youth, the difficulties of young people's meeting up face-to-face—because of parental fears for their safety, the cost of public transport, the lack of bicycle lanes or affordable places to meet up—is seldom mentioned.[33] Yet it is clear from the fieldwork that everyday physical colocation is still the primary means of constructing friendship circles, maintaining family connections, and exploring wider networks, each of which opens up different forms of social organization.[34] Who from the class lives nearby really mattered. We found the young people's social worlds to be heavily local, with unsupervised movement about or beyond the neighborhood being fairly rare. Megan said, "Sebastian lives, like, round the corner to me and Dominic and Jamie, so we'll, like, usually meet, like, either in the park or [nearby shops]. So sometimes I'll, like—usually I'll meet up with [my two best friends]. They'll come to my house, or I'll go to their house. And then we go and meet up with them. . . . And then we'll go to someone's house or go to the park." Indeed, the young people spent most of their time within a few miles of their home and school—the boys playing football or generally hanging out locally, the girls meeting up with best friends or walking to school together, possibly being more supervised. As Dilruba said, "I can't just walk out the house, no, but yes, I can just go to my friend's house." Mark's father explicitly linked the restrictions on young people's movement in their locale with their enthusiasm for social networking sites. In his own childhood in Africa, he reflected, "The village is open for everyone. You go in everybody's house, and you—in the morning, you go out, out in the field, play for 12 hours up in the mountains or somewhere, up, a suburb of the city, and it's like an adventure." But today, in the cosmopolitan city, his son's adventures are "confined within the room, which is very sad." Yet online, he added, "they are now way beyond sometimes, beyond our comprehension. They have this connection. They do online talk and play with other people as they might even—may not know, but he—they say that it's their friends, actually. They talk and they play with them, and it's going far sometimes." Even though members of the class participated in other networks beyond the school and home—sports clubs, culturally based institutions and activities, computer gaming—it was striking how often parents mediated these and, thereby, influenced which might flourish.[35] Parents were important in transporting their children to and fro. Jamie, who played tennis competitively twice a week and additionally in tournaments at weekends, was ferried about by his mother. Sara went climbing with her father on Saturdays. Dom and Nick attended the local football club, but Dom needed his parents to take him to cricket matches in the summer. Perhaps because of parental fears about the risks of city living, independent travel seemed to need a rationale—as an organized activity, undertaken in company. Sebastian now took the bus to his drama club, although it was his mother who as an adult participant had introduced him to the club.

Despite living in the suburb of a major city, only rarely did any member of the class actually travel into the city center, even accompanied by parents, although visits to local shopping centers were undertaken with close friends. The most independent person in the class was Shane, who talked enthusiastically about being off on his bike, making friends in parks or football fields across the wider neighborhood, although he was still tethered through his mobile phone:

It's like you see all kids on the street just looking at you like cautious, but when I'm day off, I feel peaceful. I can do my own thing, play football, do whatever I want, and I know what's bothering me like. I even know, like, the residents there now. Nick's mum always says, "Hi." People that I see

there in the park go, "all right?" and I'm like, "Yes, how are you?" "Fine."
Even some, like there's these days where it's a hot day, and loads of people
come out from around that area. And here are all these little kids. I even
muck around with the little kids, playing football with them.

Shane effectively conveyed an image of predigital childhood that,
for many adults, is strongly nostalgic—this is how life was before the
anxieties of the risk society restricted children to their media-rich bedrooms.[36] Indeed, as fewer and fewer children share in Shane's freedom,
the role of family in scaffolding connections beyond the tight constraints of immediate locality becomes increasingly important.

Conclusions

This chapter has used social network analysis to open up some of the
ways of relating and belonging that shaped the young people's relations
within and beyond the class. It has revealed a series of interconnecting
yet discrete networks that make up the young people's social worlds. It
has also revealed how boundaries between places and social relations
were constructed. One key border was between school and home.
Some teachers seemed to find the students' lives out of school somewhat unreal: what, they asked us in tones of curious incredulity, were
we finding about life "outside" or online? Or, as one teacher speculated
to us about how he imagined the students spent their lives, "You see
them at the bus stop on their phones. It's all meaningless social networking," adding in slightly comical fashion, "It's not as if they're on
Wikipedia learning anything." The parents, similarly, saw little of their
children's friendships, knowing only friends whom they were told about
or who were brought home to meet them. Even the class teacher, Catherine, could say little about their lives outside the class: she thought the
clique members Alice and Jenna might be friends out of school, but she
was not sure; she thought Shane was probably a loner outside school
because he seemed on the edge of things in the class. As we have seen,
Alice, Jenna, Shane, and the others had rather different stories to tell.

We pursue in later chapters whether there are costs to these attempts
at controlling such boundaries—that in effect they exacerbate disconnections across domains and thus within young people's lives. What we

have seen here is that the young people themselves tried to control access to the different parts of their lives. For instance, we saw how the clique created stronger barriers than connections between home and school, and offline and online, and we saw in other cases that what was visible at school or to parents or even to peers was carefully managed by the young people as they moved from place to place. In other chapters, we examine such disconnections more closely, to discover how identities and behaviors did not travel between home and school.

One conclusion from this chapter, with its construction and then deconstruction of the whole-class network, is that adults' fascination with the imaginary of "the class" as a coherent "small lifeworld" is significantly misplaced. In itself, it may reflect a nostalgia for a time when our social worlds had more distinct territories, shared values, high self-sufficiency, and a preordained place in the community—all of which Benita Luckmann argues to have been characteristic of premodern societies.[37] But from the young people's perspectives, their experiences of being in the class were contingent, impermanent. For sure, "the class" offered each student a meaningful learner and social role—as central or peripheral, popular or esoteric, majority or minority, and so forth. Further, the unit of the class was meaningful precisely because it brought such different kinds of people together; as a study of social relations in UK secondary schools found, culturally diverse schooling can support the development of positive attitudes to ethnic diversity among the students.[38] For this reason, in chapter 5, we examine the possible tensions between commonality and difference, as this was played out in daily life, to reveal how the school sought to construct its own version of a civil society. On the other hand, this chapter has also shown how sources of difference lie just beneath the surface; and these became all the more important when students left the school grounds.

This finding leads us to suggest that claims about the individualizing effects of the network society should not underplay the importance of spatially located social worlds structured by gender, ethnicity, and social class. Over and again in this book, we will see how these define and constrain young people's relationships in their choices of friendship. This, in turn, leads us to question the widely influential claim that traditional social structures are giving way to networked individualism in the digital age. Barry Wellman and Lee Rainie argue,

In generations past, people usually had small, tight social networks . . . where a few important family members, close friends, neighbors, and community groups . . . constituted the safety net and support system for individuals. This new world of networked individualism is oriented around looser, more fragmented networks that provide on-demand succor. . . . The revolutionary social change from small groups to broader personal networks has been powerfully advanced by the widespread use of the internet and mobile phones.[39]

Yet it is Wellman and Rainie's characterization of times past more than that of networked individualism that captures rather well the ordinary lives of the class today.[40] It is not that "the class" is itself the most important unit for the young people, but it is a key point of intersection, where their few small worlds become connected or disconnected in ways that matter. And we certainly did not see that each young person enjoyed the benefits of a "looser" and "broader" but highly "personal" or individualized network. Rather, they were embedded, more or less securely, within rather tight networks—experienced as coherent small worlds—centered on home, school, locale, and diaspora. But this is not to suggest that nothing has changed over recent decades. The young people's small social worlds were not simply those of traditional British society. Rather, they were profoundly rewritten by the effects of globalization, as shown by the mix of ethnicities and affluence represented in the class. Connections with diverse diasporas alter the geography of social relations, linking children to particular communities or subcultures in their locale as well as to relations in their country of origin.[41]

What, then, of modern notions of connection and "connectivity"?[42] Our observation that digital networks underpinned most of the social networks in the class is clearly a 21st-century phenomenon. These tended to reinforce relations of popularity and peripherality, permitting the class members to display certain kinds of public identity to each other as a class, while also facilitating other kinds of identity exploration away from the group. This leads us to wonder whether the shared space of Facebook, taking in nearly the whole class, rendered the few "outsiders" even more isolated. Or did such a space of visibility enable some to join in (and be seen to join in, however "weak" the ties) when previously they may have lacked any ready means of doing so?[43] Such questions are taken up in chapter 4. We have seen here that engaging in online networks strengthens and to some degree extends young people's connections. Yet our analysis of the ego networks drawn up by class members suggests that it did not especially increase the diversity or deepen the quality of their relationships. Rather, online communication seemed to reinforce (rather than undermine) the importance of relationships with family and local friends built primarily through face-to-face communication.[44] To develop this insight further, we next turn to the young people's own accounts of identity formation within and through their offline and online relations with peers.

4

Identities and Relationships

Having analyzed the web of social relationships that connected the young people within and beyond the class, we now focus in more detail on the texture of the young people's friendships and peer relations, asking, How do they create identities for themselves within the peer network? As the later chapters show in relation to life at school and home, children and young people live substantially in worlds not of their own making. Thus, we start with their friendships and social worlds, where they might appear to have more choice. As we saw in chapter 3, the unit of the class provides a convenient world for some young people, but for most, the friendships that matter both predate and extend beyond the class. We saw, too, that the young people often construct these friendships along gendered, classed, and ethnic lines in ways that contrast with the values of the school, which, as we show in chapter 5, is supposedly blind to difference. So what do young people's friends mean to them? What forms of sociality do they sustain, in public or private, online or offline? And how do these shape the construction and expression of identity across the sites of school, home, and elsewhere?[1]

Intriguingly, when we mapped young people's connections in chapter 3, we discovered that while members of the class had on average 500 "friends" on Facebook, when they drew us their ego network, they identified just 16 people as important to them. On the one hand, for this cohort, the heyday of Facebook had coincided with the class starting secondary school and needing quickly to establish their place in this new and much larger social world; as Nick said, "In Year 7, it was all about Facebook." On the other hand, this did not mean that young people do not know what friendship or privacy really means anymore. Indeed, when it came to people important to them, they claimed no more friends than was ever the case.[2] And the handful of friends they did claim were mostly local and all well known to them.

It seems, then, that young people sustain several intersecting social worlds. Is this simply a matter of an online world of multiple "weak ties" and an offline world of grounded, strong ties? Weak ties were originally theorized "offline"[3] as well as, now, online, so what seems new is the possibility of strong ties online. Equally interesting are the possibilities for online identity expression supporting, extending, or contrasting with what takes place offline.

Already by Year 9, Facebook had become a routine, even banal, means of keeping an eye on activity within the peer group. As Dom observed, "For us now, because we've grown up having all this stuff, it's not, like, amazing."[4] With few exceptions, the young people's offline friendships were mirrored and supported by their online networks, these playing an important role in sustaining relations with friends seen during the day but otherwise inaccessible in the evenings, given restrictions on children's movement outside the home. Part of what matters here is precisely that everyone is on it, everyone is available. Mark and Hakim said they just had not seen the point of joining, yet Mark had acquired a profile by the end of the year, perhaps reflecting his increasingly comfortable position getting along with the other boys, while Hakim may have been hampered by having the poorest internet connectivity at home that we witnessed.

For some members of the class, however, we shall see in this chapter how the online networks also significantly extended the offline ones or provided a means of presenting a successful, or different, alternative "face" to their peers. Some of these reconfigurations of social networks involved the exploration of further online services: Twitter, Tumblr, and others that lay somewhat under the radar, not least because at the time of the fieldwork, Facebook was becoming highly monitored by adults, responding to media panics and safety concerns. This suggests that it is not simply that online communication occurs away from the heavily supervised spaces of home and school but that the communication process was distinctively shaped by the affordances of online sites and services themselves—in other words, by what the technology itself makes possible.[5] We will show how these technologies make communication more visual, visible, searchable, and persistent. For example, it has not previously been possible to sort through other people's contact lists or to check one's message history among that of others in one's network, as there is no real precursor to the digital footprint, which makes much of today's communicative activity (comments, likes, images, links, etc.) visible to others.

Given the explosion of "weak ties" in the digital, networked age,[6] everyone is increasingly connected to everyone else. Yet since one cannot "really" know everyone, building meaningful social worlds seems to involve a further set of choices—how to present oneself in different contexts, how far to connect different groups of friends, and when to place boundaries so as to limit or exclude connections.[7] So how do young people manage these choices? What degrees of visibility or separation do they sustain? And where does all this leave face-to-face communication?

Visible Popularity

In chapter 3, we described the largest group in the class as "core"—the members well connected to each other and others, seemingly comfortable in their social standing. Yet further time spent with the class challenged the notion that life is easy for the core group or indeed that those who are on the periphery are more marginalized. We have already seen how the clique set themselves against any normative expectations, forming their own social world under the radar of what is visible at school. Meanwhile, for some on the edges of our diagram, the social center of gravity of their lives was simply located elsewhere.

It is also worth looking more closely at the core group itself. Take Gideon, right in the center of the class network. As we got to know him better, we saw what a lot of social effort it took to gain such status. And even though he valued this social success, it did not mean much to him in terms of intimacy. In drawing his ego network, Gideon divided his world into what he called "important people" (consisting of his extended family: "because they're family, just family"), then the friends he does lots of things with offline and online (overlapping with the core group in the class), and then the people he just hangs out with online or chats to online (who were too many to name). So, while his visible social network was important to him, it was not made up of "important people."

The people important to Gideon, we discovered, were those who helped him through what he had experienced as a difficult transition to secondary school—a time when he had difficulties with "anger management," as the school called it. This was now familiar to him as part of his self-narrative:

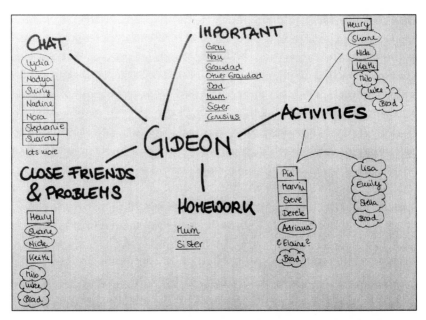

Figure 4.1. Gideon's ego network. Key: Name in bubble = member of the class; name in box = other pupils of the school; underlined name = family member; name in cloud = someone from out of school / the neighborhood.

I used to be quite small in Year 7 and 8, and I used to misbehave. The week before leaving at the end of Year 8 for some holiday, I got excluded because I got really angry at this supply teacher, and then I said to her, "Oh, you're not a real teacher. You're a fake teacher." And then I called her a stupid bitch. And then that all got [unclear], but then . . . I'm not kind of like an angry person where I'd want to hit someone; I'm kind of an angry person—I just want to have a big argument like there. But now at the moment when I've . . . since I've come back, in the summer holiday, I've grown quite a lot. And then, I don't know, I just can't be bothered to be misbehaving.

Fortunately for Gideon, both home and school responded constructively. The school provided anger-management classes and regular meetings with a mentor, although the school retained some doubts about whether Gideon himself was actually improving his behavior. Probably more significantly, his family stepped up their efforts to support him through this recent difficulty. His father took him on extended cycling holidays, and his mother contributed a series of enrichment activities, telling us, "I have to . . . there's a lot of encouragement all the time. So, you know, the summer holidays I took him to lots of things at the theater, I take him to art galleries, you know, because I want him to, sort of, be a rounded sort of person and have a bit of everything." Then, in a pattern we saw in several families (see chapter 7), his family encouraged shared media use to build family solidarity—"We like him to spend some time with, you know, even if it's just sitting watching television together. It'll be that sort of thing"—while simultaneously restricting Gideon's media use in his bedroom. Gideon had responded positively to such efforts, privately pleased that, he said, "me and my mum, we can just talk about anything. I can never keep a lie from her, or if I have to say it, later on it would just come out." Yet publicly—among his wide circle of contacts—he presented himself as a fun-loving person who takes life lightly and knows little of difficulties. Indeed, he did not discuss personal or private difficulties with anyone his own age; for such matters, he talked to his mother or his older sister.

INTERVIEWER: Have you got especially good friends . . . ?
GIDEON: I just go out with anybody. Like friends of . . . I'm kind of like, I can be friends with, like, a lot of people, if you know what I mean.
INTERVIEWER: Yes, like . . .
GIDEON: Like, I have a group of friends that I might hang out with one time and then another group. But I think everyone, apart from the kind of the nerdy people, most of the people will know each other and stuff.[8]

He described chatting via his Blackberry smartphone in similar terms:

INTERVIEWER: What kind of . . . when you're BBM-ing, what kind of conversations are you having with people?
GIDEON: With girls it's kind of a flirting type.
INTERVIEWER: Okay.
GIDEON: And then with boys it's just kind of casual.

Similarly, on Facebook, we saw him putting in considerable effort to create a successful persona, yet we had a strong sense that Facebook friendships meant little to him. He had over 1,000 Facebook friends, twice the class average, and unlike the typical, fairly straightforward self-presentation, his profile was remorselessly humorous: he was over 100 years old, cleans toilets at McDonalds, and has a huge family, with 50 friends listed as brothers and sisters. Moreover, he was very active on his profile (which, unusually, was public to other Facebook users), sharing links and happy birthday wishes, posting music, and adding new friends every few days in a manner he himself described as "addicted."

INTERVIEWER: Who do you chat with by text, Facebook, or BBM?
GIDEON: Everyone.
INTERVIEWER: Everyone? So everybody?
GIDEON: Yes, plus more people.

Facebook, like school, connected him to what he experienced as a some-what undifferentiated mass—significant in terms of scale and thus the validation offered to him but undemanding in terms of commitment. Is this projection of self as a cool, popular, and funny person part of his recovery from a difficult start? Certainly this slightly risqué image con-trasts with the boy who talks to his mother, goes cycling with his father, visits art galleries, and watches TV comfortably with his older sister. It may even be that the very notion of a friend—if this means an intimate relationship of sharing and trust—does not mean much to Gideon at present. Meanwhile, the synergy between his online and offline contacts is striking, both facilitating weak ties that are important for communi-cating popularity but are not important in and of themselves.

Private Spaces

Megan was also in the core group at school, yet she drew her social and personal boundaries rather differently from Gideon. Her ego network included 13 people who mattered to her: the nuclear family, her two best friends, several of the core group from the class, and a couple of other friends. Surrounding this tightly knit grouping, we observed the wider circle of offline and online contacts that anchored Megan in the youth culture of her neighborhood. But Megan was juggling different sides to her identity and so required a diversity of social spaces. At home, she described herself as a "daddy's girl," able to get whatever she wanted

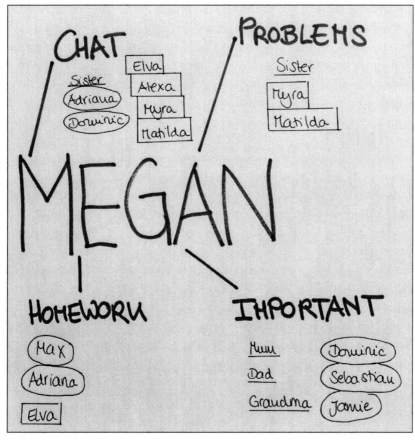

Figure 4.2. Megan's ego network. Key: Name in bubble = member of the class; name in box = other pupils of the school; underlined name = family member; name in cloud = someone from out of school / the neighborhood.

from her home-working father. With her mother, whom she could not "manage" in the same way, she was far more cautious, and we gradually saw that it was her mother who set high academic expectations for Megan, demanding violin practice, high grades, and good behavior. At school, however, Megan was "cool"—ostentatiously sassing the teachers almost beyond their tolerance, skipping classes, and missing homework (although, as demanded by her mother, she walked a fine balance to maintain high grades).[9] With her two best friends, Mandy and Mila, Megan shared intimacies, preferring face-to-face time to talk about what mattered to them, all the while missing her "best friend"—her older sister, now away at university.

Megan's tightly knit social world, then, provided a way of seeing and being seen in the class, in the neighborhood in the evenings and weekends, and also on Facebook—all coextensive insofar as they enabled gossip, flirtation, and social arrangements. Her class friends were the most visible but not necessarily the most important part of Megan's social world. The class also offered a space for getting on with boys, perhaps because there were more boys in the class but perhaps, too, because a girl who gets on with boys at this age poses a challenge to other girls ("None of the other girls talk to me. They don't like me"). Hanging out in this space involved a kind of drama, especially when conducted face-to-face.[10] "Usually I don't start arguments. I get, like—say someone's in an argument with, like, one of my close friends. I usually just get involved like that. That's the most reason, because I don't really—like, I defend people." This kind of drama somehow took the place of flirting, which, as many of the class members agreed, might be inappropriate since they had been more like brothers and sisters for the previous two years. Megan explained, "People think that, like, in our year, people flirt, like, in the years above us and, like, below us they do, but the boys and girls in my year are always arguing, like proper arguments. . . . The most like normal arguments I have is with boys."

Significantly, this was a year of transition for Megan, as she became more critical of peer influences and more serious about school, even trying out some of the after-school clubs. In the visible social spaces of school and neighborhood, Megan was stabilizing her network: "A few months ago, I used to, like—I was friends with different people then. I'm friends with other people now. I've, like, sort of changed groups, so I go out, like, more with them. I don't really stay at home that much anymore because before I would just go to, like, other people's houses and stuff or stay at home, and now I'll actually go out." This increasingly stable social scene was validated by the public nature of Facebook.[11] By midyear, Megan had pruned her Facebook contacts down to the 600 or so people whom she considered she actually knew (although this was still more than the class average), saying it was becoming more functional than expressive: "If there's, like, a party or something, because that's how people will invite someone, like, an inbox or something. But

I don't use it to talk to people that much." This was partly because she considered communication on Facebook to be public, notwithstanding that she had set her privacy settings on Facebook to be private, while Twitter she saw as essentially private (despite being a primarily public platform, its direct message [DM] function is indeed private):[12] "On Facebook, like, all my friends basically have my password on Facebook. But on Twitter, nobody does, so it's, like—so say someone wanted to tell me something really badly, they would usually DM you." This reveals one of the challenges of the peer culture: the very fact that Facebook profiles are password protected for reasons of privacy means that teens are inclined to share the passwords to signal their intimacy with their friends, even though the result is that the communication becomes public.[13]

But in addition to this public-private bonding, Megan was also searching out more personal and private spaces to try out different styles and interests, different selves even. In reflexively working out her identity, she was self-consciously following her much-admired older sister: "My sister was always different, so one time she was, like, a chav [a derogatory term for the working-class poor], one time she was, like, indie, then one time she was a Goth."[14] Popular culture—music, fandom, and the social media site Tumblr—all provided ways of constructing different selves in private, as Abby, another music lover, also told us:

I think music kind of describes a person really. So, like, if there was, like . . . if you listen to that type of music, they're kind of—they've got their own type of personality kind of, like that music, and I think if you, like, listen to, like R&B-type music, you're not exactly like [unclear] or nothing, but you kind of have the same type of personality as the music.[15]

Megan herself went on to say,

I'm, like, really, like, what people would call me is a fan girl—like, I'm a fan girl. I fan-girl everything. So I get obsessed with things. Like, I've had so many obsessions, like Harry Potter, Twilight, and celebrity, like Demi Lovato. I'm obsessed with her.

All Tumblrs are different, so you can have some which is just writing or some that is just pictures. . . . It's just random pictures, like if I send a picture, you can reblog it. But you have different things, so you can have Hipstar, Kawaii—all these different things. I used to have a Kawaii blog, which is like . . . although if I Tumblr, it's just a random—if I thought something was nice, I'd reblog it. Then I went to Kawaii, which is flashing images, and now it's gone to Hipstar, sort of indie.

Signs of these explorations of interest and self were all over her bedroom, including a shrine to Harry Potter, a muddle of music and fan paraphernalia, and a generally more enthusiastic self than was ever on view at school.

The most private space that Megan had found during our fieldwork year was on the microblogging and social networking site Tumblr (taken over by Yahoo! in 2013).[16] For the class, Facebook was a unified and simple way of making arrangements and of knowing what is new. But spaces such as Tumblr offered more aesthetic opportunities for expressive and sometimes exploratory or transgressive identity work.[17] For Megan, then, Tumblr allowed space for a self not even seen by her close friends:[18] "I don't show people, like, Tumblr. Like, I wouldn't show my parents my Tumblr. I wouldn't show my friends, really, my Tumblr. Tumblr's, like, for me, quite private. Like, that's my space for, like, my things. I don't really want people to look at my Tumblr. I find it quite awkward, like, people looking through my Tumblr." When we asked what she posted and why, she launched into an impassioned speech:

To be honest, it's like I don't know how to explain Tumblr. . . . When you first get Tumblr, you will hate it so much. You won't understand, and, like, I promise you, you will get obsessed with it. Like, it's such a nice thing to have. Like, that's your space. You can design how it looks exactly to every detail of it. You can make it perfect. But I've spent, like, five hours in a row, like, perfecting it. . . . That's, like, my space. I have everything perfect. Like, it's all correct. . . . I've been doing it for maybe a year and a half now, and I can look back how everything—the pictures I've reblogged have changed. So it sort of shows me how I'm changing. And so I'll do an hour of blogging, and then I'll look at it and I'll be like, "I've just done that," like, "I've achieved that," because I think it's good if you can't draw or something. I can't really create that myself, and I'm not that good with technology either, so I can't just do that by myself. But Tumblr gives you the opportunity to, like, express yourself kind of.

Here we surely see Sherry Turkle's "second self"—a portrayal of self that invites emotional commitment and promises perfection.[19] It seemed that, for Megan, the changes she was making in her circles of contacts at home, at school, and in the neighborhood required the solitary reflective space offered by Tumblr, as if she could concentrate on her authentic self online and then bring it into existence offline. The wealth of resources to imagine the self, combined with the absence of known others over-looking this reflective process, seemed to be just what Megan wanted.

Beyond Local Networks

Within the class, we witnessed many variations in the patterning of friendship and peer relations, offline and online. One of these variations illustrates how, even as 13-year-olds are committed to building a social circle and exploring their own identity, as we have seen, they are also beginning to look further afield. Dilruba lived in a low-income, mixed-ethnicity family of four girls and a single-parent mother; at school, she was hardworking, confident, and chatty. In her ego network, she named a sizeable group of friends from school and the immediate neighbor-hood, distinguishing those people who were important to her: extended family, her few close friends ("there's just certain people I'm close with"), and people she described as "just normal friends that I just, like, talk to, like, people in my class." In the class, these included Salma and Lydia from the girls on the edge of the class network, but while friendly with them, she did not see them much out of school.

Dilruba's inner circle, then, comprised her sisters as well as long-term close friends from primary school, so everyone was close to hand in her home or neighborhood. For these significant contacts, face-to-face communication was primary, although technology was useful for ar-ranging such occasions: "I just like to meet up with my friends. Usually my friends call me on my mobile, and then afterwards I sometime text them and talk to them just to meet up with them." Dilruba, it turned out, was someone whom others would come to with their problems:

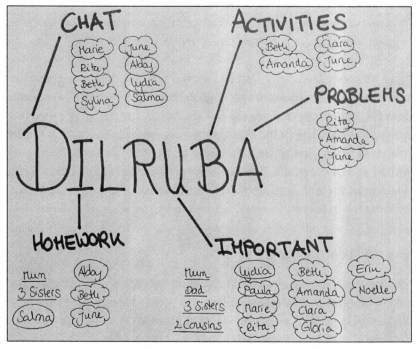

Figure 4.3. Dilruba's ego network. Key: Name in bubble = member of the class; name in box = other pupils of the school; underlined name = family member; name in cloud = someone from out of school / the neighborhood.

DILRUBA: Like most of my friends that I still have, and they like come to me and tell me, like, if they need help and stuff.

INTERVIEWER: Okay. And are you good at sort of sorting out people's problems, and . . . ?

DILRUBA: Kind of, but it depends what it is. I won't get involved if it's, like, none of my business and I shouldn't get involved, but if it's, like, something, like, personal for them, then yes.

But Dilruba's mother worked long hours, and she tended to restrict her daughters' freedom to travel far, to keep them safe. In this warmly supportive yet hyperlocal world, the internet offered a route to explore more widely. Especially since the start of secondary school, when Dilruba began to engage with more people, her after-school routine included several hours online in her bedroom chatting with friends on Facebook and Twitter. Her comment about what is or is not her business is interesting, as it turned out that Dilruba was interested in the drama of girls' friendships, as played out face-to-face and also on Facebook. She explained the way this worked on Facebook:

> DILRUBA: I do talk to them, but I'm not like close friends with them, like best friends with them. But I would add people on it.
> INTERVIEWER: Okay. Tell me some of the people you'd add to it now.
> DILRUBA: Alma because I'm cross with Amy. She just came new.
> INTERVIEWER: Okay. In one of the other Year 10 classes?[20]
> DILRUBA: Yes. I'd probably put Alma on it, and I'd probably take people off. Yes, I'd take people off.

But in addition, Dilruba was quick to see the potential of Twitter to connect with the adult word, especially that of celebrity and fashion, her twin passions. In the class, just a handful used Twitter, a then-new microblogging service that soon became more popular among UK teens. Dilruba was the most enthusiastic user, following the maximum-allowed 2,000 people, being followed by 1,000 or so, because she liked "keeping up-to-date—just, like, looking, like, seeing celebrity lives." One ambition was to be followed back by the celebrities, because "if they follow your Tweet, it's kind of a big thing, isn't it?" Regretfully, she told us, "I've never had a celebrity ever tweet back." But to encourage this, she would upload or even directly take photos of celebrities (having worked out where they might be or whom she might catch sight of) and post them on Twitter, to gather followers. She also enjoyed working out the social conventions of this social networking service as they them-selves were evolving among users: "If they're annoying, I'll just unfollow them. . . . When you reach 2,000 followers, you have a limit, so you can't follow anymore. I've reached my limit so many times, and then I just unfollowed all the people that weren't following me."

Less like Gideon, who created an inner (private, offline) and an outer (public, offline, and online) world, and more like Megan, Dilruba ex-ploited the affordances of different types of communication, including face-to-face communication, in order to engage with a range of people in different ways, thereby also enacting distinct aspects of her identity. These affordances matter; a celebrity would be unlikely to "friend" Dil-ruba on Facebook or, even, to "follow" her, but one might occasionally "favorite" her tweet, especially if she had posted a photo of him or her. On Facebook, however, even the possibility of such direct contact was remote, and thus she treated Facebook as the space for contact with her "normal" (rather than close) friendship circle. Twitter, then, permitted entry to a world usually closed to teenagers, allowing first steps in being there, even if little noticed by others.[21] Dom was another in the class who was trying this out. In his case, as a football player and fan, he would join in the adult Twitter conversations among professional football players and commentators, enjoying the chance to be part of something that he cared about but that was beyond his normal reach. Abby, too, had also worked out that Twitter could bring her closer to the music world that she hoped to join as a career, although her later declining interest in Twitter exemplified her self-exclusion from these early ambitions.

Transgressive Networking

While Gideon, Megan, and Dilruba stayed within adult-defined boundaries of experimentation with identity and relationships, our year with the class included one very difficult incident that also showed how the use of social networking sites can amplify and make visible problematic interactions. It was hard for us to get a good picture of Aiden because he was closely accompanied at school by classroom assistants and mentoring staff, having been expelled from a previous school for violent behavior. Although at school he was generally polite but reserved, seemingly anxious to avoid trouble, on several occasions, we witnessed his attempt to behave well disintegrate as he got drawn into disruptive exchanges during lessons. His family was, we were told, "known to social services" and received a range of state interventions in the form of social and health care workers. Although not evidently much poorer than some other members of the class, in the kind of housing he lived in and his material circumstances, he nevertheless brought a slightly more dangerous air of what he termed "the street" into the social world of the class.

One day in the middle of fieldwork, we arrived at VFS to learn that the school was no longer prepared to try to integrate him into mainstream education; he had, in effect, been expelled once again.[22] The trigger was an incident on Facebook, but as so often, behind the amplification of conflict on Facebook lay a "real-life" (offline) incident:

AIDEN: Basically some girl Facebooked me and said, "How did you get out at lunchtime?" And I said, "I'm allowed to go." And then she said, "Oh, I'm going to come with you." And I'm like, "Okay, cool, but if you get caught, don't bring my name into it." And then she came with me, and we were in ——, in some chicken and chip shop. And then we were playing about: she was grabbing me as a little play thing, and I punched her in her leg. And then she told her friend. And then her friend started hyping [acting "over the top"][23] to me on Facebook, and I replied back. And then I don't know how the school found out or what it had to do with them. . . . She told her friend, who was a boy, and then he started hyping to me. And then I retaliated, and I don't know how the school got involved.

INTERVIEWER: Okay. Do you want to say what kind of language you were using, or do you not want to say?

AIDEN: No, not bad language, like, just I was saying, "I'm going to punch you if you don't shut up."

Reflecting on this incident, both Aiden and his mother acknowledged that he was at fault, but Aiden was also adamant that this incident was not a matter for the school. In his view, such peer interactions—on Facebook, on the street—were played out according to social codes that adults did not understand, nor were they meant to. He put a lot of effort into managing life at school so as to keep it quite separate from life with his tight group of friends "on the street," and so he felt the school's decision was unjust.

When we visited Aiden's Facebook profile, we found that the seemingly reserved boy we had met at school had more "friends" than anyone else in the class (over 1,000) and low privacy settings, and he chatted daily with much vigor and interest. These communications revealed a curious mix—for the most part, he presented himself as a tough guy, strutting, flirting, threatening, and swearing. Yet there were also some photos of a "good boy," along with happy birthday messages, suggesting (to us) a curious switching between superficially incompatible identity performances.

Most interesting was the way in which Aiden sought to manage the boundary between personal and public spaces—through his use of language. Quietly well spoken at school to adults, at home, on the street, and online, he relished the linguistic repertoire of black London English[24] along with contemporary forms of hip-hop culture (in this case, variants of British "Grime," London-centric rap). On Facebook, nearly all expressions were in this argot, often involving highly sexist and sexual observations about women, violence, and anger, as well as solidarity with other oppressed black youth. The very frequency and intensity of these interactions revealed Aiden's investment in asserting particular identity practices, in contrast with the largely banal yet civil online interactions of most of the class on Facebook. For Aiden, unlike others in the class, Facebook offered a closed and peer-directed space for important personal expression and subcultural solidarity.

Had such interactions remained "on the street," it is possible that Aiden could have maintained the boundaries between different parts of his life—and, interestingly, his teachers tended to share Aiden's view that in-school and out-of-school spaces should be separate. But as they explained to us, once Facebook had made the out-of-school visible within school, they could not fail to take action. Indeed, several teachers had complained to us that social networking incidents increasingly opened up an unwelcome and troublesome window onto the mess and muddle (as they saw it) of some of the students' lives out of school, forcing them to deal with problems that they regarded as outside their remit. As one teacher said, "I honestly think that some students become something quite different when they are online." Then, compounding the problem, "unfortunately often that home matter spills into school, and that's where . . . that's where that tension and that difficulty lies, because we then have to call home and say, 'There's been this incident. Part of the investigation has shown that it stemmed from . . .' And then you're into home territory."

Over and again, teachers told us of incidents in which events in one location had spilled over and continued online and then all through the day, to the point that they felt they had to intervene in life out of school in order to protect the standards and values they sought to maintain in school. A particular problem was the way in which Facebook interactions leave "hard traces," making them difficult to ignore and thus demanding intervention: "Then one of the parents showed me the evidence, the rock-solid, watertight evidence, of the Facebook exchange which definitely proved [what had been claimed]." Yet these teachers knew that they could be presented with edited highlights, so that disentangling what had really happened in an out-of-school exchange might prove both technically challenging and highly time-consuming. In short, although Aiden's story is really a sadly familiar one of social disadvantage reproducing itself across generations and across sites, the digital media have complicated matters—on the one hand, creating a new space for at times rapid-fire transgressive peer interaction, while on the other hand, undermining long-established boundaries of authority dividing home and school in ways that can become troubling for all concerned.

Defining the Self and Being Defined by Others

Even in the 1970s, the term "friend" was used loosely to capture "relations of sociability, in which people visited, went out together, discussed shared pastimes, participated in an organization together, and so on. To a secondary extent, they were also intimate relations, ones in which respondents discussed personal matters—but not ones, however, in which respondents sought serious advice from the other."[25] This remains, surely, a good characterization of how young people connect online and offline today. Rather than romanticizing the notion of a friend as intensely personal—as, we suggest, the moral panics about youth culture tend to do in bemoaning today's superficiality—in this chapter, we have seen friendship claimed not only of bland "getting along" with other students but also of deep ties to the nuclear and extended family, of connections with online contacts whose names are barely recognized, and of close intimates to whom personal matters are trustingly confided face-to-face. This is less a confusion in terminology than a reflection of the diverse links that enmesh anybody: mapping the nature of the networks children and young people participate in tells us, therefore, rather little about the quality of the links since it is their very diversity that provides the wealth of social possibilities that people work to embed themselves within.

Kevin Leander and Kelly McKim followed teenagers through their various offline and online practices of identity and connection, observing that "the ongoing production of space-time is a rich process that draws upon multiple material and discursive resources, is imbued with relations of power, and is malleable through individual agency and imagination."[26] The young people in our four main case studies in this chapter have constructed the space-time contexts of their lives in particular ways, depending on their imaginations and their circumstances. Yet in the main, notwithstanding the extensiveness of connections in the network society, we have also seen that for our class of 13-year-olds, a relatively small ego network—or "personal community"[27] or small lifeworld—seems sufficient.[28]

In this chapter, we have had to work fairly hard to explicate the young people's sense of identity and relationships, not necessarily because they lacked such a sense but because they were reluctant (and it is difficult) to articulate it.[29] We have tried to emphasize how identity is constructed partly through the claims made about who is a friend or what music one likes (along with disavowals), all of this contributing to the process of positioning that preoccupied all of the members of the class. Yet we saw considerable variation in the young people's interest in exploring identity in these ways both across individuals and over the course of the fieldwork year. For example, creating a Facebook profile requires posting photos, making comments, sharing links, and so on—all of which are acts of self-presentation. But when we asked the young people what their profiles revealed about them, they disavowed any deep meanings. Dom said, "It says, like, I joke around with my friends really." Lydia said, "That I talk to a lot of people. I have lots of my friends down as sisters." Most were even less clear:[30]

> GIDEON: I'm not sure.
> FESSE: I don't know why. I just put a picture.
> MAX: I'm not 100%. . . . I don't really know, sorry.
> JOEL: I don't really put much on Facebook. It's just . . . I just sort of . . . usually I use Facebook just for, like, say, if I'm going to ask someone to do something, if they've got a contact.

Yet Gideon's profile photo was a posed gang sign, Fesse's a pensive sideways look, Max's a soft toy, and Joel's a shattered glass. None seems as random as they suggest, and each could be read as hinting at different selves not generally visible at school. Others displayed more consistent identities. Dilruba's profile was full of the fashion images that mirrored her conversation at school and home, her interests on Twitter, and the pictures on her bedroom wall. Dom's profile included images of football players and football news, reflecting his passion visible both in and out of school.

Giselle had fun choosing different screen names for her multiple on-line personae across different platforms. We asked her, "Do you see that as like a different Giselle . . . or an aspect of Giselle?" Her answer—"an aspect of me"—demonstrates a conception of identity as complex and multifaceted.[31] Yet discursively, teenagers are under some pressure to construct a unified identity, to work out who they "really" are.[32] Facebook itself seeks to enforce this by insisting on what it calls "authenticity"—a profile showing a real name and identifying information shared across platforms, whether used for work or leisure, with public and private faces seamlessly connected.[33] Undermining such affordances, we instead saw a fair degree of interest in expressing different aspects of the self on different platforms along with a host of tactics to maintain control over who saw what about you in different contexts.[34] For confident and successful Dom, this is fun: "One time in the summer, I swapped my . . . on his phone, I swapped my contacts, . . . someone else's contacts around. So I pretended I was them for, like, two days." For Lydia, all but ostracized at school, displaying a wide circle of friends on Facebook gave her power to redefine herself.[35]

During our fieldwork, the temporary dominance of one key site—Facebook—was already fading as teenagers sought out diverse platforms and services to connect with different audiences and to express different aspects of themselves.[36] Some embraced multiple platforms, others selected their niche, and a few turned their back on everything bar the face-to-face. The result complicated the communication ecology as the young people tried to remember which of their friends used which platform and for what purpose. But despite a degree of confusion or mutual incomprehension, the experiments continued, for these facilitated forms of expression and connection that the class seemed to relish. Jenna tried out using Pinterest and Twitter to follow fashion. Some Skyped their friends as an added back channel during gaming. Those interested in photography had just discovered Instagram, which mixes photo blogging or photo editing with the "follow" feature of Twitter. Each new fad, some more successful than others, hints at people's often unsatisfied desire to be in touch with each other, and if this involves platforms under the radar of their parents, so much the better.

Conclusions

Parents may be relieved to learn of the continuing centrality of face-to-face communication for young people—the class members' primary interests lay in seeing friends at school, meeting up out of school, spending time with family—and this fact should not be overlooked in the public hyperbole about digital media. This is not to say that everyone in the class was happy or sufficiently connected, as we saw most obviously in the case of Aiden, but rather that offline connections were important to all of them. Indeed, we suggest that those who struggled to sustain supportive connections offline also struggled online. It was not, therefore, that the internet was creating new problems in these young people's lives, and given that many of the digital interactions we observed were devoted to arranging face-to-face meetings, we suggest that much of the worry about young people being absorbed in social media is wide of the mark. This helps explain why, for the most part, digital networks underpin face-to-face networks rather than creating alternative connections and modes of identity. As Adriana explained about her use of her phone, "I don't just talk to people. If I want to, like, call someone up and do something, . . . I prefer to meet up with people." In other words, face-to-face communication is hardly displaced by digital media.

In the language of network theory, strong ties are primarily sustained face-to-face, while it is for monitoring the wider circle of weak ties that Facebook and similar social network services were most valued. The continual copresence[37] and easy visualization of their social networks as facilitated by Facebook enables people to see what was previously unseen—how peers engage with each other, who their friends are, and what they talk about—in turn facilitating a degree of reflexivity about their social world and their place within it. Given the expanded set of choices regarding modes of communication, it also might be that face-to-face communication is becoming re-mediated,[38] ever less taken for granted and more a positive choice for exchanges characterized by intensity, authenticity, or intimacy. It also provides, of course, a back channel for communication about school or family that leaves no trace for observing adults to find.

Our account of peer communication suggests that young people neither sharply distinguish online from offline nor find this distinction irrelevant. Rather, they are highly attuned to the particular social situations available to them, including paying close attention to the particular affordances of social networking sites—the conditions of visibility, connectivity, discoverability, amplification, and, most important, privacy.[39] The typically brief and bland interactions we witnessed over and again on Facebook, for instance, seem to mirror and extend what we analyze in chapter 5 as the "civil" school, providing a social setting for weak ties, superficial social acceptance, shared interest in popular culture, and occasional drama.[40] Tumblr was used to experiment with the self in private, deliberately disconnected from public spaces on- or offline. Twitter permitted the tentative extension of the self into adult worlds. Each bleeds into and reconfigures face-to-face interaction in different ways, with the affordances of offline situations being of equal interest. Hence, the clique of Jenna, Alice, and Max were strongly connected at home but not much visible at school or online. Giselle and Sara, the "gifted and talented" girls, were often together in the class but quite separate at home, during the rest of school, and online. The core group enjoyed the greatest overlap of connections at school, out of school, and online; possibly adopting a relatively normative and widely accepted identity generates the least need to construct alternative identities elsewhere.[41] Yet Gideon, at the very center of the core group, sustained one of the greatest disconnects between his life at school, out of school, and online compared with his inner world at home, while Megan deliberately sustained a private and anonymous life online that, seemingly, gave her the strength to convey considerable social confidence in other settings.

Across the situations or places available to young people, we have witnessed their desire both for connection and disconnection—for the tactical opportunities to escape their parents' expectations for shared family life, their school's valorization of civility, and even their peers' access to their more private explorations of the self. Since at home and school young people lack the power to manage their identity and social relations under conditions of their own choosing, they are particularly exploiting the new availability of digital networked spaces to pursue such connections and disconnections, thereby constructing and enacting different aspects of the self and, in the process, collaborating in the construction of wider peer networks that accord them a position. Therefore, we could not disagree more with the teacher who told us, "I don't think that peer-to-peer digital communication ever allows them to do anything meaningful."[42] On the other hand, we have also sought to show how what really matters is the exploration and expression of identity and relationships, and while this occurs simultaneously on- and offline, the offline is hardly being displaced, although it is, perhaps, being re-mediated in ways that will continue to unfold.

5

Life at School

From Routines to Civility

School can be a complicated and confusing place. Although it is often referred to as a monolithic institution—as in "school is boring" or engaging or repressive or enlightening—everyday experiences of school are more differentiated. On the one hand, students share the collective experience of school's day-to-day routines and rhythms of life. But insofar as their actions are also shaped by the norms and practices of family and peers, each individual student may be treated differently and will respond differently to school. This can pose a challenge to the authority of the school and to the ethos it seeks to create. Outside visitors to schools are typically struck by subtle and seemingly accepted forms of behavior and control. Our first impression of the school's day-to-day routines was influenced by the incessant scrutiny directed at the bodies of the students—what they wore, how they walked, when they were allowed to speak. Yet, although this raises questions of power and regulation of the self,[1] we were also struck by the ways that young people found spaces for informality and practiced tactics of evasion—occupying the corridors, stairwells, and corners of school buildings as well as being "disobedient" in class in ways that provided some escape from relentless institutional arrangements that dictated relations between students and teachers as well as among students.

In this chapter, we portray the texture and quality of everyday school experiences for members of the class, to ground subsequent chapters especially for readers who have not visited a school recently. Building on the snapshot of daily life in school described in chapter 2, we examine the collective identity on offer from the school and how individuals take on the roles expected of them. We consider how particular learning identities—the young people's sense of themselves as learners—were offered, although not taken up by all, a theme we develop further in chapter 6. Our emphasis is on the considerable efforts the school put into creating the norms and ideals of a civil society, constructing itself as an egalitarian community precisely by closing itself off from engagement with the diverse and potentially disruptive realities of the home.

The idea of civility has been influentially theorized by Norbert Elias's foundational work on the rise of self-restraint and self-control of speech and bodily functions in public, establishing a modern society that prioritizes manners and etiquette.[2] Certainly, schools put considerable effort into ensuring well-mannered students who conform to orderly codes of behavior. While some critics read this as imposing middle-class social norms on the potentially unruly mass, civility can also connote positive ideas of tolerating or getting on with others. As Susanne Wessendorf observes of highly urban multicultural neighborhoods, such as that in which VFS was located, these places are "super-diverse" and thus demand "civility towards diversity" as a daily strategy of their inhabitants.[3] Indeed, it is difficult to imagine forms of democracy that do not rest on a good measure of civility.[4] In this chapter, we explore the various routines of school to show how the school both recognized and avoided social difference in order to sustain a harmonious vision of a "good society" to a degree that contrasted with—and deliberately excluded—the young people's out-of-school experiences in family or peer contexts.

At the extremes, our class saw the professor's child sitting next to the Somali refugee, with students arriving at school classically from either side of "the tracks"—since a major road and rail route divided the neighborhood, more or less, according to socioeconomic status. The consequences of these efforts could be seen in the nature of social relationships at school. Managing these could be seen, on the one hand, as a matter of disciplinary regime—this was the explicit discourse of the school—and, on the other, as a key means by which the students learned to get along with others, foreshadowing an adult future of interacting with the wider world; insofar as this was the school's ultimate purpose, it remained generally implicit. The school used a range of strategies, including a rigorous focus on the life of "the class" as a unit, equally strenuous efforts to exclude external influences brought in via digital media, and ubiquitous references to popular culture as a taken-for-granted basis for sharing knowledge and forging common experiences in lesson time.

Learning Civility

Schools are expected to fulfill more roles than simply providing and accrediting learning. They are organized in ways that promote a particular way of being—as a member of the school community as well as becoming an academic learner (which we explore in chapter 6). Here we ask, What are young people learning as they adjust themselves to the school day—about themselves, about their relations with classmates, and about the institution of school? The members of a class are brought together not exactly by accident but by processes over which they have little control. They have to get on with each other, and in some cases, they have brokered what may be enduring relationships. How they learn to manage their relations with each other and with the wider community of the school will endure for the rest of their lives: we all remember our classmates even if we are not in touch with them. In what follows, we explore the mechanisms that the school developed explicitly to create membership of the school as a mode of participating in civil society.

Recognizing the wide diversity of backgrounds accommodated within the class, the school had good reason to emphasize a narrative about the students as a collectivity, as a means of addressing divisions wrought by socioeconomic status, gender, and ethnic differences. As their class teacher, Catherine, wanted to tell us, "They have a real sense of, you know, an identity as [the class], and I think that, for the most part, they're quite proud of that." Other teachers agreed; as one said, when asked about the relations among the wealthier and poorer students, "I don't think it affects, necessarily, the way they interact with each other." Yet VFS was typical of London schools for the diversity of its intake.[5] The 28 students in the class came originally from as many as 13 different primary schools, since in the English comprehensive system, everyone living within a defined radius of the school is eligible to join, and in London, this radius includes a considerable diversity of housing.[6] Thus, the class included children living comfortably in spacious houses costing one or more million pounds sitting next to children crowded into social housing and private rental accommodation.[7]

Being in the class meant that the young people had to negotiate a rather socially engineered "slice of life"; they had to learn to be citizens in a civil society. The young people were themselves aware of this expectation.

In a discussion about school rules, Gideon and Megan displayed their understanding of the school's efforts:[8]

> INTERVIEWER: Why have they got these rules? What are they about, do you think?
>
> GIDEON: It's meant to not distract your learning. You're not allowed to dye your hair certain colors so as your learning is not distracted and stuff.
>
> MEGAN: It's like being a community, because everyone is the same.

Indeed, the evident differences among students were remarkably little commented on by teachers, parents, or children. Rather, there was a strong, if implicit, emphasis on learning to get along with difficult or strange others. At VFS, we saw how the class had found a way of getting on with Toby, who had special educational needs, and its members had learned not to clash with Lydia, wary of her history of bullying.[9] Individuals had found routine ways to be more or less accepted by the group—boys kicking a football around the playground, girls chatting in pairs or small groups. Yet, as we saw in chapter 4, this often meant little outside the school, nor was it required to: the commitment being sustained in class was to more "public" allegiances, not necessarily based on personal or deep bonds of friendship.

Although the term is awkward in relation to children and young people, it seemed to us that students were learning to be "collegial," a phenomenon important to living in a large and diverse city like London. Despite the young people spending many hours together in the shared experience of school and becoming very familiar with each other's ways and problems, few terms capture the relationship that results. This ranged from polite dislike through indifference, tolerance, or friendliness to positive warmth. In the art class, for instance, Giselle and Fesse knew that they were both talented,[10] but although not unfriendly, they had no word to describe their connection: they shared an experience that mattered to them and valued the opinion of the other, yet they would hardly refer to the other as a colleague (as adult coworkers might), and they repudiated our suggestion that they were friends, without knowing what to say instead.[11] The social geographer Ash Amin talks about "collaborating strangers," although these, too, are uneasy terms with which to acknowledge that complex urban societies must find ways to enable very different people to work with each other constructively.[12]

The parents supported this vision of civil collegiality. The middle-class parents had chosen to live in a mixed neighborhood and to send their children to the local school rather than to bring them up in a more privileged context. Some of the working-class parents had worked hard to give their child this chance to benefit from a "good school"; in any case, they were glad of it. Shane lived on the edge of the catchment area, and his mother told us of her efforts to get him into VFS as a way of extricating himself from the more problematic environment of his primary school. His new friends, she told us, were "lovely boys, all well-mannered kids": "I think that's part of the reason I wanted him to go to that school—all his friends that used to go to this [other] school, . . . and I was like, 'You're not going there.' . . . I said, 'You don't realize when you go to secondary school, within a couple of weeks, you make a whole new circle of friends,' you know, which I wanted him to do. So he seems to have made a nice bunch of friends." This strategy did not necessarily provide Shane with a straightforward route to "success," however, as we will see later.

Managing Civility in Practice

Several strategies enabled this civil vision of the school community. The school sustained a principle of rational objectivity in its approach to the diverse composition of any class, employing a range of tactics. Students were generally not allowed to sit where they liked, and the beginning of each term was marked by instructions directing each individual to sit in a certain place in each classroom. Sometimes these arrangements lasted for the full school year. This varied from teacher to teacher, and some lessons, such as Design and Technology, were valued by the students precisely because they were established as more flexible, sociable situations. Catherine used deliberately to move students around each half term (so, six times a year) in order to encourage greater sociability among students who may not normally sit with each other and additionally to break up friendships that may have become too noisy for her to control. While this may have facilitated learning from the teacher, the result, as Alice explained to us, was an environment that lacked warmth and friendliness: "I don't like some of my classes, like, because . . . because we've got mixed up from our form—like, obviously, like, most of my friends aren't in my form. Like, Jenna's the only one that's really my friend in my form. But, like, I'm not with a lot of my friends in my classes." At a whole-school level, there was an online school newsletter and other forms of collective activity: a Christmas concert including dramatic performances at the end of the first term, a school fete in the summer, the Parent-Teacher Association meetings, and a whole repertoire of visits, concerts, and events. Together these practices demarcated a formal community about which we heard very little critique. Membership meant complying with a set of behaviors regarding standards of adult-youth and peer-to-peer interaction, with parents expected to support their children's adherence to these standards. In return, the school was keen to show that it aspired to high standards of academic and extracurricular performance and attainment.

In short, school life was constructed as largely self-sufficient, with its own conventions and expectations. These included a persistent discourse about "the class" itself, even though this social unit was, as we saw in chapter 4, more valued for its rhetorical appeal than as the basis of relationships among its members. There was also a persistent yet tacit avoidance of talk about "home," except in ways carefully managed by teachers or kept "under the radar" by students. The school's concern to disconnect from life at home was made explicit in its ban on students bringing mobile phones or smartphones into school, along with a ban on the use of social networking sites in school. And as we saw in chapter 4, teachers were concerned that connected devices meant that "home matter spills into school, and that's where that tension and the difficulty lies."[13]

So when Catherine talked of the class, she was positioning it as disconnected from home, given that the latter represented a world where more complex tensions might bring about conflict. As she saw it, this required a therapeutic slant; in the past, she had had to institute "quite a lot of bonding and unifying exercises": "I think they're a lot, lot better now."[14] Indeed, by the end of Year 8, the class had won the most commendations among all classes in the year group, and both their teachers and the students themselves reported to us a range of personal improvements in self-management and "anger management," which were also celebrated in discussions between teacher and parents at the midterm Progress Day and in the annual school report sent to parents.

Morning and afternoon class registration periods or tutor time were especially focused on civility and community. There was a certain amount of transactional business occupying these times—giving out letters, making announcements, and so forth—but there was also a series of rituals that worked to establish group membership and shared values. Catherine checked equipment and homework planners on Mondays. The students read their novels on Tuesdays. On Fridays, they watched and discussed the BBC news on the smart board.[15] Catherine's style was to mix conversational scaffolding with a personal interest in the students: chatting about holidays, reminders to take things seriously as exams approached, asking who would see a new film over the weekend. Occasionally, too, she told them a little about herself, often self-consciously, as if modeling a well-balanced and orderly life for her students.[16] One afternoon, she mentioned going to a birthday party and asked what the young people would be doing that weekend. Sedat volunteered that he was going to play in the garden, and the others talked about the fact that his family kept chickens, a level of knowledge about his home life that caused amusement and embarrassment. Another day, she talked about her journey to work or, bonding with Jenna and Megan, recalled crying over the film *Titanic*, just released in 3-D. Such personal interactions allowed for some differentiation among individuals, complementing their treatment at other times as equivalent members of a formal collective. To manage the interactions, students were invited to find a way to respect each other, although not all managed it. Nor were all comfortable with such performances of the personal: Lydia would rarely participate, for instance, and Sebastian expressed to us some wariness about the impersonal or staged nature of these exchanges.

Just before the students left for home, Catherine liked them to reflect on their experiences of the school day. A typical opening would be, "What did you learn today?" Depending on their mood, the students would reflect seriously or mess about. Alice and Max one day mischievously reported that they had learned in art about Frida Kahlo's bisexuality, and Dom chipped in that he had learned what a subtext is. While Catherine struggled for a response, Gideon saved her by launching into a complicated saga about a black boy in a white neighborhood seeing a black girl, saying the wrong thing, and getting murdered. Catherine took a moment to work out that he had had a lesson about apartheid but did not open up this or the previous topics for further discussion. Such apparently open discussions were, in practice, often contained by the teacher's more controlling and adult-led approach. One autumn morning, our field notes recorded this:

> Catherine does an equipment check. "You're very talkative this morning, you need to make sure your mind is ready for learning." "Make sure you've done your Behaviour for Learning target" in planner. "Class Photos are being taken tomorrow." Minor disciplinary stuff. "Maths Club starts today lunchtime"—Catherine encourages. Lydia hasn't got planner correctly completed. Nick lacks a pencil sharpener. Detentions for the five who haven't got their planner signed twice in a row by a parent.

A key point of joint ritual was the calculation at the end of each day of how many "commendations" or "concerns" (for achievement, good behavior, or the opposite, as recorded on the school information management system, SIMS) that each student had received, a topic we explore in more detail in chapter 6. This process simultaneously made visible to the class how each individual was progressing and encouraged a team spirit through explicit competition with other classes in the year group. Interestingly, given the potential for personal humiliation this process posed, the class usually responded with a mixture of good humor and indifference.

> Catherine reads out the commendations from SIMS and tries to exhort competitive enthusiasm for the class to "win." The kids are mildly interested. They veer between sneering and childlike enthusiasm. Catherine performs a sense of this being personal for her: "How Mr. X [the head of year] will sneer if I lose!"
>
> They all share in SIMS, checking who has got most commendations; Dominic plays the team captain. . . . "Well done guys." They can all see who is "of concern" on SIMS too.

These moments occasionally veered into the carnivalesque as familiarity and solidarity allowed for a certain amount of leeway with the rules. Birthdays were always celebrated by the group, along with rituals such as Secret Santa at Christmas, adding to the carnival feel: "Raucous. Catherine not there.[17] They insist on singing Happy Birthday to Salma. They all get over-excited and try to use strategies to get away with it. They have a lot of fun and games with Yusuf's name but it is all good-natured. Sedat as usual can't control himself and gets into more serious trouble than the others but it's not too bad."

Popular Culture as Common Culture

Beyond the language of behavior management and interclass competition, the teachers had found a further and more positive language for creating commonality: that of popular culture. Once we were attuned to the routine referencing of popular culture in lessons, we began to notice mentions of it everywhere. The school and the teachers seemed to imagine that the experience of watching television programs or listening to music offered a kind of common culture, shared values, pleasure, and fun, drawing the whole school together in an "imagined community."[18]

For example, to motivate students in physical education, the teacher observed that they would do the same warm-up exercises as celebrity football players do. To advertise the science club in the year-group assembly, students were enjoined to find out "how an iPhone works." To explain graphs in math, the exercises were to plot data on mobile-phone tariffs or Hollywood film profits. To judge work in geography, students were invited to act as judges on *X Factor*, a popular reality television show.[19] To pick out a tune on the electronic keyboards, students could choose the theme from *Rocky* or *Chariots of Fire* (although these choices may say more about adult visions of popular culture than the students' visions). As a strategy to build commonality, the school's endorsement of popular culture said little about the students' actual interests, which were—as we discovered later—both more current and more diverse than the somewhat dated, mainstream vision of teachers.[20] For example, favorite television programs ranged from UK soap operas (*East-Enders, Waterloo Road*), US sitcoms (*Friends, Jersey Shore, Don't Tell the Bride*), children's shows (*Merlin, Horrible Histories, Cartoon Network, Doctor Who, The Simpsons*), sports, and reality shows (*The Apprentice, X Factor, Big Brother*, etc.). Of these, we heard only sports and reality television mentioned by teachers.

High-culture references, by contrast, were rather rare, although the headteacher was keen on using these aspirationally.[21] A boy played Chopin on the piano as the students trooped into the hall for assembly. The headteacher gave a presentation of student achievements (getting into the University of Cambridge, a Shakespeare festival, etc.) to the sound of a Beethoven symphony. Just as important as raising aspirations, it seemed, was establishing a common set of reference points that could include all students, simultaneously orienting them toward the collective tasks of school life and yet acknowledging—in a contained way—their interests and habits beyond school. Certainly, it is not obvious what else the students had in common or which other cultural references could be safely brought into the classroom. Where they lived, what they believed, what they did with their time—all these could prove sources of conflict or inequality.

Pedagogically, the teachers were aware of the limits of the strategy of illustrating everything with a popular culture reference. For example, a history teacher worried that "media should only be included in lessons when it's of a high quality, . . . for example, History used Pocahontas as an illustration for something to do with the Indian people of America. How do you know at the end of it that all 27 students have made the link, and how do you know at the end of the lesson that there aren't ten kids in there that think that Pocahontas is a true story or that Disney is factually correct?" Yet we saw few critical reflections within the classroom about the use of such material; typically, film or television materials seemed to be presented as the famously misleading "window on the world."[22]

The idea that common culture offers universally shared experiences does not acknowledge social, cultural, gendered, and, importantly, ethnic or racial differences among the students. A problematic example of this was the use of some highly emotive resources to teach the history of slavery, as part of Black History Month.[23] Our field notes recorded the following in one lesson:

> The topic is well introduced—with images of slavery on the interactive whiteboard, including a present day rapper enslaved in Southern Sudan, a reference to the film Gladiator, a video of slave children in Haiti today. The lesson comes the day after news of slaves living in the UK, and the fact that slavery still occurs catches the students' attention. But the lesson

begins to go awry precisely because of the students' intense interest. Max asks why poor people have children they can't afford to care for, another boy introduces the idea that slaves are not only exploited and beaten but also raped, Megan is puzzled by an image of a pretty slave with no manacles. These are difficult issues. We notice that the teacher makes no reference to the fact that one third of the class and all the portrayed slaves (except Russell Crowe) are black.

The predominantly white teachers seemed, over and again, to ignore the diverse ethnicities present in the class. Instead, the address was generalized, substantially reliant on popular media images to draw in the students. Yet it was apparent to us that ethnicity partly shaped students' engagement. In another lesson on the same topic, the black students actually started naming their difference within the classroom in a way that challenged the teacher's authority and appeared to subvert the seriousness of the topic and, perhaps, their own claims for political recognition. In that instance, when images of lynched African Americans were shown on the smart board, as part of a film using Nina Simone's version of "Strange Fruit," we noticed that several of the black boys in the class started attaching the names of each other to the bodies on the screen. The boys then started speculating what they would do if the Ku Klux Klan came to London. The boys could be seen as subverting the gravity of the lesson. Yet they were also articulating an emotional identification with the subject of the lesson and engaging with the idea of fighting oppression. But in this instance, the teacher was more concerned with what he called messing around, although, possibly, he was also concerned not to draw attention to very different stakes that members of this class had in this subject. Some of the white students were equally irreverent—an account of punishment for slaves led Dom to ask if you can still hear after your ear is cut off, resulting in a disruptive discussion about George Weasley losing an ear in *Harry Potter*—but this was merely an attempt to distract the teacher, with little deeper resonance.

It is hard to know what lies beneath the surface discussion, but the lesson was uncomfortable for us as observers and, it seems likely, for teacher and students also. The discomfort, it seems to us, stemmed from a refusal to acknowledge difference, as social awkwardness is preferable to conflict. In such lessons, the aspirations for civility and for a disinterested approach to a universal curriculum were severely stretched by significant differences—actual and claimed—among the students. The fact that the students manifested their "otherness" through a challenge to teacher authority rather than as explicitly political acts allowed the school to avoid tackling the genuinely "teachable moment" and, instead, to support a veneer of civility.[24]

Relationships and Resistances

How did these differences within the class affect social relations at school, and how did these relationships "feel" to the young people themselves? We saw Shane's and Megan's reflections on socioeconomic difference in chapter 3, suggesting that the young people were aware of how their differences may divide them outside the school. We also saw in chapter 4 that the intersecting networks of friendships and peer relations that hold within and beyond the class were primarily consolidated outside lessons—whether in school corridors, after school, or online. In lesson time, therefore, while the young people surely retained their wider knowledge and experience of each other, they gave remarkably little sign of this beyond meaningful glances and under-the-radar chatter. This was partly because they often did not sit with friends in lessons and also because of the strategies to encourage civil attention that were rigorously practiced by most teachers. Therefore, more important within lessons than peer relations were the young people's relationships with teachers.

Abby, who lacked close friends at school, told us she cared little whether she worked by herself or with others. What mattered more was how she felt about her teachers:

> INTERVIEWER: What about—does it matter who the teacher is, about the lesson, or not?
> ABBY: Yes, I think sometimes the teachers aren't, like, very supportive, so it doesn't really help, like, in the lesson.
> INTERVIEWER: [*Asking on the basis of watching her earlier that day*] So, like, with maths, are you desperate for somebody to help you?
> ABBY: Yes, or, like, a new teacher, because I don't really like my maths teacher.

We had been asking whether the young people preferred individual or group working, thinking that collaborative working at school might be more student centered and more likely also to generate out-of-school working relations.[25] Yet like Abby, Mark expressed little interest in the social nature of the learning activities, saying he did not mind "working in a group or doing some writing" by himself. Again what mattered was whether students considered a teacher to be unhelpful or critical. This was possibly because they had little power to renegotiate their relationship with teachers if they did not find them helpful—certainly, playground discussions were often focused on highly personalized commentary about the teachers they did or did not find supportive. Gideon's account of one of his teachers revealed his sense of powerlessness over how he was treated and, therefore, how well he could learn: "It's quite weird because it's kind of confusing because one second he's really nice and supporting you, and then the next day if someone does something in the class, they kind of blame you. And then that's frustrating, and then I just get angry at that and have an argument." Megan, too, linked her relationships with teachers to her ability to learn in lessons:

> INTERVIEWER: Tell me about a teacher that you really like and really respect as a really good teacher, and tell me what's so good about their teaching.
> MEGAN: Mine's like . . . I think a really good teacher's Miss ——— because she's so nice. Like, even now she's not my teacher, she'll still say hi and talk to me when I see her. Like, other teachers, though, just, like, walk past you. But she's not even my teacher anymore, and she's still so nice. And I did learn a lot with her. . . . She, like, really helped me.

There was a lot of talk about how teachers made the students feel during lessons. Dilruba, who often appeared quietly diligent in class, revealed the importance of the emotional climate created by the teacher:

> DILRUBA: It depends how the teacher acts with you because then it affects your learning.
> INTERVIEWER: Tell me a bit more what you think about that.

DILRUBA: Because if they're, like, keep shouting at you, like, you feel like they're picking on you, and you can't really concentrate on your work.

INTERVIEWER: What's an example of that?

DILRUBA: When . . . I don't know. When you just do something, and the teacher's like he's picking you, and they don't ask anyone else, and then you just think they're like aiming at you.

INTERVIEWER: And that makes you feel bad?

DILRUBA: Yes.

INTERVIEWER: Can you explain to me how a good teacher makes you feel, then?

DILRUBA: Yes, when they're like nice, understanding, and you can just go to them for anything.

Much of the time the students appeared to feel individually vulnerable in lessons, never sure when the spotlight would fall on them, remembering for a long time how they felt when a teacher shouted at them, keeping their heads down to avoid trouble. For some of them, when relationships with staff were not good, the role of friends in classrooms became more important. Indeed, where we saw a breakdown in class discipline, it was frequently made manifest through forms of peer-to-peer socializing, as if the young people took this opportunity to display their power to choose whom they spoke with and where they would direct their energy. Thus, the somewhat exaggerated displays of friendship that we witnessed in the classroom could be seen as enacting a kind of resistance to the teacher—bearing in mind that in happier circumstances, friendship was not made very visible in the classroom. As Adriana told us defiantly, "Some lessons you just talk. That's, like, my science."

In a science lesson, we observed how Max deliberately and ostentatiously struck up a conversation with Ruth, a girl he was friendly with in the school play. Our field notes recorded that: "Max is incredibly chatty with Ruth, who openly reads *The Hunger Games* in defiance of the teacher and the lesson. Max turns his back to the teacher and adopts a righteous indignation when rebuked. He knows all the answers and what's going on. He is not uninterested in the topic." Displaying friendship in this way is as much about opposing the teacher as it is about being sociable, a point borne out in this instance by Max's continuing poor relationship with the science teacher, leading to complaints and direct confrontation later in the term.

For some of the young people, such confrontations became habitual. Shane was frequently in trouble with the school and found it difficult to shake off his reputation as a difficult student. He spent a lot of time with his seemingly hyperactive friend Kier, who was also often punished for disruptive behavior in lessons. As the term progressed, we came to see Shane as a younger version of one of the working-class "lads" in Paul Willis's classic study *Learning to Labour*.[26] Willis described how the naughty boys at the back of the class prepare themselves for a hard masculine life in factories and on the shop floor through forms of male bonding and disruptive behavior. Willis suggests that working-class youth "fail" at school as a way of preparing themselves for the actual futures that await them. We observed Shane in a PSHE[27] lesson about the United Nations:

Shane is pretty interesting throughout. He is very self-conscious when addressed and there is an underlying and on-going connection between Kier, Shane and another boy at the back. Any time one of them speaks it sparks responses from the others. Kier (who tells me he didn't know Shane before VFS) is always on Shane's radar and all of his [Kier's] actions take this into account. It makes it difficult for Shane to escape this identity if he wanted to. He seems pretty motivated and keen throughout. He volunteers that that the UN is like FIFA—that it has a model of governance he is familiar with—a point acknowledged but not developed by the teacher. He puts his hand up a lot and gets much of the answers right. He and Kier rap to the phrase, "friendly relations between nations," which gets them a frown. He asks a question about US & UK military intervention. However, he is so self-conscious that any seriousness always cracks.

But at the age of 13, Shane was still working out his options, torn between choosing to identify with the other lads as a form of identity work and not caring if he got into trouble—promoting friendship with other lads above the authorities—and the desire to succeed on the school's criteria and, perhaps, to please his mother, who, as we saw earlier, so wanted him at this school. Unlike Max's bad behavior in the science lesson, when he used his friendship with a girl, Ruth, to accelerate the breakdown in the contract between teacher and student, Shane's priority was to sustain his friendship with Kier, which he did precisely by enacting publicly how this friendship and the kind of identity that it signified for them both was of higher priority to him than the lesson was. Yet to us—who had discerned Shane's evident interest in the topic and who, on another occasion, had heard his determination to avoid trouble at school—his ambivalence was palpable.

For Adriana, who was neither overly concerned about whether she would eventually succeed nor as angry as Max with how she was treated, a third strategy was deployed. Like the others, she interwove her participation in social relations with moments of academic learning, but this time using a kind of show-off strategy that demonstrated to anyone watching (perhaps mainly to herself) that she could handle anything and everything.

> Adriana answers questions a lot, puts hand up and gets the central idea quickly. Later in the lesson I see her surreptitiously go on BBM[28] under the desk. She tells me that she is chatting with a friend in another lesson. I ask her what happens if she gets caught. She says some teachers will confiscate the phone but give it back at the end of the week, and that since it is Friday she reckons it will be ok.[29] After a bit of this, she switches back to the lesson, she asks, "Sir, what is the question" and then gives the answer. I ask her how she knows when she needs to know something, when to concentrate and how to put herself forward as a good student. She gets the question but can't explain what kind of tacit knowledge— "class-craft"—comes into play.

Adriana's somewhat insouciant attitude involved breaking school rules or behavior codes only up to a point, for she was carefully calculating just what she could get away with in her display of friendship in the classroom environment. Her point was less one of resistance to the teachers or school and more a display of "multitasking" competence to promote herself as a clever and successful student, showing command of the curious rules and regulations that students learn govern social life in school. Megan and Adriana articulated this balancing act for us with some pride:[30]

> MEGAN: I was bad and never got in trouble.
> ADRIANA: Being bad and not getting in trouble is so good.

Conclusions

Since members of the class were embedded in diverse social networks that ranged across school and home, including dispersed or transnational family and informal peer groupings that extended offline and online, the potential to challenge expressions of difference within the class was substantial. This chapter has focused on how the school as an institution organized and influenced social relationships according to both pedagogic and sociopolitical visions of who the young people "should" be, as individuals and as a collectivity. Although school is usually considered primarily as a place for individuals to learn, with the relationships among students or between teachers and students valued only when they might affect learning outcomes, we were interested in how the school contextualized young people's social identity and social relationships, even constituting its own version of "society."

We saw in previous chapters that the networks and social worlds that these young people constructed for themselves included less socioeconomic, gender, or ethnic difference than existed in the neighborhood, although this is not to say that their ego networks were not diverse. But while, out of school, they could determine who to include in the handful of people important to them, we have also seen that at school, the young people were broadly committed to the vision of fairness and inclusivity offered them by the school. However, it took a lot of teacher management to implement this vision for the whole school environment. Some of the young people experienced this management as convivial, allowing a degree of warmth, fun, and comradeship in getting along together.[31] Some found it more coercive or controlling, with students experiencing a degree of frustration, injustice, embarrassment, or alienation from the school's effort to ensure a rather impersonal sense of civility.[32]

Over and beyond the task of studying, the school's everyday routines also prioritized the task of learning to be a citizen—of comporting oneself at school in a manner that accorded with the school's values and practices of discipline, order, and getting along together. In the language of teachers and parents, this was expressed in terms of a continuous commentary on students' behavior, constantly admonishing or praising. The young people discussed this more obliquely: What is So-and-So like? Who is it best to sit with? Why do some hang out with others? Few, if any, dissented from the avowed aim of learning how to interact with very different others as integral to the civil vision of the school, whether or not they signed up to the wider moral project of public education to produce self-governing individuals able to harmonize social difference. In the "super-diverse" environment in which this very urban school was located, learning to get along with strangers was as important as academic achievement—and without it, the school would not be able to function as it wished.[33]

This chapter has identified several strategies the school employed to bring about its vision. One, as we saw in chapter 4, was to construct "the class" as a meaningful and coherent unit that confers a collective identity and sense of belonging. Another was the appeal to a shared imaginary of the wider world, as depicted in the familiar images of the mass media as a common culture in a globalized world. A third strategy involved finding ways to keep difference and conflict at bay, which in turn meant restricting what may pass across the boundary between home and school. And finally, the school made it difficult to recognize and name any kind of difference, whether economic, gendered, ethnic, cultural, or whatever, as if the very naming or making visible of difference itself could undermine the aspiration of equal treatment for all. While the microenactment of relationships among students and between student and teacher also contributed to this vision, it simultaneously opened up possibilities for tactics of distancing, renegotiating, or resistance. So, while we have used words like "control," "discipline," and "order" to refer to how power is organized at school, we have also tried to show how young people learn to consent, or not, in ways that still grant them some autonomy and personal space.[34] This, too, is something they learned at school: to accommodate institutional demands and yet also to articulate individual freedoms.

Not all the students found doing so as easy as others did. And as our comparison of Adriana and Shane suggests, social class provides differential resources from which each young person resisted the impositions on him or her. Indeed, while there is no simple mapping of teacher treatment onto student background, we witnessed plenty of occasions in which we felt, along with so many scholars of education,[35] that middle-class students received greater leeway, with teachers slower to judge Adriana, Megan, or Max, for instance, than they were to mark out Sedat,

Lydia, or Shane as, frankly, uncivil.[36] Similarly, the moments when the disciplinary regime was relaxed—for example, in top-set math, the extracurricular astronomy class, or the school play rehearsals—were all moments when the middle-class students came to the fore, positioned to benefit from such opportunities.

The school's construction of civility, then, seemed to require less overt displays of discipline for middle-class children. Similarly, how it maintained boundaries between home and school appeared to exclude what "different" (poorer, ethnically "other") children might bring to lessons and to their collective life with peers at school. In the following chapters, we shall see how these efforts excluded crucial knowledge among young people from all walks of life; but still it is likely that the school's concern to disconnect rather than connect with home life may negatively affect students from poorer homes.

However, we saw little in the school—at least in Year 9—of the disruptive forms of resistance or rebellion that some school-based ethnographies have documented in relation to the reproduction of school failure or an underclass of persistent low achievement.[37] Some of the middle-class students resisted the school's invitation to join in the common, civil space, while some of those from poorer homes enjoyed this invitation and appeared to benefit from it. Further, while most of the students had their complaints about harsh teachers or "stupid" rules, we heard no one disagree with the overarching ambition to sustain the school as a fair environment. Indeed, the absence of any single class-based opposition to the whole project of schooling shows how far all members of the class subscribed to the belief that formal education mattered and that they could rely on the school to provide it.

We have described how at VFS the vision of wider society on offer in the school was promoted explicitly and implicitly by the consistent efforts of the teachers and the institutional practices of the school. We also found that the parents generally backed this up, and as we have just suggested, so did the young people themselves. In the detailed practices discussed in this chapter, we can see evidence that supports Elias's vision of civility as a form of learned self-restraint. Elias's version of this kind of self-governing is customarily opposed to a vision of civil organization based on democratic engagement. But we did not see many deliberate efforts for democratic accountability initiated by the school—for instance, Mark was the class representative on the school council, but he and others were clear that this was all but meaningless.

There may, certainly, be other and perhaps better ways of organizing school life. But this chapter has also shown how bringing differences from home into the classroom can be hazardous. As illustrated by Laurent Cantet's 2008 award-winning film *Entre les murs*, translated as *The Class*, where the teacher did "bring the outside in" with disastrous consequences, in VFS, teachers constructed a version of civility that avoided difference, modeled tolerance, and preserved order within the bounds of the school. This can be read as an effort toward conservatism with a small *c* at a time when the relation of individuals to society is being reconfigured, accelerated by multiple macrosocial changes: uncertain labor markets, contested visions of education, global and cultural tensions, and so forth—as discussed in chapter 1. But it can also be read as a more modern response to the fact that such changes mean that, more than ever before, new forms of sociality are required. Today, everyone must relate to many others with whom they have no direct relationship. How society is imagined and how it functions is no longer governed by unquestioned convention or time-honored tradition. So for young people, school becomes a key place to develop convivial, collegial, cooperative, even collaborative or cosmopolitan values[38]—ever more important in an age of individualization when values of inclusivity, tolerance of diversity, and civility become a necessity to avoid conflict.

6

Learning at School

Measuring and "Leveling" the Self

In this chapter, we shift our focus from the social worlds of the class and the civil space of the classroom to the young people's experience of learning and the meaning of "being educated."[1] Although there are ethnographic and anthropological studies that examine how young people experience and make sense of being in school, much educational research takes an institutional or teacher point of view, often with a view to better organizing the classroom or ensuring effective learning by students. This was not our purpose. Instead, we were interested in how the school invited young people to take up their role as learners in a context in which the school itself constructs and controls definitions of learning. This led us to ask how the young people defined themselves as learners and disciplined themselves to act accordingly, including beyond the school and into everyday life.

As we shall explore, the particular ways that the school defined, measured, and recorded progress in learning dominated discussion of learning and learner identity[2] at school, and they also penetrated into out-of-school learning, a theme we develop in chapters 7 and 8 when examining learning in the home. Central to the school's conception of learning was the idea of "levels," a word used over and again throughout the school day by students and teachers to refer to attainment measured against UK national curriculum standards. But it also represented—for them and for us—a kind of metalanguage, a whole way of talking about the self that appeared to measure the intangible dimensions of growing, learning, and becoming.[3]

On the one hand, this pervasive discourse of levels articulated and made visible and manageable the process of learning in a way that permitted a degree of reflexivity, as befitted the late modern absorption in the "project of the self." Indeed, we saw many ways in which the students were invited by the school to reflect on and take control of the kind of learner they are or should be. On the other hand, this discourse risked prioritizing external markers of progression over any intrinsic value of learning for its own sake. The focus on external markers was exacerbated by a computerized system of measurement and recording that encoded not only outcomes but almost everything that occurred within the classroom, all conversation and activities becoming grist to the mill of school attainment.

There could be several reasons why VFS, like so many English schools, wholeheartedly adopted the national system of levels and leveling. The school catchment was highly diverse in social class and ethnicity, so the visible management of a fair and equitable learning environment mattered, especially for a school with an ambitious head-teacher determined to bring the school up in the national league table of exam results. At the same time, this way of encoding learning dovetails with broader social processes that homogenize "youth" and standardize societal expectations of the pathways available to them. Thus, it is at odds with a host of alternative pedagogies espoused by many educationalists, as well as by some of the class's teachers and parents. In chapter 1, we introduced the idea that the current era is characterized by increasing individualization and an attention to curating the self. The approaches to learning and education revealed in this chapter extend this argument. As will become clear, such an approach is heavily reliant on, and in some ways shaped by, the role of technology in supporting and framing a certain approach to learning. One consequence is that, although the approach has some influence beyond the school, extending the discourse of levels into the extracurricular learning undertaken at home, it more importantly acts to disconnect the school from home, establishing the school as a small world with its own norms and customs, in many ways a world apart from the learning and value discourses of family life that we explore in the following chapters.

Measuring Learning

Any teacher will tell you that the beginning of a lesson is important. Establishing control and authority is crucial, as 25 or so individuals need to be organized as one. As we saw in chapter 5, VFS was fond of lining the students up outside the classroom so that, as they filtered through the door one by one, the teacher could comment on their dress, asking for a tie to be properly tied, shirts to be tucked in, and socks to be pulled up. When the students sat down in the class, this, too, was organized by the teacher, often according to a seating plan displayed on the smart board.

This kind of discipline is generic, ignoring the particularity of different subjects or teaching styles and purposively excluding the sociality of the students. With two years of secondary schooling under their belts, the process had become ritualized. There was a kind of knowing tiredness in the way that teachers rebuked Shane or Fesse about their ties and their shirts. The students likewise, with the exception of Lydia, were not terribly serious about opposing authority in this way. Yes, Max tried not to get caught out with his top button remaining unbuttoned around his collar, but for most teachers and students, it had become a game. The students come in to class, take off their coats, get out the appropriate equipment, try to talk to their neighbors or across the room, get told off; and when the signal is given, the lesson begins.

Much of this routine was familiar to us from our own school days, but the class was also subject to another kind of discipline that did surprise us. In every lesson, even in subjects like Physical Education or Personal, Social and Health Education (PSHE), the teacher began with a review of "levels." And levels became for us—as they were for students and their families—a master metaphor for thinking about learning. At times, it seemed, the notion of levels had found its way into every aspect of the young people's lives, from their academic progress to their extracurricular activities and even their game play during leisure time.[4] The result was a routinized discourse of learning that rendered the following kind of comment (from an art teacher to her class) meaningful rather than bizarre: "Remember you've already been leveled for your work so far, so this [new task] is for your next levels."

To see how the language of levels, more than that of curriculum content, came to frame learning at VFS, we use an example from the beginning of an English lesson in the autumn term of our fieldwork. After all the business with coats and bags, the teacher set the scene thus: "We all need to start improving high levels whatever they are. The next thing to write down are, 'My Year 9 targets. My Year 9 target is . . .' The one to the right of that [referring to the chart on the smart board] is your challenging target, which is automatically one level higher. So you don't really need to write that down, 'cause it's obvious." There was no discussion of the pedagogic rationale for such target setting or, more significantly, of the value and interest inherent in the subject matter for the lesson. Instead, the class was immediately plunged into the demanding task of turning the abstract principles of progression into the explicit and practical language of levels, this, in turn, permitting a mapping of the curriculum content onto the means of assessment. The teacher continued:

> Now the fun bit! In front of you, you should have one of these [*holding up the sheet or grid that was also projected onto the smart board*]. This is the assessment criteria, the things that I use when I am marking your work. . . . So make sure it says "Reading" at the top; if it says "Writing," turn it over. . . . Now these are the three things that I am going to focus on: assessment 1, assessment focus 2, and assessment focus 5. . . . Now the left-hand column of this assessment focus 2, the one next to it is assessment focus 3, and then jump to get to assessment focus 5. . . . So that that means—everyone following me? If there's anything you don't understand, make sure I understand that pretty quick there. So [*picks out a student*], assessment focus 2, what does it say, ——? [*Student reads out loud; the teacher repeats the student.*] "Find information and use quotations" [*writing this out on board*]. Okay, that's the first thing I'm going to see that you can do. You can lift things out of the text. I flick through your essays, and it looks like you're already doing that. . . . Brilliant! But if you haven't used quotations and put them in nice quotation marks, you're not going to do very well at assessment focus 2 [*points to the level on the grid*].

To explain, by 2011–2012, the national curriculum in England required the implementation of a complicated framework[5] to support progression and assessment in state-funded schools,[6] as dictated in detail by the inspection regime run by the nationwide system for inspecting schools (Ofsted), managed by the government's Department for Education. Students progressed through various levels in each subject, and termly reports recorded both overall and subdivided levels of attainment. Significantly, rather than expecting the whole class to reach a particular level and rather than ranking students against each other or against any absolute expectations, targets were highly individualized. Each student was set target (both minimum and "stretch") levels for each subject, on the basis of their previous attainment and expected rate of progression as well as of national averages for their year. Interestingly, students were expected to know and review these levels regularly. Consequently, while every lesson began with the teacher outlining the levels on offer, since students were all at different levels, they each had to pick their own paths through this framework.

To us as outsiders, the process of defining progression by reference to the explicit criteria operationalized as levels, along with managing such a complicated numerical matrix, seemed arcane and confusing. The system was largely opaque to parents too, as we discovered on Progress Day and from talking with parents about the school (see later in this chapter). Yet in the classroom, "levels" represented an extraordinary yet thoroughly normalized discourse shared between students and teachers—a running thread throughout most lessons and the primary marker for discussing not only learning but also learner identity.

As may be seen, for teachers and students, it was not so much the abstractions that caused difficulty but the practicalities of operationalizing them. In fairness, the instructions quoted earlier were easier to follow alongside the visuals. However, as we continued to observe the English lesson, the general atmosphere in the class was simultaneously one of confusion and calm as students tried to work out what was expected of them. Yet they were accustomed to this task, and alongside the confusion, there was also acceptance: we saw little, if any, interest in the larger picture or even any questioning of students' personal targets but, rather, a dogged effort to get clear what they, as individuals, had to do. The teacher continued, "Right, what I'd like you all to do now is under assessment focus 2, find the level that you should be hitting, so that your target for the end of the year—what's your, ——, level?" A student responded, and the teacher continued:

> You're 6b, so you are up into level 6 there. So you can read that "I can clearly identify relevant points including summary blah, blah, blah, blah" [*pointing to the relevant section in the grid*] and try to find something you don't understand so that I can explain it to you. So everybody now

should be looking at the target in the assessment focus to that they need to hit, okay, reading it and seeing if there's anything they don't understand. Okay, I'm going to give you another 30 seconds, and then I will answer any questions on that.

The use of the "blah, blah, blah" is slightly less absurd given that the teacher was pointing at a section of text, but it does underline how ritualized and procedural these levels are in this moment of teacher talk and that their content and their meaning has become subordinated to the process of simply moving through them. The students accepted this as how school works.

Embedding the Discourse

We, and the students, saw this opening to a lesson repeated over and over again. As the term progressed, the lesson opening veered away from an overall view of the levels in components over the whole year toward a way that each activity—frequently contained within the time span of a single lesson and its accompanying homework—offered attainment at different levels. Few teachers made reference beyond their own subject domains: for example, although the capacity to use supporting evidence might be useful in several subjects, this possibility was never brought out. Rather, each subject was self-contained, student attainment in one subject was never mentioned in another, and the grind of constant repetition from lesson to lesson not only formatted the lesson experience as a template but also turned the concept of progression into a mantra about attainment.

Music lessons were always slightly noisier and somehow livelier than English, and students did not settle as quickly. Unlike Math, English, and Science, Music is not a core subject and so had a different status within the curriculum. Yet differences among subjects were barely noticed given the application of the discourse of levels and individual attainment across the curriculum. Here is a music teacher:

I am going to give you the more specific criteria for this assessment, but so you know, just because you've done it doesn't mean you're going to be a level 5 or a level 6. There is all the other things we are going to have to take into consideration as well. So today, if you need level 5 or level 6 criteria, then we also need to pay attention to these other things—"can you practice till you get it right?" [*quoting from the set criteria*].

By the end of Year 9, it is expected that Year 9s are at a minimum at level 5. . . . Of course, lots of you should be thinking about level 6, and some of you should be thinking, "I'm definitely level 6 on this, but the rest of it is level 5." So I want you to pick out, using these here [*pointing at a grid on the board at the front of the class*] some particular topics for you to think about, okay? Do you know that's the thing you're going to work about at the moment? Do you need to be thinking about also when we come round to do group work, about "performing independently in parts, by yourself with partners or in groups" [*quoting from the set criteria*]—that means you do your part, and everybody else does something else.

Just like the opening to the English lesson discussed earlier, students were directed to a standardized level of attainment. As part of this, a standardized vocabulary becomes the routine language of learning, signaling particular specifications of levels divorced from their original meaning in relation to the subject matter (e.g., performing independently in parts) or expectations of the relation between behavior and learning (meeting "behavior for learning targets"). Or, as the English teacher put it, "blah, blah, blah." As part of this standardized discourse, students are also frequently enjoined to reflect on themselves as learners: where their strengths or weaknesses lie, what level they are at, and what they need to focus on.

A few teachers adopted different approaches, however, and these were noteworthy, partly because they revealed a privileged position. There was little or no talk of levels or behavior from the math teacher in charge of the top set (for the highest-achieving students), for instance. Nor was there such talk in certain after-school activities: for instance, school play rehearsals were notable for their cheerful informality combined with purposeful focus, with teachers and students (again, a select group) enjoying a shared engagement in the content, skills, and performance of the drama itself. The same could be said of the after-school astronomy lessons, again composed of elite volunteer students, even though a tough examination loomed ahead.

Accounting for Learning to Parents

The more embedded the language of levels became between teacher and student, the more they inhabited a world that was puzzling, even opaque to outsiders, and this included parents. For instance, end-of-term reports to parents were exclusively couched in talk about levels rather than, say, curricular content mastered, together with a quantified account of the students' behavior and attendance: "Nick has made progress this year, meeting his target levels in four of his subjects and being just one below in several others. Notable successes have been in Geography, iLearning[7] and Science, where Nick has achieved level 6." After we read many such coded reports, it became clear that they were written by translating a database of level information into prose, accompanied by some set phrases repeated across reports. But few parents really understood the system, even though their child had been in the school for over two years, and some found it excluding.[8] Shane's mother stated, with some resignation, "I never understand those grades. It's all different to when I was at school." Even Alice's mother, a highly educated senior consultant in the welfare system, told us, "It is incredibly confusing. . . . I don't think it makes any sense at all." Although the system is designed to track individual paths without comparing students competitively, the language itself seems too alienating to communicate much at all. We asked Alice's mother how she made sense of her daughter's progress: "I don't think you ever know. And where is my child where she should be for herself or himself as opposed to the national levels? So the national levels are there, but what do they mean for the person?" Alice's mother wished to locate her daughter on the national scale, to know what her daughter had actually learned and where she ranked in relation to others, and thus she was frustrated.

Yet just as most of the students seemed readily to accommodate to the discourse of levels, most parents, too, were accepting. Adriana's father, for instance, found value in the way that the leveling system offered personal targets, without asking just what those targets referred to:

> They have—they don't give you sort of universal targets. They have targets for each pupil. Each pupil for each subject has a sort of minimum target and a challenging target, as I quote. One bit of information we don't get is how their targets—how your child's targets relate to sort of the

average target. So you don't know that. But in a sense, it shouldn't matter. So I think that is very good. I mean, not that you don't have that information but the fact that the kids are working to their own targets, without having to sort of conform to whatever is the average.

Still, some struggle is evident: Adriana's father was aware that average or ranking information was deliberately not provided, and he tried to accept the logic of this—namely, that each child is on his or her own path and should not be expected to fit a norm. Yusuf's father was one of the few parents to suggest that the levels can work diagnostically as they are intended—that is, rather than indicating actual knowledge gained, they show the degree of fit between a student's readiness or ability to learn and the curriculum content he or she is given. Talking of his approach to his children at home, he says, "Well, I don't force them, to be honest, and I always remind them to study if they are in here, [with] everything [they] need, and they can improve [their] levels. Once your level is high, you're going to get confidence and easy and enjoy it. But if you are not at a level, it's low, then you're going to struggle, which we take very seriously."

As we shall see in chapter 8, Yusuf's father envisioned his role at home as supporting that of the school, providing a domestic environment that worked to prepare Yusuf for school and compensating if and when he fell behind on his targets at school. The other parents' comments, quoted earlier, are equally revealing of their perception of their own role: Shane's mother provided space and a computer at home but left learning to the school; Adriana's parents similarly left her to get on with learning by herself, although their educated family doubtless provided implicit cultural capital, if not explicit help; and Alice's family had its own ideas about education, working to establish a strong and somewhat alternative vision of achievement that looks far beyond the narrow scope of the school. Nonetheless, it remained the case that each parent, in different ways, had to work with or work around the school's discourse of levels, and this posed challenges for all of them as they sought to support their child's learning.

Measuring Oneself

Reductionist though the discourse of levels seemed to us, and confusing though it was for the students' parents, few of the students challenged or even reflected on the adoption of levels as a way of describing learning. It seems that they regarded the school's framing of learning, along with the judgments it reached about individual attainment, as absolute. To them, the system was clear, explicit, and, therefore, manageable. Generally they knew exactly how they were progressing in each subject and were even enthusiastic in telling us what level they were performing at. According to Salma, "It's quite good because they keep what track, like, if you're going on track. All your levels, they know all your levels, and they know if you have to boost it or you're doing good. So I think it's good that they have all that information." Unsurprisingly, as one of the "clever girls," Sara had a particularly good grasp of her own progress:

> I progressed quite a bit in English. Like, I got a really good level in writing, and that was a bit surprising, like, because it was better than, like, some other people in my class that are really good. So I was, like—that was quite surprising because in Year 8, . . . I got an 8b for writing and I got, like, a 7a at the end of the year before. And it was, like, the next writing class we did, so it was pretty, like, two sublevels up, which was pretty good.

In some cases, the students' self-knowledge conflicted with our observation of their concentration in class, and this proved insightful. By February, we had spent six months watching Megan seemingly bored, disruptive, or simply absent from lessons—arguing with teachers, trying to get into trouble by putting her feet up on the chairs, and so on. Yet she told us that she was achieving rather high grades, forcing us to reevaluate her "bad girl" image as precisely that, an image deliberately cultivated: "In some subjects, 7s and for maths, I need to have a 7 by the end of this year. But I'm on 6 or 7 half the time. But I need to make it that I'm always 7. On English, I'm a 7. History and geography I'm a 7. But then Spanish I'm a 6a, so I need to get to 7." This self-assessment led to a fascinating interview in which she explained that Year 9 was the last year she thought she could get away with her "bad girl" behavior, before the formal exam preparation began, and she planned to enjoy her moment of freedom. But this did not mean she took her eye off the levels she was gaining.

Even in response to our occasionally leading questions, we encountered very little explicit critique of this system. The most evident sign of resistance or opposition to the system was expressed as apathy or ignorance. The few students who did not know what levels they had achieved tended to be low achieving and not greatly engaged in school. Lydia would go silent when asked what level she was at. Sedat did not have a clear idea what level he was at, and neither did Shane. Some students wrapped their answers in modifiers: "I think I'm at level 7." This may have been modesty or reluctance or perhaps a lack of confidence in situating themselves within the language of the school.

Life as a Level

The language of levels extended beyond the curriculum and was used to describe attainment in a range of organized activities outside school. Jamie, a keen club tennis player, used an almost identical language to describe his achievements—in this case, the goal being to get into the competition. Jamie's mother explained it best:

> He trains twice a week now for two hours each time, and two before. . . . Coming back into some tournaments, what you also do is you do match plays to bring up your ratings because there's a system of ratings that you can go up. You've got to go up so many wins before you can go up to the next rating. So you're trying to get up to 1.1 basically. So at the moment he's, like, a 7.2. So, you know, he's got a way to go. It goes 7.2, 7.1. 6.2, 6.1 . . .

Max took piano lessons and was entering the grade examinations offered by the Royal College of Music. As we discuss further in chapter 9, for Max, the focus of extracurricular learning seemed to have become the externally validated levels themselves, more than any intrinsic pleasure in music.[9] Even Lydia, our most resistant class member, was engaged in an activity measured in terms of levels, although she herself disavowed any commitment to this measurement. Interviewed with her best friend, Kimberly, it was indicative of Lydia's disengagement from measuring progress of any kind that it was Kimberly and not Lydia who could articulate how good an ice-skater Lydia was:

> INTERVIEWER: So you don't do the levels [the grade exams in ice-skating], but do you sort of know where you are? Could you say, "I'm a level 7 or a level . . ."?

LYDIA: Not really.
INTERVIEWER: Could you say where she is?
KIMBERLY: She can, like, skate forward and—think, like, level 3.
INTERVIEWER: Okay. So she's got a way to go?
KIMBERLY: Yes, because she can skate forward fine, but I don't think she knows what the tricks are.

Our point here is more to demonstrate how the language of simplistic numerical attainment has penetrated into forms of social activity beyond the school. And to support this contention, we have further examples of Sara talking about her climbing and progress in Taekwondo. Yusuf described his experience in mosque school of working his way through the sura (verses) of the Quran (see chapter 8), and Dom and Nick talked about achievements in cricket and football—all in terms of levels.

The most explicit and common use of leveling outside school is in the world of computer games, where attainment in the game and entry to more advanced play is managed in terms of levels. Here is Shane talking about a football game:

INTERVIEWER: What level are you in?
SHANE: 24.
INTERVIEWER: And what—Nathan was in 8 division or something— what division are you in?
SHANE: What division am I in? I'm in 5th, I'm a higher . . . I beat Nick at this, like, four times.

Levels here serve several discrete purposes. They allow for direct competition and, to Shane, the measurement of progress and achievement. Adam was proud to tell us of his gaming accomplishments:

ADAM: I'm a Nord in dragon scale armor, and this . . .
INTERVIEWER: How are you playing that character?
ADAM: This is my own character. I'm level 51.

Not all out-of-school activities extended the concept of leveling into leisure time. Sebastian attended a drama club with quite a developed timetable and infrastructure that allowed for a series of performances but also enabled him to move between different levels aimed at younger and older children. He was clear that the pleasure of attending this club was that it did not offer any form of certification or other ways of marking progress, as we noted in a field note: "The playing of the games was clearly enjoyed for its own sake. In this sense the kind of activity on offer was very different from the remorseless pressure to improve levels that we observed in school." In the interview following this observation, Sebastian reiterated the pleasure of participating in something to be enjoyed for its own sake. Similarly, Giselle enjoyed her music lesson for its own sake, and she and the teacher explained to us (further developed in chapter 9) that they had explicitly rejected the idea of doing the grade examinations. Our field note records,

> We talked about the challenge of developing progression in these flexible and semiformal situations without having to mark progression in traditional sense. This was like her music lessons because Giselle told me she didn't want to work for grades. She didn't like that system and into the point of it but she was very motivated to develop musical skills. This was part of her overall scheme to become some kind of performer in the future so her interest in music was to an extent dictated by future sense of self as much for its expressive pleasures.

Both these examples come from the arts field, where a rejection of external authority in favor of internal judgment frequently characterizes the nature of arts learning.[10] It is difficult to say whether this rejection of levels was simply a way for Sebastian and Giselle to postion themeslves as different from the norm or whether such a rejection was used more as a way of defining their "artistic" sensibilities. We also note that in both of these instances, it is young people from middle-class homes who display the confidence to define alternative markers of significance for themselves and their achievements.

Encoding Discipline

Beyond academic attainment, the school and its digital information management system also encoded attendance and, especially salient in the life of the class, behavior—both "good" and "bad." The history of schools has seen the deployment of a series of methods to record progress and to discipline students, so as to facilitate learning. Megan Watkins's study of the development of writing examines how the young child is taught to sit still, to hold writing implements, and to concentrate.[11] Other established systems of control include termly reports to parents, yearly examinations, and other forms of information collation over the student's school career. But what was striking in our observations was how the class was almost constantly under surveillance, recorded, and evaluated—both interpersonally and digitally.

VFS, like many other schools, employed a computerized and networked information management system that underpinned and extended the discourse of levels. Although the students were constantly reviewing their minimum, target, and achieved levels in each subject, these did not require frequent updating. Their behavior, by contrast, was updated by teachers and recorded in the same database, several times in the course of every day. Although behavior was coded in simple binary terms: good behavior (such as timely homework, compliance with a teacher request, or a show of interest) received a "commendation," and poor behavior (lateness, rudeness, incomplete work, interrupting a lesson) received a "concern." This encoding of behavior resembled that of levels in its persistent quantification of activities at school. Whether talking of attainment or behavior, the constant counting seemed to overtake consideration of what these counts might refer to or what might motivate them.

In the case of VFS, the information management system used was called SIMS, and talk of "SIMS" figured routinely in students' and teachers' accounts of the school day.[12] While the desired effect was to demonstrate to the teacher that the student could enact "being a learner" over the course of the school day, some students, of course, became inured to performing quite the opposite.

Teachers entered and extracted information about any student's progress or behavior throughout the school day via a range of computers available to them across the school. We observed that each student might attract between two and ten entries in any day, resulting in a detailed database. This was, unsurprisingly, onerous for teachers, who devoted a fair amount of class time to the ongoing process of recording students' attainment, ill discipline, or lateness. Yet it was also valued, as a teacher explained: "For the day-to-day things of just flashing up commendations, you can filter who's gone on concern, who's been silly. That's brilliant. . . . I always have it up on the board at the end of the day." The same teacher went on to explain, "If I've got a kid who's on concern three times in a week, I pass that name on to the head of year. They keep them in detention, and they have a note."

While information was often written on the whiteboard or occasionally projected onto the smart board, for the most part, individual records were not available to the young people or their parents.[13] But teacher control over the database did not mean students were unaware of its contents because accompanying the discourse of levels was a discourse of SIMS-recorded data that similarly infused everyday interactions between teacher and student. Teachers often commented on the records they were creating and were equally likely to refer to a student's record. This was partly intended to be encouraging: as one teacher called out to the class, "Who's going on praise? Who's doing the right things?" It also ensured that students knew where they were "going wrong": one day in Shane's life, for instance, recorded separate incidents of his being disruptive, bullying, being uncooperative, and being rude.[14]

The daily accumulation of commendation and concerns was also, as we saw in chapter 5, reflected back to the class as a way of trying to instill a sense of collective identity. Commendations were translated over the school year according to a set calculus into the possible award of a bronze, silver, or gold badge, celebrated in the school newsletter.[15] Meanwhile, concerns were translated, this time on a weekly basis, into detentions, leading to direct intervention by the head of year. This system was well known to the students. As Nick explained, "If you got three concerns on the class sheet in a week, you would get a detention. Then it would be one thing on SIMS. But now you would get four, because you would get the detention plus the three concerns." Megan added, "If you got three praises, that's one commendation." But any system may be misapplied, misunderstood, and, of course, gamed. Max was vocal on this point: if he did not receive a commendation, he felt his hard work had been overlooked. We witnessed him playing a tactical game when, once, a teacher promised a commendation for each good answer, at which point, having been bored throughout the lesson, he started putting up his hand and was duly rewarded. Yet he was not entirely cynical. Asked "Are there any subjects where just the satisfaction of the work would be good enough, you kind of don't care about the commendation?" he replied, "Yes, like, in maths, she doesn't give them, but that's okay, because, like, . . . because we do some hard topics." The language of SIMS was internalized by other students too, and they oriented their behavior toward its priorities. We frequently heard students asking for commendations or trying to negotiate the "concern" so that it could be struck out, and a few students told us that their parents rewarded them with pocket money if their metrics improved.

Perhaps most interesting was the willingness with which the young people adopted the language as a means of self-understanding. For instance, Gideon calmly measured his own progress toward maturity in terms of SIMS metrics: "In Year 7, I just didn't care. Every lesson, I'd just be getting in trouble, and sometimes I'd get, like, a concern in every lesson. And then Year 8, I became a bit better. But I'd still probably get one or two concerns in a day, and regularly, every Thursday after school, I'd have detention. . . . [Then], through the summer holidays, I don't know, I just came back, and I wasn't getting on concern that much."

The teachers saw SIMS as highly effortful but also useful. In principle, they could gain a thorough view of each student across time and across subjects. Yet as they also observed, the data were more often used for disciplinary purposes than mined intelligently for diagnostic uses. In some eyes, it had offered an efficient and even fairer way of doing what teachers have always done. Few saw it as affording new opportunities for understanding student progress, however. And some were more cynical, recognizing the computer science principle of "garbage in, garbage out." An English teacher explained to us, "I think it's quite rubbish, actually. . . . It's almost like the data's stored, and that's what it's for. . . . What happens with it after that I don't think is very well managed at all. Do you see what I mean? . . . I feel I spend far too much putting stuff in and far too little time taking stuff out, if you see what I mean."

While the process of data collection for SIMS was, in itself, significant for its visible process of encoding everyday activities, databases are especially potent insofar as they can be mined for learning analytics.

For instance, SIMS could be scrutinized for the progress of each student or each class by subject over time (and it could also be used to monitor the effectiveness of teachers). Yet being a proprietary piece of software, certain analytics were built into the system, and others were not.[16] Just as levels have had an impact on defining how this population came to understand what learning is in epistemological terms, so the encoding of discipline through SIMS shaped the experience of learning at school as a process of negotiated surveillance.

Conclusions

This chapter has sought to get to the heart of how schools normalize a particular vision of what learning is and to understand how the young people respond. Different schools do this differently, with implications for "what learning counts and what counts as learning."[17] Schools in England follow a distinctive approach to characterizing and managing learning that may be unusual in an international context. But in many contexts and cultures, recent decades have seen increased emphasis on testing regimes, school inspection, and competitive school league tables, together transforming the ways that learning is understood, regulated, and measured.[18]

Although it may be an unintended consequence that this approach should generate a particular discursive framework for classroom interaction and self-knowledge, it was striking in our fieldwork how the discourse of levels came to stand for the process of learning as understood by the families and the young people in the class, even to the exclusion of other and different approaches to learning.[19] Indeed, the processes of encoding, measuring, and reporting learning proved so demanding that they seemed to evacuate the intrinsic value of learning itself. Attention centered on extrinsic markers of learning rather than the pleasures, fascination, or value of the knowledge being gained. Learning, as defined by the school, is disembodied, disconnected, and abstracted from everyday activities. We saw how the young people themselves have learned to perform under these circumstances, although in other cases, the identity work that motivated them pushed back against the prescribed forms of subjectivity that they were being encouraged to adopt. Yet somewhat to our surprise, we heard relatively little criticism of the system. Rather, students, teachers, and parents were variously preoccupied with managing the system so that it worked best for them. Once the system was mastered, that seemed to bring its own satisfactions, leaving little interest in asking how learning could be different with regard to process, content, or outcome.

Models of education are grounded in particular assumptions about intelligence and knowledge, from academic models to what Jerome Bruner has called "folk theories," the commonsense and normalized everyday assumptions we all hold about how the mind can learn:[20] leveling fulfills this role as a way of defining learning. As we have noted, teachers were often ambivalent about the penetration of this discourse into virtually all aspects of classroom management and pedagogy.[21] Nonetheless, the idea of learning held out by teachers to students is, we have suggested, one that prioritizes the regulation of progression above other qualities such as intrinsic interest and engagement. If leveling comes to stand as a new kind of folk theory of mind—that this is how young people learn today—then this will have consequences for all who are involved in understanding the meaning and purpose of education. Most obviously, the discourse of levels displaces two discourses that one would have expected to figure more prominently: one, the content of the curriculum, the subject matter to be learned; the other, the students' own interests and motivations to learn, whether shared or individual.[22]

In VFS, the master metaphor of leveling appeared to offer clarity for both teachers and students. This was thoroughly embedded not only discursively but also through the operation of a digital and networked school information management system, SIMS. As we have seen, the system digitally encoded the students' attainment at the same time as ensuring a constant monitoring of their behavior. Without SIMS, it would have been difficult to operationalize the complex government-mandated system of levels and the many sublevels by curriculum component on a day-to-day basis. Not only did the sheer effort of inputting into SIMS have a transformative effect on the classroom interaction between teacher and student, but digital systems have their own particular affordances, most notably ubiquitous networking, encoding and quantification, and surveillance (or accountability). All of these factors could be seen to shape the learning process at VFS.[23]

At first, we had thought the practice of making visible each student's progress to others would be a source of embarrassment or competitiveness. But on observing how Catherine ended many school days by reading out the list of students in receipt of commendations or concerns, it became evident that students mostly took this in good part. At the end of one day, she checked SIMS, congratulated the class ("Well done, we got 33 commendations today"), and then read out who got how many commendations, concerns, and, last, detentions. Far from seeming to humiliate, this seemed to give the class a chance to point out inaccuracies or to comment on perceived injustices; they were particularly vocal when commendations or concerns were seen to be given too easily or unevenly.[24] And contrasting with our perception of this system sustaining an "empty" pedagogic discourse,[25] parents also liked it, seeing it as offering a guarantee of fairness through the use of a common (and seemingly culture-free) metric. Thus, when asked about SIMS, Adriana's father said, "Given the kind of school it is and the kind of intake it has, . . . you know, they have to be fair. And they can't just sort of selectively be disciplinarians for the people who they think might be trouble and let the others do what they like." Inequalities beyond the school gate are, he suggested, kept out of the classroom precisely because the system is so standardized, ensuring accountability of teachers and fairness to students.

Visibility brings not only accountability but also reflexivity. As we have seen, students were consistently encouraged to reflect on their own progress through levels from task to task and from lesson to lesson, thus encouraging the idea of consistent and observable progress. Moreover, much of the talk about levels was designed to ensure that the responsibility for learning was shared between teacher and student: students must always know what level they are at in any subject and be actively planning how to meet their targets. Yet such reflexivity was limited: talk of learning and of learner identity focused on attaining levels or gaining commendations, not, say, of new areas of a subject to discover or the pleasures of meeting the next educational challenge or of becoming a particular kind of learner. Moreover, the system could be seen to normalize the expectation of surveillance: everyone was being constantly monitored, and everyone knew how everyone else was doing.

Surveillance tends to result in standardization, as the majority fit their behavior toward the norm. Learning was understood as linear, taking one step after the next, and as singular, with everyone on the same path (although not all expected to travel the same distance along it).

We have argued that the discourse of levels impedes a constructive or flexible connection between learning at school and elsewhere.[26] To be sure, extracurricular activities have long used levels prior to the introduction of the National Curriculum framework. Not only do many pursuits, especially sports, involve forms of self-measurement and competition, but one might also even argue that the development of any expertise involves the capacity to self-assess and to "level up." Our argument, however, is that these scaffolding mechanisms have lost their scaffolding function and have been folded into measurement for measurement's sake. Some families in our fieldwork—largely for reasons of cultural capital or socioeconomic status[27]—managed to assert alternative visions of learning, although these are largely fostered at home (see chapter 8) and found little scope for expression at school. While it is not new to suggest that teachers and schooling confuse and exclude large swaths of the population, we are suggesting that the peculiarities of the discourse of "levels" limited the kinds of connections young people could make with learning experiences outside the school, and this is newly constraining in a digital age that precisely fosters such connections.[28]

We could have written this chapter to argue how the school exemplified the inexorable logic of a mediatized institution of surveillance and control, imposing a relentless regime of discipline and the standardization of learning that reduced knowledge to test results. But our sensitivity to the acceptance of and willing participation in the system of levels and SIMS, on the part of students, parents, and teachers, led us to think again. Thus, we found ourselves pondering the anxious experience of growing up in an individualized risk society where traditional anchors have become disembedded and the struggle for success, or even survival, is acutely felt. Why, one might ask, would we expect people to jeopardize a system that seems to deliver, even if it is controlling, hierarchical, and narrow in its conception of learning and its specification of roles? New models of education experiment with teaching practice and student learning. They take risks with unproven forms of assessment, and they confuse expectations of parents. Thus, we are inclined to conclude that the class members' acceptance of the learning process we witnessed in our fieldwork hints at an underlying anxiety characteristic of the risk society, one that is warded off by endorsing so totalizing a system. We return in the book's conclusion to the idea that all concerned signed up to this system for its predictable conception of learning and its much-needed promise of reasonable exam results, notwithstanding that alternative possibilities are thereby excluded.[29]

7

Life at Home Together and Apart

Many of the anxieties of the risk society—as expressed in the mass media and by politicians and as felt by individuals in their daily lives—center on "home" and "the family."[1] As government, welfare organizations, and schools affect daily life in increasingly intricate and personal ways, the burden on parents for children's upbringing becomes ever greater. This chapter focuses on the young people's lives at home, complementing previous chapters examining their lives with friends (chapter 4) and at school (chapter 5).

To the school, and even to the young people's friends, life at home is often the most inaccessible part of young people's lives. Yet home and family generally have the largest influence on their habits, values, interests, and expectations. Viewed from the school, home seemed a rather vague, even problematic place. Among the teachers at VFS, we heard both curiosity and skepticism about family life—seen as time wasting, ineffective, or just plain mysterious.[2] As the school saw it, students moved beyond its control as they left the school premises each day, although the homework tasks, planners, phone calls to parents, and injunctions to students were all designed to ensure that the rigor and ethos of school reached into the home. From the young people, however, we heard a collective sigh of relief as the last bell of the day rang, with the noise level rising rapidly as they jostled in the corridors, gathered in their friendship groups, and chatted on their way to the bus stop, the parental car, or the walk home. What happened next is the focus of this chapter.

At 13 years old, the young people were in transition—about to make more serious academic choices, increasingly immersed in their immediate and wider peer culture, and yet still strongly anchored in life at home. Although they attended the same school and lived in the same neighborhood, their families were all very different. These differences were shaped by social class, cultural factors, and the many personal circumstances that make up family life in ways that are hard to classify or predict. We wanted to understand how the young people developed and expressed aspects of themselves at home, possibly in contrast to those expressed at school or with friends. And we were interested in how their parents sought to construct the home and its resources.

We should first acknowledge that the very notion of "home" is open to interpretation, with scholars describing it as more of an imaginary than a geographic place: home is where we feel we belong. It is invested with our personal meanings and narratives and shaped by cultural and personal histories.[3] Thus, "home" was not always a straightforward location for members of the class. Max divided his time between his mother's and father's houses. Adriana spent a lot of time in the "family home" in Spain. Jenna seemed happier outside hers. Who lived with the young people and what relation they all bore to each other—this, too, could be complicated. Within the home, too, spaces might be demarcated for particular people or activities. For Mark, space was shared, and he struggled to understand our question about whether he had a special place to do his homework. As researchers, we struggled to understand Dilruba's bedroom, since there was only one set of everything, including the bed, yet two teenage sisters peaceably sharing everything.

Indeed, the more we came to know of the young people's lives, the more interested we became in the dynamics within families as well as the variation across them. For example, even though the home is commonly conceived of as "private," a place away from the public realm, within the home, there was much discussion about how to further demarcate domestic spaces or times as public and private or communal and individual.[4] Also high on families' agendas was how much of their economic and cultural resources to devote to "enrichment" activities or, explicitly or tacitly, to leave children to their own devices. Parents and children have unequal power in such decisions. Drawing on the work of Michel de Certeau, we can say that parents have strategic power to set the space-time parameters of life at home, while children must resort to tactical power if they wish to renegotiate or subvert these parameters.[5] The time line of family life is also important; we entered their lives at a certain point in their personal histories, and we discovered some of their present dilemmas to be shaped by a history of past troubles (and pleasures).

Since the arrival of electronic media in the home half a century ago, they have become a key resource for managing domestic space-time relations, their schedules and contents variously demarcating family time or dad's time or bedtime and so forth, just as their positioning in particular rooms is used to demarcate child from adult spaces or public from private spaces. In consequence, the use of media at home—along with the baggage they bring from the wider society regarding "good" and "bad" uses of time and resources—is a key point of contention between parents and children. Parents are particularly exercised by the never-ending task of embedding the latest technologies within family life, linking them to rewards and punishment and framing them in terms of deeply felt ambitions and values.[6]

Continuities and Discontinuities

As we planned the home visits, we had a host of school-based impressions of the students, but how would these hold up outside school? Would Sedat always play the clown, or did he have a serious side? Why was there a troubled atmosphere surrounding Lydia? Would Dom be as confident at home as at school? How disorganized was Fesse's home given his continuous lateness in getting to school? And what of those seemingly sullen white, middle-class children, Alice and Adam—what would they be like at home? Entering their homes was a key moment in our year, revealing a host of contrasts with what we had seen of the young people's lives at school.

Virtually all of the homes were expressive in one way or another, with photos and certificates on display, evidence of particular commitments or talents, a sense of tradition revealed through accumulated artifacts or activities halfway completed. Some were laughingly chaotic, with piles of clothes whisked away to allow us to sit down. In some, we were more formally entertained in the living room. In others, we were plonked down in the kitchen and plied with tea and snacks, with conversations casually interrupted by siblings to see what was going on. There were the more "open" homes, where family and friends variously popped in or even stayed for extended periods of time. There were also a few rather sparsely furnished or largely silent homes. How the young people and their parents constructed their accounts of family life revealed something of how the family lived and also the diverse range of ways of valuing "family."

Having formed our impressions of the young people from observing and talking to them at school, we were curious to see continuities between the school and home identities. Several of the young people showed different sides of themselves. Fesse told us about his art and music interests, of which only the former was visible at school, while Sedat proved much to our surprise to be a skilled musician. We explore their musical interests in chapter 9.

We have already noted in chapter 3 that the members of the clique all seemed to have personal reasons for banding together so firmly. Jenna, for instance, was more forthcoming and seemingly happier at school or with her friends than she seemed—at least to us—at home. Indeed, visiting her home was a somewhat difficult experience: the worn and cluttered living room dominated by a constant loud television offered us little space to sit, and there were few artifacts revealing family interests or commitments. Most striking to us was the absence of any soft toys or girlish customizing of the tiny bedroom she shared with her older sisters.[7] There was also a language barrier between Jenna and her single-parent mother, revealing a pattern we saw in several families, in which only the older but not the younger children of immigrant parents would speak to their parents in the language of origin, meaning that the older siblings played a key role in parenting the younger children in English.[8]

For Jenna's best friend, Alice, the opposite was the case. Alice had puzzled us at school, often looking bored, withdrawn, or sulky. Yet in her middle-class, bohemian home, Alice turned out to be chatty and confident, delighted at our visit and cheekily pressing us for indiscretions about what we were finding out about the class. Her life proved one of the most civically engaged: she played a leadership role in the Guides (Girl Scouts), helped her mother with local charitable activities, babysat for neighbors, and joined the rota for cooking family supper. She was also one of the busiest, with many extracurricular activities, including singing, ice-skating, and digital photography. Her bedroom was the messiest we saw, with evidence of diverse hobbies: several digital devices, broken and operational, along with books and music, the placard from the family's participation in a political protest, even her father's drum kit. Her mother's philosophy was one of self-reliance, as revealed when we asked about social media: "I don't check on Alice that much really. They're going to have to make their own judgments about it, actually, and given they do everything else, so it doesn't stop them going ice-skating. You know, they actually go to a lot of things outside, so I already see them managing it reasonably well." Although Alice was not without her problems—one problem was being overshadowed by a high-achieving older sister[9]—within the clique, she seemed to have the warmest home life; hence her invitation to Max and Jenna to share some of it with her. Nonetheless, the Alice we met at home and with her friends was quite different from the one that we and her teachers saw at school.

Joel, by contrast, was much the same boy at home and school, but he never seemed particularly happy. Our field notes describe visiting the house as follows:

> The house is messy and disorganised. There is loads of stuff all over the place. Mainly to do with music and bikes. I get a sense of a more isolated social world. This is where Joel's life revolves. He has little personal space. Despite the Bohemian ambience, this is most heavily regulated domestic space so far with time limits and weekend internet use being proscribed and controlled. There are loads of cultural resources here but it's not always clear how they are drawn on.

The school had told us that his mother had died and that his father had recently remarried, so maybe we saw a "new" family working hard to make itself whole. We had wanted to pursue Joel's seeming interest in digital technologies—he played the keyboard and experimented with a digital camera—but this turned out to be merely part of the stream of stuff, along with a skateboard, roller skates, and more, that his parents bought him during our year with the class. But Joel's interest in engaging with these technologies did not persist, illustrating an emerging theme across this book, namely, that young people's initial interests would stop and start, frequently meeting obstacles and so not being developed, often seemingly without explanation.[10] The warmest moments we observed centered on homework, perhaps because here the demands on Joel were both sustained and valued, also drawing in his stepmother's expertise at art. Joel told us, "They just help me a little bit, like, but usually I'm fine. But my dad's usually the one that checks my home-work. My stepmum is like, a bit . . . I don't know. She sometimes looks at it and sometimes my planner, but she—it's like she's usually helping more where we have to, like, build stuff for [art or design]." In turn, Joel helped his little sister with her homework, and in this way at least, the efforts they were all making to construct a sense of successful family life were positive, if rather self-conscious. But an effort it did seem, in contrast to, say, the easy management of independent or overlapping activities that made up the lively hubbub of Alice's home.

Family Difficulties

Understanding the contrasts between life at school and home took some investigation, and fortunately several families were open about the prob-lems that shaped their child's experiences, giving us an insight into how trouble at home could affect life at school and vice versa. For instance, at school, an aura of misery hovered around both Abby and Lydia.

Abby was sometimes focused in class but often disorganized or just blank. Sometimes she was boisterously friendly with a group of girls; at other times, she was withdrawn, on edge. At home, she was far more relaxed and forthcoming, revealing some serious musical ambitions. She took her homework seriously, working conscientiously in her room and calling on her older sister or father to help when needed. Her father un-burdened himself about their problems almost as soon as we entered the house, first about his once-successful professional life that had ended in bankruptcy and homelessness, then about Abby, a once-happy, sporty girl who was badly bullied when she entered VFS, resulting in a crisis that necessitated professional intervention. He saw their stories as linked, because he was rehabilitating himself by devoting himself to his family:

Last year in school, she just switched off. She wouldn't react, she wouldn't respond, she wasn't working, she was doing no homework, you know, and she was getting an awful reputation at school as far as somebody who was going nowhere. So people weren't bothering with her, which is not ever any good, and . . . but she's determined—she was determined for herself, and she said to us before the end of the school year as from Sep-tember last year, this year, this current year, "I will work, and I'm going to make it happen." And we've supported her with that, and, bless her, she's done it, you know.

He stressed a family narrative revolving around fierce emotional support:[11]

ABBY'S FATHER: There's a lot of family around. There's cousins in at the moment, yes. Abby's mother has two sisters that live very close by, both groups, and all the families have got . . . and we've had some family holidays together, which have been great fun.
INTERVIEWER: You're very positive; most people think family holidays are their idea of a nightmare!
ABBY'S FATHER: Absolutely not. We took 13 of us up to the Lake District for a week, which was great, a couple of years ago.
INTERVIEWER: I bet you planned it.
ABBY'S FATHER: I did, yes. . . . I think that's important. I think family is important in life anyway, yes. It's part of the ethos, I guess, of this family, of this household.

By contrast, the family narrative about Lydia was more uncertain. Her school report recorded that she had received the most "concerns" in SIMS (see chapter 6), and we observed her at school to be painfully shy with adults, sometimes in tears, or rude and unresponsive, in trouble for forgetting homework or flouting uniform rules. The class tended to give her a wide berth, and she generally sat alone. From the start of secondary school, she was excluded several times. As she herself told us, "I used to do bad things. Like, they used to say that I bullied people, but I didn't." Her head of year told us that things came to a head when an online "hate Lydia" group was set up. He recognized that she was the victim, yet he also told us how she used the "full array of tricks" for getting under people's skin. Indeed, Lydia admitted that since people "wind her up," she, too, "winds people up."

Lydia's mother, living in a modest and charming house complete with roses around the door, had her own painful story to tell. Lydia's parents had separated just before she transferred from her familiar local primary school to the much-larger secondary school, and her father maintained no contact, leaving the family with significant financial problems—nearly losing their home—as well as considerable anger and sadness. Ever since, it seemed, the school was constantly phoning Lydia's mother to express concern about her behavior. To account for what was happening, Lydia's mother narrated the painful history of the family breakup and resultant poverty. Yet in so doing, she subtly seemed to side with the school rather than her daughter (perhaps because her own escape from all these troubles was work she loved in another school).

We had known that Lydia was keen on athletics, but since she no longer ran, we had not paid much attention. The field note describing the moment when we entered her bedroom revealed our surprise—and her own pride in a very public success: "Pride of place on the chimney breast in the centre of room is her large display of running medals—her preferred distance is 100 metres, she tells me." It turned out that she had engaged in athletics at a high level for much of her life, culminating in participation in the London Youth Games and leading her London borough as a runner, while also being an "excellent swimmer." This was narrated positively as a family tradition. As her mother explained, "I was good, her father was good, my father was excellent, my mother. Jason [Lydia's older brother] continued it." Yet this family narrative, along with the culture that sustained their shared athletics, was all focused on the past, and apart from the medals and the stories, there was little that was positive that the family seemed to share in the present.

Lydia's coping strategy involved something of a break with her own family, leading her instead to "adopt" that of her best friend, Kimberly. She would go early to Kimberly's house for breakfast before the girls caught the bus to school together. They often went back to Kimberly's after school, messaging friends outside school, before Lydia went home around 5:30 p.m. Lydia's mother, who juggled multiple part-time jobs, was relieved: "I mean, it's lovely because Kimberly's got a big extended family, great-grandmother, grandmother, and she's very nurturing. Lydia, she loves little ones, so Kimberly's got two little sisters, so Lydia is just there." Lydia described how, once home, the evening meal was eaten "separately but at the same time." In other words, "My mum will cook something, and then I'll sit in here, my brother will go upstairs, and my mum's in the kitchen." "Here" was the living room, where Lydia ate while watching television, explaining that her loud eating annoyed her mother.

So while Abby's father told a story of the family rallying round and supporting Abby, there was no positive narrative for Lydia's mother to address her daughter's problems at school or home. This is not to say that she had given up on her, as there had been a period of professional counseling and, more recently, a new puppy, but none of this seemed sufficient to alleviate Lydia's downward spiral from a once-happy and successful little girl.[12]

Mediating Private and Shared Lives

Perhaps because the use of digital media and communication technologies is relatively flexible, resonant with possibilities, they tended to crystallize tensions over shared versus individual lives within the family and between the home and the world beyond. While parents and children might hesitate in telling us of their worries, arguments, or values, they readily regaled us with the dilemmas, squabbles, and emotions surrounding the media at home. The popular linking of the internet to discourses of risk added to parents' concerns.[13] For their children, the media offered rich resources to explore and express their growing independence, as well as to engage in pleasures that were not always favored by their parents. Analyzing the "domestication" of media in everyday life thus offers a lens through which processes of socialization and individuation become visible—to us as researchers and to the families themselves—stimulating parents to reflect on how their children's childhoods differed from their own.

In the history of domestic media, from the radio or television to the computer or mobile telephone, the trend over recent decades has been from shared to personally owned goods and thus from large, showy objects with fixed locations to ever-smaller and more-portable goods. When it comes to content, the trend is from mainstream genres shared by the nation (from soap operas, news, and sporting events) to more variation and niche (yet globalized) markets (although popular fads may suddenly grip a cohort to briefly bring people together around a soap opera or boy band or sports competition or YouTube meme).[14] For parents trying to manage the socialization of their children just at the moment when their children wish to individuate from them, this complexity adds to the options and tensions of family life.

Typical of UK homes in the early 21st century, all the young people's homes contained a diverse array of broadcast, printed, and digital media, and all had a computer or laptop and access to broadband internet at home. But the management of these media through location and rules of use was variable and complex, depending partly on household income and also on family composition (the single children had more personal devices, for instance) and parental values. Are the media to be shared, or are they personal possessions? Are they to be used in full view in the family living room, or can the children use them as they please in their bedroom?

We have already examined the young people's bedrooms as opportunities for identity expression.[15] But parents set the basic parameters. In table 7.1, we classify the young people's bedrooms to reflect parental choice.[16] In working-class homes, more media are generally seen as a good thing, if they can be afforded. For the middle classes, economic and cultural capital often clashed: thus, the better-off homes might lack the largest or latest technologies, especially when it came to goods located in children's bedrooms. Consequently, not all the middle-class youth had as many private media possessions, although the common areas of the house were generally media rich. Nor were all the working-class youth lacking in such possessions, since media represent a means by which

TABLE 7.1. Media Use by Members of the Class

	Who	Typical possessions
Media-rich bedroom	*Wealthier home:* Adam, Alice, Gideon, Max, Megan *Poorer home:* Dilruba, Fesse, Nick, Salma, Shane	Two or more internet-enabled devices (PC, laptop, tablet, games console) or one internet-enabled device plus a television; also one or more of second games console, hi-fi, digital camera, keyboard, MP3 player, smartphone, peripherals
Average bedroom	*Wealthier home:* Adriana, Jamie, Sebastian *Poorer home:* Abby, Aiden, Mark, Sedat, Yusuf	Either a television or an internet-enabled device (PC, tablet, or games console); usually one of MP3 player, smartphone, other peripherals
Media-poor bedroom	*Wealthier home:* Dom, Giselle, Sara, Toby *Poorer home:* Deyan, Hakim, Jenna, Joel, Lydia, Sergei	No desktop computer/laptop or tablet; usually one of smartphone, MP3 player, television, hi-fi

even relatively poor families can try to "keep up." Thus, domestic media were determined as much by parental cultural capital as by economic capital, given the middle-class tendency to prize books over screens and quality time to concentrate or be creative over displays of the latest technology.[17]

The arrangement of media goods at home was the outcome of past parental strategies and youthful tactics. But this was not simply a matter of parents seeking to control their children and children to escape their parents. Rather, all members of the family sought time both together and apart; the question was how this was managed and on whose terms. Adriana's mother captured many parents' sense that the acquisition of multiple devices was not quite under her control: "In the past year, suddenly the house has been filled with more things, and I think for a long time we didn't have many. Even we used to have a very tiny TV, and suddenly—I guess with the girls becoming teenagers—and suddenly more things came." Although each purchase has its own rationale, the emergent effects on the household can be unanticipated. Devices bought for one purpose may be used for something different. Or devices bought to reduce conflicts between the children in the living room enable a dispersal of children to the bedrooms, resulting in new conflicts with parents. Population surveys show that parents employ several strategies to manage domestic media, including active mediation, in which parents discuss or interpret media with their child; co-use, in which parents share a media activity with their child; and restrictive mediation, in which parents set rules or restrictions on their child's use.[18] The choice of mediation strategy reflected parents' wider values (or dilemmas) regarding family life.

Restrictive practices are often the simplest to justify. For example, explaining that Mark must prepare for exams, his rather-strict East African father restricted media technologies to weekends because, he said, "I don't see the point of it, to be honest." Although watching television, especially football, was also a shared common family experience, even more so was the importance to Mark's parents of going out to visit family friends. The concern of middle-class Max's mother was more global: "I didn't want them to be box kids. . . . I think it's very dangerous. I think it penetrates a life, their lives, without them knowing that. I think it penetrates the life of a family." Rather than imposing simple restrictions, her strategy was more subtle, involving the temporal and spatial arrangements of family life. First, she divided the after-school period into individual time (in which Max completed his homework and also used the computer before she returned from work) and family time, when, she said, "we discuss the day and what's happened and what's going on. So then it's not ideal for you to be sitting with your headphones on, on your iPad." After a family meal, then, Max often watched television with his mother and older sister. Second, she arranged their rather elegant, arty home so as to have no other screens than the television set in the living room, although they were permitted in the bedrooms. While she drew on a discourse that links cultural capital, quality time, and the value of restraint, in some other middle-class homes, the same discourse was used to justify the opposite strategy—few media in the children's bedrooms, while living spaces contained several screens.

Limiting "screen time," however achieved, was a particular concern in virtually all homes. Yet, at the same time, all sought to avoid conflict. In Abby's family, where we have already seen an effort to generate mutual support, multiple personal devices were acquired to avoid domestic clashes, allowing partially parallel lives to be lived under the same roof:

> INTERVIEWER: If I were to hang out here for a week, would I see
> everyone here every evening watching the telly together?
> ABBY'S FATHER: No, because there's another telly upstairs, so we
> would . . . you would see different programs operating upstairs and
> downstairs, and you would even see TV on the computer as well.
> INTERVIEWER: Are there rows that go on in this household around
> what to watch on telly or too much Facebook or . . . ?
> ABBY'S FATHER: Yes, but then we've got—that's part of the reason
> we've got more resources for that to be able to happen in different
> places upstairs, downstairs, whatever.

A more complex ambition for many families was that of "being together" in a sustained, enjoyable, and preferably voluntary way. To achieve this, the media, especially television, were often given a positive role in family life. Adriana's family was fairly typical, using computers for separate interests (including professional work on the part of her parents), while television was used as a source of commonality. In that family as in others, it was the children growing up that necessitated a rearrangement of the bedrooms to alleviate tensions:

> ADRIANA'S MOTHER: We decided to separate the girls in different rooms to have their space.
>
> ADRIANA'S FATHER: Well, the three of them used to share a computer, and that sharing of a computer was one of the main sources of conflict in the house. And basically we got two other computers to avoid that conflict.[19]

Then, to avoid family members each being alone with their own screen, the parents constructed a positive "life of the living room":

> INTERVIEWER: So in a typical evening, is everyone on their own laptop, or is everyone . . . ?
>
> ADRIANA'S FATHER: It varies a lot. I mean, sometimes—last night, we were the four of us. . . . The boy was upstairs reading a book, because we wanted to watch a film together that was not appropriate for him. So we were watching here a movie together. So it varies a lot. Sometimes each of us is in their own, in front of their own computer doing their own things, and some other times we do something together or we play a game. It really depends on the circumstances or how tired they are, how tired we are, and that kind of thing.

In Alice's family also, watching television brought the family together, while using the internet separated them, even when everyone was in the same room. Her mother explained: "There are times when [Alice's father] and I can be watching telly, and we'd have both our laptops, you know, like doing notes while we're all there. And actually there have been times perhaps when all of us have had our laptops. I mean, it's a bit bizarre, I think."

In some families, the worry about fragmentation is more poignant. Giselle's father, who worked as a designer from home, describes a very similar resolution to that of Adriana's family. But in this case, the parents were trying to sustain family life for the children despite their own recent split:

We keep trying to limit their computer time. . . . There are times when we just want them off the screen, and they'll fall off the computer into the iPhone or the Touch or something. . . . I think it's a bit sad really. There are times now when sometimes we gather as a family—and we're a bit of a fractured family, because [Giselle's mother] and me are actually separated, although we're all under the same roof—where we kind of say, "Come on." . . . In the past, it was "Let's not watch any . . . ," you know. Now it's "Come on, let's watch a movie together and get off the computer to watch the telly."

Sustaining togetherness was also a challenge for Nick's family, since he was coparented by a single mother who worked long hours and his grandmother who lived abroad. Rather than banning or restricting technology, Nick's grandmother embraced a strategy of active co-use, both face-to-face when she was in London and by Skype when she was in Sweden:

We are not leaving him alone all day long, you know. We ask, "What are you doing? What's that?" I'm sitting with him. I think, for me is very interesting. I have time for him, to see what happens, how he plays World of Warcraft or whatever. So he explains for me. [Then] with Skype, for example, we are sitting and talking about everything and about also topics at school and really . . . so we just . . . it's a, kind of, being together.

So when Nick and his grandmother were physically colocated, his grandmother normalized their shared use of the computer so that this could be comfortably continued when they were apart, their mutual online interests helping to sustain their relationship.[20] It may be that the computer will increasingly displace television as the chosen medium of togetherness—computer gaming seems to be the practice that enables this. For example, Sebastian's dad would join him in playing the popular game Call of Duty, creating a sense of togetherness over an activity that, for Adam and his father, pushed them apart. Here again, the particular narratives of different families can be important.

Adam's favorite games—Call of Duty, Grand Theft Auto, Assassin's Creed—were rated for over 18 years only, and this upset his father, as his mother explained:

ADAM'S MOTHER: This is because [Adam's father's] parents were German war babies; they grew up through the war. He's first-generation postwar German. He has very strong feelings about anything martial, anything military, anything . . . because for him that's a very real history.

INTERVIEWER: Okay, so the idea that he's got a son that wants to go round shooting people for pleasure . . .

ADAM'S MOTHER: Is abhorrent to him, deeply abhorrent to him. I respect that. . . . I don't have quite the same position. That's his position, that's my position; we've had to work this out.

So, while Adam's mother was fully aware that he used the games as "a very, sort of, buoyant, active social tool, although he's up there on his own, you can hear him, you know, partying," and although she herself liked to remain open to digital media,[21] she felt as a parent that she had become locked into an anxious framing of Adam's activities as part of her role as mediator between Adam and his father. She tried a compromise designed to please them both: "To keep a . . . so my position, I keep a theoretical eye on it, so I say—you know, I've made a rule. I've just said I don't want anything sadistic in the house. That's it. It can be violent, it can be aggressive, but it can't be sadistic."

This discussion about games led into a deeper appraisal of Adam's academic interests and motivation. Adored by his middle-class parents but seen as lazy by his teachers and as sleepily disengaged by us, Adam described himself as a practical rather than an abstract or creative learner, even as "kind of stupid." Whether this had frustrated the aspirations of his middle-class professional parents we did not discover, but they told us of his history of anger and school refusal. In his mother's view, "I think it's because he's not a driven person, he's not a motivated person. . . . He just sort of does what's in front of him or resists it, but he's not . . . he doesn't seem inspired by anything at the moment. . . . It seems to me that the thing that totally engages him is the gaming. The thing that doesn't engage him is school"—hence her need to find a compromise between the father who hated violent games and the son who found little else motivating. She was not, however, entirely successful in her efforts, and Adam remained critical of his father's position, which he considered inconsistent and unfair:

He doesn't want me to have 18s [age rated] either, although I don't understand why. But he lets me watch war films, and he says it's because it's like educational and it's like real things: "You should learn about stuff." And I say, "Oh, my gosh." And so he doesn't let—well, he doesn't want me to have those games, and then I say, "Surely if I buy it with my own money, then I could have it." And then he says, "No, because I don't want it in my house" and stuff like that. It's just really annoying. So I sometimes buy them off my friends and, yes, because like half my friends are just playing CoD [Call of Duty] all the time and war games that my dad wouldn't let me have.

The result was a degree of subterfuge on Adam's part about his computer game playing, creating a distance between himself and both his parents. However, when we revisited him at the end of the year, this moment seemed to have passed. He had reorganized his bedroom so that instead of having separate gaming and "work" equipment and spaces, the consoles and computers were brought together on the one desk, and he clearly felt that his gaming pleasures were now more understood by his parents.

The potential risks of today's digital media pose further challenges, again either pushing parents toward simple restrictions or, when it could be managed, to more communicative strategies that sought to respect and support their children's own capabilities. Here is one example:

SEBASTIAN'S MOTHER: Basically I was brought . . . you know, my parents trusted me, and I trust my own child.
INTERVIEWER: Yes, and that's an attitude as a way, yes.
SEBASTIAN'S MOTHER: And then, you know, basically, you have to have these experiences in your teenage [years], don't you?
INTERVIEWER: Right. So you . . . that's a deliberate strategy to expose safely to risks, as it were?
SEBASTIAN'S MOTHER: I think he's . . . I think he's quite open with us.
SEBASTIAN'S FATHER: Yes.
SEBASTIAN'S MOTHER: I mean, he'll sort of say, "Oh, come and look at this thing I've seen on YouTube," and you might think, "Ooh, that's a bit . . . isn't it?" But he's . . .

Megan's father took a similar line when her older sister saw Megan acting provocatively on Facebook, resulting in a family row; but her father responded that this was to be expected of a 13-year-old, and simply talking with Megan was a sufficient response in his eyes. Yusuf's father took a more autocratic approach, dealing with his concerns over internet content by only sustaining internet connectivity in the main living room space and explaining this in religious terms: "As Muslims, we are restricted to go to—we can't go [on] every website we come across."

While the media were sometimes presented to us as a problem in the family, requiring management, we also saw the media proving to be a resource that families called on to solve more fundamental problems in their lives. After all, it is a robust family that can sustain long periods of positive face-to-face interaction. Giselle's dad seemed to speak for many parents in welcoming the safety of gathering around the television as a way of being together despite underlying tensions. Yet even when, as he poignantly put it, "we're trying to be a nuclear family" in front of the television, "I'll be checking my emails, [and] the kids will also have things shuffled away—it's the phone or the Touch or the iPhone or something knocking about." Sustaining togetherness can never be fully achieved, and for the most part, we were struck by these families' commitment to engage in a form of continuous "work" to make it so.

Conclusions: Living Together and Separately

In the 21st century, coming together "as a family" is ever more a matter of choice than of necessity, often seen as a task to be managed rather than taken for granted. Parents operate with varying norms and expectations for themselves and their children, and they face a range of problems depending on their circumstances. These problems, and their resources to cope, are both socioeconomic and social-psychological in origin. In chapters 3 and 4, we have already seen how young people use their limited free time to exercise control over what they do and with whom, seeking out moments in their often-full days to be alone or to hang out with friends on- or offline. Those who have expressively customized, media-rich bedrooms have recourse to a bubble of privacy even within the family home, although those who lack their own space at home could achieve a similar result by using earphones, for example. Yet when parents construed the living room as an opportunity for the family to come together, often around the television set, their children generally responded positively even while seeking—before and after—a measure of separation within the home to enable privacy and to avoid conflict.[22]

We might speculate that, just as schools are tempted to regard new technologies as offering a route to solve some long-standing problems with schools, so parents seize on these as resources to reshape their domestic practices in ways that can reduce conflict and enhance family harmony. In both cases, the driving factor is young people's evident interest and pleasure in digital media, as it is this motivation that, the adults around them hope, can be harnessed to fulfill larger goals. Hence, we disagree with Sherry Turkle, who despairs, in *Alone Together*, that "we are increasingly connected to each other but oddly more alone."[23] Indeed, we saw little evidence that young people—or their parents—are becoming so obsessed with their personal screens that they no longer have time for each other. It might be said, however, that our class of 28 young people is too small for us to counter this claim, or maybe our 13-year-olds are still too young.

Our fieldwork did lead us to conclude that, while parents certainly worry that their family risks living "alone together," a better account is that families are finding ways to "live together separately," as Patrice Flichy has put it.[24] This familial desire for "commonality" differs from the notion of civility, which, we have argued, is valued by the school (see chapter 5) and by the young people themselves online (see chapter 4). Although both civility and commonality demand that, for certain purposes, the group's concerns are put ahead of the individual's, civility applies in the public realm where genuine differences among people connected by weak ties threaten to undermine the larger concerns of society. By contrast, the commonality that we see families concerned to sustain is centered on the emotional depth of strong ties among people bound together, even as their children move toward greater independence. Civility enables the public good despite fundamental differences. Sustaining commonality within the family may provide the confidence for individuals to express their differences in public.

This chapter has explored personal narratives of family life, finding that explanations for the time-space patterning of family interactions, and the ways in which digital media fit within these, have deep roots. Rather than interpreting media use as indicative of attitudes to the media per se, therefore, we see media use as a way to move on from past problems or to find strategies to achieve deeper family goals. However, in pointing to the importance of diverse family dynamics, we do not mean to underestimate the importance of social class, gender, or ethnicity. But we do find that mapping these structural features onto particular families is not straightforward.

Lynn Schofield Clark identifies two increasingly polarized types of American family. Among upper-income families, she observes an "ethic of expressive empowerment," visible in the ways that they encourage media use for learning and self-development while discouraging distraction or time wasting (as they perceive it). Among lower-income families, she notes an "ethic of respectful connectedness," where the emphasis is on media uses that are respectful, compliant, and family focused.[25] While these two ethics are convincing, they do not readily account for socioeconomic difference in our study. For instance, the challenge for Abby's (very poor) father was to encourage his shy daughter to find expressive confidence outside the home. Middle-class Giselle's father was trying to sustain both ethics, seeing the connected family as precisely what gives each member the confidence to go out and to succeed in his or her own way. Lydia's and Adam's very different (poorer and richer) families were each tryng, in their way, to manage just a little more respectful connectedness and empowerment. Adriana's middle-class family was quietly confident of her future success and so focused on respectful connectedness, as this seemed to them more at risk as the children grow and so go their own ways. This is not to say that socioeconomic differences make no difference. As we explore in chapter 8, these shape the resources available at home, including the time and expertise on offer from the young people's parents and their own take-up of a range of activities.

Living together, then, remains the bedrock of family life, but recognition of the individualization of modern lives, including the rights of children to explore their own interests and the complexities faced by parents with their own pressures and desires, demands a degree of separation within the home. This is intensified by the limitations on young people's freedom of movement beyond the home, as noted in chapter 4.[26] The panoply of shared and personal media devices within even relatively poor homes aids the exercise of choice over how time and space within the home can be used to support a particular balance between the individual and the communal. Digital media also mean that the boundary of the home is ever less a bar to communication beyond the home—as children come home and use social networking sites, staying in touch with relatives abroad or even saying good night to each other via the phone while forgetting to say the same to their parents downstairs.[27] Being together, in the media-rich home, is significantly a matter of choice, involving more negotiation, some conflict, and a general openness to the possibility of sharing. Flichy describes this as a kind of lifestyle juxtaposition, with family members colocated but each attending to his or her separate screen or physically dispersed but connected to each other through their screens.[28] The result is an often-mediated but still-genuine togetherness that sustains the fragile balance between individuality and commonality required in the modern "democratic" family.[29]

All families, in varying ways and degrees, seek to sustain both the warmth and respect of family life and the self-development and life chances of their children. But there are many pressures on families' capacity to do this. In today's often-busy, "time-poor" families, time not already allocated to homework, housework, or earning is precious. No wonder that "family time" has become an explicit category to be planned for and protected[30] or that, as we will see in chapter 8, homework and extracurricular activities have become a new burden for parents as they adopt pedagogic roles.[31] Since whatever remains as free time is, therefore, even more under pressure, it is no wonder, too, that the media—with their capacity to structure the lifeworld both spatially and temporally—have become a particular focus of contention in families, for what they bring, what they promise, how they organize social relations, and what they displace.

8

Making Space for Learning in the Home

The modern family varies in how it balances the desires of its members to live together and yet also separately, as we saw in chapter 7. One way is to exploit the flexibility of contemporary digital media to structure domestic time and space, building common rituals and yet allowing for individuality. But as we have also argued throughout this book, considerable flexibility is increasingly demanded of all the institutions that structure young people's lives, including family, school, and community. In this chapter, we explore the changing arrangements surrounding the nature and place of learning outside the school and in the home.

We build on the argument of chapter 1 that the forms and ways of knowing in society are diversifying, complicating the traditional activities of schools (along with libraries, universities, museums, and other repositories of information and expertise). Education—frequently conceived throughout the 20th century as a public good to be managed by the state—has begun to fragment into a series of local, national, and (in the case of universities) international markets.[1]

Markets in education encompass not only schools but also ancillary educational services, some of which seek to supplement schools while others appeal directly to families. In recent years, a host of publishing and educational technology companies both offline and online have developed in this marketplace.[2] Yet this mixture of entrepreneurial markets, which place a heavy emphasis on the responsibilities of the individual and on establishing comparable and measurable outcomes, by no means results in a simple or singular narrative replacing older values (variously humanist, meritocratic, social justice oriented) around learning and education. Taken-for-granted boundaries between educational institutions are being rethought, as are the relations between institutions and individuals, motivated by a sense of global opportunities and yet an intensified culture of anxiety over academic attainment and labor-market competition.[3]

Taken together, these shifts are reconfiguring the risks and opportunities that young people—and their parents and teachers—must engage with. In turn, this impacts on parental attitudes toward the authority of schooling and how families reconstruct the home as a new kind of "learning provider." Since digital media pay little heed to physical boundaries of home or school, such technologies are often harnessed by commercial and policy rhetoric as the solution to deliver these new opportunities for out-of-school and lifelong learning.[4]

But do parents give time to reimagining the education system? They know that they must ensure their child gets to school on time, ready to learn. They know they must check their child's planner and attend the periodic parent-teacher appointments. Many parents ask daily, "How was school?" even though the answer is often a grunted "boring." Many set aside a time and place for homework, and most regard it as their responsibility to provide their child with internet access, even if they have never used it themselves. As Abby's father told us, "It is the communication media of the age at the moment, so . . . if they can't be switched on to that, they're going to be in trouble and they're going to miss out." But some go much further in supporting learning at home and school, hinting at the general uncertainty facing parents: what support is most useful, and how much is enough? We explore their strategies in this chapter, bringing out how these reflected families' differential economic, cultural, and social resources. Moreover, as the existing research literature makes clear, the more it seems that we are living at a time when fewer and fewer people trust schools, and so the more the responsibility for education falls heavily on parents.[5]

This chapter explores these themes by examining how different families construct opportunities for learning physically (how they arrange rooms and resources, especially technology), socially (how they establish habits and rhythms), and conceptually (how they see the purpose and nature of learning). As will become clear, varying conceptions of the relation between home and school learning were evident across the families, and these depended on their cultural capital. Although the idea of cultural capital is contested, we find it the most useful way of capturing the mixture of social-class-based assumptions, values, and beliefs that we observed to distinguish the families.[6] Attitudes to education are passed through the generations, and they are also shaped by cultural beliefs.

While they are often instrumentally oriented toward employment, families are also concerned with their children's well-being, happiness, and fulfillment, however defined, and they may or may not rely on the school to deliver this broader vision. Thus, the value that families accord to school depends on how they calculate its relevance to their children's possible futures (not necessarily just a question of qualifications) and, in turn, on how they frame their hopes and aspirations more fundamentally.

As we spent time in the class members' homes, we were provoked by research showing not only that middle-class families benefit more than other social groups from educational opportunities, formal and informal, but that they are responding to the competitive pressures of the risk society by striving ever harder to maximize such benefits, seeking distinction (in Pierre Bourdieu's terms) for their child by multiplying enrichment activities as a deliberate strategy of what Annette Lareau has called "concerted cultivation."[7] While the existence of such middle-class anxieties is widely asserted in popular discourses, with growing evidence for concerted cultivation especially in the US,[8] we were curious as to whether similar practices were evident in the UK. And we were even more curious about what we would find in the less privileged homes, for Lareau's contention that working-class families simply conceive of their children's development as a "natural" process seemed at odds with the widespread efforts of families over recent years to gain computers and internet access or to respond constructively to labor-market uncertainties.[9]

Respecting the School's Definition of Learning

Yusuf was the eldest of four children in a devout Muslim family that had emigrated from East Africa when he was little. His father had been a trained nurse but in London could only obtain work as a railway ticket inspector. His mother spoke very limited English, although the rest of the family was fluent. At school, we saw that Yusuf worked quietly and conscientiously in lessons. He was in advanced classes for math and science, which he enjoyed, although he received remedial attention for English and had previously received it for math and science, as well as being screened for learning difficulties.

When we visited him at home, we found that two distinct learning practices were high on his parents' agenda. First, his twice-weekly atten-

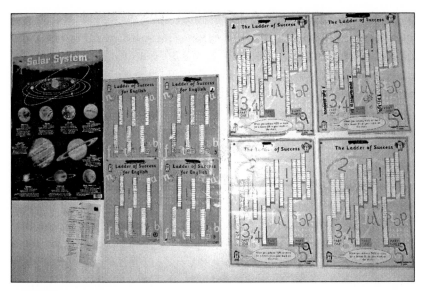

Figure 8.1. Yusuf's "study."

dance at Quran school, which involved a considerable amount of rote learning (in Arabic) that he did not always fully understand, as well as more open discussion of moral and social issues. Here, progression was measured by learning the suras (verses of the Quran) by heart.

Second, his father had purchased an integrated series of math and English programs on CD for around £3,000—a considerable expenditure for any family and especially for one with such modest means as Yusuf's. The CDs provided a series of graded activities and tests; when a certain number of tests have been passed, the company that makes the CDs issues bronze, silver, and gold certificates. At home, one of the bedrooms had been turned into a "classroom," with large wall charts marking the children's progress through the tests along with a careful arrangement of further educational resources: CDs, books, worksheets, and test materials. Yusuf's father referred to himself as a sort of head-teacher, and each child was expected to complete a certain number of tests weekly, filling in the appropriate cells in the wall chart. This demanded considerable discipline since Yusuf's father was often absent on shift work, and his mother could not communicate well with the children.

Both the Quran school and the home investment in educational technology mirrored the emphasis on structured learning tasks and quantified indicators of progression that we saw at school in its implementation of national curriculum levels (chapter 6). Yet the school was unaware that Yusuf was engaged in either of these learning activities out of school. Nor was it clear to us that the family's investment particularly aided his achievement at school or his learning for its own sake.

While Yusuf's family, especially his father, went to great lengths to mirror at home their conception of learning at school, most families took a more moderate stance. One common strategy was to carve out one small part of the home and arrange it to look like school, building a home-school link through spatial design. For example, Shane's mother had done her best to support Shane's learning by dividing his bedroom into distinct activity zones: the bed in one corner, a small air-hockey table and a boxing punch ball in another, an Xbox in a third, and placed diametrically opposite it, a PC. This distinction between work and pleasure was repeated in several of the boys' bedrooms; implicitly, a computer is for work, and the Xbox or PlayStation 3 is for fun.

Yet Shane barely used his PC, and when he did, it was mainly for fun. When we visited, he could not show us any software he used other than the browser, and his history revealed searches for YouTube, shopping, and Facebook. Moreover, the house had few books, and the only talk of focused practices that could be classified as learning concerned his serious engagement in sports, both organized and informal. Shane's mother had come to a similar conclusion:

> INTERVIEWER: Okay, what do you think are the positive benefits of all the time he spends on the computer and the Xbox and stuff like that?
> SHANE'S MOTHER: Don't know, really.
> INTERVIEWER: So what do you think he gets out of it?
> SHANE'S MOTHER: I don't know, really. It's all for his personal use, isn't it? I don't think it's educating him, really.

While not all the parents had reached the point of disillusion, it was common that conversations about technology faltered when we asked what was good about it, what they hoped their children would gain from it. The fear of "missing out," it seemed, drove the acquisition of such goods more than any particular vision of their benefits.[10] We were led to conclude that a positive vision of how technology—or, indeed, any other informal or extracurricular activities—might foster learning of various kinds was, in large measure, a matter of cultural capital.

Contrasting with both Yusuf and Shane, whose families were both relatively poor, was Adam. All three boys were obtaining grades around the middle of the class, but while Yusuf's family in particular regarded this positively, Adam was considered by his teachers and parents to be under-performing. We have already seen in chapter 7 how Adam's computer gaming had led to conflict in his family. As we then hinted, the problem was more than one of how to regulate his engagement with violent media but was also one of how to build on his enthusiasm for computer games since this was so at odds with his lack of motivation at school. His mother—an artist who welcomed unconventional ideas—was generally familiar with current claims that playing computer games can offer new and exciting ways to learn and even have a place in formal education.[11]

Does the attitude of Adam's mother account for our observation that Adam's game playing was qualitatively different from that of the other young people we interviewed? Adam had access to PC gaming as well as an Xbox and was as interested in more exploratory, open-world games—like Skyrim and a skating game that allowed him to experiment with moves and sequences and to be led by the qualities of the game. The first time we visited Adam's home, he was less concerned with leveling (proceeding through the levels of a game to define his progression) or with the social interaction facilitated by game play compared with the other boys and more focused on exploring the possibilities of the game. He showed us magazines, websites, and other resources that he drew on, suggesting that his gaming represented an organized and systematic form of knowledge acquisition.

Thus, it appeared to us that, for both negative and positive reasons, Adam and his family sought to construct his interest in game play as a form of learning, one that stood in opposition to what school offered. Yet this was a fragile construction, risking the accusation that they were finding justification for his troubling performance at school. Nor was it clear to any of them what exactly was being learned or where it might

Figure 8.2. Adam's bedroom, showing places for work and play.

lead. As we also noted in chapter 7, when we visited Adam at the end of our project, he seemed to have moved on in two senses: first, he now positioned game playing as just a way of connecting with his friends, and second, he had become more involved in his schoolwork. For instance, he took one of his public (GCSE) exams early, obtaining a high grade, and was more positive about—and more successful in—school. Perhaps in consequence, his computer gaming no longer seemed a point of conflict at home.

Unlike Adam's mother, neither Yusuf's father nor Shane's mother had any way of framing learning beyond that of the school. In this respect, cultural capital, as conceived by Bourdieu, matters: Yusuf's and Shane's families made certain investments to aid their children's educational prospects, but they did not create a culture that recognized pedagogic values other than the instrumental. For example, although like Adam, Shane was a keen computer gamer, he lacked a language to talk about what he knew or how he might seek to improve his game performance, nor was he interested in metatextual practices such as reading magazines about gaming or looking up game cheats.

In short, although Yusuf's and Shane's cases exemplify different kinds of continuity with school definitions of learning, these boys did not find a way to escape that paradigm. Rather, their parents accepted the school's highly instrumental approach to knowledge and, with little cultural capital to contest or qualify it, created a domestic environment that, to a greater or lesser degree, mirrored the school's emphasis on external indicators of achievement.

Deploying Cultural Capital

Dom and Sara both came from affluent middle-class homes with parents in high-status professional occupations. Dom was a serious athlete, playing for the local cricket and football clubs as well as the school teams. Sara had several hobbies and interests, including taking an additional qualification in astronomy and performing in a Shakespeare workshop, both offered by the school as extracurricular activities. For their parents, the school was necessary but not very interesting, while home life took a lot of investment to support their high-achieving children.

The notion of investment here needs careful unpacking. Lareau's account of middle-class parenting in the US paints a picture of a stressful schedule of enrichment activities that is highly demanding of both children and parents in the competitive struggle to maintain distinction. Yet we found that Sara and Dom had more flexibility and no less free time than Yusuf did. Moreover, unlike Yusuf, both were encouraged to undertake a wide range of activities, not simply for instrumental reasons, to develop their "curriculum vita," but also from deeply held beliefs about the importance of a childhood that includes diverse forms of learning and engagement, beyond "just" academic success.

For instance, Dom's progress in sports was considered as important as his progress in academic study. Shane played as much football as Dom did, but Dom was much more serious in his preparation for games, commitment on the field, and collegial relationships with team members, regarding all of these—as well as actual football skills—as a focus for continual improvement. Dom's club football coach had made him player of the year precisely because of the way that Dom concentrated during the game and was consistently serious in considering strategy and talking to, encouraging, or leading his teammates, as well as in paying attention to the work rate of the whole team. In a similar fashion, Sara was encouraged by her family to take her hobbies seriously. When we first visited, she was making a whole series of Play-Doh sculptures, approaching this with a similar level of intentness that she did her academic work. While the family was obviously aware of the difference between earning a qualification in astronomy and making Play-Doh figures, it was noticeable that her family supported and respected all kinds of participation that provided opportunities to develop new interests—as exemplified by the array of cultural activities Sara enjoyed, including a visit to the Charles Dickens museum and National Trust properties.

For both Dom and Sara, access to technology was helpful: Dom liked to follow expert football commentary on Twitter; Sara would photograph and then upload images of her Play-Doh sculptures to Facebook. But it was neither relied on as sufficient in itself as a route to achievement nor especially prominent. Despite living in an affluent home—and with a father working in IT—Dom, his brothers, and his mother shared two computers between them as a deliberate strategy to encourage sharing, to regulate potentially antisocial behavior, and to mitigate against ob-

Figure 8.3. Photographs of Sara's Play-Doh creations uploaded to her Facebook profile.

sessive solitary game playing. Dom's bedroom was one of the few that had no screen, although the family did have an Xbox in a dedicated playroom for the boys. Sara had largely given up the struggle against her Facebook-mad little sister for the family laptop and would go online from her iPod Touch when she needed to look something up. Indeed, her bedroom was largely dominated by her Sylvanians (a cute range of animal toys with human characteristics), legitimating a space for childhood play along with her books and her new telescope.

Sara's father described the process of seeking out enrichment opportunities: "For quite a number of years, I've tried to get them interested in various sports; and we've gone through a whole gamut of sports and, yes, from swimming to tennis. But a few . . . about four years ago, we stuck at climbing, and Sara's become quite good at that." It is noteworthy that more like Yusuf's than Adam's experiences, the climbing was part of an accredited scheme that provides qualifications measured in levels. Sara was persistent at this activity, although a little frustrated at how slowly she was progressing: "You have to move on to the next level and stuff, and it's . . . and I still haven't moved on, but it's just—it's really long. They haven't even got a level 5 at our climbing center. But I'm level four, at the moment, so it's, like, I can't give up now. So I'm going to just keep doing it, hopefully, get to level 5. I think . . ." By trying a range of activities, Sara had developed the ability to self-assess realistically, recognizing that she was not "sporty" or arty, for example, and coming to terms with her limitations in rock climbing after watching fellow climbers.

Such talk might give the impression that Sara was more average than is the case. However, she undertook the broadest range of activities in the class, working hard and obtaining A grades. It may be that to fit in with her peers she had learned not to shine too obviously, although it is also surely an achievement in itself that she had learned to recognize where and when to concentrate her efforts effectively. Two instances hint at the secret of her success. On one occasion, she had to research child mortality in Swaziland for a model United Nations competition: "I'm on the committee for child mortality rates, so I had do so much, like, research for it. And in the end, Dad just like—I'm just ringing up the consulate in—from the UK to Swaziland. So he just rang them up, and I was like, 'You can't just ring them up, can you?' And then he was like, 'Oh, here's the government website, just . . .'" Not all fathers have the confidence to phone a consulate to help with their daughter's homework, and so this example nicely illustrates Lareau's claim that middleclass families teach their children to stand up for themselves, to demand the resources they need. Still, since any moderately experienced internet user could find this information easily, we found it interesting that high-achieving Sara did not, suggesting that she was more hardworking than used to taking initiative. For example, to be accepted on the after-school astronomy course, students had to promise to undertake what the school called "independent learning," since the amount of formal teaching offered was limited. We asked Sara if this involved a different kind of study:

> Not too much. It was relatively all right, but, like, because they gave you all the resources to find out anyway and a lot—like, we didn't actually cover that much in class. A lot of it we did have to study at home, but you didn't realize you were studying it, because what we were doing is we'd get our homework, and it would just be a set of questions, and then,

if you answer them, you don't realize it, but every single one of them is, like, related to a topic that will come up on the test. And so it was quite nice how, like, you can study it yourself, and you can understand it at your own pace and stuff. I really, like, I really felt that was good.

We asked her about searching online for additional information or resources—for instance, whether she had visited the NASA site, a well-known source of astronomy knowledge geared toward students. But such exploration had not occurred to her, and she evinced no qualms about not checking any of these out.[12] As she saw it, the facts required for the tests were conveniently available on a single recommended site, and there was no need to look further afield. Yet her account of studying astronomy in the evenings is one of positive engagement; she found school learning pleasurable and rewarding and thus welcomed its extension into the home.

Dom's approach to learning was a little different: he tended to generate a kind of running commentary to accompany his activities, as if performing his own learning experience. We saw him to do this in tutor time, speaking aloud the class's rate of awarded commendations as if he were a sports commentator; we might even see his way of following and commenting on the experts' football discussion on Twitter in a similar light, and we saw him doing it during football practice, as our field note recorded:

Dom is very focused in the skills-based sessions. He is clearly competitive; at many points he made jokey remarks about beating other opponents but not excessively so. He is conscientious and does as he is asked and will rebuke others if they mess around. He is very involved in the action though not by any means the most aggressive or evidently talented show off. When [the coach] gave advice or instructions I noticed it was Dom who picked up on this first. . . . He does offer a little bit of a commentary in a humorous and engaging fashion—I mean he is always trying to involve others in the narrative. So: saying "well done," "man on," ooh's and ahh's, screams of pleasure etc. These are all ways of vocalising and narrating the experience for the group. In the game they played in the baseball arena kicking the ball as if they were making runs in a skills-based complicated activity; he immediately set up a commentary, a

> dialogue with other boys—a jokey banter as a form of competition. They all do this but he is inventive, witty and consistent in this.

When we asked him about his player-of-the-year award, Dom explained, "I just realized that obviously I'm not the best in the team, but if I try hardest, I can make myself look like I'm the best in the team." As with Sara, Dom found he could achieve beyond his actual expertise, because excelling was as much about performing as a type of learner as it was about displaying knowledge. In their different ways, we can interpret both Sara and Dom as having grasped what it takes to excel, having made a realistic assessment of their personal strengths and weaknesses, and having found a self-regulating strategy, perhaps even a personal pedagogy, that worked for them.[13]

Dom and Sara exemplified young people who had learned or were in the process of learning how to make the "choice biographies" introduced in chapter 1.[14] Support for theoretical claims about the changing nature of identity in the modern age can be glimpsed in the daily efforts of these two youngsters as they went about developing the kinds of identity that were supported and rewarded by both their family and school and that, surely, would help them "succeed" in the future. The ways in which they had embraced these subtle and unstated aspects of being good learners stand in strong contrast to the attitudes of Yusuf and his father, who still operated with a top-down notion of the teacher-managed student, and of Shane, whom we saw to be puzzled, aware that no great burden of expectations was imposed by the school yet unaware of the self-regulating model that could take its place. As the year progressed, we saw Adam managing to integrate forms of learning that were marginalized with those deemed central. Also significant was the way in which Giselle's family, and some of the other "bohemian" families, had access to alternative discourses of learning, allowing them to sidestep the school's vision of learning.[15]

Alternative Visions of Learning

Although far from high earning, Giselle's parents were a highly educated, bilingual couple, each self-employed in creative enterprises.

Giselle drew, performed, played music, and had a sense of herself as an emerging artist, strongly supported by her parents. She told us how, on vacation with her mother, a trained artist, she and her brother used dedicated sketchbooks as part of the holiday ritual. Giselle's mother had also run a small after-school club for art when Giselle was younger. These professional practices—using a sketchbook, critiquing art together, or talking about photography—were normalized within day-to-day family activities. This same structure of support framed Giselle's technological pursuits: her creative use of Tumblr, a management role on her cousin's Minecraft server, her production of witty videos uploaded to YouTube.

Although Giselle's father did not play Minecraft, he had observed Giselle and her younger brother's game play—usually prominently conducted in the living room—and had developed a view of how it incorporated a range of learning processes. Unprompted, he spoke to us about how the play developed technological fluency and social skills to participate in a virtual social world. Giselle and he talked about some of the game's design issues, such as developing customized skins for building textures. Unlike Adam's mother, Giselle's father had a vocabulary and set of concepts about learning that derived from his work as a self-employed creative within the digitally connected economy. This outlook and values framed his and Giselle's mother's beliefs about learning, leading them to treat Giselle's participation with a certain equality and seriousness, recognizing that it involved a degree of responsibility on her part. Meanwhile, Giselle learned to conceive of her game play and her use of Tumblr as an extension and development of her other embedded artistic practices.

Here, then, was support for a vision of learning that integrated Giselle's different skills and interests, drawing on wider discourses about aesthetics, taste, and expertise. This contrasted with the siloed approach of the school to art or music or information communication technology (ICT), instead allowing for an approach to learning that was reflexive, pleasurable, and interest driven and that made no artificial divisions between "academic" and "play" or "just games." The result was a degree of disconnection between home and school in which home was superior in providing creative and flexible opportunities to learn:

INTERVIEWER: Do you feel that what [Giselle] does here in terms of creativity is recognized in the school, is welcomed by the school, is completely separate from school perhaps?

GISELLE'S FATHER: I don't know what happens in the school really. I mean, I know she's good at art, and they've acknowledged that. I know . . . when it comes to music, I think it always sounded like music is a bit chaotic generally at school and isn't really the place to really . . . the music classes aren't really the place to do much at all other than . . .

INTERVIEWER: They have those rooms full of digital electronic keyboards.

GISELLE'S FATHER: I don't know what happens in there though. It does seem—I don't know, music classes—I ask about music, and she goes—sort of, it just seems to be a bit of a struggle getting through music, because there's just too many people doing too many things. And it sounds like the music teachers have trouble controlling the kids. I imagine they realize that she's quite a creative person, but she's also good at maths and that sort of thing, it turns out. So I don't know how the school view her, sort of, creativity.

In this exchange, Giselle's father stops short of direct criticism of the school, although he is clearly confident of his own views: he knows Giselle is good at art, that she is creative, and that her extracurricular music lessons are superior to those provided at school. As we explore in chapter 9, the expectations established at home are less concerned with measurable achievement than with cultural expressivity. Supporting and deepening Giselle's creative and cultural engagement, therefore, is not something her father expects of the school, but he is confident of providing it for her at home.

Contrasting Learning at Home and School

Comparing different families' conceptions of learning gives us a wider insight into what has been called the "habitus" of the home.[16] Learning, as we have analyzed it, is not so much or not only an inner, psychological process but is grounded in and constituted through a whole set of activities, experiences, and resources that vary across contexts. At school, as we saw in chapter 6, priority was given to a single definition of learning as progress through a series of explicit and measureable levels, although in a few more relaxed moments—the school play rehearsals, some of the after-school activities—we saw signs of less instrumental, more intrinsically motivated conceptions of learning. But for the most part, the school operated with a conception of learning that paid little heed to learning located outside its boundary, unless that learning could be translated into its own terms—in other words, made visible at school and accorded commendations or other markers of value that the school could recognize.

Yet families, as we have shown, are strongly oriented toward learning, investing their resources and arranging their homes and timetables to support, complement, or provide alternatives to the learning they perceive to take place at school. Thus, the home introduces children—explicitly and implicitly—to other ways of valuing and making sense of learning, to which individuals respond in different ways. How much is this a matter of individual choice, or is it the workings of social class, resulting in the social reproduction of advantage and disadvantage?

As argued in chapter 1, traditional notions of social class were tied to a stratified and stable labor market (unskilled, blue collar, office workers, management) that is now in flux, although far from obliterated. So although social mobility has hardly increased over recent decades in Western societies, many observers argue that, on the one hand, middle-class lifestyles have become more uncertain, while working-class solidarity is all but lost as the trade-union movement has been undermined, and many people even among the poor now self-identify as middle class in their values and politics.[17] Matters become even more complicated when we add in the effects of immigration and multicultural living, as we saw some of the most determined efforts to support children's education and attain social mobility among the minority ethnic families in the class.

It is in this context that researchers are rethinking social class less as a matter of labor-market positioning and more as a cultural ethos. For example, Lareau argues that middle-class families focus on enrichment and self-assertion as part of a strategy of "concerted cultivation," leaving ever further behind the working classes whose ethos of "natural growth" offers their children more freedom over their lives but at a long-term cost in achievement.[18] And as discussed in chapter 7, Lynn Schofield Clark contrasts the higher-income family's "ethic of expressive empowerment" with the lower-income family's "ethic of respectful connectedness." Clearly some cultural differences are to be expected in family life, given strong sociological evidence for the persistence of social class differences across the generations. Yet just as in chapter 7 we could not neatly map our families onto Clark's two ethics of family life, nor can we neatly map our families' approaches to learning onto the two ethics of Lareau.

The cases of Yusuf and Adam are perhaps the most striking: Yusuf's relatively poor and marginalized family was making striking efforts to ensure that Yusuf would achieve educationally, while Adam's professional parents, having lived through a painful year of his school refusal, were doing their best to stand back and not push.[19] Equally, we have contrasted Sara and Giselle, two "gifted and talented" girls (as labeled by the school) who sat together in the class but who turned out to live so differently at home. Both were middle class and both were provided with many learning opportunities, and yet Sara's learning at home singly conformed to the school's conception of learning, while Giselle additionally pursued an alternative model of learning at home.

Only in Shane's case might we agree with Lareau's concept of "natural growth," his mother having set him up with a computer but having little idea how he might use it, instead leaving him free to play the games he wished or to bicycle around the neighborhood at will. Yet over and again during the fieldwork, we found ourselves discussing Shane in terms of how the school seemed to have labeled him as a "bad boy," even though, in their different ways, both he and his mother—Shane with remarkable patience, his mother with some frustration—seemed to wait for better support from the school, an institution they respected precisely for its expertise regarding education.

Sebastian's middle-class parents demonstrated a type of "concerted cultivation" when his mother rather ruefully listed the activities he had now given up: "we went through a lot of [musical] instruments," he played rugby for a local team, he gained a brown belt in karate, the family used to go skiing, and so on. His mother worried that "he's recently dropped virtually everything that he was doing, because he wants to be with his friends," even though she had warned him he would need extracurricular achievements for his CV. While accepting that teenagers are not always very malleable, we were more struck perhaps than his mother was that Sebastian had followed her lead in excelling at drama and singing, both of them participating in a successful local drama group.

Overall, there was little doubt that most of the parents, irrespective of their social class, were well aware of the intensifying competition for qualifications and employment that awaited their children. Equally, they were familiar with the supposed value of extracurricular activities—as witnessed by the alacrity with which they joined forces with Catherine on Progress Day to encourage their child to take on more, to achieve more.[20] To check out what the young people did, in a short in-class survey, we asked them about their past, present, and future extracurricular activities. This revealed a broad mix of musical, performance, sporting, and cultural activities, as is typical of British young people. Some of the impetus for these activities could be seen to come from the school, which provided lunchtime and after-school activities on-site. More, however, came from the home, and here lies the potential for social inequality, as on average, the young people from middle-class backgrounds did three or more organized activities (by which we mean activities that require arrangement, payment, or infrastructure), while those from poorer backgrounds did nearer two.[21]

Linking Home and School

So far, this chapter has examined the notion of learning from the perspective of the home, contrasting it with the school's approach (in chapters 5 and 6). We have described the efforts that parents make, according to their own conception of learning and education, to prepare their child for school and for the wider world thereafter. Both here and in previous chapters, a sense of the disconnections between home and school persists, with each operating according to different logics. It seems that parents, teachers, and children do not always understand the efforts that each makes with respect to learning. Such misunderstandings risk undermining innovative policies to connect home and school, to engage parents with the life of the school, or to integrate diverse processes of informal and formal learning.[22]

The school's predominant focus on curricular learning, measured by a complicated system of levels and integrated with a stringent system of behavior management, was in itself simultaneously respected—as clear, fair, and effective—by parents and students and yet problematic. For parents, it was often opaque and confusing, difficult to contest, and frustratingly insensitive to what they saw as the individual needs and circumstances of their child. For the young people, it kept school life predictable, but they resisted its invitation to offer up their out-of-school lives to its all-encompassing forms of measurement, recognition, and management.

For teachers, too, the desire to retain authority over their own domain proved stronger than the desire to link up with their students' home lives. Indeed, few, if any, expressed to us much respect for what occurred at home—as they saw it. For example, we asked an IT teacher if he thought that young people's use of digital media at home could aid school learning, only to receive a scathing reply:[23]

> They do very little in terms of anything remotely academic at home that could be related to our curriculum. So the things we do in our curriculum, they do almost zero of it at home. So within that scenario of what they do at home, nothing appears to me to be remotely academic or related to the IT curriculum—certainly nothing to do with robotics or game design or designing their own games or video editing, which we do, graphic design, elements of programming, HTML script, web design of their own. Some of them occasionally venture into designing web pages, but that's about it.

The home, as we have periodically observed in this book, was not generally seen by the school as a place of valuable learning, partly because, as in this example, the school did not have access to any way of understanding learning beyond its own metrics.

In the early 21st century, many hopes are pinned on digital networked technologies, for these surely can connect what has previously been disconnected, creating constructive linkages and new flows to circumvent familiar barriers.[24] Yet in some ways, this is a naïve view of technology as a neutral conduit and of information as uncontested, so that it can somehow be shuttled between homes and school and other places in a simple and unproblematic fashion. This chapter has shown that learning itself is best thought of as a range of different practices, habits, values, and disciplines that lie at the heart of different class dispositions. On the whole, schools find it difficult to accommodate this kind of diversity, and so, as Basil Bernstein showed 25 years ago, they adopt a series of linguistic mechanisms to frame, classify, and categorize knowledge deliberately to maintain control and authority over "what counts as learning."[25] In some ways, the teacher just quoted is doing no more than rehearsing this process of marking out the boundaries of these knowledge realms. But if this is the case, how can we expect the new digital networked technologies to be able to operate in such a highly contested and jealously guarded series of domains?

Over the year, we saw how this confusion between means (network technology) and forms of knowledge (how learning is understood differently in different places) repeatedly clashed and confused teachers, families, and the young people too. Nowhere did we see this more clearly than in the various fragile or halfhearted attempts to construct deliberate, and often too-simple, one-way digital linkages between home and school. For example, our fieldwork coincided with a new initiative to use email to strengthen communication between home and school. This failed, the teacher in charge explained to us, because although the school worried that parents were "hard to reach," the teachers were "very nervous" that establishing email connection would unleash a flood of queries and demands from parents. In other instances, it was the students who resisted the intrusion of learning into their free time at home (for instance, when teachers set up subject blogs that they imagined the students would access out of school).[26]

To be sure, the school and the families were willing to cooperate on certain set-piece exchanges: weekly, via the paper planner that the students carried between school and home, transmitting notes, marks, or instructions as needed; annually, via Progress Day (the face-to-face parent-teacher consultation near the start of the year) and the end-of-year school report, itself heavily coded (see chapter 6); and on an ad hoc basis, when either teacher or parent had something directly to communicate to the other. But this did not mean either was open to further or more flexible forms of interchange. In the main, efforts to make connections were ineffective when conceptualized in ways that might extend or transform learning but were more effective when they contributed to the efficiency of authorized and school-sanctioned communication.[27]

The main link between home and school is, of course, the young people themselves. Every day, they traverse the boundary between school and home, and yet, famously, they communicate little of the interests or concerns of either to the other. There is nothing new in this, but it encapsulates the challenge for those who wish to improve relations between teachers and parents and between formal and informal learning. As Catherine reflected ruefully, "On the whole, there's too many assumptions or preconceptions about teachers but also about parents and what they will bring. I think we're both guilty of it."

Conclusions

The abstract idea of learning was conceptualized by families in the class in a variety of ways. Yet whether they sought to extend what they saw as the school's vision into the home or to enact a complementary or alternative vision of learning, there remained a notable disconnection between home and school. "Home" is a rather vague and problematic place, as seen by the school. "School" is an equally vague and problematic place, as seen by parents. Yet although efforts are made on both sides to overcome this disconnection—with teachers and parents seeking ways to connect formal and informal places of young people's learning—at the same time, it is actively reproduced, with school and home each keen to retain control over their own domain. We saw parents making a rather greater effort to second-guess how best to accommodate the expectations held of them by the school than the reverse. As a European survey of teachers' use of ICT concluded, digital resources are rarely used "to communicate with parents or to adjust the balance of students' work in new ways."[28] Or, as Lyndsay Grant concluded even more critically from her research, "the requirement on parents to deliver the school's agenda in the home comprehensively conceals any contribution that children's home practices and discourse make to their learning."[29]

The key symbol of learning in virtually every home we visited was that of the screen: computer, tablet, or mobile. We have already observed that asking parents if we could visit their home to talk about digital media and learning was successful precisely because parents were keen to discuss how they were variously appropriating new technology. Indeed, we were led to conclude that the significance of technology was not merely the entry point to thinking about learning, but in many cases, it had come to stand for learning itself, thereby encapsulating parental dilemmas about their responsibilities in relation to their child's learning. To be sure, families have long sought to provide a quiet place, perhaps a shelf of books and a convenient table for their child's homework. But the far greater demand of investing in a computer; rearranging the home to accommodate it; making decisions about printers, speakers, scanners, and other peripherals; getting their heads around first dial-up and then fixed broadband and then Wi-Fi at home—all of this has engendered a degree of reflexivity as to its purpose. Does playing computer games involve learning? Is access to a computer or internet-enabled device helpful? How many extracurricular activities is enough?[30]

Yet in families' development of strategies for supporting their children's learning, they are very unequally resourced. Differences in cultural capital, as we have shown, result in significant variation in the ways that families understand what learning is, in their attitudes to authority, the pleasures of discovery, the autonomy and independence of the learner, and the wider social values at stake. We hesitate, on the basis of one class, to draw categorical conclusions regarding the likely future outcomes for the young people on the basis of their very different socioeconomic and cultural backgrounds. But we have observed a general tendency toward the social reproduction of advantage or disadvantage, while also noting the contrary cases among other complexities. And this general tendency makes us cautious in the face of the undoubtedly exciting calls to reimagine education in ways that rely on families to support and extend learning, for these risk exacerbating socioeconomic inequalities. In chapter 9, we explore the uneven distribution of cultural capital in more detail as we look into music making outside the school. We will see not just how some families deploy traditional cultural capital but how bohemian and community-facing families draw on alternative kinds of cultural capital in supporting their children's learning.

9

Learning to Play Music

Class, Culture, and Taste

Chapters 7 and 8 have explored how families organize and structure the lives of their children, with an emphasis on the parents' as much as the young people's perspectives. In this chapter, we look in more depth at how some of the young people themselves established their own "learner identities" through the ways they developed expertise in out-of-school activities.[1] We have chosen the particular domain of music learning as our case study, because opportunities to learn and play music span formal, informal, and out-of-school settings. Music can connect experiences, engagement, and expertise across the various places of young people's lives. Examining informal music making allows us to see how ways of learning developed in school may or may not be carried across into cultural activities outside school, demonstrating both connections and disconnections in discipline and habit.[2] Learning music can be child led (or "interest driven") or adult led (part of "concerted cultivation") or both. It may be taught or self-taught, although, being usually a more "optional" subject, how the child or young person learns to be a learner is surely central.

In short, music learning offers a means of bringing together many of the threads in the previous chapters. What kinds of possibilities for learning music did our class encounter? What was the range of pedagogies on offer to them, across different situations of music teaching, learning, and provision, and how did they respond? How do families build on youth-led interests to develop particular forms of cultural capital? In what ways does learning to be a learner in out-of-school contexts reveal the development of cultural capital as young people practice habits and ways of behaving that reach beyond narrowly defined academic achievement? And because learning music—in particular, learning to play an instrument—is to a great extent voluntary and privately financed, what does it reveal about how inequalities in social class and wealth are mobilized?[3]

At Progress Day, described in chapter 2, Catherine was keen to ask the parents about whether their child was learning an instrument, whether through the instrument lessons offered by the school or privately. Such discussions were not about music in general—itself a field of considerable importance that engaged virtually all of the young people with varying degrees of intensity. Indeed, they listened to music frequently, most of them every day. However, many of their preferences found little resonance either at school or in out-of-school music lessons.[4] The more street-wise boys preferred "Grime" (London-centric rap). Several of the girls listened to "Top 40" (mainstream popular hits). Abby, Dilruba, and Salma liked Top 40 but focused on black artists, especially women such as Rhianna and Beyoncé. Sebastian and Dom liked mainstream "Indie Pop," Sergei liked "Dubstep," and Joel liked "Retro Rock."[5] But Catherine's questions were about how the students might demonstrate the playing of an instrument as an accomplishment, recognizing that out-of-school lessons were conventionally focused on classical music. If they were playing an instrument, Catherine invariably asked what grade they were at, referring to the examination system controlled by the Royal Academy of Music or similar bodies, where students progress through graded examinations that are often taken as markers of achievement.[6]

While all members of the class had group music lessons at school, just nine told us that they were currently learning to play or perform music outside the school. Several more said that they had had lessons when younger but no longer pursued music. This was, in itself, a far from equitably distributed privilege, as shown in table 9.1. Although the table's classification by relative wealth may be too simple, it shows stark differences regarding which young people had access to the possibility of music lessons and who was excluded.

The picture is clear. The opportunity to learn music is heavily influenced by social class, unsurprising insofar as all the young people currently learning music were learning it out of school, where lessons are relatively expensive; no one in the class was taking up the school's offer of lessons at a subsidized cost. There were more girls than boys taking these lessons, suggesting that playing an instrument

Table 9.1. Private Music Lessons Taken by Members of the Class

	Has never learned music	Used to learn music	Is currently learning music
Wealthier homes	Dom Gideon	Adam Jamie Toby (plus several of those who were currently learning, who had previously tried a different instrument)	Adriana Alice Giselle Max Megan Sara Sebastian
Poorer homes	Aiden Dilruba Hakim Joel Lydia Mark Nick Sergei	Abby Jenna Salma Shane Yusuf	Fesse Sedat

may still be regarded as a gendered accomplishment. It is interesting that the two boys from poorer homes currently learning music were both from minority ethnic groups, which, in one case, revealed the importance of Turkish cultural practices. Several who said they would like to learn music in the future were notably from poorer homes, including Abby, Dilruba, Joel, Nick, and Sergei, suggesting that the barrier for poorer children is less lack of interest than the resources to sustain music learning.

As we got to know the young people and started visiting them in their homes, we found out more about the place and meaning of playing music in their lives. This chapter develops the stories of some of the nine who are currently learning music. Three were following grade examinations, and we begin with Adriana and Megan, two middle-class girls reluctantly learning the piano and violin, respectively, because their parents wished it. We contrast their cases with the case of Max, a middle-class boy learning the piano in a traditional and highly structured way. Then we turn to three young people whose music learning was not framed by the national system of grades and was instead primarily self-motivated: Giselle, Sedat, and Fesse.[7]

In different ways, our discussion of these three young people elaborates and complicates the nature of cultural capital by revealing how different kinds of pedagogy—or relations between ways of teaching and the knowledge being learned—contribute to what cultural capital might mean. In chapter 8, we outlined how forms of cultural capital in the form of resources, attitudes, and understanding of learning were bound up with social class. Here we expand on that discussion by outlining three types of cultural capital that we call traditional, bohemian, and nonconvertible. Traditional cultural capital is the typical goal of efforts toward "concerted cultivation"[8] often pursued by the middle classes and is here illustrated by Adriana, Megan, and Max.[9] By contrast, Giselle, although also from a middle-class home, exemplifies "bohemian" cultural capital, where an alternative approach to learning is deliberately derived from artistic practices.

As discussed in chapter 8, the learning practices evident in the poorer homes were also far from homogeneous. In relation to music, we were particularly interested in what we might call "nonconvertible" subcultural capital, rooted in minority ethnic cultural practices. We examine how Sedat's playing of the *saz*, although it seems to include mainstream learning practices in its discipline and habits, is so rooted in cultural events not recognized by the school that the value of his learning does not "convert" to achievements that are recognized beyond his community. The chapter ends with Fesse's story of determined "self-teaching," a wholly interest-driven endeavor that, partly because it demands few resources and gains no credentials, also is not publicly visible and so makes little claim to convert into value that can be recognized outside his home.

Parental Ambitions and Reluctant Children

Adriana had completed Grade 1 piano and was now working toward Grade 2. She was uncomfortable with the idea of us watching her play the piano, so we did not accompany her to her lesson. At home, she told us that practicing the piano was a source of tension between her and her mother: "I used to have so many [arguments]. . . . I'd scream at her. I had to go to anger management and all this stuff. But I don't have . . . and now I don't have arguments with my mum at all, only for piano."

We did not get to see Megan playing her violin either, although she was about to take her Grade 2 exam the month after we interviewed her. She framed her violin playing as a matter of filial duty, with music being traded against language learning in the family calculus of achievement:

I don't really care. I just do it to keep my mum happy really, because, like, I do classics as well. So I do violin, classics. And I was going to stop doing violin a while ago, but my mum was like, "If you want to change Spanish to RS [religious studies]," then I have to keep it up. So it doesn't, like, bother me having to do violin. It's just like . . . and to be honest, I actually do quite like—when I think of violin, I don't like the sound, but then, when I go, I don't mind it. Like, I'll enjoy it. It's just because it, like, it ruins my evening because it's at the most awkward time and it's just . . .

Unsurprisingly, perhaps, the girls' parents saw matters differently. In Megan's case, they were articulate about the skills, technique, and knowledge involved in playing an instrument. Megan's parents not only knew much about the technique and learning processes involved in the teaching and learning of instrument playing but saw in some way an essence of their child's unique abilities realized through these disciplines. Her father explained,

She's natural at it, you know. She's very good at sight reading, but for her, it's something that she has to do, and it's not something that . . . She doesn't come home and say, "Great, I want to play some violin." It's "You will do some practice now," and she'll do the minimum. And you listen to her, and you think, now with the bare minimum she, you know, she can play, you know, nice enough to make you think, "Oh, that's such sad music," "Oh, that . . . ," and it's pleasant to listen to.

Clearly he was perfectly aware that Megan did not see her practice as he did; rather, he hints at a parental philosophy in which the parent holds that he or she has the better grasp on the child's long-term interests. Adriana's mother, who may have shared some of these desires, was more worn down by the power struggle that this process entailed:

We've been quite persistent about that [piano lessons]. But have to kind of drag her to do the activity, because again with the sports, she doesn't—she says she doesn't like sports, which you have to respect to some extent. But I say, "You have to do some kind of physical activity." So for—in the past few years, she did a bit of ballet and dance and other activities, but again, if she doesn't go with a friend, she doesn't want to go. So that's one of her difficulties, doing things on her own. And her plan this year is to do tennis lessons with a friend. So now that the weather is getting nicer, maybe she will start that.

Adriana's mother was herself an expert in dance, so it is unlikely that her expectations of Adriana were solely about CV-worthy achievements. But the value of music learning in and for itself easily gets lost in parent-child struggles of the kind we see here. As Adriana's mother implies, beyond the value of engaging with music lies her belief that the very process of music learning involves the development of character (involving planning, doing things on one's own, being self-motivated). As with Megan's father, the challenge is to respect the child's expressed wishes in the present, while believing as a parent that long-term benefits may accrue with persistence.[10] And, indeed, Megan herself had taken on this language of self-determination in relation to music learning: "Before you've done your first grade, it takes two years maybe, because you're just starting to know how to play the violin. But then if you want to start an exam, it will take about a year to plan for it." Listening to these girls talk about music lessons at school reveals how little—as they see it—learning music at school supports its learning at home (or vice versa):

ADRIANA: Music, I don't do anything. We just talk.

MEGAN: Music is actually [*overtalking*].

INTERVIEWER: Music—I saw everyone was in the same room with the keyboard, and no one was really doing anything. . . .

MEGAN: It's fun in the practice room, because you do whatever you want.

GIDEON: Everyone goes on their phones.

MEGAN: The teacher will come in for, like, five minutes of the lesson; the rest of the lesson we do [*overtalking*].

We observed a fair few music lessons at school in which the tasks set—especially for those who had instrumental lessons—were rather simple. As we saw in chapter 6, the discourse focused more on matters of levels and behavior than on the analysis or performance of music itself. Moreover, we witnessed very few lessons in which the students' extracurricular knowledge of music—whether their broad interest in music listening for leisure or their specific expertise gained through out-of-school lessons—was specifically recognized by the teacher or drawn into the flow of the lesson. This is not to say that the teachers did not know who was studying music, but they depicted out-of-school learning as a curiously random and uneven form of knowledge, one that the students themselves were unclear about:

> There are quite a few kids whose parents are in bands and stuff, and they've done some song writing. So they've probably got software at home that they've had a play around on with. I don't think they realize . . . when we ask them in lessons, "What experience have you had of music technology?" and then some of them go, "Actually, I do know how to do this, because I've had a bit of a go at home." There is the odd one or two who sometimes come out the woodwork and seem to be quite easy at picking up a different model or a different program.

Possibly, too, home learning is difficult to build on in lessons because those lessons are varied and constructed around national curriculum levels and tasks that do not fit with the grade system used to evaluate learning out of school.[11]

Obedient Children

Max played the keyboard and piano. He was happy to allow us to attend a lesson at home one evening in his well-decorated flat with lots of family and wedding photographs. The teacher, Adrian, arrived late and seemed uninterested in having an observer as long as it was not an official inspection. He rushed in, did the lesson, got paid, spent two minutes talking with us at the end, and rushed off. Before the lesson, Max had explained that he had begun playing the piano in Year 6. He had taken it up because he liked the idea of being able to be a virtuoso. However, he explained his motives in instrumental terms, saying that it would look good on a future CV. He was working toward Grade 4 and had an ambition to get to Grade 8. We recorded in a field note,

> He seems to practise prior to the lessons, so not every day—this is partly to do with him not liking the keyboard at his mother's house. Whilst he

isn't incredibly keen, he is dutiful and well organised in preparing for the lessons. He was a bit vague about discussing his musical taste. I think he liked a group called Octopus. He said his musical taste was not the same as his friends and was quite happy to be different. The grade system allows you to choose from a repertoire but he does not listen to classical music.

The lesson itself was intense, focused and technical. There was very little praise or negotiation about what Max was doing. Adrian has now taught him for 3 or 4 years so they are both used to this. Max went and got the money (I think £30) for Adrian. Like Dominic knowing how much the football costs (and unlike Nick) the affluent middle-class children are confident and informed about financial transactions.

They worked through the Grade book. They changed activity 3 or 4 times, working on sections of bits of music in order to get the technique correct. At one stage they did a sight-reading exercise. Whilst Adrian hummed a bit and obviously enjoys the music none of this came across from Max. Unlike Giselle [see later in this chapter], the emphasis is on complete technical accuracy rather than the experience of the whole piece or song. It is clearly anatomised, broken down into openings, middle parts and so on, all of which are treated repetitively to get correct. They worked a lot at the music itself, marking the stages, talking about notes, sorting out finger positions and at times talking about overall phrasing (preserve *legato*). Adrian wrote on the text a lot. It is about getting things right. Max rarely asked questions. Most of his talk in the session was apologizing, saying sorry or confirming "I get it," to demonstrate to Adrian that he knew what he was supposed to do and it was just a question of making his fingers do the work. There was a lot of self-correction, which Adrian supported tacitly. (Afterwards Max did admit that he thought my presence may have made him slightly more anxious about performing.) Altogether I was struck by the shared focus and understanding mediated through mastery of the symbolic language of music.

Praise was reduced to comments like "You're sounding confident here" and the occasional "good." As I commented to Max afterwards, in some ways this was a harder and more critical examination then he would experience at school. I think he agreed with me here. Adrian is very direct and instructional, "fingers, fingers, 2nd." Adrian makes all the decisions. "That's all we're going to do this week," "Let's do this piece now." He also makes the judgments about quality, about when it's good enough to move on. I didn't hear him involving Max in this process of judgment making and although he asked him several times whether it sounded right, to an extent Adrian is the authority and it wasn't clear how Max learns to know when it is right or good enough.

At the end it was "Right we are done," "More practice." Target setting and homework. If anything, I thought this was more school like than school itself—certainly more disciplined and challenging.

Two features of this episode are particularly noteworthy. First, there is the relationship between learning to play an instrument and the young person's own musical tastes. Here, there seemed to be a complete separation between high and low cultures, with Max's own music consumption having no bearing on the lesson. However, unlike Giselle (see later in this chapter), Max did not question this value system, and it did not seem to impact on his motivation to become a proficient pianist. Indeed, in contrast to the other young people discussed in this chapter, this capacity to separate himself from his tastes suggests an understanding of how cultural values work more broadly. In other words, it seems that Max has learned to operate with a notion of disinterest rather than just to be led by his own personal tastes.[12]

Second, there is the lesson's pedagogy.[13] Unlike Adriana or Megan, Max did not question the formal, transactional, and heavily top-down approach taken. This was not a school environment, and yet Max was clearly accustomed to being obedient and obliging. He was quite happy to show mastery of the symbolic notation and was comfortable exploring these concepts. However, as in lessons at school, he was not encouraged to take much responsibility for the direction of his learning. His tastes and motivation were not considered relevant to the work at hand, nor was he invited to self-assess his progress or to suggest any of the strategies or content of the lessons. Despite the personalized, one-to-one nature of the relationship with his piano teacher, the feel of the occasion was of an impersonal adult-child relationship. However, Max seemed to find it clear, focused, and purposive, possibly because the teaching was precisely tailored to his developing expertise—something that he rarely experienced at school—and possibly because it provided very clear scaffolding for his steady progression in a way that suited him. Indeed, such a disciplined experience out of school may even have contributed to his frustrations at school, as we showed in his concerns with his science teacher in chapter 5.

Structured Alternatives

We have already discussed Giselle and her family's "alternative" or "bohemian" pedagogy in chapter 8. It will be no surprise, then, to learn that this was also evident in relation to her music learning, where the system of grades had been tried and rejected. Instead, Giselle and her teacher, Rachel, had developed a pedagogy that situated Giselle's tastes at the heart of their jointly constructed curriculum. Here is our field note from her lesson:

> In the car on the way over to [a leafy suburb on the outskirts of London] where the music lesson takes place we talked about a number of things. Giselle's mother told me the story of how she found Rachel the music teacher and about her struggles to set up a business and also how she worked as a part-time art teacher working with a few kids in an after-school setting recruited through friendship groups.
>
> Giselle told me she didn't want to work for grades. She didn't like that system and couldn't see the point of it, but she was very motivated to develop musical skills. This was part of her overall scheme to become some kind of performer in the future so her interest in music was to an extent dictated by future sense of self as much for its expressive pleasures.[14] The lessons seem to cost about £30 for the session. The family isn't that well off so clearly this was a serious investment. Giselle has a big input into choosing which music she works with. She likes folk, country and a bit of Indie.

We already see a rather different orientation toward the act of learning and playing music than we saw with Max. The fact that Giselle was quite interested in and capable of engaging in discussions (both with us and with Rachel and her mother) about the theoretical challenge of constructing progression in informal learning situations says much about the reflexive nature of her family discourse. The directly personal way that Rachel welcomed and interacted with both Giselle and her mother was also very different from Adrian's transactions with Max. Then there was the contrast between Giselle's deliberately developing an artistic sensibility compared with Max's interest in what would be recognized by and impress others. While we can see this emerging from the family habitus, Giselle herself knew she needed to develop a set of practices to turn her dreams into reality. Rachel had constructed a series of progressions with Giselle to give them something to work toward. The field note continued,

> The lesson was split into four distinct activities. First Giselle plays the piano and Rachel accompanies her on the guitar. Then Giselle takes over the guitar while Rachel instructs on how to do some fingering. Giselle then sings at the piano and Rachel accompanies her on guitar. Finally Rachel sets up GarageBand on a Mac in the room and tries to teach Giselle how to lay down tracks. Giselle hasn't done this before but she gets the hang of it. She first lays down a piano track. Then she sings while listening to the piano being played and tries to lay down vocals. They listen and debrief and agree to continue this work next time they meet. I think they are using an Adele track to work on. It's a powerful song either way and Giselle doesn't seem inhibited, giving it strong vocalisation and emotion.

This process was both more tailored to Giselle as an individual and more varied in its roles and activities than we saw with Max. However, the discipline of repetition and accuracy was perhaps similar for both. The pedagogical relationship was also distinctive in giving Giselle the responsibility for her own learning:

> There are a number of features to the way that Rachel interacts with Giselle. She has a persistent questioning tone and when she issues requests she always frames it as a question rather than as a direct instruction. "Can you please . . . ," "How about . . ." those sorts of directions. Giselle is quite self-correcting and often reprises sequences in order to get them accurate of her own accord. At one point Rachel gets Giselle to write the chords for the guitar onto the piano script in order to develop Giselle's notation abilities. At another point she says she's not going to be that prescriptive; in other words, Rachel is not going to force accuracy

at the expense of getting it. This gives Giselle a real sense of engaging in a joint project rather than just having to get something correct and which she is not in control. Virtually all the playing is, to an extent, a collaborative activity, even when Giselle is being recorded, Rachel is then acting as the studio engineer, or when Giselle plays the guitar, and even when Giselle is singing, Rachel accompanies her. All through the session Giselle is very confident about her own abilities, every now and again she does say "I can't do this" but most of the time she actually says, "Yes I can do this," "I will do this."

Again, in comparison to Max's lesson, there was a greater sense of equality between teacher and pupil. This emphasized the idea of making music together rather than the teacher taking a judgmental role. Rachel worked hard to set challenges in a supportive fashion through the way she questioned rather than instructed. Although they were not working within the framework of a recognized and accredited curriculum like Max, this did not mean that there was less sense of rigor or progression.

Notably, we had not seen this kind of pedagogic relationship in school at all.[15] Indeed, Giselle said of music lessons at school, "They don't allow you to do anything interesting; they seem silly and a waste of time." Possibly her disavowing school music as "pointless" helped to valorize the kind of experience we had just witnessed, but it is also one of the ways in which cultural capital is given shape and form. On the way home, we found out that Giselle knew about the reputation of schools across North London and had a sense of the kinds of career pathways that people might follow. This discussion showed how she was beginning to adopt a deliberately bohemian artistic identity, a position that requires critiquing mainstream schooling.[16] For this, she drew on her family's cultural knowledge and her out-of-school experiences to look beyond life as a school pupil and to envision a possible creative future for herself.

Nonconvertible (Sub)cultural Capital

In contrast to Giselle and Max, Sedat found school difficult, as we saw in chapter 5, and he tended to play the class clown. Few fieldwork moments were more striking than that in which we discovered Sedat to have considerable expertise in playing the *saz*, especially since this achievement clearly earned him respect within the highly organized context of a cultural institution.

Sedat's family is Turkish and comes from a rural background. He came to the UK when he was six years old and frequently visited "home," as he referred to it—indeed, he considers himself Turkish rather than British. He appeared to have the best English in the household. The family are from the Alevi minority (a branch of Sufi from the Anatolian region) but not ethnically Kurdish, unlike many Alevi who have migrated to the UK. On our first home visit, he told us about playing the *saz*. On that occasion, he played for us in front of the family to demonstrate his prowess, and his family proudly told us about the musicians on his mother's side whose tradition he was continuing. *Saz* playing has a cultural importance for the Alevi minority, accompanying songs performed at key ceremonial events such as weddings and circumcisions, as well as signifying political resistance against Turkish hegemony. Musicians are often political leaders and possess considerable cultural authority. In other words, this kind of music has a different meaning from that of learning classical music in Western culture and certainly significance beyond that conceived by the subject "music" at school.

Sedat had started playing the *saz* when he was very young, as is traditional, and continued learning when the family came to the UK. He attended an Alevi cultural center in a disadvantaged neighborhood where he went twice a week for two-hour lessons. Our observation of his lesson revealed significant cultural capital, although, in comparison to Giselle's or Max's, it seemed likely to offer little potential for his educational trajectory, hence our characterization of it as nonconvertible. In addition to the lessons, Sedat practiced for at least an hour a day, suggesting a self-discipline that contrasted markedly with his behavior in school, where he seemed unfocused and often received bad marks for behavior. We managed to negotiate taking him to one of his lessons at the cultural center, a journey that left behind the green, middle-class location of the school for territory that hinted at a different cultural and community significance for what playing the *saz* might mean for Sedat:

This is a depressing journey. Georgian gives way to very poor run-down public housing. There is significant police presence and gangs of youths on the streets. Sedat observes this with great interest. We enter a light

industrial area. There are many people around—I see number of travel-
ler families and small children in vans around junkyards. It is a different world. The cultural centre is in a converted warehouse. There was a
gaggle of children and young people hanging around outside—some of
whom had been primed to meet me, it seemed to me, and who rushed
over to shake my hand and introduce themselves. Everybody is generous,
polite and friendly.

The differences in social context also extended to the relationship
between the teacher and his pupils:

Sedat's class, they tell me, is the most advanced. The teacher smiles and
clearly is happy to for me to be there. Nobody speaks much English; indeed the whole session is really conducted in Turkish. Everybody trans-
lates for my benefit when necessary. There are seven boys and three girls
including Sedat. There is an atmosphere of considerable discipline, order
and respect, especially for the teacher. Relationships appear warm and
generous but clearly hierarchical. We talk about this in the car on the way
home and Sedat tells me that the teacher never gets cross with him and
clearly respects him; he contrasts this with his schoolteachers.

The educational transactions that unfolded contrasted with the sophisticated student-centeredness of Giselle's experience and even the
transactional directness of Max's.

The room is small; kids are arranged in pairs in rows with small tables in
front. Many, but not all of the kids have folders with music and during
some of the songs they do look at these but I am also struck by how much
of this behaviour is about memory and repetition. The first 20 minutes
are spent sitting almost in silence. There is very little backchat and very
little talk between the kids. A girl brings each child's saz up to the teacher
and he tunes the instruments in turn. The age range must be from 12–17.

For most of the session the teacher would tell them what song they
were going to play, with some requesting of favourites. The teacher would
play the tempo they were to play the song at and give a few instructions
and then the whole group launched into these orchestral pieces. I say orchestral, because some of the sazes are bass and some tenor and therefore

there was an element of harmony. For most of the songs most of the students sang as well. In some cases I noticed a very devout mode of singing with eyes closed and an intense ecstatic focus. This is clearly a learnt performance style.

This is a very different mode of self-expression compared to some of the music lessons I have seen. The class is invested in their cultural heritage; at break time many of them spoke about being proud of their heritage, using such language explicitly. The teacher plays along with the class and gives a little feedback at the end of each song. There seems very little individual attention. The kids tell me that because this is an advanced class they don't get that kind of tuition. There is thus a sense of professional competence at work here.

This lesson was in many ways highly conventional in educational terms, as the pedagogy emphasized rote learning, repetition, and memory. The teacher's address was to the group, emphasizing collective practice and trying to reach a certain kind of shared standard rather than to develop individual ability or recognize individual performance, as in the lessons for Max and Giselle. In contrast to any of the other lessons we observed, the absolute discipline instilled by the teacher derived from an older, different tradition of authority and respect.[17]

In the break we go to the cafe and Sedat is insistent that he buys me a cup of tea. I chat with the teacher who has played in Paris and seems to have an international reputation. A number of the other boys join us. One of them talks about right- and left-wing politics, about music being oppressed in the 70s, about protest songs and about how some musicians are leaders of revolution and independence. The boy talks about being racially discriminated against in Turkey. The music and the maintenance of the cultural identity clearly play a key role within this struggle. He tells me about all the other Alevi cultural centres in London. They show me pictures of musicians on the wall, and tell me stories of atrocities and discrimination. They tell me that as well as learning the music they also discuss the text and the meaning of the songs in the classes.

The whole episode was as equally remarkable for introducing us to a Sedat—serious, disciplined—whom we did not see at school. There are a number of reasons why the Turkish community and in particular boys underachieve in the current English educational system, of which difficulties with language are key. His identity as a learner in this context was embedded in both his family narrative, with its particular musical heritage, and a wider cultural narrative and set of cultural and social activities that were able to include and respect him and his expertise. We might even suggest that, rather than seeing his *saz* learning as "extracurricular," it was rather as if the school was itself somehow outside or additional to the educational trajectory developed by this community. The inability to convert such learning back into the school environment, given the school's preference for classical music, standardized measures of progress, and different kind of pedagogic relationships, locked these experiences as a form of cultural capital away from mainstream pathways within the English educational system.

All By Himself

Just as Sedat's playing showed us a completely different side to his character that we could not have imagined from observing him at school, so, too, with Fessehaye, known as "Fesse." On our first visit to Fesse's home, he told us that his main activity at home was playing the guitar and that he was teaching himself. Being self-taught is not in itself unusual—within studies of informal music making, there is quite a long history of young people teaching themselves to become quite competent musicians[18]—but in subsequent visits, we became intrigued by the principles and practices underpinning this autodidacticism. At school, Fesse was recognized for his abilities in art, but he had a reputation for being disorganized and, again like Sedat, had a tendency to play the clown that sometimes got him into trouble. Although we had observed him concentrating well in most lessons, we could not have anticipated his self-discipline in music learning at home. We made an extended visit after school one day:

> Fesse was quite happy to see me. He assured me, supported by his sister, that coming home, sitting in the living room and playing the guitar was a common everyday experience and that he really tried to play guitar every day. We all agreed that me being there was a bit odd but that it wasn't

significantly altering a normal everyday experience. His sister told me that he often got so wrapped up in playing his music and that he would forget to come to eat—a family sacrilege.

He went and got his electric guitar although he doesn't have an amplifier for this. There was a Krar (Ethiopian guitar) behind the settee. Fesse demonstrated this a little bit and when his father did pop in I was treated to a quick tune by dad. The dad told us how his father had been a musician. This is why the father can play the Krar. In my first visit, his father's musicality had been, they said, the source of Fesse's guitar playing. It may be that his father encouraged him when he was younger.

As for Sedat, there was a family narrative about inherited musicality and how this ability is passed down through the generations. And as with Giselle's artiness, it seems that children's learner identities can be greatly influenced by prevailing family beliefs. Over the next hour or so, we observed Fesse's approach to learning, discussing this with him on and off as he practiced:

For about an hour maybe longer, I sat in the living room. The TV was silenced though running all the time and Fesse played the guitar. The first thing that struck me was his incredible discipline and concentration. Not only does he get wrapped up in the music, but also he is sufficiently self-motivated to practice on a regular basis. Indeed much of his leisure activities show this desire for mastery. He cannot read music. He has a vague memory of some private lessons when much younger, and it may be that his father will be arranging some lessons for him in the future. His whole approach is playing by ear. He is completely fascinated by the Red Hot Chili Peppers. He basically tries to play their repertoire. He practises each song. He repeats phrases and sections until he gets the song right. He will often skip repetitive sections in order to focus on the more ambitious solos. He does like some other music but his taste is distinctive and unusual. He talked about wanting to be a musician and perhaps choosing music GCSE. The unusualness of his tastes, referenced by name-dropping bands, shows a considerable independence of spirit.

He was very interested in learning how to record on the computer but has had no experience. However, digital technologies are very important in his musicianship. He downloads music, one of his older brothers showed him how to do this online and these are obviously unpaid for—unlike Max or Dominic. He puts the music on his phone. At several points in the conversation he used music from the phone to make this point. He does not use music as background mood but listens to it actively. He clearly knows all the words to the songs that he played me and these are important—we talked about this—but he refused to sing along for me. He does use YouTube tutorials and he talked about learning where to put his fingers.[19]

He has a strategy of how to deal with frustrations when he cannot get it correct and a way of pretending to play to an audience in order to be explicit to himself about what he's doing. For the most part he is left alone playing on the sofa. At one stage I did ask him to bring down the acoustic guitar. He finds this more difficult as the neck and frets are more physically demanding. He was happy on the un-amplified electric. He clearly hears the music in his head. At this stage he does have a notion of progression, of improving himself and some sense of the repertoire he would like to be able to play. He did play me a few riffs—his own composition—but was by no means overly ambitious about wanting to be a songwriter. At the moment playing other people's music accurately is what he wants to do.

As with Giselle, Fesse's interest was driven by his taste, which came across as a form of deep cultural attention. This was part of his distinctive individual confidence, a sense of taking himself seriously—imagined as a future musician—which enabled him to transform this pastime into a serious educational project. The strategies he had developed, pretending to perform to an audience, repeating, using tutorials, and so forth, may have been drawn from school-based experiences. But he demonstrated a mature ownership of these processes that was not—or perhaps could not be—exercised at school, where the teacher generally retained authority over learning in the classroom.

Conclusions

In different ways and for different reasons, Max, Giselle, Sedat, and Fesse exemplified an energy, drive, and enthusiasm as they began to exert independence in relation to their music making and music learning.

The relation between the teaching style on offer and the development of their learner identity was strong for all four, with Max and Giselle fully aware that they were building an identity and expertise that would be useful to them in the future. For Sedat, participation in his culture of origin was crucial as a source of meaning and belonging, while Fesse was more intent on pursuing an individual vision of who he wanted to be, albeit one that, as for Sedat and Giselle, also drew on family traditions and values. The efforts of all four revealed how pursuing out-of-school interests[20] can have a positive influence on young people's sense of themselves as successful and independent learners.

While the school and the young people's families professed willingness to support their ambitions, it was often difficult to steer a line between practical encouragement and realistic aspiration—and in Megan and Adriana's cases, it seemed that matters were not going well.[21] Although Giselle, Sedat, and Fesse were learning music successfully, in a manner stimulated by their musical interests, this was little recognized by the school because they were not pursuing the standard exam grades. Meanwhile, Max, who was doing well within the traditional grading system and seemed to be thriving in a personalized one-to-one learning context, was often distanced from or critical of school. Thus, for him, too, there was little constructive connection between in-school and out-of-school learning, although, as he was well aware, his music grades were valued by the school.

At the end of Year 9, the students chose further courses of study for the national public examination system. Interestingly, none of the children discussed in this chapter chose music GCSE, although Sedat had chosen music BTEC (the more practical, vocational option). Of course, following music in the academic setting of the school is only one possible avenue for further development, and it is likely that these musicians will pursue their interests into the future. Yet at this point in their lives, it was difficult to see such interests and expertise being recognized by or transferred into school learning: the experiences remained rooted in the particular social and cultural context in which their practice was developed.[22] The stories in this chapter also reveal a disconnect regarding pedagogy. As we have sought to describe, the four whose music lessons we observed encountered distinctive and diverse pedagogic practices that could have—and perhaps did—facilitate their learning in school. But such experiences remained largely unknown to the school and so could not easily be recognized or developed there. Furthermore, there were hints that positive out-of-school learning experiences led the young people to be more critical of school pedagogy, adding to the distance they felt from the school's approach to learning not only in music but more generally.

This chapter has concentrated on music as a domain in which diverse pedagogies, differential cultural capital and resources, and youth-led interests and identities all intersect.[23] It would also have been instructive to contrast the array of learning experiences gained by each individual.[24] For instance, our account of Giselle's music learning in this chapter bears considerable similarities to our account of her artistic and gaming activities in chapter 8; the "bohemian" form of cultural capital fostered in her home clearly shaped her learning activities—and her identity and ambitions—across the board. A similar point can be made about Sedat, who, on another occasion, we observed going to his boxing class. This, too, was a club populated by young Turkish men, and it was also highly structured and directed in its style of teaching. The boys were made to repeat and rehearse the boxing sequences until perfect, and as in the *saz* lesson, the feel was caring but impersonal and disciplined, with individual interpretation.[25]

In these and other cases, we could see how out-of-school pedagogies supported young learners to take responsibility for their learning, engaging them in forms of repetition and practice that were not oppressive and in which the learner understood exactly what he or she needed to do to progress. In different ways, these learning practices contrasted with the school's vision of learning as a matter of conformity to a prescribed and abstract set of expectations and regulations, as described in chapter 6. This understanding of pedagogy only became clear from our observations out of school and the ways in which we could follow learners across these different social contexts.

It just so happened that our six case studies in this chapter included two middle-class girls who were learning music as a matter of duty, "concerted cultivation" as Annette Lareau would call it, this learning being designed to get them "ahead" but with little pleasure or real achievement. Similarly, it turned out that the class included two boys from poorer, minority ethnic homes who loved music, were supported by their families' enthusiasm and skill, and were also highly intrinsically motivated, along with a boy and a girl from relatively wealthy, arty homes who nicely illustrated the traditional exam-based and alternative or bohemian approaches to music learning, respectively. Overall, then, our six cases illustrated different learning contexts as they relate to cultural and economic capital, possibly revealing generalizable trends.

What, then, can we conclude about the relation between learning and cultural capital? In Pierre Bourdieu's theory of cultural capital, he contrasted the traditional or bourgeois and the avant-garde positions, both found among the middle classes but not the "proletariat" and revealed through taste in classical music. Updating Bourdieu's account, Tony Bennett et al. argued, first, that classical music is no longer the domain through which cultural contestation occurs, although it still symbolizes elite status among those who can convincingly display their knowledge of it, and second, that cultural capital is now symbolized by "omnivorous" tastes across all types of music, along with some enthusiastic "knowingness" about particular genres or subgenres, all in contrast to what they call the more "restricted" tastes of the working class.[26]

But these distinctions fit poorly with the young people's interest in music, as we have discussed in this chapter. To be sure, wealthier families are more likely and able to invest in classical music lessons as a means of distinguishing themselves and their children from the majority, now and in the competitive future that may lie ahead. But that does not explain why this strategy was working better for Max than for Adriana or Megan; and to understand this, we can only turn to the kinds of individual factors that introduce variation into all typologies. Then, we would hesitate to call Giselle's family "avant-garde" in that it did not seem at the cutting edge of a movement.[27] What matters more than the label, however, is that this form of cultural capital resists the pressures toward concerted cultivation or competitive individualism that oppressed Max as well as Adriana and Megan. Finally, it seems imperative to make some distinction among the cultural positioning of children from poorer homes too—calling their tastes "restricted" may apply to some but surely undervalues the commitment, expertise, and knowledge of both Sedat and Fesse—hence our identification of their musical expertise here in terms of nonconvertible (sub)cultural capital.[28]

These various concepts of cultural capital help to nuance the distinctions evident in the class, both with regard to young people's music learning and, looking back to chapter 8, in how parents try to equip the home so as to support school learning. In chapter 10, we examine how the young people's experiences of school, home life, friendship, and their associated pleasures, successes, and failures enabled them to reflect on their emerging sense of themselves as learners as they began to make choices for the future and to look back over the year we spent with them.

10

Life Trajectories, Social Mobility, and Cultural Capital

We spent over a year with the class, and this allowed us to reflect on the importance of different timescales in the young people's lives.[1] Building a learner identity in terms of leveling took place over several years of constant yet mundane repetition in the classroom (chapter 6). Gaining a musical or artistic identity, as we explored in chapter 9, could take rather longer. The roles that children take on within family narratives not only develop over their entire childhood but may also have longer roots back into earlier generations (see chapters 7, 8, and 9). Learning to get on with strangers in a civic or public sense may last a lifetime (chapter 5). Playing with the performance of different identities online, by contrast, is often momentary and intense (chapter 4), yet this, too, might have longer-lasting significance for the "project of the self." In short, growing up, "being socialized," learning to learn does not occur in a uniform way or on a single timescale.

How, then, do young people themselves tell their stories? Are certain moments or perspectives important to how they construct and reflect on their personal narratives? How does their sense of self influence how they see the future? In the introduction, we observed that these 13-year-olds no longer viewed themselves as children, aware that they were already making decisions that would be significant for their life chances. For instance, in the year we spent with them, they had to choose their options for the formal examinations they would sit at the end of Year 11, two years later, having followed the same course of study together up to this point.[2] The "options" process, as the school called it, offered students a menu of subjects from which they had to choose how and where to specialize (e.g., performing arts, science, or design). Such decisions could also restrict their future trajectories (for instance, if they chose to do a single science course rather than all three of biology, chemistry, and physics or if they did or did not choose to study languages).[3]

This process represented yet another timescale as the students had to envisage their academic careers over the next few years, anticipating how this might set the foundations for further study. Outlining this in year-group assembly, the deputy headteacher challenged the young people to think hard about the decisions they faced: "Where do you think you're going to be in three years' time? That seems a really terrible question to be asking people who are coming up to be 13, 14. It's quite a hard thing to think about, where you want to be in that many years' time. But if you don't get your choice right at GCSE, that may well affect what you then have a choice to do later on." This language brought into stark relief a key narrative about young people: their future.

In chapter 1, we commented that young people are often denied an ontological status in the here-and-now, instead being referred to as the people that they will become.[4] School discourse is absolutely drenched in this talk. Competence and expertise is measured in terms of the opportunities they open up in the future rather than what they facilitate in the present, and there is a consistent pressure from teachers and families as they look forward to the next stage of qualifications: so GCSEs (taken at age 16) lead to A-levels (taken at age 18) and thence to university (for some) and then to employment (it is hoped). Even though this route is clearly not going to be followed by the whole school population, the whole edifice of attainment and achievement is built around the idea of progressing in an orderly fashion into an imagined future. Of course, the future is just that: an imaginary construct.[5] But as the school conceived it, at least in its official discourse, progress is possible for all children so long as they can shake off the limiting visions held out for them by others. In the options assembly, the year head explained, "Today is not about who you're sitting next to or who your friends are. Today is not really about what your mum and dad are saying at home or what advice they're giving or what they're saying you should do. Today is really about you, sitting there, thinking about your own choices, thinking about your own interests, thinking about what you want to do in your life. This is about you." The point being driven home is that the students are responsible for forging their own individual path, and advice from friends and parents risks swaying them from acting in their own interests.

This chapter explores how the different young people of the class imagined their futures, how they reflected on the way they had grown up, and what the process of imagining tells us about the building blocks of their aspirations. This focus enables us to discuss the class in two key ways. First, we address the mechanisms by which young people learn to become the kinds of reflexive individuals who imagine and enact their "project of the self," as discussed in chapter 1. Reflexivity implies a sense of oneself that is separate from experience and is important to the way people learn to be individuals in contemporary society.[6] Second, in the process of examining the emergence of reflexivity, we also gained some insight into how the process of reflexive identity building is more difficult for some young people, possibly because of their socioeconomic position or life circumstances.

In this book, we have seen how the young people acted so as to meet, more or less, the expectations held of them at both home and school. For many of them, this is experienced as desirable and unproblematic, although we have also noted Lydia's and Abby's gradual silencing and isolation along with Aiden's more disruptive exclusion.[7] Equally we have highlighted what scholars call "intersectionality," in which issues of ethnicity, social class, and gender all intersect with each other in ways that make it difficult to draw neat conclusions about particular groups.[8] We have also seen—especially with the case of the clique (chapter 3)— how these dimensions of difference do not always explain the friendship or other social configurations that the young people enter into. Nor do they necessarily dictate young people's expression of identity (chapter 4). This is partly because processes of individualization shape young people's actions and partly because explicit talk of social class or ethnic difference is publicly difficult and seen as potentially racist or prejudiced or as undermining the vision of civil society.

In the young people's—and our—reflections on the relation between past, present, and future, many of the themes explored in this book come together in the effort to understand growing up in late modernity. Most fundamentally, there are strong pressures on young people to internalize and adopt expectations that, in practice, result in social reproduction. Those from more wealthy homes were already by the age of 14 asserting different versions of the future than were those from poorer ones; and ideas about choice and agency that hold out the promise that young people can affect the course of their lives already apply more to some than to others.

The language used to point to these processes of change over time tends to be spatial: we talk of routes, trajectories, vectors, and pathways.[9] A major purpose of education, it is widely held, is to promote "social mobility," despite Basil Bernstein's 40-year-old warning that "education cannot compensate for society."[10] In class-stratified societies such as the UK, one key metaphor is of moving "up" the social scale, allowing future generations to trump their parents' standards of living. Another is that of "leveling the playing field," a social-justice-oriented vision of using education to give all children a fair chance. Yet, as we saw in chapter 1, both of these goals are becoming more difficult, more implausible than ever.

Uncertain Futures

The young people were constantly being required to imagine their futures; it is one of the burdens of youth. Their school progress reports speculated about future grades, classroom talk focused often on subject choices or careers, and there was a constant buzz about the lives they were going to lead once they had left school. Parents, too, were increasingly concerned about such matters. But how did the young people themselves conceptualize their futures? Some could not imagine a future at all, finding it difficult to talk to us about next year, let alone five or ten years hence:

> INTERVIEWER: Okay. What kind of future do you think . . . what do you think you want to do?
>
> GIDEON: I don't know what I want to do at the moment. I want to get on with lots [*unclear*]. Definitely.

It is difficult to capture the hesitancy and silences in these kinds of exchanges. We could see that young people are used to such questions, and so many had developed pat answers. But we also heard plenty of nonanswers and stumbling replies, and these are inevitably hard to transcribe coherently. As we saw in chapter 7, Gideon's recent efforts had been focused on overcoming difficulties at school as well as on growing his social network. So the fact that he did not know the answers to these questions led him into a self-knowing state of anxiety:

GIDEON: I want to do good.

INTERVIEWER: Yes.

GIDEON: But I'm confused about what I want to do for GCSEs. . . .

INTERVIEWER: Just one thing, have you got any sense of what you
want to do?

GIDEON: No.

INTERVIEWER: But are you very worried about this?

GIDEON: Yes.

Not knowing what you want to do at all is existentially troubling, especially if you are constantly expected to present yourself as a person with a clear vision of your future. Some young people clung to earlier family narratives, even though they were no longer convincing. In a family of keen tennis players, Jamie had been seen as promising, albeit not as successful as his elder brother, and the family had come to recognize that Jamie had reached his limits. Yet when pushed, Jamie gave us the answer he was used to giving:

INTERVIEWER: So can you see ahead past GCSE, can you see to
A-level, what you're going to be studying?

JAMIE: No. Not that far.

INTERVIEWER: Are you going to be a scientist, or . . . are you going to
work in the world of sports or . . . ?

JAMIE: I'll try and get a scholarship in tennis, because that's what my
brother [*unclear*] do. Yes, so I'll just try and do that.

At this time, neither Gideon nor Jamie was doing especially well at school, and not having a clear pathway to a socially accepted future seemed unsettling for the family:

INTERVIEWER: Do you imagine he will go to university?

JAMIE'S MOTHER: We'd like him to, but I don't know. Again, if he's in
that mind of, you know . . . he might find once he's done his GCSE
subjects, you know. He's thinking of doing Business Studies, ICT,
and Media Studies I think. Maybe within those subjects he will
find something that he will say, "Right, I like that, and I want to do
something."

INTERVIEWER: Do you think he hasn't really found his mojo, in that kind of sense?

JAMIE'S MOTHER: No, I don't think so. I mean, he says he likes English, and he likes some of the science things. Maths he's okay with, but I know that I need to, sort of, help him, push him a bit for that. So it's just finding . . . and obviously computers he enjoys because he's on it all the time kind of thing.[11] But to find something for him to do in life, and it's going to be difficult, I think.

There is a sense of waiting for a spark to ignite, of hoping that Jamie will "find something" that motivates him.[12] There is also a sense of his being closely watched so that if and when "something" is found, his parents could swing into action. However, while Jamie's mother hoped he would go to university, she seemed to regard this as Jamie's decision, not hers. In other words, in the modern democratic family, her role is delicate: she can help, even push a little, but the outcome must be Jamie's own choice. This is something of a burden for Jamie as well as for his mother, and not surprisingly, perhaps, as we saw earlier, he expressed himself as willing to fit in with the family preference for a tennis career.

Gideon's mother was also anxious about the lack of a special passion or ability. While Jamie's mother tried not to compare Jamie to his older tennis-playing brother, Gideon's mother found the comparison with his successful older sister particularly worrying.

INTERVIEWER: Yes. And do you think he'll go to university?

GIDEON'S MOTHER: I don't know. I used to think maybe he wouldn't, but I don't know. Now I think I don't know, you know, whether he will or he won't.

INTERVIEWER: Okay.

GIDEON'S MOTHER: He's . . . I think he's quite a hard one to read, and the fact that he's a late developer. When my daughter was this age, I knew that she would.

INTERVIEWER: She was . . . okay.

GIDEON'S MOTHER: And I knew, again, because she was very focused, even at a young age, on what she wanted to do. With Gideon, not so much so, but I think it's just because he's developed late, and things will sort of dawn on him perhaps, you know, later on.

As we saw in chapter 4, Gideon presented a highly social, fun-loving face to his peers, only revealing his problems at home, where, it seems, he was seen as "a late developer." Again, there is a sense of being suspended in this moment in time without a future pathway, of having to wait for "things" to "dawn on him." These middle-class parents with high-achieving first children expressed the waiting as an anxious time.

Realistic Futures

By contrast, Shane, whose single mother had the benefit of little education or income, was more realistic about his situation. On the one hand, he had the insight to realize that it was still too early to decide his future path:

> INTERVIEWER: Yes. Are you looking forward to the options stuff next year, the new subjects, or don't you care really?
>
> SHANE: Not really because, like, it's a big thing, if you know what I mean. It's a big step forward from just going and doing normal lessons.
>
> INTERVIEWER: So not really in a sense that you do care?
>
> SHANE: Obviously I care, like, obviously I want to try them out, but it's a big step forward.
>
> INTERVIEWER: And have you got any thought what you want to do beyond GCSEs?
>
> SHANE: Not really, like, I haven't really thought about that yet.
>
> INTERVIEWER: Have you got any ambitions . . . about jobs or anything like that you want to do in life?
>
> SHANE: Not, I haven't really thought, but when I was younger, I wanted to be a footballer. But it's not as easy as people think it is.

At first, Shane seemed to say he did not care what would come next, but what he meant was that he was not trying to control what could not be controlled: he knew big changes were coming, he declared himself ready to try out different options, but he would not try to anticipate the outcome. Unlike Jamie's or Gideon's anxiety, Shane did not seem to feel inadequate for not having a mapped-out pathway, even though growing out of the childhood fantasy of becoming a football player left him in limbo for the present. A few months later, at the start of Year 10, we saw a keener sense of economic realism about what might come next than in the unformed aspirations of many of his classmates: "I'm basically guaranteed a job with my uncle, but if not, I'd rather be a carpenter or like something designing stuff, making wood. My uncle's work is, like, it's his own company. Basically, you know, gas on the roads, like doing the things. But my cousin used to do; he said it's quite enjoyable because it's all family, so you get along. But if not, I'd rather be a carpenter." Here we have an ambition, to be a carpenter (a craft occupation), and a fallback plan, to work with his uncle as a more unskilled laborer. While the former was more motivating for Shane, the latter offered a comfortable alternative, and both plans fitted the expectations of his family and school.

Lydia similarly had worked out her answer to the question of what she will do in the future, thus seeing off further adult inquiry or anxiety:

LYDIA: I want to work harder at school, so I get good GCSEs.
INTERVIEWER: What will you be able to do with the GCSEs? Do you know what you want to do when you . . .
LYDIA: Child care.
INTERVIEWER: Okay, so you like small children?
LYDIA: Yes.

Although Lydia was struggling at both home and school, she had found a role in looking after her best friend Kimberly's little sisters. Shane's and Lydia's practical and realistic understanding of what the future might hold contrasted with the often-inflated language of possibility and aspiration that occupied many families as well as the school. Shane's vision of joining the male working class and Lydia's intention to take up a traditional female role contrast with the seemingly gender-neutral, individualistic, university-focused aspirations of the school and the middle-class families.

Planning a Career

Some of the young people from middle-class homes had also developed ideas about their future, but these ideas focused more on the stepping-stones required to get them to their goal than the goal itself. As they had found, faced with the question of "Who do you want to be when you grow up?" they had found it counted as a sufficient answer to say, "I want to get to university, and then I'll see what happens next," taking economic imperatives for granted. Sara, who we have described as hardworking and academically successful, explained her plans to us at the start of Year 10:

> SARA: Yes. I think if I had to . . . if I would say now, like, if I had to pick my A-levels right now, I would probably say biology, physics, chemistry, maths, and Spanish or something, because I love science and so I just . . .
> INTERVIEWER: And do you have ambitions, serious . . .
> SARA: Yes, seriously I want to be, like, a scientist or something when I grow up. I don't know what kind of scientist because it, like, fluctuates, but sometimes I'm, like . . . in a biology lesson I'm, like, "Oh, I love biology so much," and then you go to physics and you're, like, "Wait, I love this."

For a girl who has only just begun her GCSE course, she was already clear about the next stage (A-levels) and knew that this clarity would buy her time, allowing her to be vaguer about her longer-term direction, provided that she conveyed enthusiasm and determination. Her strongly expressed love of science may also be designed to rebut skeptical responses from others aware of how few girls choose science. This may also be why she had kitted out her bedroom to match this view of herself:

> SARA: I really want to do something with science, but I don't know what. Like, if you look in my room, I have a lot of science things. I've got, like . . .
> INTERVIEWER: Point out the science things in your room.
> SARA: I've got an elements calendar.
> INTERVIEWER: You have, yes.
> SARA: Yes, and I've got the visual elements.

And most important, she had her new telescope, dominating the relatively small room.[13]

In Sara's mapping out of the steps and qualifications needed for each stage in her projected future, she was fully aware of the social status she aspired to. While Jamie and Gideon suffered from comparisons with successful older siblings, Sara was herself the successful older sibling, and over the course of the year, we heard several disparaging comments made about her little sister. As she told us in this interview, "[I want] a job that I want to do, because like, I don't want to end up like working in McDonalds. God forbid. . . . [My sister] is like, 'Yes, I want to do that,' because she wants French fries." By such confident talk about loving science and being different from her Facebook-obsessed sister, Sara worked to repudiate any stereotypical expectations of being girly and frivolous.

Moreover, in Sara's already planning the steps of her career, she showed herself very different from Jamie or Gideon in her determination and from Shane and Lydia in her ambition. Unlike them, Sara understood that working on her learner identity was crucial to her hoped-for future. For Sara, this was a wholehearted commitment and one that rewarded her parents' considerable investment in her. A comparison with Sebastian's plans for his future raises a doubt over whether we can call Sara's approach the result of "concerted cultivation," however. At school, Sebastian was diffident, even though he performed well. In his out-of-school drama and singing group, he showed passion aplenty, along with a confident swagger and the admiration of an enthusiastic bunch of friends. He knew, too, of the value of this activity for his future plan:

INTERVIEWER: But you're telling me that you don't actually do it, because you think you're going to be an actor, or you're very good at it . . . that's not what this is about.

SEBASTIAN: Because it's fun, doing . . . I think if I put on a CV, "Oh, I've . . . I did drama, and I've done shows at . . ." Like, I could say I've sang at the Royal Festival Hall. It would look quite good on a CV, you can show that you can do something.

INTERVIEWER: But you're not doing it because it's something just for the CV. You're doing it [*overtalking*].

SEBASTIAN: I'm doing it for the fun. It's a lot of fun.

INTERVIEWER: Yes, yes. Okay.

SEBASTIAN: It's very enjoyable.

Sebastian kept the two rationales separate: drama was fun, *and* it would look good on a CV. While the pleasure he took in drama was motivating in the here-and-now, he also knew that present pleasures can be calculated with an eye on the future.

Fulfilling Lives

For some of the young people, their present interests and pleasures offered a way of imagining their future that combined recognition of what motivates them as a person (the spark that Jamie's and Gideon's mothers were hoping for) with knowledge of the stepping-stones needed to realize their vision (as we saw with Sara and Sebastian just now). This was more typical of those from artistic—or what in chapter 9 we called "bohemian" backgrounds—and, therefore, of more middle-class youngsters.

Megan, for whom social life and personal interests were a priority now, had mapped out the next few steps—A-levels (Sixth Form), university—but had not thought beyond that: "I think, like, all my group have decided that we're going to VFS.[14] Obviously maybe one or two of us won't, but I think, like, the majority of us will carry on going to VFS. I'm going to do . . . well, I'm either going to do history or English, I haven't decided yet, and then drama. And I think I'm going to go to Liverpool, so then I'm right near my family and stuff, and, like, my cousins went there and stuff." Here Megan explained the considerable uncertainties before her by establishing some continuities: keeping the same friends and staying at the same school as she enters the next phase, selecting a university town where relatives live, anticipating subject specialisms that she already enjoys. As for where this might lead her, Megan was torn, already aware that her dream of becoming an actor could prove unrealistic, but unlike Shane's hope of becoming a football player, she was also not willing to put these dreams aside. Instead, she offered a rationale for why acting could be a plausible career for her, plus a more prosaic alternative in case it fails.

> MEGAN: That's why I would do, like, history or English with it [acting]. So then I have something to, like, fall back on.
> INTERVIEWER: Yes, but you're going to give it a try, then? You're going to try and be an actor?

MEGAN: Yes, like, I love acting.

INTERVIEWER: Are your parents going to support you in that?

MEGAN: Yes, like, my mum's, like, happy that I'm doing drama. But, like, since I've been little, I've always been, like—you know, you do the school plays, and, like, primary school, I was always, like, the lead character because I think it's just because I'm not afraid to, like, talk, and I think I can act.

By contrast, while Fesse harbored similarly artistic ambitions, he was less articulate in their defense:[15]

INTERVIEWER: What kind of future do you imagine for yourself?

FESSE: Either a designer or a musician.

INTERVIEWER: Okay. So what kind of life do you think that means?

FESSE: Like, just doing my, like, doing what I enjoy.

For these young people, then, lifestyle preferences in the present provide a guide to plausible futures built on desire more than concrete expectations about career or even employment.[16]

However, social class makes a difference, not only in formulating ambitions but also in convincing others of their feasibility. Max, who we have seen under some pressure in earlier chapters, had not reached the point of knowing what he wanted to do either, being more focused on escaping school to a world of his own choosing than on elaborating on any particular future. Thus, he told us, "[I will] probably go and take like a year off or something, get some money and then go to university, if that's . . . I think I might go, if I still want to go in, like, five years." But while the future remains uncertain, as indeed it must for a 14-year-old, he has learned a convincing answer to the question "What will you do?"—one that is likely to satisfy middle-class questioners.

Transitions

When we revisited members of the class at home at the end of our project, we invited them to reexamine the ego networks they had drawn for us six or so months earlier. Few were as explicit as Megan that life was not going to change: "I think my life's going to be like this until the end of secondary school. Like, I've never been in a completely different friendship group. Since Year 7, I've had, like, basically the same friends of—like, the boys I hang out with have been the same since Year 7, and Mandy and Mila have been my friends since Year 7. So I don't really think it's going to change that much." In general, the young people made few changes: the important people then were still important, and there were few additions or omissions. But there were exceptions. Giselle had stopped playing Minecraft and had gained a boyfriend. Lydia had fallen out with Kimberly, her main source of support. Sedat's family had been rehoused to a much poorer estate, and they had had to leave their vegetables and chickens behind. Nevertheless, our overall impression was of stability and continuity despite the constant talk of growing up as being all about change.

While few of the young people saw Year 9, the year we were with them, as possessing any great existential significance, the institutionally determined transition from primary to secondary school loomed especially large in their personal narratives. Other pivotal moments revealed the gender work important to teenagers. Sebastian, for example, recalled a ski trip organized by the school in Year 8. As a slightly self-conscious and sensitive young man, Sebastian never quite felt part of the class or indeed the school, perhaps because he lived on the edge of its catchment area. However, he had been skiing for many years with his family and was an accomplished skier. The school trip gave him the chance to assert his physical prowess, allowing him to put his relations with the other boys on a different footing: "I just shared a room with them. The original room I was in, because I sat on the top bunk, and I think something sort of snapped, so I don't want to sleep there. So I moved into the other room that was, like, full of Dom and Albie and Anton [two other boys in the year group]."

For Nick and Adam, being inducted into different kinds of gaming circles proved the key to a new social life. Getting an Xbox marked a more grown-up status for Adam, allowing him to communicate with friends and to evade the anxious scrutiny of his parents (see chapter 7). Nick talked about his early entry into console game playing watching his father (from whom he was now separated):

When I used to live with my dad, in his flat, I always used to watch him play, like, you know, Dragonball Z. Yes, and then my cousin came over, and I remember, I used to get . . . I didn't like losing. Like, I still remember one time when he kept on firing fireballs, so I kept getting knocked down. And I was getting really angry, and that just encouraged me to get more gaming experience and, like, try to beat him one day.

Nick's narrative was that his personal qualities of persistence in and commitment to game playing derived from this early experience, and thus, like Adam, entry into game play stood as a marker of adult masculinity.

The most repeated trope about teenage rites of passage was gaining a profile on Facebook (see chapter 4). Joining Facebook for this cohort was the central means of managing the difficult transition at 11 years old from a small, local primary school to a much larger secondary school, full of older teenagers. With Dilruba and Salma, we discussed how this transition marked a shift to a more social self, increasingly turned outward toward the world.

> INTERVIEWER: When did you join Facebook?
> DILRUBA: I think when I was in . . . wait, what day was it? I think when I was in Year 7.
> INTERVIEWER: So was part of like coming to secondary school part of doing Facebook kind of growing up like . . . ?
> DILRUBA: Yes, because everyone else had it.
> INTERVIEWER: Okay, what about you?
> SALMA: Yes, I joined Facebook in the start of Year 7.
> INTERVIEWER: Do you think you joined because everyone else was on it, and you kind of felt like you'd be left out?
> DILRUBA: Yes . . . no, not . . .
> SALMA: You started it later. She done it like . . .
> DILRUBA: I started it later than you. Wait, I was like . . . I started when I was like end of Year 7.

This talk of girls "starting" their teenage social life seems rather gendered, hinging on the moment when they joined the social scene.[17]

The boys also told stories of getting on Facebook, but they more often narrated their personal trajectory to a more grown-up self through an account of a fight or confrontation of some kind. Sedat, Shane, Gideon, and Yusuf all told us stories about getting into trouble and having fights. In each case, these were serious incidents, resulting in temporary exclusion from the school, reinforcing the idea of a masculine rite of passage.

We saw in chapter 4 how Gideon described overcoming his anger and disruptive behavior (although for the school, his anger was not yet firmly in the past). Gideon's mother also saw his struggles in gendered terms: "You know, he's a young boy trying to find himself, his way in the world, and perhaps, you know, going around with people who were not really his sort of people and perhaps behaving in a way that he thinks people expect that he should behave. And I don't know, maybe as he's getting older, he's becoming more comfortable in who he is, you know." Shane, too, had learned to tell the story of his difficulties, putting them firmly in the past, although, again, the school found it harder to put his reputation in the past:

> I used to get like angry, like, really quickly, and, like, some teachers were just, like, start shouting in my face, and they didn't understand that makes me more angry. Then they just go, like, "Take five minutes outside and, like, just calm down." But, like, also with Ms. S. was one of my favorite teachers. Do you know Ms. S.? . . . Like, she's the only one—like, them four teachers were the only ones that understood that if, like, you shout in my face, like, they knew I'd retaliate. So they would just tell me to calm down outside.

Shane's speech, with its hesitant "likes,"[18] hints at his determined struggle to express himself clearly. He is reflexive here about methods of self-regulation in the social situation of the school (although on other occasions, both he and his mother tended to blame individual teachers rather than attributing any fault to himself).

Both Gideon and Shane had reflected on and sought to put right their troubled reputations, recognizing that this was part of the task of realizing a different future. Both boys narrated a sense of growing up and working through a specific kind of institutional difficulty as young men marking out a transition for themselves as well as one that has been articulated by the school and their families. But this task was not a purely private struggle. Although it was rare to hear the young people talk about each other's reputations, they gave sufficient hints for us to see how watching and comparing themselves with others was significant in their own self-development. For example, Nick commented on how Dom had been a very different kind of person at the football club in previous years and how he had changed his persona to someone far more active, leading the team. Sara expressed surprise that Adriana behaved as if she was more stupid than she was, again possibly positioning herself in contrast to displays of frivolous femininity and not knowing, as we did, that Adriana was reveling in what she saw as her last year of being irresponsible before knuckling down to the task of fulfilling her parents' (and her) expectations. The clique (Max, Alice, Jenna), among others, talked about Lydia's reputation as a girl with problems in the past as well as someone who was still difficult to get on with.

Conclusions

In this chapter, we have concentrated on how individuals draw on different discourses to narrate stories about themselves. These stories articulate the individual's sense of themselves and their actual or possible trajectories, variously framed by the norms of gender, family, school, and the wider society. With greater or lesser degrees of reflexivity, optimism, and anxiety, the class was beginning to look backward in order to grasp their present and to meet the practical task of developing a socially acceptable response to the ever-present question "What are you going to be?" For, as we argued in chapter 1, having a credible story to tell both about and for oneself is vital to the larger task of identity construction (itself a never-ending task, although particularly intense in adolescence).

While there is widespread recognition that the social, economic, and cultural trends through the 20th century have wrought significant changes in the conditions under which children grow up—longer education, less secure employment, increased social stratification, the consequences of globalization and commercialization—there is less agreement on what this means. Whether such changes are really generating a new life stage ("emerging adulthood") or new life tasks ("the choice biography," "the project of the self") and whether these in turn are evidence of a grand historical shift (individualization) or a new historical epoch, late modernity (or the risk society or network society), remains hotly contested. In this chapter, we have tried to listen to how the young people talked about themselves with these concepts and claims in mind, but we return to these bigger questions in the conclusion to this book.

Although we have contrasted Gideon and Jamie, Shane and Lydia, Sebastian and Sara, Megan and Fesse, we could have selected others in the class. With the exception of Lydia, the young people were willing to speculate about themselves with us. They were all to some degree self-reflexive, taking the opportunity of our interviews to conduct their own identity work and to check out our responses. Is it possible to explain the ways we have grouped them according to their gender or social class? Jamie and Sara, for example, come from equally affluent and well-educated families, yet they could not have been more different in their confidence about the future. Fesse's strong desire to do things he likes—an expression of personal self-fulfillment—might not have been expected from knowledge of his social background. Shane's self-assessment was, perhaps, more predictable from his home circumstances, but it would not do him justice to call this simple social reproduction; and we have tried to capture the thoughtful determination with which he and, in different ways, Abby (see chapter 7) have sought a path through their difficulties. Megan's self-aware effort to negotiate a plausible artistic future (as we also saw with Giselle in chapter 9)[19] drew on her family background, where her willingness to embrace uncertainty derived from her speculative interest in prioritizing creative fulfillment over economic comfort.[20]

We saw in chapter 5 how the school's vision of civility seeks to efface social, ethnic, and gender difference, in the interests of fairness.[21] But it is hardly surprising that, for example, young people seek to construct gendered identities for themselves and thus frequently came up against the supposedly gender-neutral values of the school, which they met with exaggerated forms of gendered resistance such as fighting and rudeness (mainly by the boys) or flouting school uniform rules (mainly by the girls). Why did they focus on these particular aspects of masculinity or femininity in this context, and how will these forms of identity serve them as they grow into adults? We could read the gendered images and expectations of society as offering the much-needed (if not ideal) resources for constructing identities. Similar arguments could be made about social class or ethnicity, although society is keener to disavow classed imaginaries as resources for the self, and it is ambivalent about the significance of ethnicity and cultural difference. In a society that tries to efface difference and celebrate the individual, it is hard for young people to recognize who they are or imagine who they could be: the project of the self seems potentially content- and context-free.

However, we should not overstate the case for generational or historical changes in late modernity, not least because we cannot know what the future really does hold for our 28 young people. Interestingly, there are a small number of scholars who have formed long-term relationships with young people in their research, following them over years, even decades. What can these studies tell us about the trajectories of their participants as they have grown into adults?[22] How do participants' senses of their own futures stand against long-term analyses of social change?

Most of these studies end up telling a story about large-scale social change and are almost epic in scale. Lois Weis's study, for example, of young women coming of age around the end of the 20th century tells a story about the declining employment prospects in postindustrial economies for the male working class and its mixed effects on women's family roles and their economic independence. In Jay MacLeod's decade-long study of "aspirations and attainment in a low-income neighbourhood" in the US, social class disadvantage is thoroughly perpetuated, but this occurs differently among his "white trash" group and his group of poor black boys. To summarize briefly, the former group was deeply pessimistic and so barely tried to "succeed," resorting to anger and racism, while the latter did try to gain academic results but failed, internalizing this as their fault; yet they stayed hopeful even years later.[23] Given the rhetoric of the American dream, Mac-Leod captures his findings as showing "social immobility in the land of opportunity." For this, he is highly critical of the school for devaluing the boys as deficient and for failing in turn to recognize their cultural capital, especially compared with its positive valuation of the middle-class white kids. Annette Lareau reaches similar conclusions in her ten-year follow-up, although her explanation lies more with the differential role of the family than the school: "Although all parents wanted their children to succeed, the working-class and poor families experienced more heartbreak. The middle-class parents' interventions, although often insignificant as individual acts, yielded cumulative advantages."[24]

But unlike Willis's boys, who learned to labor, or MacLeod's boys, who never expected to "make it," our class was hopeful. This may also explain why we saw relatively little or only minor forms of resistance. Have things changed in recent years, or is our class naïve, yet to "wise up" (they were, it should be said, a little younger than those in these more pessimistic studies)? Arguably this chapter has identified some of those seemingly insignificant, if microlevel, processes that will, over time, increasingly distinguish the life chances of young people from wealthier and poorer homes: the parental ambitions and resources, the school's perception of a child's potential, learning to map the concrete steps required to attain a long-term goal, learning to present one's aspirations in ways that will convince others, becoming reflexive about the tasks ahead, and aligning one's personal narrative with an imagined future.

From this point of view, an attention to learning is important because it emphasizes those moments of agency and control when individuals can exert their own power (or not) over the influences that envelope them. Rachel Thomson and her colleagues pay attention to what they call "critical moments,"[25] drawing on perspectives from narrative theory to focus on these significant yet time-bounded, even momentary, experiences, as we have done in this chapter (and as the young people themselves were keen to do). Yet they argue that, still, structural determinants prevail since "critical moments" are interpreted in ways that are heavily structured by lifeworld contexts. This would suggest that the reflexivity that we have highlighted in this chapter does not so much offer the young people an intrinsically advantageous vantage point on their own experience in the ways that forms of self-knowing have been privileged in the past but, rather, is simply the discourse that contemporary society expects them to be able to use.

Also complicating conclusions about social reproduction is the fact that, in a multicultural, late modern society, social class differences are themselves no longer clear-cut (as discussed in chapter 1).[26] In chapters 8 and 9 especially, we have divided the middle-class families into those who rely on more traditional economic and cultural resources and those who adopt a more alternative or bohemian approach. The poorer children—whom we cannot even label as "working class" in the taken-for-granted sense of this term—may lack traditional forms of economic and cultural capital, but, we have found, some benefit from nonconvertible but still-significant forms of (sub)cultural capital or from determined parental input; and the individual consequences cannot be easily predicted. With all these intersecting influences at home as well as in the wider society, no wonder that the young people—and we as researchers—give some credence to more individual visions of the self and of the future, being reluctant to conclude that social inequalities will inevitably reproduce themselves in familiar ways.

We worked with the class only over the period of one year. We were not able to see how the young people's lives unfolded after our time with them, so our conjectures about their trajectories must remain immanent. We have seen how the young people were subject to a range of expectations and aspirations that at times verged on the pressured and oppressive. We have seen how they were preoccupied with the "work" of positioning themselves within desired, prescribed, or problematic trajectories so that they could make sense of present experiences in relation to narratives of the past and prospects for the future. Whether or not life circumstances have been different at different times or in different cultures, for those who are growing up in the 21st-century Western city, it could hardly be otherwise: the modern self must tell stories about who we are and why and how we imagine the future. But the stories that young people tell betray their origins.

Most often, we saw young people learning an identity that fitted the future that others had planned for them. Whether they will be fully prepared for this inheritance, and whether the possibilities that are laid out for them are real or imagined, is something we will have to return to in 20 years' time.

Conclusion

Conservative, Competitive, or Connected

In this book, we have portrayed the lifeworld of a class of 13-year-olds throughout a year of their learning, family, social, and online lives.[1] Now we bring together the threads of our arguments. In chapter 1, we asked, What is distinctive about the texture of young people's lives today? What is it like growing up in a hyperconnected yet anxiously competitive world? How are young people navigating the at times conflicting demands from school, family, peers, and community, and how have these institutions and relationships themselves changed under contemporary pressures?

Our ambition was to reconcile young people's everyday experiences with the many hopes and fears about youth in the digital age. We open this conclusion with an account of one of the extracurricular opportunities offered by the school to the whole year group. For us, the World Challenge epitomized the tensions that we have found to connect and disconnect the social worlds of young people at home, school, and elsewhere. Particularly, it reveals how the promise of harnessing connection is largely sacrificed to a mix of conservative and competitive pressures that maintain the status quo.

The World Challenge

The World Challenge, offered at the beginning of Year 9, promised a two-week trip to Malaysia to introduce students to the rainforest and to the conditions experienced by people living in developing countries. It was a commercial enterprise, packaging together the necessary travel arrangements and local services for schools and families. There is nothing new about school trips, but such exotic trips are not always on offer to everyone regardless of circumstance. Outsourcing educational activities to a global company is also new, as is the World Challenge's efforts to link individual and collaborative activities across school, home, and community, locally and globally, through digital networks.

The invitation to 250 members of the year group arrived early in the school year, promising that "students who participate on a World Challenge will embark on an amazing journey of self-discovery. The life skills they learn will not only aid personal growth, but help secure university places and impress future employers."[2] A tough competition followed close behind, there being only 16 places available. Students were invited to write a proposal about how they would each raise £2,000 toward the cost of the trip, no mean feat for a 13- or 14-year-old and far more than poorer families could contemplate for a holiday. We saw around a third of the class preparing their entry forms, working hard to find the words to represent themselves as young people with the right kind of interests, ambitions, and all-round life skills. The teacher in charge, Julie, then checked applicants' school records for attendance, discussed their character with colleagues, and aimed to select "self-starters" or those with "a passion" for the effort—criteria that emphasized individualized competitiveness. She found this hard, describing the selection process as "horrific." We, too, watched as some members of the class succeeded while others had to deal with the disappointment of rejection.

Gideon's case was interesting, as Julie had had to argue him in as a reward for leaving behind his troubled past (chapter 7), as his school record was insufficient.[3] Indeed, despite the school's professed values of fairness and equality, the World Challenge turned out to be a rather privileged experience: the four who were selected from our class—Max, Giselle, Gideon, and Sara—were all from middle-class families. This was not intended, but the process contained its own logic. Julie had had to persuade the skeptical headteacher that the project was feasible, making her highly risk averse in selecting students and managing the project— hence her scrutiny of the school records for each student. But these, as we have seen in earlier chapters, are influenced by different social backgrounds. And the plan to raise such a lot of money was itself risky: we asked Julie what would happen if the students could not manage it, only to learn that it was assumed that the affluent families would make up any shortfall.

This one instance encapsulates what we have seen over and again in this book. The discourse of opportunity is presented as fair and inclusive, and teachers, parents, and young people all subscribe to it. The process of taking up such opportunity is one of individual competition, seemingly a matter of personal interest and expertise. But the contextual factors that shape both the school's offer and the students' uptake result in social reproduction: the already-advantaged gain more than the relatively disadvantaged.

So far we could have been describing a process from any time in recent decades: school led, local, privileged. But the rhetoric surrounding the World Challenge was that of the digital age. The young people had to connect to each other to coordinate shared activities and monitor progress. And the school could connect to the wider international project, with schools in many countries engaged in parallel efforts. Yet what we witnessed remained a highly local effort. The young people met face-to-face after school to review their progress and to discuss the next tasks. They organized fund-raising events at school (a parent quiz night, a cake sale, an Easter egg hunt) and in their neighborhood (babysitting, washing cars, packing bags in an upscale supermarket).

As we have seen throughout this book, although "the digital" was always present, it made less difference in practice than the rhetoric promised. Digital connectivity can link home and school, youth and adults, local and global spheres. But as we have documented, both teachers and young people have a lot invested in keeping their spheres of interest and identity separate, under their autonomous control, and away from the scrutiny of the other. This was illustrated by the catalogue of minor failures that resulted from Julie's attempts to organize the fund-raising activities via digital platforms. These were seemingly practical: when Julie tried to demonstrate the World Challenge website to the young people, on one occasion the school's internet went down, and on another she had forgotten her password; and when she posted meeting minutes on the school's intranet, it turned out that the students did not know how to access it. Such minor yet persistent struggles over the World Challenge reminded us of a host of other digital struggles we witnessed during the year—for instance, the teachers' difficulties in establishing subject blogs to engage their students at home (chapter 8).

But this was not a school that could not manage technology; the school's information management system worked with considerable efficiency (chapter 6). So why, then, did it seem to fail to recalibrate other or new kinds of home-school relationship? In part, both teachers and students exercised personal autonomy and control. For example, we asked Julie and the students if it would be helpful to set up a Facebook group to coordinate World Challenge activities. Julie thought this a good idea but worried that it would give the students access to her profile, her personal life. Unbeknownst to her, however, the young people had already set up a Facebook group—they did not want to give a teacher access to their profiles either. As we have learned in this book, young people are heavily invested in not connecting the spheres of their lives.

Disconnection was also favored over connection to preserve the school's authority. For Julie, email provided an efficient means of arranging meetings, issuing instructions, and setting deadlines; she posted information on the school website and sent text messages to the students and newsletters to their parents. Her preference—along with that of the school more generally—was for unidirectional, one-to-many communication. Receiving many responses from students or parents or being drawn into multiway negotiations not only would be time-consuming but would risk the school's authority.[4]

The World Challenge's invitation to participate in a global effort was particularly unsuccessful. The global vision on offer proved obscure and unclear to the young people. To sustain interest and get things done, they preferred to meet each other face-to-face. None of them took up the invitation to "meet other Challengers" or to participate in the World Challenge website (via Facebook, LinkedIn, YouTube, Twitter, etc.) or to engage with "people living in developing countries."[5] Only at the very end did the project become publicly visible as a record of the school's achievement, with photos of a successful trip uploaded to Facebook and celebrated in the school newsletter.

Although digital networks now reach across long distances, it was the visibility and intensity of local links that counted for these young people, as we saw in chapters 3 and 4—attesting to the persistence, perhaps "re-mediation," of face-to-face communication, valued for intimacy and discretion.[6]

To be clear, it is not that the digital made little difference to the young people's lives. We saw effective use of technologies at school to track individual attainment and deliver one-to-many content in the classroom.

We argued in chapter 6 that this facilitated an unprecedented normalization of quantification, standardization, and surveillance of the self-as-learner. We also saw the effective use of technologies at home, especially those that enabled the radical personalization of media consumption among family members who, nonetheless, put considerable effort into the communal as well as the individualized dimension of "living separately together." In the peer group, we saw how digital communication enabled more subtlety in communication choices and identity work. Our point is that we saw remarkably little use of technologies to connect people or activities *across* these places, especially in ways that opened up new opportunities to learn or participate.

The promise of a more connected society remains; but it seems just that, a promise. And it is not necessarily a promise that young people themselves wish to see realized. Indeed, digital technologies were as much valued for how they could disconnect (keeping teachers and students in separate spheres, for instance) as for their potential to connect given that home-school communication was still more likely to be face-to-face or by telephone or letter. Distant links in the young people's ego and online networks were relatively rare, and when they did exist, they generally stemmed from extended family or the places where the young people had lived previously (see chapter 4).

The main exception was young people's considerable use of technologies—via gaming and social networking sites—to sustain sociality when they were separated from each other for reasons of cost or safety (notably, parental anxiety about their children's freedom of movement in the neighborhood). This in itself tells us something: where adult boundaries are imposed unwillingly on young people, they welcome the potential of digital networks to reconnect them. But where adults themselves initiate connections, young people seem more likely to evade than subscribe to them whether they are digital or not.

Finally, the World Challenge illustrated a threat to the school's vision of itself as a civil and fair society. Not only did it privilege a small group of already-privileged young people, but it also represented the developing world as an exotic "other," an object of study rather than part of "our" world. Possibly to mitigate this threat, the selected group worked hard to foster trusting relations with each other. Gideon told us, "You're kind of making friends with people, like, I probably wouldn't have made friends with before because you're all kind of connected and working together." However, not only was the group more socially homogeneous than the class in general, but the global "other" was absent—displaced from the group camaraderie. Similarly absent from explicit discussion were the students who had not been selected or who had not applied because they were not interested or had judged that they would not be included.

Yet, as with the civility constructed within the school, this sense of "working together" proved useful for the duration of the World Challenge, even if it did not extend much further. This too seemed to us symptomatic of the civil space constructed within the class: it was important for day-to-day sociality and, justified with reference to the longer term, for socializing the young people into getting along with very different others. But as the whole-class network discussed in chapter 3 showed, such civility did not extend very far. This is not to say that incivility broke out regularly but rather that social class put the young people on rather different tracks, and these were more often sustained than challenged by the school and among peers.

The World Challenge typified tensions between opportunity and exclusion, connection and disconnection, democratic and competitive values. How it played out was also symptomatic of late modern life: in the eyes of the school and the selected families, this was a successful activity, but we also saw it as fostering an individualized and competitive sense of achievement, mediated through the disciplinary processes of the school and privately financed by middle-class parents. Possibly some parents, teachers, or the young people themselves might agree with this analysis. But in practice, it was tacitly accepted as a reasonable compromise that talk of unfairness, thwarted ambition, or overidealistic aspiration should be set aside so that the young people involved could complete the tasks well and have a good time.

Living with Social Change in Late Modernity

We saw in chapter 10 that young people commonly evade incessant adult questioning about the future ("What do you want to be when you grow up?"), anticipating only more demands in the present. While schools, heavily focused on the business of sorting and stratifying, prioritize a philosophy of "becoming," parents try to combine wanting the best for their children's well-being in the present with a concern to prepare them for an uncertain future. Yet in the face of adult efforts toward competitive and instrumental imperatives,[7] the class seemed generally sensible, thoughtful, and not overly anxious (unlike some of their parents). They lived in smaller and more private worlds than the rhetoric of the network society might imagine, prioritizing face-to-face communication and valuing time with their families. They were broadly respectful toward the school, hopeful of their learning, and accepting of their likely paths ahead.

How, then, can we relate these young people's experiences to the efforts of sociologists, psychologists, educationalists, technologists, and others, outlined in chapter 1, to analyze the social changes, perhaps even historic transformation, through which we are living? We have tried to sustain a double focus, integrating a close-up exploration of everyday experiences while also setting our account of these young people in the wider context of sociohistorical shifts. We noted in chapter 1 that neither the claims for accelerated change in late modernity nor for characterizing our times in terms of individualization (including the individualization of risk and the destabilization of traditional stratifications based on social class) are sufficiently proven through empirical study.[8] Insufficient evidence certainly characterizes the grander claims about young people's present and future circulating in public and policy discourses, whether optimistic or pessimistic.

Late modern theorists say remarkably little about young people's experiences, childhood activities, or the institutions that address children themselves.[9] This blind spot extends also to questions of family, learning, and socialization. Theorists' enticing yet rather abstract discussion of how children's relations with parents are altered in today's "democratic" (rather than the "Victorian") family asserts, improbably in the light of our findings in chapters 7 and 8, that family life is now freer than ever before from the dictates of gender, generation, or social position, with the "pure relationship" satisfying for its authenticity and freedom from social constraint.[10] Hence, we have worked to make visible young people's own voices and experiences. After all, the project of the self is one in which young and old are all equally absorbed. The effects of the risk society are likely to burden today's youth more than older generations, well into the future. And children and young people also experience—and have views about—the democratic family, the hopes invested by society in its children, and the individualized burden of risk. Much rests on how they adjust to society's pressures and on their capacity to respond positively.

In interpreting the subtle ways in which people live with and respond to social change, we must remember that change occurs over a longer timescale than can be observed in a single year of research. Any putative cause of change—even the recent adoption of digital technologies—has long roots, and there is often little good evidence available for reliable longitudinal comparisons (after all, what was family or school life really like "before"?). Then, any change is multiply caused, with changes in schooling or family demographics or labor-market opportunities not always linear in nature, and all occurring on different timescales. Last, change is often less than transformative because pressures toward change generate their own counterpressures as individuals and institutions try to hold onto established practices and preferences. These conservative counterpressures are most apparent in the effort that the school and families put into maintaining separate spheres of influence or resisting moves to connect learning across sites, for instance. They are also apparent in relation to social reproduction, with the parent generation trying all the harder in the face of change to secure for its children the values and resources that it holds most dear.

Competitive or Conservative?

We hazarded in the introduction that faced with a measure of social change, people might adopt competitive or conservative practices in response—either to try to succeed within or to slow down the effects of individualization and the risk society.

From the foregoing chapters, it has become clear that young people do not generally share the phenomenological experience of the breathless "rat race" of individualist competition claimed by the theorists of late modernity.[11] When asked, the class members generally struggled to imagine their various futures and tended to draw on what they already knew from home to anticipate lives much like those of their parents' (chapter 10). But they were only 13 or 14 years old, and as we saw in chapter 1, surveys show that young teenagers are generally fairly optimistic about the present, although around 15 or 16, the transition to adulthood begins to loom larger. Significantly, surveys also show that, for the first time in some decades, today's teenagers doubt that they can improve on the life situation achieved by their parents, hinting at a new fatalism.[12] This too we saw some evidence of.

By contrast, chapters 7 and 8 reveal rather more anxiety and uncertainty among the parents, often triggered by questions about the use of digital media at home and its implications for family values and possible futures. Interestingly, many of the families were themselves undergoing transformations with regard to social class, ethnicity, migration, and family composition, on a timescale varying from months to generations. This in itself complicated the norms and expectations within family life, resulting in a fair degree of flexibility toward children but also anxiety about whether the parents have made good decisions.[13] Perhaps for this reason and perhaps because of wider anxieties about the future, parents' views of the school were significantly risk averse, appreciating rather than criticizing its efforts to protect its pedagogic and disciplinary autonomy by reinforcing its boundaries rather than meeting change by experimenting with alternative pedagogies or reaching out to embrace and integrate with home or community life.

The school, meanwhile, prioritized a regime of individual measurement and competitiveness while maintaining a rigorously civil internal culture (as argued in chapters 5 and 6). This regime of individual competition, welcomed by risk-averse parents yet surely disappointing to progressive educators, was sustained by erecting barriers to the possibility of collaborating or connecting across different places and forms of knowledge. This civil culture could be read as conservative in claiming fairness (within the school walls) while masking hidden processes of social reproduction (extending from home into the school). But we also read it as a progressive contemporary response to the challenges of multicultural or cosmopolitan city life.[14]

Young people's own experiences are, in various subtle ways, marked by adults' embrace of either competitive or conservative responses to the pressures of late modernity. Indeed, their actions are contributory, since relations at home and school are coconstructed through everyday practices and mutual understandings. For instance, despite the public hyperbole about the opportunities of youth and education, the young people had broadly accepted the conservative "deal" on offer from the school ("if you accede to our discipline and measurement, we will get you sufficient grades to succeed in what comes next").

Taking this idea a step further, we saw young people's ready internalization of standards and metrics, into their everyday talk, interactions, and sense of self. Education has long been measured, but the shift we see today is an internalization of these values on a different scale. In chapter 6, we captured this as a shift from measuring the curriculum in terms of levels to one of measuring the students as being "leveled" (as in the discourses rife within the school: "I'm a level 5b" or "Have you been leveled yet?").[15] We conjecture that by internalizing such metrics, young people (and their parents and teachers) gained a sense of control over the expectations and pressures that surrounded them, even though doing so simultaneously excluded attention to young people's intrinsic motivations to learn or the possibility of exploring alternative conceptions of knowledge and ways of knowing.[16]

However, the young people had set a significant condition to their acceptance of the school's regime: that it should not extend beyond its boundary into "their" places—interstitial, domestic, or online spaces of living and learning. Conveniently, this condition suited the school for related reasons, as we saw earlier in relation to World Challenge and in chapters 4 and 5.[17] Thus, we observed the care with which the young people sought to contain (rather than resist or reject) the ever-encroaching adult demands to accede to rigorous regimes of measurement, narrow conceptions of the knowledge worth learning, and civil relations with their highly diverse classmates in public (in the classroom, on Facebook).

The young people tried to protect their personal autonomy by seeking out unsupervised places or times in their day (the walk home from school, their bedroom, certain online sites). Their friendships were conducted face-to-face when possible, as this—still—optimizes flexibility, authenticity, and reciprocity. Insofar as friendships were also conducted online, doing so already represented a response to adult control over their physical freedom of movement; so most emphatically did not wish to engage with adults in their online spaces.

While friendships tended to be more socially homogeneous than the school population at large, we also saw several friendships built around popular media interests (sports, gaming, fandoms), and some of these, also as a matter of choice, bridged divides of gender, social class, and ethnicity.[18] We saw the pursuit of forms of learning, too, that evaded the scrutiny of or valorization by the school, with several young people refusing the chance to "shine" or obtain "commendations" for out-of-school activities in school precisely to keep their spheres of interest and activity distinct. We cannot say with confidence that among this group of 13-year-olds, such signs of independence hold out great promise for future pathways that are neither competitive nor conservative. Nor can we say that they do not.

Reconfiguring Home, School, and Peer Culture

The relation between social change and social reproduction has been a theme throughout this book. While the middle-class families were fairly easy to identify, the class contained few, if any, young people from working-class or blue-collar homes (as traditionally defined), although many of them struggled economically. As we saw in chapters 8 and 9, when we look more closely at these families, they cannot simply be identified in terms of traditional conceptions of social class; for this is late modernity, and economic and cultural resources are no longer so tightly linked and the one no longer neatly predicts the other.

Nor did social class neatly predict responses to the demands of late modernity. For instance, some of the middle-class families were content to endorse the authority of the school, while others sought more "bohemian" alternatives, although they tended to sidestep rather than directly contest the quantified standardization of learning at school. Some migrant families were also pursuing different paths to that of the school, concerned to value and sustain their home cultures. These alternative or subcultural pathways were rather quietly trodden, with rich subcultural knowledge gained outside the school sometimes making little impact on the bounded life of the school or, at this stage, despite the potential benefits to the learner, without converting into capital that could be recognized more widely. Moreover, since all concerned acceded to the standardized, supposedly fair, and generally civil discourse of the school, refusing the language of social class or even of inequality, it seemed difficult to articulate any critique of the unequal outcomes that sociologists continue to document.[19]

In contrast to earlier ethnographies of school life, we could not identify either "hidden curricula" or the processes of "learning to labor" that implicitly validate middle-class children while working-class children are allocated to the factory floor or seek tactics of resistance.[20] This is not because the school was as fair as it claimed but, rather, because the discourse of individual competition and success was made explicit rather than tacit. Differences in opportunity or achievement were not seen as either controversial or unfair—quite the contrary. Thus, it seems that a sense of collective classed identity is giving way to an uncertain and ambivalent recognition of status differentials, understood as a matter of individual talent or luck, good or bad. The long-term outcome— that social advantage or disadvantage persists—is little changed from 20 years ago,[21] but the means by which it comes about and the implications for identity and social relations are reconfigured.

Relatedly, we have traced ways in which family lives are being reconfigured: as the transition from child to adult is extended,[22] as the value of the resources that families can provide their children are increasingly uncertain, and as the home becomes saturated with media of many kinds, to the point that highly flexible, increasingly personal digital media use encapsulates what it means to feel "at home."[23] The continued importance of family, along with young people's respect for their parents and comfort in the security of home, is perhaps only surprising to those who believe the popular hyperbole about an alienated and superficial digital generation.

But the meanings of family and home are, nonetheless, subtly different from what they used to be. Managing the balance between time together and time apart is high on most families' agendas, with tensions about commonality and privacy accentuated by the habitual use of shared and personalized media. As we put it in chapter 7, rather than family members "living alone together," isolated under the same roof, we found them more often "living together separately." By this, we mean that, in the modern "democratic family,"[24] the interests and desires of each family member are respected as a matter of individual rights but that even when everyone is in a separate space or using a different technology, they still feel connected to each other. Furthermore, most of the families put a lot of effort into finding ways to come together. The media, especially television, although sometimes computer games, often underpin shared times "as a family," and each family had stories to tell about how this was managed.

One reason the young people's desire to spend time alone at home was accepted by their parents was on account of their reduced freedom of movement outside the home. Most members of the class stayed within a narrow radius of home when they were outside and often stayed at home once they had returned from school. It is no wonder that they liked to delay the return home, dawdling and chatting or dropping into the local shops. For 13- to 14-year-olds today, going online once they are at home to hang out with friends on Facebook or Xbox or the like seems to have taken the place of long phone calls or hanging out on street corners, activities typical of their parents' own youth. As a result, the home—and especially the bedroom—has intense individual meanings for the young people that are ever less determined by parents, becoming increasingly a place in which friendship, gossip, and flirtation can occur, albeit online more than offline.

At the same time, and in various ways, the values, logics, and practices of school have progressed further into the home, with parents widening their responsibilities for their children's present and future success by ensuring that particular places, times of the day, and technologies are used not only for homework but also for varieties of informal learning, enrichment, and school-related activities. As young people's developing interests are increasingly conceived as a matter of choice for them to pursue according to personal preference rather than mandated by economic or cultural position, the task of sustaining their interests often falls to them personally even as the importance of these interests grows in the minds of parents and teachers. The young people in the class, even by their early teens, could already recite a list of activities (musical, artistic, sporting, etc.) that they had tried and dropped. Since each activity had represented an investment on the part of family or school, this apparent failure was regarded with growing frustration and, in some cases, anxiety by their teachers and parents.

Yet we also saw only unevenly sustained support from those same parents and teachers to encourage young people's intrinsic interests, to find ways to recognize small achievements in meaningful ways, or to overcome the many obstacles that might seem minor or temporary to adults but often proved significant for the young people (a missed class, a friend leaving the group, a teacher they did not like, loss of time for relaxation). Such interests are not simply the hobbies of old but, rather, are increasingly framed as the source of personal drive and self-direction required to compete in the tough race for success that lies ahead. Some of the middle-class parents, realizing this, took it upon themselves to support interest development: this was more successful when done as part of family activities, for intrinsic motives, and less successful when it was reduced to a similar system of reward or punishment that the school also operated. Engagement in creative digital media activities—creating minivideos to upload to YouTube or experimenting with a digital camera or music—seemed particularly short-lived, even if it was enjoyed in the moment. This points to the need for social and institutional support for informal learning activities, which was often most readily available among families whose lives were already embedded in a rich cultural world, ranging from Giselle's art to Sedat's music. It was seemingly least recognized by the more individualized families—wealthy or poor—who lacked such a local culture and who tacitly accepted the notion that success is a matter of individual striving and character. In sum, the choice biography is problematic, inasmuch as it imposes a responsibility for managing it well (thereby generating anxiety for the young, their teachers, and their parents).

Throughout this book, we have asked how young people construct and enact their identity (or aspects of identity) in a high-pressure, digital age. We mapped a range of social spaces within which identities and relationships are imagined in different ways. In the super-diverse society of 21st-century London, civility online and offline proved unexpectedly important—unexpected because most academic discussion of civility concerns adults and, when applied to young people, is seen as oppressively disciplinary. Yet our class was keen to endorse civility as an ethical outlook—tolerance, fairness, inclusivity—albeit seeing these as values primarily relevant to public places. In private, young people tried to keep their desires and friendships more under the radar of adults, some experimenting with aspects of their identity, selecting friends like them, and trying to deal with daily difficulties and upsets. Their online lives largely mirrored rather than opposed both public and private senses of self, underpinning, extending slightly, and intensifying the experience of their more public and also their more private networks.[25] At the same time, we saw ways in which face-to-face communication—for long the only form of communication available—is prized for intimate talk. In other words, since online interactions may or may not be private—and, arguably, uncertainty over privacy online will surely increase—face-to-face interaction becomes increasingly valued.

Connections and Disconnections

Throughout this book, we have drawn attention to connections and disconnections: the social relationships among members of the class (chapter 3) and how these are underpinned by digital networks (chapter 4); how these relationships contrast with the relatively closed world of the school (chapter 5); and the usually small worlds of individual families (chapter 7). We have identified some of the structures and norms that make each place particular and that facilitate or close off connections with other places, people, or activities (chapters 6, 8, and 9). While the metaphor of the network—local and global, social and digital—has proved helpful in this book in revealing the connections and disconnections among young people and their spaces and activities, our analysis has also pinpointed some limitations of this metaphor, especially its tendency to emphasize ever-extending links and connections.[26] Indeed, we have found the idea of places or spheres of activity more persuasive as way of capturing the texture of everyday life than that of the immaterial network.

In the class, connections between people and places were most sought out among peers (locally or online) and most avoided between home and school. With regard to activities and interests, we saw ways in which art, music, and sports could link home, peers, and community in various ways, but this was not always acknowledged or valued. Parents' efforts to bridge the home-school divide by organizing learning at home were unrecognized by or even problematic for the school,[27] while teachers' efforts to bridge that same divide using digital technologies were fragile and short-lived. We have drawn attention to the disciplined practices of the school to support civility, showing also how young people and their families supported this emphasis on inclusivity, transparency, and fairness, and we saw such civility replicated by the young people themselves on Facebook.[28] But few civil bonds extended beyond the school gates, with traditional social (with a few idiosyncratic) groupings shaping the construction of smaller social worlds at home and in the neighborhood.

Yet there were small signs that digital technologies altered the young people's possible connections with the wider social world, even if other forms of connection at school or in the family did not. Dom's forays into Twitter or Megan's burgeoning use of Tumblr may have ended up maintaining their immediate social world rather than forging new kinds of links with others, but for these young people, the scope of the network had changed. Similarly, Giselle's embryonic role as a moderator on the family's Minecraft server had introduced her to the management of risk with random outsiders and learning to interact with people she did not know, giving advice and direction and thus inducting her into a new way of relating. Shane told us that on open game play during Call of Duty, he disliked what he called "racist Americans," whose commentaries he actively opposed, reinforcing his pride in belonging to a racially diverse family (with black cousins) and actively encouraging him to take antiracist stances. Here access to wider networks changed—for a time at least—the social horizon.

But overall, we saw more effort invested in controlling access to the networks the young people were in rather than extending their reach. We have interpreted this as a reasonable desire to limit their networks more in line with other "conservative" responses to pressures for change, introducing this label with a small c in the sense of conserving the status quo rather than resisting change.[29] Indeed, we have recognized the identity commitments that the young people—and also their parents and teachers—invest in particular places, relationships, and activities. They defend these commitments because they matter to them.[30]

Policy makers or others who seek to cross established boundaries and multiply connections will need careful negotiation to consider the likely costs as well as the benefits of doing so. There are additional difficulties in harnessing digital networks as part of this effort to connect. These technologies offer unprecedented possibilities to connect people, places, and ideas, and so teachers, parents, and young people alike are now highly attuned to questions of privacy and trust. Indeed, the principles and practices involved in regulating or restricting the scope of digital networks has become a public preoccupation, protecting particular spheres of influence and interest even at the cost of experimentation, collaboration, and cooperation.

The class members were still very young, and few wider opportunities have yet come their way; so this insularity is hardly surprising or, arguably, problematic. But in trying to puzzle not only how connected the class was but also what difference any such connections might make, we struggled to relate our emerging understanding to the burgeoning body of theory and practice that insists on the benefit of bringing wider opportunities into the lives of teenagers. In this work, the value of the network is almost always perceived as a good thing, mainly because of the belief that more connections will benefit youth and also society at large (see chapter 3). Making connections, it is held, harnesses young people's often-untapped creativity, advances social justice by combating disadvantage and exclusion, and contributes constructively to changing conditions of knowledge and expression, cultural and economic production, and transnational understanding. In some ways, the motivational, creative, and collaborative potential of digital technologies has come to stand for this deeper and wider thesis of the "benevolent network" and thus enhances learning outcomes even if the pedagogic and political visions driving such efforts are not always clear or agreed.[31] In these visions, changing education has come to stand for a way of changing society at large, irrespective of the kind of analysis that has permeated this book.

Harnessing Connection

Given a public rhetoric that suggests unlimited potential for connectivity, we have described some of its practical and desired limits. Yet the public and policy enthusiasm over varieties of (digital and global) connection is framed as an alternative to both competitive and conservative responses to late modernity. Specifically, against competitive individualism, calls for more connections—as in connected learning, connected communities, a better-connected world—assert the values of inclusion, collaboration, empathy, and civic engagement. Against conservatism, calls for connection invite creative thinking about ways of living that could leave behind established forms of exclusion or exploitation and meet future challenges with fresh thinking. Here dreams of a digital future connect with older traditions of progressive interventions for social change. During our year with the class, thinking about these possibilities often led us from observing what the young people were actually doing to imagining opportunities that they might be missing. And so in this final section, we think through some of ways that connections might be "harnessed" for social change for ordinary young people like those in the class, by applying the logic of late modernity we have used in the preceding chapters to assess what kinds of change (if any) might be possible (or desirable).

For many schools and parents (and, doubtless, governments and employers), the question is not only whether harnessing connection could bring improvements but whether pursuing it is worth the risk of getting it wrong. What was striking about the parents' and young people's endorsement of the school's approach to measuring learning via standardized levels (as minutely tracked on the school information management system) was not that anyone thought it an especially stimulating approach to learning—for they did not—but that they were not willing to risk its predictable delivery of adequate results by contemplating alternative approaches. As pressures on education and uncertainties over employment grow, the more conservative (rather than flexible or experimental) we predict parents will become. For schools, too, the benefits of alternative approaches would need to be firmly established to wrest them away from a tried-and-tested approach to schooling, one that manages external pressures, fends off rather than embraces the messiness of home, and locks down rather than opens up uses of technology by students.

The risky opportunities of "the digital" seem especially to breed conformity as much or more than experimentation. The convergence on a single proprietary platform, Facebook, is one such instance. Fears about new contacts and reluctance to explore new pathways to participation are another. But most important is the lack of motive, of purpose, or of a reason to do things differently. Young people could use the internet to get to know almost anyone, but they stick to their own kind. They could explore esoteric forms of knowledge, but they stick to the top-ten

Google hits, and their favorite sites include Amazon and eBay.[32] They could create and remix their own content and become "produsers,"[33] but they actually consume stuff made by others. As we have argued, this is partly a concern about the individualized burden of risk and lack of a safety net and partly a lack of knowledge about the alternatives.

And as for the alternatives, the exceptional cases are much celebrated. Henry Jenkins writes about Flourish, a girl who published her first online novel at age 14, thereafter mentoring many other hopeful writers twice her age. Mizuko Ito and colleagues highlight the case of 17-year-old Clarissa, an aspiring screenwriter whose friends introduced her to a role-playing site online where equally enthusiastic peers pooled their creative and critical resources to the point that Clarissa could use her newfound expertise to get into college. Mark Warschauer and Tina Matuchniak describe how 14-year-old Max produced humorous videos and posted them on YouTube, gaining so much fan mail that his video aired on mainstream television.[34] But the point is that these are, precisely, exceptions. Should we wish that these opportunities existed for everyone? What effort should society put into making this a reality? Members of the class had encountered little of this, with a few exceptions: Megan, Giselle, and Sergei had uploaded home-produced videos to YouTube, and Joel and Alice experimented with their digital cameras, for instance. But even these activities were rarely sustained or developed, and most of the young people did not seem to feel the lack of such opportunities.

But before simply seeing a lack of change as missed (or rejected) opportunities, we need to be wary that we do not fall into the trap of blaming individuals for their own failings. Many scholars have critiqued alternative or nontraditional approaches to learning as implicitly middle class.[35] Connecting learning across school and home might seem beneficial for everyone, but given the different resources that families can call on, in practice it opens the door to socioeconomic inequalities.[36] Further, shifting the burden of responsibility for children's learning from school to (also) home compounds already-heightened parental anxieties over children's increasingly uncertain educational and employment prospects.

Also troubling is the claim that promoting and designing flexible opportunities to harness the power of networked technologies to support self-motivated paths to living and learning is an enterprise that aligns closely to the needs of an insecure, exploitative, and precarious labor market where risks are borne individually, not collectively.[37] Indeed, against the call for connection, critical voices fear that connectionist talk seems to overplay individual agency and commercially driven populist visions of the ideal society. Connectionism underplays the importance of the state's vested interests in retaining the power to frame and judge people's everyday activities while appearing to devolve governance processes to ordinary people, as well as disguising commercial efforts to coopt public discourses in companies' extension of proprietary and profitable networks.[38] Certainly there are plenty of initiatives that use the discourse of connection to market edutainment products to parents and digital creation or coding resources to schools, just as there are many that seek to profit from the more conservative desires to manage "the digital age" safely by minimizing risk.[39]

Such concerns might lead us to consider framing connection in negative rather than positive terms. Yet watching young people and the adults around them take everyday actions designed to disconnect rather than (or as well as) to connect instead provoked us to rethink disconnection in positive rather than negative terms.[40] These everyday actions, along with the simple fact of a persistent and practical lack of connectivity across places and activities, led us to look more deeply at the deliberate and inadvertent impediments to greater connections, digital or otherwise. People's everyday actions, we learned, often affirm the positive value of separation— as facilitating spheres of autonomy or trusted spaces rather than as failing to take up the promise of connection.

But even this is insufficient reason to reject the promise of better-connected alternatives. At their best, they offer a humanist vision for living and learning that could challenge the injustices of contemporary society. And from this perspective, digital affordances[41] may yet facilitate communication that is creative, civic, collaborative, and experimental, potentially linking spaces, respecting voices, building self-efficacy, supporting interests, acknowledging expertise, and scaffolding learning. Will these positive visions combat the risk-averse responses of both individuals and institutions? If the potential of connection is to outweigh the appeal of disconnection in the future, we must directly address the risk-averse fears and self-protective practices that stand in the way of rethinking society in the digital age. But for our class—and the many other classes of ordinary young people—initiatives that address structural and widespread reorganization remain rarely available or sustained, and with respect to outcomes, they are, at present, ambiguous at best.

But is it digital connections that are really needed, or are these a (currently fashionable) means to achieve a more familiar but hugely important end, namely, to support connections among people and places more generally? It perplexed us that neither the school nor the families could imagine what goes on outside their immediate gaze, leaving young people to move from home to school and back each day without the adults responsible for their opportunities really seeing how their lives do or could better fit together. We have uncovered a series of reasons why the situation is as it is, but we remain unsatisfied. So we still wonder whether there are ways—digital or otherwise—that teachers could (or should) know more about their students' lives, for the benefit of all young people. Must such knowledge inevitably become incorporated into top-down, standardized conceptions of traditional learning, neatly measured according to the logics of digital systems?[42] Could not small changes make a big improvement over time? What if Sedat's musicianship and discipline could be credited; if Fesse's independent concentration could be acknowledged and developed; if Giselle's wide-ranging knowledge and accomplishments could be built on; if Mark's sense of social isolation could be more directly addressed; if Yusuf's extraordinarily committed out-of-school life could be brought together by all the adults concerned for him; if Alice and Jenna and Max's friendship around literary appreciation could be developed; if ways could be found to value and trust in Shane's mature, reflective, and honest appraisal of his own capabilities? If the school had recognized the young people's out-of-school lives without seeking to manage or measure them or limit their value, parents, too, might have found ways to focus their own role without either simply approving or sidestepping or misunderstanding the life the school constructed for their children. And then perhaps young people might have more reason to welcome than to resist such efforts.

But what can schools or teachers do about the determining influences of social class? How can greater agency be granted to young people? How could changing ways of conceptualizing learning alter such seemingly overdetermining social structures? These questions have haunted almost every study of childhood and youth, and in varying degrees of explicitness, they underpin most countries' education and family policies. While investigating young people's lives in the round might seem only to deepen our knowledge of these challenges, we also believe that it reveals some chinks in the processes of social reproduction, at least for some young people in some circumstances. By paying attention to the ways that young people develop and enact their identities within particularly enabling or constraining contexts, our project has revealed not so much cruel fate as society's lack of imagination and resources about creating alternatives. We recognize the considerable and entrenched inequalities that stratified the lives of the class. But these were not wholly determining of young people's realities and prospects.

Thus, we remain optimistic about a progressive project that seeks creative ways to engage people—as individuals and institutions—in imagining alternatives that can expand their vision of future opportunities and of the possible pathways by which such opportunities might be reached. But our year with the class has also taught us that such a project can only work if it engages with people's identity commitments to how things have been until now and with their often-justified fears about a risky or threating future.

Appendix

The Young People

The 28 young people in the class were all 13 to 14 years old during the academic year we spent with them, 2011–2012. While there is much that we came to know about each individual, we have omitted some details to protect their anonymity. Providing even a short sketch of each child was not straightforward. Noting who was a boy or a girl was simple, and so was birth order, although the reconstructed families made for complications, as several of the children had older step- or half siblings living elsewhere.

Our choice of pseudonyms tried to capture something of the social class and ethnicity of each individual. However, in providing further information, we acknowledge that ethnicity and religion are too complicated to represent in a simple label, and we are fully aware of the dangers of either under- or overestimating the significance of these or other descriptors. The school provided information on religion, but we do not always know what such affirmations of faith meant to the families. Many of the young people spoke several languages, so here we have simply recorded whether their first language was English. For those brought up to speak a different language, which encompassed quite a range of European, African, and Asian languages, all spoke excellent English except Deyan, who had arrived in the UK only recently; he, too, was fluent by the end of the year.

Social class is no simpler. Researchers and governments traditionally assign social class on the basis of the occupation of the "head of household," but nearly half of the poorer families and a fair number of the wealthier families were headed by a single mother. It is fairly straightforward to note whose parents were homeowners and those who were in receipt of free school meals, standard indicators of wealthier and poorer households, respectively.[1] More impressionistically, we estimated economic and cultural capital on the basis of our knowledge of parental occupation, home location (postcode), and our observations of parental cultural knowledge and resources, especially noting the level of education reached by mothers.[2] While judging economic capital was a reasonably evidenced estimate, in judging cultural capital, we made a deliberate decision to recognize what has been called "subcultural capital" as well as the dominant cultural capital of the white indigenous middle classes. For example, as we discuss in chapters 8 and 9, we recognize Yusuf's family's investment in a Muslim education for their children and Sedat's family tradition of music making in the Turkish community. We also sought to recognize the fact that some of the migrant families had well-educated parents who, following their arrival in the UK, had not been able to obtain employment commensurate with their qualifications.

Finally, Sergei's parents declined permission for individual research, and Toby did not wish to be visited at home; so they are included only to describe the class as a whole but with no further details.

Members of the Class

Abby: girl, mixed African, first language English, youngest child
Parents: couple, Christian, low economic capital, medium cultural capital

Adam: boy, white European, first language English, youngest child
Parents: couple, other religion, homeowners, high economic and cultural capital

Adriana: girl, white European, first language not English, middle child
Parents: couple, no religion, homeowners, high economic and cultural capital

Aiden: boy, black Caribbean, first language English, middle child
Parents: single mother, Christian, free school meals, low economic and cultural capital

Alice: girl, white English, first language English, younger child
Parents: couple, Christian, homeowners, high economic and cultural capital

Deyan: boy, other European, first language not English, older child
Parents: couple, Muslim, low economic and cultural capital

Dilruba: girl, mixed other, first language not English, middle child
Parents: single mother, Hindu, low economic and cultural capital

Dominic (Dom): boy, white English, first language English, middle child
Parents: couple, no religion, homeowners, high economic and cultural
   capital

Fessehaye (Fesse): boy, black African, first language not English, middle
   child
Parents: couple, Christian, free school meals, low economic and medium
   cultural capital

Gideon: boy, white English, first language English, younger child
Parents: couple, Christian, homeowners, high economic and cultural capital

Giselle: girl, white English, first language English, older child
Parents: separated, no religion, homeowners, medium economic and high
   cultural capital

Hakim: boy, other European, first language not English, older child
Parents: single mother, Muslim, free school meals, low economic and cultural
   capital

Jamie: boy, mixed Asian, first language English, middle child
Parents: couple, no religion, homeowners, high economic and cultural capital

Jenna: girl, black African, first language not English, middle child
Parents: single mother, Muslim, free school meals, low economic and medium
   cultural capital

Joel: boy, white English, first language English, older child
Parents: reconstructed couple (mother died), no religion, free school meals,
   low economic and medium cultural capital

Lydia: girl, mixed Caribbean, first language English, younger child
Parents: single mother, Christian, homeowner, low economic and medium
   cultural capital

Mark: boy, black African, first language not English, older child
Parents: couple, Christian, free school meals, low economic and medium
cultural capital

Max: boy, white English, first language English, younger child
Parents: separated, Christian, homeowner, high economic and cultural
capital

Megan: girl, white English, first language English, younger child
Parents: couple, Christian, homeowner, high economic and cultural capital

Nick: boy, mixed African, first language not English, only child
Parents: single mother, other religion, medium economic and cultural capital

Salma: girl, Asian, first language not English, younger child
Parents: couple, Muslim, free school meals, low economic and cultural
capital

Sara: girl, mixed Asian, first language English, older child
Parents: couple, Hindu, homeowner, high economic and cultural capital

Sebastian: boy, White English, first language English, only child
Parents: couple, no religion, homeowner, high economic and cultural capital

Sedat: boy, other European, first language not English, youngest child
Parents: couple, Muslim, low economic and medium cultural capital

Sergei: boy, other European, first language not English

Shane: boy, white English, first language English, older child
Parents: single mother, no religion, free school meals, low economic and
cultural capital

Toby: boy, white English, first language English

Yusuf: boy, black African, first language not English, oldest child
Parents: couple, Muslim, low economic and medium cultural capital

Social Class in the Class

As figure A.1 illustrates, through a simple scatterplot, the households were broadly divided by socioeconomic status according to a dividing line running from the top left to bottom right of the graph. But there was no perfect alignment of economic and cultural capital, and there was also considerable variation within each grouping. For this reason, in this book, we prefer to talk of wealthier and poorer homes, as this is both clear and yet carries less baggage. However, when it seems justified, we do refer to wealthy or educated homes as "middle class."

Further complicating matters is the strong association between social class and ethnicity. The young people in the upper right of the figure are mainly white, although this includes several with parents from the European Union (EU) whom we have identified as white European in the list; and Sara and Jamie each had an Asian (Indian and Chinese respectively) and a white parent. In the lower left of the figure, most

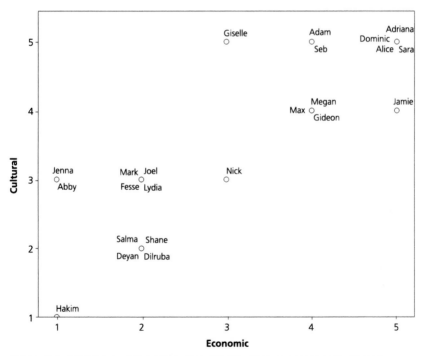

Figure A.1. Members of the class classified by their parents' cultural and economic capital.

of the young people were black, mixed black or other European (from eastern Europe or Turkey). Indeed, only Joel and Shane fitted the classic image of the white working classes supposedly indigenous to the UK.[3] While it is likely that more children would have fitted this label had our school been located outside the urban conurbation, it is typical of the ethnic and social class mix to be found in city schools, as well as many others, in the UK.

The English State School System

At Victoria Forest School (VFS), students followed a curriculum consisting of English, Math, Science, Geography, History, Art, Music, Design and Technology, IT, Religious Studies, Personal, Social, and Health Education (PSHE), and Physical Education (PE). Around 40% of curriculum time was devoted to the first three "core" subjects. Attainment in each subject was measured on a series of levels from 1 to 10 (see chapter 6), with students being expected to progress around one level per year of their schooling. In England, students automatically progress each year, with the term "year" describing both the period of 12 months and the cohort that each child is a member of. In Year 9, the class was set one or two hours of homework per night.

During Year 9, students select eight to ten subjects to study over the next two years for their national qualifications (GCSEs; General Certificate of Secondary Education). Such decisions depend on interest, achievement, and future ambitions and are made by the school and parents/student together. This decision in turn affects the choice of three to four subjects studied in the following (and last) two years of secondary school. And these then determine the level and content of any postsecondary vocational or tertiary education.

Around 93% of children and young people are educated in the public (i.e., state-funded) school system of England, although that figure is lower for London. Children attend primary school from the age of five (covering what the English call "years" and the Americans "grades," Years 1–6). They leave these often small, local schools in the year they turn 11, entering a much larger secondary school (usually between 1,000 and 2,000 students, covering Years 7–13). The school leaving age was recently raised from 16 to 18, and most secondary schools offer an integrated place for learning for young people aged 11 to 18, although there are exceptions. We worked with 13- to 14-year-olds in Year 9—in other words, the third year of their secondary education.

School catchments are largely determined by geographic proximity, although other criteria also apply (notably, exceptions for young people who have siblings already attending the school or who have designated special educational needs). A small proportion of schools select by ability, and this is an important battleground in contemporary educational policy as more and more schools are choosing what is known as "academy status," which means that they are funded directly from the central government rather than via the local authority. In many areas of the country, however, pressure on places at successful schools has intersected with housing prices within the catchments of these schools, arguably further exacerbating the gap between "good" and "poor" schools as well as the gap between education received by better-off and worse-off children.

The Education Reform Act 1988 divided the curriculum into five "key stages": Key Stages 1 and 2 cover Years 1–6 (at primary school), and Key Stages 3 and 4 cover Years 7–9, and 10 and 11, respectively (secondary school). Key Stage 5 covers learning in Years 12 and 13 (from 16 to 18 years old). Formal school qualifications (via nationally managed examinations) usually take place in Years 11 and 13 (with some also in Years 10 and 12). Year 9, our focus in this book, is thus the culmination of Key Stage 3. Graduation across school years is not dependent on grades or examination results.

There is no tracking, as found in the US, but many schools employ processes of selection and streaming by ability within the comprehensive framework. Students may be tested and then put into "sets." This is more common in Math and Science. Not being in the top set means that it may be more difficult for individuals to advance in those subjects, which may reduce their chances of a more academic career.

Perhaps more than any other country in the developed world, England has been a national crucible for continuous persistent educational reform for the past 25 years at every level of the education system, from governance to curriculum to teacher education to pedagogy. In the lead-up to the period in which we conducted our research and during the year we spent with the class, the then Conservative secretary of state for education continued in this tradition, creating headlines, confusion, hatred, and admiration in equally explosive measure.

Race and Ethnicity in Modern Britain

Around 12% of the British population describes itself is from a minority ethnic group (as categorized in the decennial national census). This figure rises for children and young people, being 21.5% of 0- to 19-year-olds in the 2011 census. Further, this population is far from evenly distributed across the country: around 40% of London's population is classified as a member of a minority ethnic group, and as in all postcolonial countries in the global North, the politics of ethnicity, race, and multiculturalism are complicated. Although parts of London contain concentrations of people from a particular minority ethnic group, it is more common to find a high degree of diversity in many London neighborhoods, so that frequently a school population may speak between 30 and 40 languages at home.

Because of Britain's postcolonial past, many minority ethnic groups tend to come from the Indian subcontinent (including people from India, Pakistan, and Bangladesh) and the West Indies. However, because much immigration took place over 40 or 50 years ago, most forms of categorization now also allow for hybrid identities, notably, British Asian, British African, or British Caribbean. In the UK, the term "Asian" usually describes people from the Indian subcontinent, unlike in the US, where it usually refers to people from Southeast Asia. Besides the obligations of postcolonialism, two other immigration patterns define contemporary Britain. The first is the rights of fellow members of the EU to the free movement of labor, so that there are now significant populations from other European countries in the UK, with, for example, nearly half a million people from Poland at the time of writing. Second, despite increasing harsh entry requirements, the UK does admit refugees from war-torn countries such as those of East Africa. There are also populations seeking economic improvement from countries all over the world in a cosmopolitan city like London, as well as older immigrant traditions including Jewish and Irish people.

With respect to academic outcomes, the UK's minority ethnic groups are far from homogeneous. Children whose families originate from India or China do the best.[4] Black Caribbean and black British children do less well. White British children come somewhere in between.[5]

Research Methods

The first phase of our fieldwork, conducted mainly during the autumn term at the beginning of the British academic year, centered on the school. Spending our time in and around the classrooms, this phase was heavily observational. As well as observing, informally chatting, and generally capturing what goes on at school, toward the end of this phase, we also interviewed members of the class individually or in pairs, as well as interviewing a fair number of their teachers. We collected background data from the class using structured minisurveys, and the school gave us the behavior and achievement records for each student. The purpose was to capture how learning is organized, from the perspectives of both students and teachers, to see what kind of knowledge and competence is credited or undervalued. We were interested in how members of the class performed in different subjects, creating for themselves an identity as a learner. And we asked the students about their lives, their school experience, and their interests in digital media.

By the end of phase 1 (see table A.1), we had observed about 80 lessons between us, making a point of observing each child in each subject, given that the members of the class were split for all of their subject lessons across four other classes in the year group. It turned out that Catherine did not always have the tutor time fully planned, so we could address the class every now and again, letting them know how the project was going and what we would do next. We used this time to administer short surveys on their media use; they completed three in all, each just a page or two long, helping us gather useful background information. Although the initial process of gaining access to the school had been tricky, once we were "in," the school gave us access to the school management system, permitting the collection of individual data, over time, on grades for each school subject, along with the school's record of "commendations" (reward points) and "concerns" (for poor behavior). Last, we took advantage of whatever else was going on: a school trip, school play rehearsals, extracurricular activities, parent-teacher progress meetings, and so forth.

The second phase of fieldwork, conducted mainly during the spring term, centered on the home. Again we observed family life, noting the domestic setting, family dynamics, and any digital media used at home. But in this phase, interviews played a greater role, and we interviewed

TABLE A.1. Research Design Overview

Phases of the research	Activities
Phase 0: Preparation, summer 2011	Preparing research ethics permissions and interview and observation protocols, negotiating access to the school
	Initial meetings with the headteacher, "gatekeeper" teacher, head of year, class teacher, and the whole class
	Collecting information about the school and its locale
Phase 1: At school, autumn 2011	Observations in 80 lessons, in tutor time, extracurricular clubs, and around the school (total: 100 hours observation)
	Individual (and a few paired) interviews with members of the class ($n = 26$) for 15–60 minutes each
	Interviews with 17 teachers for 15–45 minutes each, plus informal chats with teachers, gatekeeper, headteacher
	Three short media-use surveys administered to the whole class, each with around 20 questions
	Collection of (school-produced) achievement and behavior data for class members ($n = 27$) at four time periods over the school year
	Observation of whole-class events, e.g., the parent-teacher "progress" meetings, a class trip, year-group "options" assembly
Phase 2: At home, spring 2012	26 interviews with parents (20–30 minutes each)
	26 individual interviews with the child (20–30 minutes each), plus "show and tell" about internet use, on the child's computer (15 minutes), child-led tour of the home, focusing on places, people, media (chatting, taking photos; 15 minutes), individual (private) completion of social networking survey (for the whole-class network), and an interview about the construction of the child's ego network (15 minutes)
Phase 3: Community, summer 2012	Observation of "interest-led" events (e.g., sports, music lessons; 14 in all), with interviews in the various locations (15 students)
	Focus groups at school (three held, discussing mobile phones, Twitter, and the World Challenge; 20–30 minutes each, 11 students in all)
	Digital footprint mapping (as researchers, we searched for publicly available online traces for each class member)
Phase 4: Closure, autumn 2012	Exit interviews with 25 class members either at school or home (20–45 minutes)
	Collection of end-of-year reports (produced by the school for parents) for 27 students

each child separately and also one or both of their parents. While we talked to the parent, we asked the child to leave the room to complete the online social network survey. Each child was then invited to give us a tour of his or her home, telling us what happened in each room, noting media/technology-related uses, and also taking photos.[6] And to complement the students' whole-class social network survey, we also asked them to complete an ego network survey, discussing with us all the people they were in touch with; to their pleasure, we lent them our smart pen for this task. Last, this phase included a child-guided "think aloud" exploration of their internet usage, including their browsing habits, main online activities, Facebook, and other profiles and homework practices. We asked for and were given permission to "friend" each child on Facebook for a week. The purpose in phase 2 was to explore the everyday lifeworld of the students. We considered the role of learning and school in their lives at home and how the rhythm of connecting with family and friends was organized and maintained. We looked at the ways that parents and life in the family envisioned futures for their children and therefore what pressures they were either responding to or placing on the purposes of school. We explored how independent or dependent these young people were, and we looked at the organized and semiorganized activities they participated in outside school, in order to gain insight into how young people relate their learning across formal, semiformal, and informal settings. This revealed what motivated or engaged them as well as inviting wider reflections on how they were developing as learners and on their sense of themselves as energized, motivated, and disciplined.

Phase 2 segued into phase 3, which was more locale based, with fieldwork conducted during the summer term and the summer holiday that followed. Phase 3 was probably the hardest to arrange, partly because young people were not always at ease with the idea of our coming with them to out-of-school activities and partly because of the need to arrange informed consent procedures with others who were likely to be present. As a result, this phase was spread over the summer term and summer vacation, giving it a somewhat leisurely feel; and arrangements were hard to fit in, as holiday plans made life complicated. We had aimed to accompany each child to at least one additional site outside school or home, as befitted his or her interests and activities, although we did not quite manage this for everyone. In the event, we found our-selves at out-of-school music lessons, a drama group, and several sport-ing activities. We also visited the children at home with their friends to play computer games or to talk about subjects as diverse as Harry Potter fandoms, preparation for the World Challenge, attendance at mosque school, or interest in art. Last, we held small focus groups talking about mobile phone and Twitter use, to focus in on the digital dimension of their leisure activities.

A chance mention by one of the young people of a digital platform we had not yet asked them about led us to do some searching online for their "digital footprints."[7] This revealed several points of interest. First, about half the class could be seen to have contributed to their teacher's math blog (on https://edublogs.org), and some figured on a public Slide-Share announcing the school's sporting achievements. Then, beyond their nearly ubiquitous presence on Facebook (including a few additional profiles with playful or false names), Sedat and Giselle had their own YouTube channels (two, in Giselle's case), several were on Twitter (Dom, Megan, Dilruba, Sebastian), Tumblr (Giselle, Megan, Sebastian), and Pinterest (Jenna) as well as a mix of other sites. We asked about these in phase 3 and 4 interviews to follow up, for example, eliciting an interview from Megan about how much Tumblr meant to her (compared to every-day Facebook; see chapter 4).

Phase 4 was not planned originally, but during the project it be-came obvious that an exit interview with all the children would create closure in our relationship with them and with the school and, sub-stantively, would invite their reflections on the year past. These were conducted at school or home as children preferred, in the autumn of their Year 10, allowing us to fill in gaps in our knowledge, check our interpretations and emerging conclusions, note any reflections on the project itself, and gain the students' own perspectives on their lives and learning over the past year. We ended with an invitation for them to look ahead, which they found hard, and to imagine the world with-out the internet, which they found impossible. Who knows if we will return to them. It is notable that several projects have returned even a decade later;[8] we, too, hope to meet the class again.

We end this discussion with a note on the limits of our gaze, for there were some things that we did not see and some that we saw but have not included in these pages. In relation to the omissions in what the young people told us, two stand out. First, although we heard a fair bit about the problems or painful experiences in their lives, they told us of these only after the event, once they were safely in the past. So, while teachers and parents might have alerted us to present pains in the young people's lives, they themselves were reserved about such matters. Second, although clearly the young people were going through adolescence, they rarely discussed this with us beyond occasional conversations about boyfriends and girlfriends or starting to shave.

Transcription Conventions

In preparing this manuscript, we have quoted faithfully from the original texts, but we have applied our judgment to making what was "talk" communicate clearly on the page. This means that occasionally we have cut or reduced some phrases, for example, making verb endings agree.

Social Network Visualization

In order to create the whole-class networks presented in chapter 3,[9] each student was asked nine questions in relation to every other student in the class. Q1: Who is your "friend" on Facebook? Q2: Who have you asked to help you with homework? Q3: Who do you hang out with out of school? Q4: Who would you call a close friend? Q5: Who do you chat with by text, Facebook, BBM, or MSN? Q6: Who have you asked for help or advice about a personal problem? Q7: Who have you done an out-of-school activity with, like sports, music, drama? Q8: Who have you flirted with? Q9: Whom do you spend time with online (e.g., gaming, Facebook)?

The students completed the questionnaire online by themselves, thus ensuring confidentiality. In the event, three students (Aiden, Sergei, Toby) did not complete the questionnaire, although as Sergei was included in the questionnaire, others could link to him (but not vice versa). Also, almost everyone was friends with everyone else on Facebook, and no one admitted to flirting with others in the class; so these two questions were omitted from the overall whole-class network. Separately, all the children were interviewed face-to-face to obtain their ego network: they were asked the same nine questions, but the answers were open; and so each listed a range of people who were recorded as individuals and also classified as members of the class, the year group, the family, or someone else.

Ego networks were hand drawn by each child. By contrast, to produce the whole-class network, JUNG (Java Universal Network Framework) API was used for data visualization, where each node represents an individual and each connection between the nodes is a link (or "edge"). For the overall whole-class network (based on questions 2–7 and 9), links were weighted with a value of 0.2, if a student answered yes for another student (for a single question); if a student answered yes five times, the score was aggregated to 1.0 and shown in the network as a thicker line. If nodes have higher connectivity, they cluster together in the network (although the space between nodes does not reflect actual distance). For example, Giselle and Sara have higher connectivity between them, and hence they are closer to each other. The same is the case with Max, Alice, and Jenna. The nodes for Fesse, Gideon, Nick, Jamie, and Sebastian are in the center because they have highest connectivity with each other. For ease of comparison, each whole-class network (based on the separate questions) uses the positioning of nodes established for the overall network.

Notes

Introduction

1. In the British school system, this is Year 9. In the US, it would be eighth grade. For US readers, Year 9 describes both the whole cohort and, in addition, a level of schooling.

2. The idea of studying a class was partly inspired by Laurent Cantet's 2008 award-winning film *Entre les murs* ("Within the walls," translated as *The Class*; see www .imdb.com/title/tt1068646), which follows a year in the life of an optimistic young teacher of a class of 14- to 15-year-olds as he seeks to recognize the students' diverse family contexts within the classroom. While his aim is well meaning, namely, to connect sites of knowledge to enable a holistic conception of learning, the result is disruptive and upsetting, leading the school to reassert the traditional separation of home and school.

3. Schools will typically mix up the new intake from their "feeder" primary schools (although often keeping close friends together), and they may distribute them according to a rough ability banding while also ensuring that children with designated special needs are not clustered together.

4. We are aware that this notion of a class varies among educational systems within and across countries. In some countries—for example, Denmark—students may spend all day together as a single class up to and beyond the age of 13. In other countries—for example, the US—students may each traverse an individual path through the day, depending on lesson assignment or subject choices, with no single teacher who knows them well or no shared association with a meaningful group that meets in the "homeroom." But whatever the system, there is always a balance struck between individual pathways and shared school experiences, and it is this balance that we seek to depict through our focus on one (British) class of students.

5. Recognizing the ubiquitous nature of the digital media environment is to imply not that everyone has access to the Internet but rather that everyone is accessible to the satellite communications that scan, record, and connect all parts of the globe, along with the pervasive economic and political logics that shape those communicative connections and their consequences. See Lievrouw and Living-stone (2006).

6. As the critique of technological determinism makes clear, technologies may only be said to "afford" particular user practices—by shaping behavior or setting the boundary conditions for how a technology can be used. See Bijker et al. (1987), Mansell and Silverstone (1996), MacKenzie and Wajcman (1999), and Hutchby

(2001). And Nancy Baym (2015, p. 175) reminds us that "people are adaptive, innovative, and influential in determining what technology is and will become." Once we stop seeing the digital as a distinct and external influence on society, then we can begin to recognize the mutual coevolution of society and digital technologies over decades or centuries.

7. As William Davies (2014) explains, while definitions and evaluations of neo-liberalism vary, the term is widely used to capture the modernizing forces of capitalism, especially in the global North, as they seek to bring institutions that lie outside the market within it, privatizing or regulating them according to an ethical and political vision that promotes competition and considers inequality as necessary. See also Belfiore (2012) and Couldry (2010).

8. Consequently, critics are increasingly concerned that behind the popular rhetoric of connection lies a far-less-emancipatory reality. For example, see Couldry (2010) and van Dijck (2013a). For a critique of neoliberal forces in relation to education, see Loveless and Williamson (2013).

9. As we discuss in chapter 1, Anthony Giddens (1991) introduced the notion of the project of the self, while the psychologist Jerome Bruner (1991) talked of self-making. See also S. Hall (1996) on the importance of pluralizing identities. The extension of our project over a year adds a temporal dimensions, allowing each young person we interviewed to tell and retell his or her story of the self.

10. James Clifford (1983) critiques efforts to create a coherent ethnographic narrative with an overarching viewpoint for reader and author. For ethnography is interpretive, multivocal, and messy, and its readers, now more than ever, cannot and should not be easily controlled.

11. Generations matter too; when we have given talks during the writing of this book, younger and older people view the material from different vantage points, looking back to their own youth, reflecting on how things have changed, or comparing with their own present, and this is central to our concern with the nature of contemporary societal change.

12. In placing the emphasis on the everyday, the ordinary, we have been greatly influenced by what Raymond Williams (1961a) called "the whole way of life," seeking to capture "the kaleidoscope of daily life," as Janice Radway put it (1988, p. 366); see also Drotner (1994).

13. This means immersing the researcher (and the reader) in the worldview and daily routines of the researched (see, for example, Duneier et al., 2014) while also recognizing the dialectic between insider and outsider perspectives on the life of a community or cohort (Bohman, 1991).

14. We recognize that the structures of living and learning for our class are in some ways peculiar to the UK at the start of the 21st century, although many of the forces shaping both school and home have a longer history and a wider resonance beyond London. For instance, educational policy was highly contested in the political sphere, with an unusually dynamic secretary of state for education changing policy wholesale at frequent intervals. Educational practice was

affected by the influx of educational technologies, from the Smart Board or use of YouTube at school to personal digital devices designed to bridge school and home and a host of commercial products for homework and out-of-school learning. Yet efforts to create order and solidarity of purpose within the classroom are as old as school itself, the ambition of fostering home–school links has been advocated for some decades, and debates over how the boundaries of education—to deliver curriculum knowledge or to shape "the whole person" as a citizen—have ebbed and flowed in different places at different times.

15. We prefer the more everyday notion of in-between places to the more heavily theorized sociological notions of third spaces or liminality (Mitchell 1995), drawing on the empirical study of childhood places easily overlooked by adults. See, for example, Holloway and Valentine (2000); see also Olwig and Gullov (2003).

Chapter 1. Living and Learning in the Digital Age

1. Technically, "the digital" refers to the process of encoding information in discrete symbol systems and transmitting it across connected switching devices. But the social significance of the digital is much debated. It is vital to understand how it is imagined and used, as this embeds particular values, political interests, and normative practices in emerging communication infrastructures. See Mansell (2012).

2. Other changes affecting childhood exacerbate these anxieties—the recognition of children's rights, growth in leisure time, emergence of youth subcultures, huge growth of marketing to children and young people, and increasing restrictions on children's freedom of movement and opportunities to play. See Cunningham (2006) and Children's Society (2013).

3. Corsaro (1997), James et al. (1998).

4. For Jürgen Habermas, as Outhwaite (1994, p. 86) explains, the lifeworld "is the 'horizon' within which human beings refer to items in the objective, subjective and normative worlds." The concept thus captures the mutuality of individual and environment, thereby avoiding what Habermas sees as the reductionism of phenomenological approaches that prioritize the intersubjective realm of interpretation over wider societal structures.

5. While the popular sense of such claims is too simple, changes or even fragmentation in identities are discussed by Anthias (2002), O. Jones (2012), and van Zoonen (2013).

6. Coontz (1997), Osgerby (1998). This stability meant that when television first entered family life, a set of practices and concerns became established that, in retrospect, were particular to their times. Yet these have cast a long shadow of expectations over today's diversified domestic media ecologies (see Livingstone, 2009b).

7. Late modernity, the most recent stage of change in Western societies since the Industrial Revolution, is shaped by the longer history of modernity including the rise of capitalism and the onward flows (and counter- or cross-flows) of

globalization—as seen in the often conflict-ridden spread of Western democratic ideals and in the consolidation of political and commercial forms of power around the world. Although the theorists of late modernity are often pessimistic about the future, they are not determinists or fatalists, and questions of agency run through many of their writings. Late modernity has also been called "second" or "reflexive" or "liquid" modernity. We do not address the differences among these labels but would point toward Beck et al. (1995), Castells (1996), Tomlinson (1999), and Jessop (2002).

8. With the notion of a "sensitising concept," Blumer (1954, p. 7) pointed out how concepts in the social sciences often lack a clear-cut definition but instead give us "a general sense of reference and guidance in approaching empirical instances," sensitizing the researcher about where to look rather than defining precisely what exists a priori.

9. Lash (2002).

10. Lukes (1971).

11. Lash (2002) theorizes this in terms of "disorganised capitalism," arguing that modern institutions (the school, the family, community, etc.) have lost their purpose and significance. We wonder what this means for generational divides—when structures still meaningful to parents and teachers are seen as mere legacy structures by young people.

12. Indeed, media scholars are beginning to conceptualize a process of "mediatization" that parallels the other core processes of modernity (globalization, individualization, commercialization); see Krotz (2007) and Lundby (2014).

13. Beck ([1986] 2005, p. 183).

14. Lash (2002, p. xi).

15. Bauman (2002, p. xv).

16. Ibid., p. xvi.

17. As Bauman puts it, pessimistically, "The other side of individualization seems to be the corrosion and slow disintegration of citizenship. . . . The concerns and preoccupations of individuals qua individuals fill the public space. . . . 'Public issues' which resist such reduction [to the individual concern] become all but incomprehensible" (ibid., p. xviii).

18. Beck and Beck-Gernsheim (2002, p. 2).

19. Ibid., p. 11.

20. See Sims (2012) for an equivalent account in New York.

21. Bauman (2002, p. xix).

22. Beck and Beck-Gernsheim (2002, p. 23).

23. Chisholm et al. (1995), James and James (2008).

24. Hence, the postwar period, especially since the 1970s, has seen more mothers in paid employment, older parents, lower birthrates and so fewer siblings per child, more children born to single parents and to unmarried parents, more marriages ending in divorce, and more children brought up in reconstituted families. See Hill and Tisdall (1997) and Chambers (2012).

25. Hagell et al. (2013); see also Beck and Beck-Gernsheim (2014) and Nayak (2003).

26. Hagell (2012). The proportion of 16- to 18-year-olds in education or training rose from two-thirds in 1985 to over four-fifths in 2011 (see also Hagell et al., 2013).

27. See Livingstone (2009a), Arnett (2011), Henderson et al. (2012).

28. Coontz (1997, p. 13).

29. See Livingstone (2002).

30. For example, poorer children can rely on less social capital to generate supportive peer relations and a sense of belonging at school, for instance, than better-off children can (see Stevens et al., 2007).

31. Hagell (2012). As Cribb et al. (2013, p. 6) observe, "there are now much larger gaps between the richest and poorest individuals in families with children," as the result of a decades-long rise in income inequality that today's parents have lived through, just as they have lived through rising school achievement pressures and future job uncertainties. For instance, the social gap is widening in educational attainment at A-level and access to top universities, as well as among youth reoffending rates (see SMCP Commission, 2013).

32. Hagell et al. (2013).

33. UNICEF Office of Research (2013). This figure is, however, lower than in many southern and eastern European countries and three times lower than the figure for the US. Ethnicity and deprivation are strongly linked; see Jivraj and Khan (2013).

34. As Ulrich Beck and Elisabeth Beck-Gernsheim (2002) observe, even social reproduction is no longer predictable, having become precarious. See also Ito et al. (2013). The Timescapes qualitative study of parenting found that the more affluent the parents, the more uncertain and worried they were about how to anticipate and plan for their children's employment futures. It seemed they felt the pressure, and the fear of failure, if their children could not sustain their own improvement in circumstances (see Backett-Milburn et al., 2011).

35. Edwards and Weller (2011); see also Arnett (2011) on the notion of "emerging adulthood" as a new life stage.

36. Social Attitudes of Young People Community of Interest (2014).

37. Hagell et al. (2013) show a sharp rise in all these indicators from 2000 to 2011. See also SMCP Commission (2013). For equivalent figures for the US, see Ito et al. (2013).

38. See Furlong and Cartmel (2006).

39. As many scholars have observed, rather than calling young people apathetic, it seems more appropriate to recognize that they struggle to find political efficacy (the sense that they can bring about change) in a world that pays them little attention. See Couldry et al. (2010).

40. Such beliefs are borne out by the evidence (Putnam, 2015).

41. Social Attitudes of Young People Community of Interest (2014).

42. See Ochs and Kemer-Sadlik (2013), Clark (2013), Lareau (2011), among others.

43. We note that UK surveys find that teenagers are generally satisfied with their lives, especially with their friends and family, and four in five are also relatively

happy at school. Children's Society (2012); see also Beaumont and Lofts (2013), Social Attitudes of Young People Community of Interest (2014).

44. JWT (2012). See also Chamberlain et al. (2010), whose large national survey of students in Years 6, 8, and 10 found that 51% worried about schoolwork and exams, followed by career choice, friendships, and physical appearance. Currie et al. (2008) found that half of 13-year-olds felt pressurized by schoolwork. See also Hagell, Sandberg, et al. (2012). Whether the level of worry is new is contested: psychologists report that anxiety, depression, and emotional problems among adolescents have risen over the past 30 years (Collishaw, 2012), but the increase has halted in the past decade, along with a steady decline over decades in risk behaviors—smoking, drinking, drugs, and crime (Children's Society, 2013). Still, an estimated one in ten children and young people is affected by mental health difficulties of one kind or another, and a similar proportion says in surveys that they feel they cannot cope with day-to-day life (see Nuffield Foundation, 2012).

45. Hagell and Witherspoon (2012, p. 167). Looked at cross-nationally, Britain is a little below average on subjective well-being (children's self-reported happiness and life satisfaction), although it is far above the US; see Bradshaw et al. (2013). Over the first decade of the 21st century, the situation for Britain's children has slightly improved across a range of indicators (while it has worsened in the US, Canada, and several European countries); see Martorano et al. (2013). It is interesting to note, given our focus on 13- to 14-year-olds, that the Children's Society's *Good Childhood Report 2013* (2013) found measures of life satisfaction and well-being to decline over the ages from eight to 15 but then rise again after the age of 16.

46. Scribner and Cole (1981), Luke (1989), Levinson et al. (1996), Alexander (2001).

47. See Alexander (2009), Williams (1961a), Hunter (1994), and Somekh (2000) for a UK focus; Bowles and Gintis (1976), Pope (2003), and US Department of Education (2010) for a US focus; and Green and Luke (2006) and Whitty (2010) for wider reflections.

48. Goldin and Katz (2008).

49. Schuller et al. (2004).

50. See, for example, Nussbaum (2012).

51. Biesta (2011).

52. See www.oecd.org/pisa/aboutpisa. At the same time, nonacademic outcomes built on experience and "craft" have also been undervalued despite powerful and pertinent social and economic arguments. See also Sennett (2008), J. Rose (2001), and M. Rose (2009).

53. Furlong and Cartmel (2006, p. 24).

54. Indeed, such contradictions may have always been present, as Raymond Williams suggested in his account of social and cultural life in the 20th century (1961a).

55. Thomas and Brown (2011).

56. N. Rose (1999).

57. Edwards (1997), Chisholm (2008).

58. J. Thompson (2011, p. 61). We hesitate to use Homi Bhabha's notion of a "third space" in this discussion insofar as this refers to the dialectical or transcendent resolution to conflicts among other places or relationships (Mitchell, 1995). Nonetheless, it is intriguing that Gutiérrez (2008) uses this concept in combination with Vygotsky's zone of proximal development to theorize productive interactionally constituted learning spaces.

59. Social science has come to recognize the coconstructed nature of the spaces, times, and social relations of childhood, since young people's imaginings, actions, and reactions shape their interactions with others and, thereby, the social contexts in which they live (Corsaro, 1997; Qvortrup, 1995; Holloway and Valentine, 2000; James et al., 1998; James, 2013).

60. See, for example, the sections on "human beings and human becomings" in Lee (2001) and James et al. (1998). As Qvortrup (1995) has argued powerfully, Western societies have a deeply ambivalent, even paradoxical, approach to children: they assert a positive view of them while simultaneously devaluing or neglecting their needs and experiences; children are disenfranchised within the public sphere yet castigated for being apathetic; they are subject to increasing surveillance yet seen as subversive; their imagination is valued, yet their lives are increasingly controlled; their protection is widely promoted, yet society allows many children to encounter serious risk; and so on.

61. Willett et al. (2013); see also Goetz et al. (2005).

62. See Corsaro (1997), Holloway and Valentine (2000), and Olwig and Gullov (2003). See also Livingstone (2002), on children's "bedroom culture," an account that draws on the "domestication" tradition of theorizing family, home, and media. See also Morley and Silverstone (1990), Bakardjieva (2005), and Silverstone (2006).

63. See, for example, Scollon and Scollon (2003) and Leander and Sheehy (2004).

64. Heywood (2004).

65. The particular sites that wax and wane in popularity with the young continue to change. At the time of this writing, UK national surveys show Facebook to be by far the dominant site (see Lilley and Ball, 2013; and Ofcom, 2014), with over a billion users worldwide and a near monopoly among young people in the global North (see Lenhart, 2015, for US findings). While Facebook and MySpace are social network sites, Twitter and Tumblr are defined as microblogging sites, with the relative emphasis on short text messages and visual images, respectively. Generally, although not always, social network sites prioritize communication among people who know each other or who share a social circle ("friends"), while microblogging sites prioritize sharing content anonymously (among "followers").

66. Bolter and Grusin (1999).

67. Livingstone (2008), d. boyd (2014).

68. Bruner (1991), Sundén (2003).

69. Arnett (1995); see also Buchner (1990).

70. d. boyd (2014).
71. Benwell and Stokoe (2006, p. 6).
72. Bauman (2002, p. xv). This is conceptually distinct from "commonsense" notions of identity, which suggest a stable, continuous, persistent notion of personhood.
73. S. Hall (1996). See also Shotter and Gergen (1988) and Gergen (2009). As van Zoonen (2013) argues, because identity is not what we are but what we do, it is multivocal and context dependent; see also Somerville's (2008, p. 31) account of how second-generation migrant youth particularly "describe a fluidity of identities, and a myriad of ways in which their identities are expressed as a direct result of shifting ethnic and national contexts."
74. Goffman (1959).
75. See de Certeau (1984). In other words, in common with others who lack institutional or collective power, children and young people exercise such power as they possess through seemingly unimportant everyday actions that may reinforce a desired adult response or rework an apparently fixed arrangement or renegotiate the meaning of a practice in a way that better suits their interests.
76. Becker (1972), Hunter (1994).
77. Bowles and Gintis (1976).
78. Willis (1978).
79. Weis (2004).
80. Our approach is influenced by studies of schooling conducted in the Foucauldian tradition that examine how the interplay of forces in social environments shapes how individuals, in turn, shape themselves. See, for example, Sullivan (1994), N. Rose (1999), and Baker and Heyning (2004). As Sullivan explains, by this self-shaping or care of the self (or what N. Rose, 1999, calls "governing the soul"), Foucault (1988) meant to advocate a self-scripting of one's life, positioned not within a hierarchical society but rather within a complex society with multiple and distributed centers of power—we might now call this a network society in which people are more connected, not withdrawn. In this society, the cultivation of the self is defined not by ideology but by a new "stylistics of existence" (Sullivan, 1994, p. 8).
81. Bourdieu and Passeron (1990), Bernstein (1973); see also Ball (2013) and Wortham (2005).
82. Coleman and Hagell (2007), Hill and Tisdall (1997), Social Attitudes of Young People Community of Interest (2014).
83. Henderson et al. (2012).
84. Stanton Wortham's analysis of "learner identity" parallels this analysis by focusing on school. His yearlong study of a class of US middle schoolers showed that forms of social identification (gender, social class, ethnicity, etc.) are inextricably part and parcel of academic learning, with the social self constantly referred to or called on in situations that are ostensibly purely concerned with the curriculum. Drawing on Jay Lemke's work on time scales (2000), Wortham (2005) showed how this occurred by tracking the to-and-fro between local, short, and

longer-term forms of identification across the hour of a lesson and the full length of the academic year. Early UK studies of similar depth and influence include Hargreaves (1967) and Rutter et al. (1979), and for a recent US study, see Putnam (2015).

85. Henderson et al. (2012, p. 19). See, again, the analysis in Furlong and Cartmel (2006).

86. Henderson et al. (2012, p. 24).

87. Wilkinson and Pickett (2010).

88. As Giddens adds, "disembedding mechanisms depend on two conditions: the evacuation of the traditional or customary content of local contexts of action, and the reorganizing of social relations across broad time-space bands" (1995, p. 85). Beck and Beck-Gernsheim agree, defining "individualization" as the gradual process by which people's everyday lives have become partially detached (or "disembedded" or even freed) from traditional structures of gender, social class, nationality, and religion: "'individualization' means disembedding without reembedding" in new traditions (Beck and Beck-Gernsheim, 2002, p. xxii). Chambers (2013) traces the consequences for friendship, which, she argues, we come to rely on ever more for intimacy and meaningful ties to others.

89. See Giddens (1993), Beck and Beck-Gernsheim (2002), and Buchner (1990).

90. Cultural geographers have argued that we have reconfigured the familiar and secure neighborhoods and places of our lives within new global flows and migrations; see Massey (2005).

91. For example, see Atkinson (2007), Brannen and Nilsen (2005), Elliott (2002), and Woodman (2009). Identifying the relevant evidence may not lead to clear conclusions either way, however. For example, in reviewing 30 years of annual surveys from 1983 to 2013, the British Social Attitudes report tracks a series of shifts among adults that show, as predicted by the thesis of individualization, that they have become progressively less attached to traditional religious and political affiliations; but the findings for social class identification are more equivocal (see Park et al., 2013). Predelli and Cebulla's (2011) interviews with adults and their parents offer more support for Beck's thesis, showing that individualization, future uncertainty, and the choice biography are more salient to and more discussed by the younger than the older generation.

92. On the pernicious effects of rising social inequality, see Wilkinson and Pickett (2010), Piketty (2014), and Dorling (2011).

93. Beck and Beck-Gernsheim (2002, p. xxiv).

94. Ibid., p. 39.

95. O. Jones (2012), Savage (2010).

96. See Savage (2010) and Bennett et al. (2009). One outcome is the identification of further segments of society—not only the underclass but also the service class, the "precariat" or "hipsters," or the new elite, and so forth.

97. For recent debates in the UK context, see Atkinson (2007), Bennett et al. (2009), O. Jones (2012), Biressi and Nunn (2013), and Skeggs (2013).

98. Brown et al. (2011). There is little evidence of change in social mobility, although this varies by country. UK government data show that social mobility reduced considerably (and inequality rose) during the 1980s but has neither improved nor worsened since (Cribb et al., 2013; Kennedy, 2010). See also Hills et al. (2010) for a major review showing that while differences across social groups remain substantial, there are also considerable differences in income and employment within groups (e.g., by gender, ethnicity, or class). Corak (2013) shows that mobility is lower in the US than in parts of Europe and Canada. Piketty (2014) concurs that the 20th century saw little social mobility, with even less in the US than in Europe; he particularly contests the belief in "American exceptionalism" among US sociologists that they alone in the West have high social mobility (p. 484). See also Putnam (2015).

99. Becker (1972), Bourdieu and Passeron (1990).

100. Bernstein (1990). Bernstein writes further of the "pedagogicization" of society, referring to the spread of school-like forms of educational organization, knowledge, and subjectivity beyond the boundaries of traditional learning institutions, notably into the home. For a discussion of the use of pedagogy in relation to informal learning in the home, see Bonal and Rambla (2003) and Buckingham and Sefton-Green (2004).

101. Buckingham et al. (2001); see also McLaughlin (1996).

102. See Bourdieu (1984).

103. Hey (2005). The notion of the child as a "production" by middle-class parents is theorized further by Skelton and Francis (2012) as "the renaissance child," whose "all-rounder" curriculum vitae will help him or her to win; Beck and Beck-Gernsheim (2002) are perhaps more sympathetic in attributing such parental efforts to the desire to "re-enchant" their own lives. See also Jenks (1996, p. 23), who argues that "children have become both the testing ground for the necessity of independence in the constitution of human subjectivity but also the symbolic refuse of the desirability of trust, dependency and care in human relations." Demerath's (2009) study of how school can become complicit in this process of seeking advantage is relevant here too.

104. Meanwhile, Lareau suggests that in working-class families, "the cultural logic of child rearing at home is out of synch with the standards of institutions" (2011, p. 3), and thus "social class dynamics are woven into the texture and rhythm of children and parents' daily lives" (p. 236). Such processes result in social reproduction of dis/advantage, the opposite of that idealistic vision of a constructive and fair relation between home and school. For a somewhat different view, see Clark (2013).

105. We are especially thinking of the work of Pierre Bourdieu (1984), along with the many scholars following in his tradition who question how far social class relations are changing and in what ways. Although they have effectively articulated the subtle ways by which institutions (how they are organized, the languages they use, and the habits and procedures they follow) interact with individuals so as

to reproduce rather than alter social hierarchies of power, they have tended to envisage a rather stable society with clearly stratified occupations and recognized hierarchies of taste and wealth.

106. Berlin (1978, pp. 114–115).

Chapter 2. A Year of Fieldwork

1. Up to that point in the term, our observations had been rather general, focusing on the class as a whole rather than on individuals. This was, then, a crucial moment for our project: we requested formal permission to interview the students individually at school and explained that after Christmas we would further request permission to visit the family at home.

2. This also affected their power relations with us, with these young people mediating our efforts to gain parental consent for our research. As things turned out, however, virtually all the parents deferred to their child when deciding whether to allow us to visit them at home. It even seemed that the young people had already constructed us as advocates for them in some way, although, as it later emerged, parents appreciated the opportunity that the research provided to reflect on their childrearing practices and challenges.

3. The *saz* is a stringed instrument used in Turkish and Near Eastern music; see chapter 9.

4. Case studies triangulate multiple methods to offer a rich account of a phenomenon, with full awareness of its wider implications; see Flick (2014) and Yin (2014). Linking case studies to reflexive social science in a way that we are sympathetic to, Michael Burawoy (1998, p. 30) calls for research that takes "context and situation as its point of departure . . . and seeks to reduce the effects of power—domination, silencing, objectification, and normalisation." Specific methodological considerations apply when conducting research with children and youth, as argued by Heath et al. (2009), Graue and Walsh (1998), and Greig and Taylor (1999).

5. We draw in particular on two ethnographic traditions: ethnographies of childhood and of school life. Among ethnographies of childhood and family, we were most influenced by Bakardjieva (2005), Seiter (2005), MacLeod (2009), Pugh (2009), Lareau (2011), Henderson et al. (2012), Clark (2013), and Ochs and Kemer-Sadlik (2013). Among school-based ethnographies, we would note Hargreaves (1967), Rutter et al. (1979), Ball (1981), Hammersley and Woods (1984), Eckert (1989), Pollard and Filer (1999), Bettie (2003), Pope (2003), and Davidson (2011).

6. Benwell and Stokoe (2006).

7. Methods for tracking such spaces need to be attentive to young people's own perspectives. In a recent study, Thornham and Myers (2012) gave teenagers digital cameras to video the architecture of their school as they saw it, revealing not only its surveillant design but also their tactics of reappropriation; this construes space "less as a finite and separate entity that produces behaviour, but more as a fluid, continual process of negotiation, that is both lived and imagined" (p. 797).

8. Marcus (1995).

9. Horst and Miller (2012, p. 3) propose several useful research principles to guide ethnographic research in the digital age. Most important is the emphasis on sensitivity to the ways in which the digital "intensifies the dialectical nature of culture" by materially altering everyday processes of mediation (but not increasing them, since culture is always, necessarily, mediated). They further advocate research that is holistic yet not homogenizing and that recognizes the indeterminacies and ambivalence of everyday life.

10. UK government statistics list schools according to their size (school enrollment), proportion of children with educational special needs, proportion of families whose lack of resources qualify the student for free school meals, the percentage of students who achieve five employer-recognized qualifications at age 16 (A–C grades at GCSE), whether the school has a sixth form (Years 12 and 13), and whether it has a specialism (usually in technology, science, languages, sports, or performing arts). Hence, we took all these factors into account.

11. There were also differences in our intellectual orientation. It was more evident to Julian that school-based research is often vague about domestic and familial practices at home, while Sonia became increasingly surprised that research based at home says little about the fact that children spend much of their lives at school.

12. Indeed, after we began our fieldwork, the school was upgraded by the government's inspection body, Ofsted, from "good" to "outstanding."

13. Measuring distances by walking instead of driving time is more typical of European than American suburbs, as Fishman (1987) insightfully discusses. This is, of course, especially important for children.

14. Vertovec (2007) has coined the term "super-diversity" to capture the complexity of cultural identities that, more than ever before, characterize late modern societies. See also Beck and Beck-Gernsheim (2014) on the notion of "world families." We try to avoid marking out minority ethnic children as "other," as cautioned by Gutiérrez's critique of "white innocence" (2005–2006).

15. This is a common feature in neighborhoods that have female single-sex schools, allowing parents to opt to send their girls to an all-girl school and so leaving more boys in coeducational schools.

16. School uniforms are common in England—with its tradition of fee-paying private schools—unlike in many other countries around the world where a uniform is seen as an infringement of students' rights. In recent decades, successive governments have advocated a return to school uniforms as a way of marking a particular kind of discipline (despite the lack of scholarly evidence) and of stressing a return to the kind of rigor lost in the allegedly "permissive" sixties.

17. The computer-controlled electronic "blackboard" (or interactive whiteboard) displayed at the front of each classroom.

18. Ofsted (Office for Standards in Education, Children's Services and Skills) is the government body that carries out inspections to ensure compliance, with standards for English and Welsh schools (see www.ofsted.gov.uk/about-us).

19. For a handful of the students, the end of school registration was followed by detention, in which they were kept behind for minor infractions.

20. In this context, it is worth noting the considerable decline in the proportion of British children permitted to travel to school independently in recent decades (along with similar declines in unsupervised outdoor play and weekend travel without a parent); see Shaw et al. (2013).

21. Throughout the book, we have lightly edited the verbatim quotations from young people, pruning some of the repeated terms such as "like" and "sort of." Abby, for instance, told us, "Sometimes I hang out with my friends, like, and then or, like, and then when I get home, I'll go, like, on my phone, or, like, on, like, the Internet and stuff like that or maybe go out." These terms become intrusive when written, even though they go largely unnoticed when spoken.

22. We met a few challenges: parents who spoke little English or who confused us with the teachers or who insisted on listening to the interview with their child or even answering for them. There were some practical difficulties: missed appointments, broken laptops, or nonworking internet connections. Sometimes children checked that we would not tell parents what they said before revealing something. A few bedrooms were tidied, instruments practiced, or internet histories cleared before we arrived. And we found that some young people texted each other our questions while we traveled from one house to the next.

23. See the appendix for the adoption of digital devices by teenagers in the UK generally and in the class in particular.

24. Minecraft is a construction game often played collaboratively; see https://mine craft.net/.

25. This is an indication that Dom was in the vanguard, the microblogging site Twitter being only recently popular among UK youth at the time; see Mascheroni and Olafsson (2014); for US findings, see Hargittai and Litt (2011).

26. Weekends also offered another opportunity for young people and their parents to fit in extracurricular activities. Giselle told us, "Weekends, I have piano and tennis lessons, so I do that. And on the weekend, I—we normally—me and my friends normally go out, like, maybe take the bus to [the mall]." Salma, too, was busy, with Saturdays spent swimming, horse riding, and trampolining, all of which she was confident in.

27. Undoubtedly, there was a link between social practices on- and offline. Just as multitasking homework with Facebook allowed the young people to mix learning and peer identities in a way that suited them, playing computer games together depended on parental approaches. For example, for Shane, playing computer games with friends meant getting together over pizza at his house, while for Nick, whose mother did not want a bunch of large, loud teenage boys in her home, computer games were primarily an online experience.

28. Livingstone (2002), d. boyd (2014). For example, Lydia and her best friend enjoyed the "teen scene" in a local leisure facility most Saturday evenings. Initially, Lydia's mother was worried about this, and so she checked it out, saying,

"Twenty-five years ago, it was like pretty rough up there on a Friday and Saturday night. It was just sort of groups of youths hanging round trying to get the girls. And I was thinking, 'No, you're not going to start that; you're too young.' But, actually, we've both been up there, and it's absolutely fine. There's little ones and there's grown-ups, and there's teenagers up there as well, but it's all pretty—it's all right."

29. See, for example, Carrington (2006).

30. There was an opportunity at the start of the following year to correct choices that did not turn out as anticipated.

31. This film was designed to mirror the BBC's *Britain in a Day* and even director Ridley Scott's *Life in a Day*. See www.bbc.co.uk/programmes/poookqz5p and www.youtube.com/watch?v=b2k4nIARvS8.

32. Since the film could not be posted online for reasons of student privacy, this was one of many small examples we witnessed of how fears about the risks of digital media worked to constrain the opportunities that such media could bring in practice (see chapter 6).

33. Connections among the diaspora meant that summer holiday destinations were shaped by where relatives lived, and again, social class stratified experiences. Salma had fun with cousins, freedom, and sunshine in Lahore. Jenna went to Kenya but expressed little pleasure in this. Adriana and Gideon went frequently to see grandparents in Spain, as did Adam in Germany and Nick in Sweden. Two of the poorer children—Lydia and Joel—did not go on holiday at all in the summer before our exit interviews. It seemed that being part of an immigrant family ensured that young people from poorer homes got to travel abroad, but certainly the wealthier families traveled more.

34. As Neale and Flowerdew (2003, p. 189) observe, only through longitudinal qualitative methods can one grasp "the time and texture—or the interplay of the temporal and cultural dimensions of social life"—that are so crucial to understanding "the process of 'growing up.'"

35. We have omitted some of the identifying details or events that could break our promise of confidentiality or anonymity, even though they might contribute to the overall picture.

36. Or, as Pink and Mackley put it (2013), while life is hardly centered on media, it is saturated with media, making media banal and yet crucial to the contemporary feeling and structure of life at "home." See also Lievrouw (2004).

Chapter 3. Networks and Social Worlds

1. Ito et al. (2013). Yet the countervailing view is also strong—that society is becoming more fragmented, with individuals more isolated from their communities and disembedded from traditional ways of life, left only with the weak ties typical of the individualized network society. See Granovetter (1983), van Dijk (2012).

2. Varnelis (2008, p. 145).

3. Furthermore, today's conceptions of social network analysis draw heavily on the sociometry of the 1950s. One value of that earlier analysis is that social network analysis respects but also goes beyond the particularity of each individual's experience, since a network encompasses multiple vantage points from which to view links among participants. Significantly, although networks are built through human action, no individual may fully grasp the larger network within which his or her life is lived. For example, individuals may or may not recognize their position in the network (e.g., near the center or on the edge), and they may not recognize the network effects that transcend the intention of any individual (e.g., how networks sustain forms of social capital or social exclusion). See Marcus et al. (2011).

4. See the appendix for an account of ethnicity in the British context. See also Williamson (2004). Thorne (1994) remains a primary source regarding the development of gendered identities, and we draw especially on her insight that the expression of gender is complex, sometimes surprising or contradictory, and not always even salient, although at other times it is central to children's talk and play.

5. Monge and Contractor (2003), Scott and Carrington (2011). For an earlier application to children's social worlds, see Belle (1989).

6. The use of Facebook was thoroughly embedded in the young people's daily routine. Fesse logged on every day, Alice never logged off, and Abby turned it on as soon as she woke up, to "just, like, check what's, like, happening on Facebook or something or, like, talk to people." For Giselle, it was important when she came home from school, to coordinate her social life: "If I'm organizing an event or . . . quite often there are group chats."

7. As George (2007, p. 127) observes, "Black girls . . . carry the dual yoke of sexism and racism," so there is much to encourage their banding together, although they may be very different as individuals.

8. When the survey was done, Deyan had just arrived, so he seems isolated, although he quickly built links with Sergei, Sedat, Mark, and others (and he shared a home language with Sergei and Sedat). Sergei's parents chose not to participate in our project, so we did not include him.

9. Pat ball is a playground game that involves knocking a tennis ball against a wall with the hand (as opposed to soccer).

10. Sebastian was eloquent about the difficulty of negotiating potentially hurtful social interactions: "My parents actually told me that when I went to the secondary school, they said everyone's going to be really cruel. And I try not to be cruel, but sometimes if someone's nosey, you'll just be mean to them."

11. See Thorne (1994).

12. From their school grades, it seems that the friendship groupings were not necessarily homogeneous by grades, although Sara and Giselle both got high grades. The mix of grades within the other groupings is striking. It should also be noted that the class was divided for their academic work, so friends from the class may not have been pursuing the same homework tasks.

13. The question "Who do you spend time with online?" more or less mirrors the pattern of chatting via digital technologies, although the network is a little less connected.

14. The boys on the periphery included Joel, Sergei, and the new boy Deyan, although Deyan was building connections fast, with nearly 400 Facebook friends, for instance, by his second term in the school.

15. Reich et al. (2012) compared the overlap in teenagers' friends for friendships maintained face-to-face, through social networking sites, or by instant messaging. Most online contacts are already known offline, and for the most part, teenagers used online communication to reinforce offline friendships; but there was far from total overlap in the friends contacted in each of these three ways.

16. Clark (2005).

17. Ling (2008).

18. Leurs (2014).

19. In an ego network, the respondent answers the same questions as for the whole-class network; but answers are open-ended, so they can answer about anybody they wish. This then reveals the social world as seen by the individual.

20. We have not labeled these young people "the cool kids" in the way some American readers suggested they might be, partly because they did not call themselves this and partly because of the contested conceptions of what might count as "cool" by others in this network. For further discussion, see Eckert (1989), Murray (2004), and Ito et al. (2010).

21. Their communication problem was linguistic—it seemed that Jenna's mother had worked to bring up her older two daughters speaking her language but had lost the energy for Jenna and her little brother; nor had she managed to learn much English since arriving in the UK, although this is not to say that the family lacked warmth or understanding.

22. Pottermore is a privately owned website, a collaboration between Sony and the author of the *Harry Potter* series, J. K. Rowling. It contrasts with the Harry Potter Alliance, a website run by fans, which offers considerably more creativity, interactivity, and community organizing. See Jenkins (2012).

23. Jenkins (2006).

24. At the time of writing, two of the most popular crossover child/adult book series were Suzanne Collins's trilogy *The Hunger Games* and J. K. Rowling's seven-book *Harry Potter* series, centered on life at Hogwarts School of Witchcraft and Wizardry.

25. Ling (2008, p. 182) characterizes such social worlds as offering "bounded solidarity," situations of reciprocal affirmation that close off ties to the wider network. Horst (2010b) talks of the ways in which teenagers segment their social world, employ tactics to suspend connections, or reduce integration as part of the continual dynamics of power in the family—and, we might add, the school and peer group.

26. For more on this important theme, see Silverstone (2005) and Siapera (2014).

27. By contrast, Yusuf attended a mosque school twice a week but, unlike Sedat, did not use this experience as a means of socializing, making it clear that he did not hang out or see the students from that school in his leisure time.

28. See Strand et al. (2010).

29. See Witteborn (2012). In ethnographic research on the communicative practices of migrants, Witteborn observes how they talk of "connecting" in several ways, when referring to Facebook and other online practices: to mean reaching distant others, engaging with diverse ideas, participating in communities of interest, positioning themselves in relation to others. These practices she calls "translocal," following Kraidy and Murphy (2008). See also Madianou and Miller (2012).

30. Licoppe (2004).

31. Dom, for instance, put "the cricket team" in his ego network, while Gideon wrote "cousins" in his. The categories also blur boundaries. "In school" groups together those in the class and those across the year group, with most of the young people having more friends from across the year group than within the class. "Out of school" combines nuclear and extended family, out-of-school friends, neighbors, and both adults and children known through drama or sports or other activities.

32. While this suggests a degree of contentment in family relationships, it may also underscore the fact that these were young adolescents. Possibly much was set to change in the coming years.

33. Holloway and Valentine (2000), Gill (2007).

34. See Moje (2000) for a discussion of these "levels" as ways of defining community membership.

35. Few children included in their ego networks any other adult relatives, teachers, or mentors who might introduce them to new interests or skills or diversify their social experiences. Even the names of their music or sports teachers often escaped the youngsters at the moment of recollection, suggesting that it was their role that mattered more than any more personal identity.

36. Livingstone (2002), Shaw et al. (2013).

37. Luckmann (1970).

38. Stevens et al. (2007).

39. Wellman and Rainie (2012, p. 8).

40. The theory of networked individualism is possibly more convincing in relation to adults, although the concept is intended to capture changes in society as a whole. In fairness, we note that advocates of the theory of networked individualism do not intend the conclusion that the Internet is somehow transcendent, replacing offline relations and practices. Rather, as Hogan and Wellman (2011) argue, mass use of the internet is intensifying longer-run changes toward individualization, personalized lifestyles, and the undermining of social cohesion. So, as with other theories of late modernity and the risk society, the analytic task is one of deciding whether the direction of travel has been insightfully identified by such theories, even if the pace of change is somewhat overclaimed.

41. Complexities and contingencies of economic and cultural capital are such that these small worlds do not simply ensure social reproduction of advantage or disadvantage from generation to generation (see chapters 8 and 9).

42. Although these terms are often used interchangeably, increasingly with reference to digital networks in particular, their meanings remain contested. For the OECD (2012, p. 15), connectedness "is the capacity to benefit from connectivity for personal, social, work or economic purposes." By contrast, Turkle (2011) writes of "connectivity and its discontents," lamenting that our absorption in digital technologies means that "we are increasingly connected to each other but oddly more alone" (p. 19). Differently again, van Dijck (2013a) sees connection as a matter of human communication, while connectivity is the commodification of such communication by major technology companies (for instance, transforming affiliation into "likes" and then monetizing them). At the heart of this debate is the question of whether certain values are embedded into technologically mediated networks so that their increased importance in underpinning social relations also shapes those relations.

43. On the basis of a longitudinal analysis of social networking practices among university students, Steinfeld et al. (2008, p. 434) concluded that "those with lower self-esteem gained more from their use of Facebook in terms of bridging social capital than higher self-esteem participants."

44. As social network scholars have also found for the adult population, physical location remains a crucial factor shaping social networks—not merely in determining their nature but also as a source of diversity in networks: "Place is not lost as a result of the affordances of new technologies, but place-based networks are reinforced and made persistent" (Hampton et al., 2011, p. 1046). In a survey of US teenagers, Reich et al. (2012) reached similar conclusions, finding that use of social networking sites reinforced friendships forged offline rather than significantly extending their range of contacts. See also van Cleemput (2011).

Chapter 4. Identities and Relationships

1. In chapter 1, we discussed how identity is not fixed or given but instead is continually reconstituted through discourse, individually and culturally (S. Hall, 1996; Gergen, 2009).

2. Fischer noted (1981), albeit among US adults, that in the predigital era, people claimed to have, on average, 11 friends, of whom seven people, most of them kin, were called "close."

3. In Granovetter's original (predigital) formulation (1983), weak ties were no less important than strong ties but were important for different reasons: strong ties nourish the self emotionally; weak ties build the wider network and deliver social capital by bringing the resources of a larger social network within reach.

4. Banality is important since what is taken for granted reveals the communication infrastructure (Lievrouw, 2004). Young people have come to regard technology much like any other public utility (such as electricity or water), and thus socio-

technical conventions, priorities, and standards have become embedded in the lifeworld (Star and Bowker, 2006).

5. In discussing the affordances of social network sites, d. boyd (2008) focuses on persistence (since content is recorded, always visible online, and difficult to erase), scalability (since simple interactions can be rapidly made available to vast audiences), asynchronicity (enabling tactical interaction management), replicability (permitting seamless editing and manipulation of content), and searchability (both extending and permitting specialization within networks of information and relationships). These result in uncertainty regarding the audience for any message now and in the future and the collapsing of traditional context boundaries (most notably between public and private). Baym and boyd (2012, p. 328) elaborate the consequent "socially mediated publicness": "an ever-shifting process throughout which people juggle blurred boundaries, multi-layered audiences, individual attributes, the specifics of the system they use, and the contexts of their use."

6. Hampton and Wellman (2003).

7. Strathern (1996, p. 530) writes of "cutting the network," since "in practice one does not trace connexions for ever; conversely the most intimate group is also open to discovering contacts they never knew existed."

8. In chapter 3, Gideon said, "Boys don't really have close friends. Like, it's girls that have close friends. Boys kind of all go together." His mother confirms this sense of "casual" friends: "He doesn't seem to have that many friends. I mean, he says to me—he, you know, . . . he's very popular. . . . But unlike my daughter—maybe because she's a girl, I don't know—she's always had a very little, close-knit group of friends as much as she's had wider friends, whereas Gideon doesn't seem to have had that in this school."

9. The class teacher, Catherine, describes Megan as "flying under the radar" with regard to the school's record of her "concerns" (for the school's management of "bad behavior," see chapter 5).

10. For Marwick and boyd (2014), drawing on Goffman's early analysis of social interaction in dramaturgical terms (1959), Facebook is well suited to teen drama.

11. Kupiainen (2013) argues that Facebook is a prime instance of school-based "networked publics" (Ito, 2008) for young people, making visible the school community to itself although not necessarily facilitating the "affinity spaces" (Gee, 2004a) required for more intensive or creative or civil collaboration.

12. As d. boyd (2014) argues, teenagers enjoy "social steganography" or "hiding in plain sight" by communicating with peers in technically public places yet in ways that become private in practice because the adults around them do not understand the message.

13. The point is that, for teens (and many adults), privacy matters most in relation to people you know rather than in relation to a wider or unknown public. This is often misunderstood as indicating that young people do not care about their

privacy, but the key point is that privacy means control over one's information rather than keeping that information secret from everyone. See Livingstone (2005).

14. For definitions of these types of youth subcultures, see www.urbandictionary .com; see also Ziehe (1994).

15. We develop the relationship between popular taste and identity in chapter 9.

16. Just a few years earlier, older teens were choosing Facebook, while younger teens preferred MySpace. But now, by the age of 13 or 14—the age when they were officially "allowed" on Facebook—our class was already losing interest, keeping a Facebook profile mostly as an address book to monitor action among their peers. The once "grown-up" blue-and-white layout had come to seem too straight-laced and public to be exciting or transgressive, while what teens had previously enjoyed about MySpace could now be found elsewhere on Tumblr or Instagram—notably, trying on possible selves by playing with stylized cultural tropes, decoration, and moods (Livingstone, 2008).

17. Massey uses the concept of "throwntogetherness" to capture the diverse constituencies, even the "clash of trajectories," evident in major cities such as London. But we can apply this to the experience of social networking sites. She explains, "Insofar as they 'work' at all places are still not-inconsiderable collective achievements. They are formed through a myriad of practices of quotidian negotiation and contestation; practices, moreover, through which the constituent 'identities' are also themselves continually moulded" (2005, p. 154). See also Leurs (2014) on "digital throwntogetherness."

18. However, Tumblr had become very time-consuming: "Tumblr takes up—like, it's a massive part of my life. I'm on it a lot, like . . . I can reblog up to, like, 1,000 things a day. . . . I spend up to, like, two hours doing it at a time. But say I have nothing to do, I always have Tumblr."

19. Turkle (1984).

20. This conversation took place in our final interview at the start of Year 10.

21. Facer et al. (2003) observed over a decade ago how technology contributed to "flexible childhoods" by reconfiguring how children could enter adult worlds.

22. Afro-Caribbean boys are disproportionately represented in exclusion statistics (see www.nmhdu.org.uk/silo/files/black-and-ethnic-young-education-disadvantage.pdf).

23. See www.timwoods.org/the-london-slang-dictionary-project

24. See Back (1996) and Rampton (2006).

25. Fischer (1981, p. 306).

26. Their concern was to challenge a simple binary between online and offline, especially insofar as the online is popularly seen to detract from or undermine the offline, since "online and offline spaces are dynamically co-constructed and interpolated" (Leander and McKim, 2003, p. 222; see also Horst and Miller, 2012). They draw on Miller and Slater (2000) in calling for a "connective ethnography."

27. Spencer and Pahl (2006).

28. Chambers (2013) argues that in late modernity, the relationship between intimacy and privacy is being reconfigured such that we can rely ever less on traditional ties (to family, community, or work), and so the voluntary and flexible ties of friendship are more intensely important. This may be true for adults; but for teenagers, friends have surely always been the relationship most under their control, so we see little grounds for claiming a change.

29. Anthias (2002, p. 492) makes a related point in her study of Greek Cypriot–British youth when she notes that "asking someone a question about their 'identity' often produces a blank stare, a puzzled silence or a glib and formulaic response. This is not only because research subjects have not understood the question, but also because they cannot easily provide answers."

30. These responses are collated from individual interviews. Lydia's response suggests a common way in which girls and boys delineated inner ("family") from outer circles of contacts. Images showed the profile owner in everyday or sassy poses, with smiling groups of friends, social or sporting activities, jokey memes, and occasional news items (about Obama, Kony). There was lots of visible peer support ("love you all!!," birthday wishes, exclamation marks, and smiley emoticons), although a few complaints enter the mix ("why don't you answer?"; "you're annoying"); but these were generally mild in tone, even when the jokes become rude ("faggot," "fuck off").

31. Goffman (1959), S. Hall (1996), Anthias (2002), and Elliott and du Gay (2009).

32. Cote and Levine (2002).

33. Facebook CEO Mark Zuckerberg said, "Having two identities for yourself is an example of a lack of integrity" (van Dijck, 2013b, p. 199), but young people would disagree, precisely wishing to explore and express different identities in relation to particular social groups or situations. Van Dijck critiques the supposed emphasis on personal integrity, claiming that social networking has shifted from self-expressive communication to sustain connection among people to the promotion of the idealized (and quantified) self within a corporate context driven by the monetization of connectivity. So, while users choose what personal information to curate and share, data companies are mining the signs they give off naively or unintentionally, the better to target advertising; and for this purpose, a unique identity across sites is optimal (van Dijck, 2013b, p. 202). Yet, among the 13-year-olds in the class, we saw few signs of the self as a brand, many signs of resistance to Facebook's more intrusive or determining features, and a strong sense that what matters are one's relations with a circle of more or less known peers.

34. Contradicting popular prejudices that young people care little for privacy, see Nissenbaum's contextualist conception of what is public or private (2010).

35. George and Clay (2013) note how few resources are available to the girl who is excluded by others and how problematic it is that school cultures tend to identify "the problem" in the girl rather than in wider peer dynamics.

36. At the time of writing, there was much discussion in the media of Facebook's declining popularity with teens, reminding us to focus on how young people act

and interact as much as on the particularities of any one platform. See, for example, www.huffingtonpost.com/2013/10/23/facebooks-teen-trouble-in_n_4150940 .html.

37. "Continual copresence" means even when people are physically apart; see Gergen (2002).

38. Bolter and Grusin (1999) argue that as a new medium of communication becomes commonplace, the social significance of already-established media is altered. But this is not to say that face-to-face communication is displaced by digital communication (as argued most recently by Turkle, 2015); indeed, one interpretation is that it thereby gains a greater intensity of meaning.

39. This is not to say, however, that social networking sites can always be made to work in young people's best interests. Aiden's story reminds us that online activities can be recuperated within established practices of control and supervision.

40. We observed the interactions on the class's Facebook profiles over a period of several weeks. The young people seemed to prioritize a generally courteous to-and-fro of posts, likes, and brief comments, with most posts receiving little or no comment. Moreover, few interactions involved more than a handful of turns, and few of the several hundred contacts were in active communication.

41. There were anomalies: although Adam was connected to the core group in our analysis, his actual friendship behaviors as gleaned from interviews really revolved around his ego network, with less interest expressed in the class; Adriana's life was more separate, too, due to her frequent visits to the family home in Spain.

42. As d. boyd (2014, p. x) comments, her study was inspired by the fact that "teens' voices rarely shaped the public discourse surrounding their networked lives."

Chapter 5. Life at School

1. See, for example, the essays collected in Albright and Luke (2008), N. Rose (1999), and Ball (2013).

2. Elias (2000).

3. Wessendorf (2014, p. 392).

4. As R. Boyd (2006, p. 863) argues, "contrary to the many critics who see civility as a conservative or nostalgic virtue deployed to repress difference and frustrate change, it is argued that civility should be understood as democratic, pluralistic and premised on a sense of moral equality," especially in the contemporary city. Contini and Maturo (2010, p. 1544) put the positive case for civility yet more urgently: "school can have an important role in the development of cross-cultural competences, in the formation of social bonds and flexible and inclusive belonging and in the building of a multiple and shared citizenship, that implies the recognition of individual rights and universal values, to promote the living together in a multiethnic society."

5. A report on young people's social networks for the Department for Education (DfE 2008) found that most students had a lot of friends, largely from the same school, and that those with fewer friends in school also had fewer friends out of school.

6. There are exceptions to this principle, especially for young people with designated special educational needs and also if siblings already attend the school, but in general, it is the idea of neighborhood that underpins the principles of selection. The school used a form of rough ability banding to select pupils of different abilities and also to mix up (but also to sustain a few paired friendships) from the young person's first school at primary or elementary level.

7. There were a few tower blocks in the locality, but most social housing and private rented properties were in low-build estates usually interspersed with privately owned houses.

8. The view—clearly endorsed by VFS—that teachers should identify and prevent "classroom incivility" is articulated by, for instance, Feldmann (2001). Yet, as classroom ethnographies have long shown (Erickson, 1984), such efforts risk teaching middle-class children to "play the game" while provoking poorer or minority ethnic children into tactics of resistance.

9. In relation to Toby especially, although arguably Lydia also, we could call this, following Goffman (1966), "civil inattention." Cahill (1987) examines how children are taught the subtleties of the deliberate withdrawal of attention as a tactic to demonstrate unobtrusive recognition of the other.

10. See Sefton-Green (2015).

11. See Pahl (2000). In practice, a range of words is available although not in common use among teenagers. Heil (2014) discusses discourses of conviviality, cohabitation, and neighborliness, for instance, as ways of instantiating equality and respect for others. As his ethnography reveals, such discourses must be continually enacted through practices of interaction, negotiation, and translation, as the configurations they facilitate remain fragile, with cooperation always liable to give way to conflict. See also Wessendorf (2014).

12. Amin (2012); see also Sennett (2012).

13. As this teacher went on to explain, dealing with trouble from the children spilling over into school was one thing, but it was far worse when the parents became involved. For the teachers charged with welfare responsibilities, home life impinged on life at school in a host of problematic ways: students smuggling distracting or disruptive devices into class, "inadequately parented" teenagers being unpleasant to each other online, angry parents complaining to the school, addicted teens staying up too late gaming or social networking and so missing homework or school. As more and more of teachers' time was taken up with untangling conflicts, checking screen shots of claimed hostilities, or even calling in the police, it is no wonder that they saw digital technologies—and the out-of-school lives of the young people that they represented—as a problem to be

controlled rather than an opportunity to be harnessed constructively. Such difficulties led Grant (2011) to advocate the creation of "virtual third spaces" where a compromise between the logics of home and school learning might be reached. See also Crook (2011), Attewell et al. (2009), and Cramer and Hayes (2010).

14. See Ecclestone and Hayes (2008) for an extended critique of the extension of therapeutic discourses into educational settings.

15. It used to be the children's news program *BBC Newsround*, but now the class demanded "adult news" (as Gideon said, *Newsround* "was all about penguins").

16. Hochschild (1979) captures the kind of "emotional labor" that Catherine does here in her analysis of how "work" increasingly demands a performance of the private self for the benefit of others.

17. On that day, a teaching assistant was holding the fort in Catherine's absence.

18. See K. Jones (2009) for an analysis of how, in late modernity, popular culture now stands in for common culture, especially that formed by collective class experiences, in English schools, identified by earlier theorists such as Williams (1961b) and Hoggart (1969). There is, in any case, no way to keep the world beyond the school out of the classroom, as Wortham (2005, p. 1) argues: not only do the "social identification, power relations and interpersonal struggles" of daily life occur in the classroom as anywhere else, but they intersect with the academic learning that also occurs there. Wortham is particularly interested in the explicit and "common pedagogical strategy of building an analogy between students' actual or hypothetical experiences and the curricular topic" (p. 2). Since building these analogies is doubly hazardous—both because the teachers know little of the students' lives at home and because these are themselves very diverse—popular culture is often positioned as a shared body of experience by which teachers can bridge what students are presumed to know already and what they need to learn.

19. The use of popular culture genres such as *X Factor* in class can be appreciated as a step toward what Ladson-Billings (1995) calls "culturally relevant pedagogy." But the practice is criticized by Lefstein and Snell (2011). Their detailed linguistic ethnographic observation showed, on the one hand, that the practice was motivating to the students, encouraging them to participate, but, on the other hand, that when the genre of the show took the lesson away from its pedagogic objectives, a degree of contestation and messiness entered that confused the learning. Most interesting is that, in the lesson Lefstein and Snell analyzed, the loudest students were those who usually dominated; so this teaching strategy did not manage to include otherwise marginalized students.

20. The gap between popular culture references selected by teachers and those favored by students is, in itself, indicative of the difficulties inherent in trying to build a shared framework from a teacher-led perspective. As Dover (2007) found, in her ethnographic study of playground talk, children talk about popular culture constantly; it is just that they pick their own references, for their own purposes.

21. Alvermann (2012) contests this normative distinction, while noting its widespread endorsement by teachers, especially insofar as digital literacies may enable students to find pleasure in "high culture," making it "popular." See also Jenkins and Kelley (2013).

22. Such critical knowledge is often lacking from classroom discussions that draw on popular culture (L. Hall, 2012). While it should especially come from media studies, although as an optional subject, for older students, such debates are not usually part of the common curriculum. See also Buckingham (2004).

23. See http://en.wikipedia.org/wiki/Black_History_Month.

24. Seiter (2005) observes how often teachers avoid "teachable moments" because of their expectations of what the children should value, which often exclude the messy and conflictual realities. She cites Audrey Thompson (1998) on the "color-blind" model of teaching adopted by teachers that ignores the class's experiences of race and racism, saying, "It is a disservice to students to exclude from classroom discussion issues of class and race that they are negotiating throughout their everyday lives" (p. 24).

25. This idea is suggested by studies such as O'Hear and Sefton-Green (2004), National School Boards Association (2007), Thomas (2011).

26. Willis (1978).

27. Personal, Social and Health Education, taught once a week, a subject that included formal civics.

28. Blackberry Messenger, a form of instant messaging via Blackberry smartphones that was popular among teenagers at the time.

29. The school always returned confiscated phones at the end of each week.

30. Cahill (1987) would call this "ceremonial deviance," the point being that while Megan and Adriana push the boundaries of classroom behavior as far as they can, they do not transgress too far; thus, they sustain their independent image for themselves and the class without this being overtly challenged or having to leave the situation.

31. Several of the scholars cited earlier in the chapter are eloquent on the positive pleasures of civility; see, for instance, Sennett (2012) for a careful critique of Elias's critique of self-restraint.

32. As R. Boyd (2006, p. 870) reminds us, civility encompasses an acknowledgment of distance and difference without entailing intimacy or strong obligations. Rather, it merely—but importantly—allows "diverse populations to live side-by-side in mutual peace and accommodation." As the school recognized, this goes beyond mere tolerance and, rather, requires continual, if small, displays of mutual respect. For Calhoun (2000), civility must be visibly communicated or displayed if it is to be more than mere tolerance; regulating visible behaviors was a matter that the school took seriously, irrespective of how the students might feel "underneath."

33. We might note that the school was tacitly supported in this effort by the wider culture. As Watson and Saha (2013, p. 2020) put it, drawing on Stuart Hall's

earlier work, in the 21st century, "multicultural drift . . . captures the sense of an ordinary, humdrum and lackadaisical set of changes that are neither dramatic nor exoticized, but that take place in a willy-nilly, quiet and hotchpotch way in suburbs across British cities." In other words, it is becoming ordinary for diverse cultures to live in close proximity, with some tensions, some shared pleasures—a kind of "mundane multiculturalism" that suggests little to celebrate but no great failure either.

34. We refer to the work of Michel de Certeau here (1984), as he proffered an analysis of the tactics people use in everyday life to resist and negotiate dominant order across many levels of social activities.

35. There are many studies exploring this theme; see, for example, Reay (2006).

36. Recall Catherine's comment about Megan (in chapter 4) that she managed to stay "under the radar" with regard to gaining "concerns," despite her poor record of attendance and homework completion. Catherine presented this as a matter of Megan's skill in not attracting teacher disapproval rather than reflecting on what this meant about the school's differential treatment of students from wealthier and poorer homes. Such injustices did not escape the young people themselves. As the middle-class Dominic told us, "Like with Shane, because he used to be really badly behaved, like last year, like teachers would think the worst of him. Like, if something's happened, they would usually blame Shane."

37. There is a vast literature on school failure, so here we just note the more ethnographic studies that influenced our thinking: Hargreaves (1967), MacLeod (2009), and Willis (1978).

38. This is not the place to develop an analysis of such various concepts, but it is noteworthy how many scholars (several of them cited in this chapter) are devoting their intellectual and normative efforts toward forms of communality or solidarity as the historical process of individualization advances.

Chapter 6. Learning at School

1. Levinson et al. (1996).

2. By "learner identity," we refer to how forms of social identification become part and parcel of academic learning. A school is both a formal institution to ensure learning and also a particular social context with its own norms, habits, and ways of being. Students' identities are constructed in part through the ways that their teachers refer to them or group them in particular ways and through the ways that students in turn enact certain identities within the classroom. See Wortham (2005).

3. See also the current interest in the idea of the quantified self, the counting and display of one's diet, health, sleep, and other dimensions of daily life; see Lupton (2014); see also http://quantifiedself.com. Although the quantified self is generally thought of as voluntary rather than imposed, what surprised us was how accepting the students were of the quantification of their learning.

4. This seepage into gaming and from gaming into learning lies behind some of the principles of gamification—turning and using structured games play in education; see, for example, http://badgeville.com/wiki/case_studies.
5. National curriculum testing in terms of levels was introduced in 1991 by the UK's now defunct National Assessment Agency (NAA) arm of the Qualification and Curriculum Authority (QCA); see www.nfer.ac.uk/shadomx/apps/fms/fmsdownload.cfm?file_uuid=67EAAF91-C29E-AD4D-07F1-A9373EA17105&siteName=nfer. Each subject was divided into core elements: for example, English was divided into Reading, Writing, and Speaking and Listening; and Music into Performing, Composing, and Listening. Criteria defining attainment were specified for each element for each of ten levels, with each level further subdivided into a, b, and c. In principle, students in Year 9 were meant to achieve between levels 5 and 7. In practice, at VFS, the ability range stretched from 4 to 8. A degree of complexity entered when creating the overall scale, since "a" was higher than "c" but 6 higher than 5. This meant that, for example, students in the class might be striving to rise from 5b to 5a and then to 6c followed by 6b, 6a, and then 7c.
6. Certain kinds of school were exempt, but not VFS.
7. iLearning is otherwise known as ICT (information, communication, and technology).
8. There is a further level of confusion in that in Year 10 students start their GCSE courses, and these have a different form of grading (A, B, C, etc.) that map onto levels 8 to 10—an additional dimension that bothered some parents during their meetings on Progress Day.
9. Recall the exhortation to "shine" through outside achievements that Catherine urged on all the young people on Progress Day (see chapter 2).
10. Eisner (2004).
11. Watkins (2011).
12. SIMS stands for "school information management system" (see www.capita-sims.co.uk). The technology was developed and is owned by Capita, one of the largest private providers in the UK education market. This ever-growing and never-forgetting system of record keeping integrated detailed accounts of incidents during lesson times with other information held about students by the school: their family structure, special needs, or the involvement of social services, as well as correspondence between the school and the home. Other systems include IsisBehave (formerly iBehave). The normative expectation, among educational policy makers, is that such a system can support improved teacher and school decision making; see Breiter and Light (2006).
13. While in theory the young person's family could access student records, and Catherine told us that this was the school's original plan, this does not seem to have happened at VFS (and as Catherine hinted further, it would have necessitated the teachers rewriting a number of the entries for public consumption).

14. During each lesson or immediately after, teachers entered commendations and concerns into their computers. Some wrote the names of students deserving of punishment or reward on the white board during lessons. These might be transcribed later into SIMS, but sometimes they merely acted as a form of visible control during the lesson. Alongside this system of recording good and/or poor performance, lesson teachers would also record formal attainment in terms of levels.

15. Badges (gold, silver, bronze) were awarded for 150, 100, or 50 commendations, respectively, and were announced to all in the school's newsletter.

16. As we discovered, teachers generally lacked the time or skill to exploit the wealth of information available. They were intrigued, for instance, that we, as researchers, managed to calculate levels across subjects in order to track the class's progress by socioeconomic background. Although we did not inquire at the time into the legal and ethical aspects of this information management, as such systems raise issues in regard to student and parent rights to access or correct information and about how schools manage privacy rights within the school or with the software provider. Interestingly, by the time of writing, a US equivalent of SIMS, inBloom, was unceremoniously closed down due to legal privacy concerns. See Herold 2014 and Balkam 2014.

17. Green and Luke (2006).

18. See Alexander (2009), among others, for an extended critique of how the management of schools is negatively affecting attention to questions of curriculum and developing learning.

19. Leander et al. (2010) talks of the traditional model as instantiating the "container classroom," for instance, noting that this is now challenged by mobile technologies.

20. Bruner (1996), M. Rose (2009).

21. See, for example, projects led by Brenton Doecke examining teachers' professional identity in Australia: National Mapping of Teacher Professional Learning project, http://apo.org.au/research/national-mapping-teacher-professional -learning.

22. Chouliaraki (1998, p. 6) observed a parallel process in a UK classroom some 20 years ago in relation to the then-progressivist discourse of child-centered pedagogy, when she found that "individualized talk did not serve the pedagogic purpose of 'fine tuning.' Instead, it had primarily, a *regulative function* in (a) controlling each pupil's rate and quality of activity, and (b) constructing pedagogic knowledges which avoided content input and emphasized procedural tasks."

23. For an account of digital affordances, see Lievrouw and Livingstone (2006). For an account of the "mediatization of education," see Rawolle and Lingard (2014). What remains unknown is how such data systems, likely to become more rather than less common, will develop in the future. Perrotta (2013, p. 119) is pessimistic, arguing that "powerful techniques to manipulate data can be easily co-opted to serve the restrictive frameworks of competitive, hyper-controlling, managerial accountability that characterise current cultures of summative assessment in

many countries." By contrast, Visscher et al. (2003) were disappointed to find that school information systems are more often used for clerical rather than strategic educational purposes.

24. This practice was not universally approved, especially when coming from an unpopular teacher. As Salma told us of a teacher she disliked, "He always tells us, 'Oh, you're underachieving your level,' like, 'You're not doing your level good,' and he just like tells everyone in front of everyone. It's like embarrassing. It's just rude."

25. Chouliaraki (1998) here cites Bernstein (1990) on how an "empty" discourse sustains an institutional order—in this case, in the school—that is cut off from any relation to actual learning, supposedly the primary purpose of the institution. Hence, talk of levels in the class becomes ritualistic, meaningful within the classroom but disconnected from an engagement with knowledge.

26. See the arguments in Schuller and Desjardins (2007). A critical argument that school is "colonizing" the domestic lifeworld is pursued by Nocon and Cole (2006).

27. Levinson et al. (1996).

28. Ito et al. (2013).

29. Just a few months after we said goodbye to the class, the UK's Department for Education announced the abolition of levels in the national curriculum for all schools in England starting in 2014, stating, "We believe this system is complicated and difficult to understand, especially for parents. It also encourages teachers to focus on a pupil's current level, rather than consider more broadly what the pupil can actually do" (DfE, 2013a). Exactly how policy and practice unfold—and how far these reflect political struggles between government and the education profession—is beyond the scope of this book. Certainly our fieldwork year coincided with an ambitious secretary of state for education, determined to change the British school system substantially during his tenure. This particular change positions much of what we have documented in this chapter as potentially wasted with regard to both teachers' efforts and, more significantly, the students' sincere attempts to construct their learner identities in the ways required of them by the school. It is as yet unclear what more stable set of practices might replace those we observed or how this pronouncement will impact on inspection regimes, which in themselves are far more influential than policy speeches in determining what actually happens in schools. But at the time of writing, it was already clear that changing so entrenched a culture of learning was proving a struggle for many schools (Commission on Assessment without Levels, 2015).

Chapter 7. Life at Home Together and Apart

1. As discussed in chapter 1, for many children, the notions of family, household and home do not necessarily coincide. See Livingstone (2002).

2. This is partly because teachers fear that the many hours spent with screen media at home undermines children's concentration, their academic interests, and even their skills in writing. See Common Sense Media (2012).

3. See Morley (2000), Hoover et al. (2004), and Brooks (2011).

4. As J. Thompson (2011) observes, what we call private spaces are defined less by their physical spatiality than by the contextual norms that define their accessibility and visibility. See also Cunningham (1995).

5. Children's tactics should not be interpreted in cynical or manipulative terms; tactics are, more simply, the means available to those who lack the power to intervene in more systematic or structural ways. As Corsaro (1997) shows, children's tactics are often creative or witty, and they may also be effective in renegotiating the domestic environment. See also Brannen (2005), de Certeau (1984).

6. Over the past century, the media have adapted to these domestic concerns, seeking to accommodate family preferences in order to better shape and profit from them. But it is important to see media goods and contents not simply in the terms of their developers, distributors, or marketers but, rather, to inquire into how households appropriate and make sense of them in their own particular cultural and personal contexts. Domestication theory emphasizes the active, interpretative work that goes into the temporal, spatial, social, and material conditions of "home," including the ways that media technologies are appropriated and made meaningful so as to sustain particular interests and meanings. See Buckingham (2000), Livingstone (2002), Oswell (2002), and Berker et al. (2006).

7. We did not discover whether this was a matter of religious prohibition, poverty, or aesthetics.

8. This is not to say that Jenna was neglected; her mother was ambitious for all the girls. Impressively the older sisters were gaining university degrees, and Jenna had a tutor for math and English because, she said, "my mum wants us to be best at stuff." As researchers of immigrant families have shown, having parents less attuned to the host culture can offer children particular power in brokering (via language or media) the community or state resources required by their parents. Katz (2010) draws on family systems theory—the notion that a family is more than the sum of its parts and, further, that it is self-organizing in its dynamics—to examine how migrant families seek to balance the need for intimacy, on the one hand, and differentiation or mutual independence, on the other.

9. The pattern of "practically perfect" older siblings, as understood in the family discourse, was a challenge for several members of the class.

10. As we often had cause to reflect, the young people's initial interests frequently stopped, with few new interests sustained to the point where they became self-organized or part of the young people's identity and core motivation, as this takes considerable resourcing over time from the family, school, or community. See Hidi and Renninger (2006). Parents tended to identify the transition to secondary school as a moment when the development of interests was disrupted, either because the young people embraced change as part of growing up or because peer support was lost or because institutional provision was age related.

11. As Fiese and Sameroff (1999, p. 3) put it, "family narratives move beyond the individual and deal with how the family makes sense of its world, expresses rules of interaction, and creates beliefs about relationships." Bohanek et al. (2006, p. 41) explore how family narratives are important for young adolescents, who are concerned to create "self-continuity and a more complex sense of self."

12. Rather speculatively, we would note that both Abby and Lydia at this age were rather overweight, mixed-race (white/Afro-Caribbean) girls with a past prowess in sports who had experienced difficulties with their peers since the transition to secondary school. This parallel made us want to ask whether sporty girls encounter particular problems in adolescence for failing to fit the gendered norms of their peers.

13. For example, the clinical psychologist Steiner-Adair (2013) articulates a host of popular anxieties in her guide to parents, *The Big Disconnect: Protecting Childhood and Family Relationships in the Digital Age*. She worries that screens are "sucking us in," making us all addicted, as we all fight over digital devices, with misunderstandings becoming endemic as we prioritize our relationships with technology over our relationships with each other. Interestingly, however, her suggestion of developing "a family philosophy about using [technology] that reflects and supports the family's values and well-being" (p. 269) echoes the conclusions of Hoover et al. (2004) from their in-depth studies of mediated family life, as well as a strategy often attempted by the parents of the class.

14. Scannell (1988), Spigel (1992), Flichy (1995).

15. Bedroom culture was originally analyzed by McRobbie and Garber (1976). See also Steele and Brown (1994) and Bovill and Livingstone (2001). For an artistic exploration of girls' rooms, see http://bankstreet.edu/occasional-paper-series/30/out-of-school-at-home/a-girl-and-her-room/. Such an analysis builds on the importance of lifestyle in late modern societies. See Ziehe (1994).

16. This analysis follows Livingstone (2002).

17. As Pugh (2009) observed in her ethnography of American families, poorer families tend to invest in "symbolic indulgence," while wealthier families tend to practice "symbolic deprivation."

18. Livingstone and Helsper (2008).

19. To counterbalance this increase in individual access to the internet, Adriana's father installed parental controls on all the computers, which he monitored actively. So had Dom's father, while Salma's father kept an eye on her computer use (by "friending" her on Facebook, checking her "history," etc.).

20. This use of Skype is emerging as common practice for sustaining geographically separated families; see Madianou and Miller (2012). For the notion of digitally mediated copresence, see Baym (2015).

21. She told us, "My relationship to it I would've said wasn't blocked at all because I'm quite . . . because of the whole art thing, you tend to be open to different media, you tend to be looking for cross relationships. But I'm aware of having, sort of, compartmentalized what he does as a different—which I'm not pleased. . . . It's one of the reasons I let you into the house is because I don't really like that

attitude in myself." For her, the research project was an opportunity to reflect on how her role in the family had become one of mediating between Adam and his father, as Adam grows up, no longer a child for whom, she said, "we dictated what he was doing, and we decided what he could and couldn't have."

22. As Horst (2010a) observes from her fieldwork with families, this "coming to-gether" need not be tightly planned by the parents but, rather, is subtly orches-trated by creating flexible places in the home and casual times in the family schedule so that they can "hang out" or "mess around" or even "geek out" (p. 171) with their kids as a shared pleasure.

23. Turkle (2011, p. 19); see also Steiner-Adair (2013) and Turkle (2015).

24. Flichy (1995, p. 158).

25. On the basis of an in-depth study of 46 American families, Clark (2013) showed how families draw on public scripts or discourses about media effects that guide their appropriation of new media at home, including the ways in which they consider themselves accountable—to researchers, to their children, to themselves. She argues that our society as a whole values the ethic of expressive empowerment over the ethic of respectful connectedness, so that the privileged children's media uses resonate with other institutions, unlike those of the poorer families, thereby exacerbating social inequalities. The resonance works in both directions; the "moral economy of the household" (Silverstone et al., 1992, p. 9) also has implications for the wider society. The irony, as Clark points out, is that the middle-class families find themselves envious of the respectful connectedness and warmth in the working-class families but cannot give up on their competi-tive, individualistic aspirations sufficiently to emulate those families more closely or even to recognize the hidden costs of their high-stress lifestyles.

26. Clark's (2013) research also showed how American parents' time-poor lifestyles lead them to create media-rich homes. But their children are often less time-poor, so digital media provide a workaround given their heavily regulated access to spaces outside (and, indeed, within) the home or school, permitting a pathway to a certain kind of independence. See also Boneva et al. (2006).

27. Taylor and Harper (2002).

28. Flichy (1995).

29. Giddens (1993, p. 184); see also Beck and Beck-Gernsheim (2002).

30. Hence the notion of "quality time"; see Brannen (2005) and Kremer-Sadlik et al. (2008). See also Robinson and Schulz (2013). Indeed, Gutiérrez et al. (2010) worry that children, especially the children of working middle-class families, have little unstructured time at all to play or be creative.

31. Wingard and Forsberg (2009). There are cultural variations in the meanings and uses of time. See also Kremer-Sadlik et al. (2010).

Chapter 8. Making Space for Learning in the Home

1. Ball (2007); see also Skelton and Francis (2012).

2. Buckingham (2007), Selwyn (2013).

3. Brown et al. (2011).
4. See Bradbrook et al. (2008), US Department of Education (2010), Luckin et al. (2012), OECD (2012), European Schoolnet (2013), and Aspen Institute (2014).
5. Paus-Hasebrink et al. (2012); see also Halford and Savage (2010) and Warschauer and Matuchniak (2010).
6. For the notion of cultural capital, see Bourdieu (1984). For an extended analysis of cultural capital in the British context, see Bennett et al. (2009). For critical analysis of the idea of cultural capital, see Fine (2000).
7. Annette Lareau's book was first published in 2003, with a ten-year update on the families published in 2011. See also Hey (2005), Pugh (2009), and Clark (2013).
8. Over the past four decades, family spending on so-called enrichment activities for their children has risen only slightly for those in the bottom income quintile, compared with a nearly three-fold increase among those in the top quintile. Inequalities, therefore, are to be found not only in the absolute level of expenditure (which is itself substantial) but also in the growing gap between the richest and poorest families. For US data, see Ito et al. (2013). For UK data, see Holloway and Pimlott-Wilson (2014).
9. See, for example, Facer et al. (2003), Becta (2009), and Davies and Eynon (2013).
10. As Clark et al. (2005, p. 421) have observed, technology is popularly associated with particularly individualistic notions of "success," with parents "adopting the familiar rhetoric linking access to ICTs [information communication technologies] and their appropriate, industrious use to the ability to prosper in an information-based society."
11. She did not cite any examples, knowing only the general principles. We would note, for example, Gee (2004b), Salen (2008), and also the Quest to Learn schools, at http://q2l.org.
12. Warschauer (2006) compared information literacy practices among students Sara's age and younger in more and less privileged schools. In the more privileged schools, some sophisticated practices were already in evidence, with students learning to search and evaluate a range of primary sources to produce an integrated result. In the less privileged schools, however, students would simply take the first source from a Google search and cut and paste the information into their assignment. Similar findings regarding students' instrumental searching were obtained by Rye (2013).
13. As Hammerberg (2004, p. 375–376) observes, "the training of independence is closely related to levelled curricular outcomes and a sense of what is 'meaningful' in terms of cognitive, psychological goals," adding that such training values "techniques for operating on the self in ways that appear independent, authentic, or meaningful [but] are, instead, rigorously trained and curricular."
14. The term is from Giddens (1991). See also the discussion in Archer et al. (2010, ch. 4). See Buchner (1990).
15. Other studies confirm that this is a largely middle-class phenomenon. See Schwartz and Arena (2013).

16. The term "habitus" is most associated with Bourdieu (1990) and is usually taken to describe the relatively stable and taken-for-granted mix of values, dispositions, and expectations of social groups that arise from the experiences and activities of everyday life.

17. See, for example, Brown et al. 2011.

18. As Lareau (2011, p. 3) says of working-class families, "for them, the crucial responsibilities of parenthood do not lie in eliciting their children's feelings, opinions, and thoughts." Rather, they instantiate a strong boundary between child and adult and issue directives rather than trying to persuade their children of desired actions. The result is that "the cultural logic of child rearing at home is out of synch with the standards of institutions" (ibid.).

19. As Chin and Phillips (2004) have also observed, while there are, indeed, social class inequalities in parents' ability to support their children's development of interests and skills, this should not be interpreted as evidence of differential desire: poorer parents may share wealthier parents' wish to support their children but lack the finances or know-how to do so effectively.

20. In chapter 2, we described how, on Progress Day, Catherine met each parent with his or her child for an intensive ten-minute discussion to review academic attainment, in-school behavior, and extracurricular activities. As we observed, this meeting was fraught in a number of ways. Parents often did not understand the system of levels by which attainment was measured (see chapter 6). Nor did they always accept the school's account of their child's behavior, with parents aware of the personal extenuating circumstances that teachers might not know or take into consideration. This made us all the more surprised when teacher and parent teamed up to exhort the young people to take on more so as to "realize their potential" and "shine" at school, in the face of marked reluctance from the young people themselves. We interpreted this partly as a manifestation of the young people's desire to protect their "free time" and also as reflecting their awareness of how an informal and pleasurable learning activity could be transformed by fitting it into the calculus of the school—with commendations, public commentary, and pressurizing exhortations to achieve more.

21. This level of extracurricular activities among poorer families is not insignificant, however. As Robinson and Schulz (2013, p. 545) concluded from their US-based research on ICT use, "insufficient attention has been paid to disadvantaged families . . . [for] parents from all socio-economic backgrounds can take an active interest in guiding their children's ICT use for capital-enhancing activities." In general, boys' engagement in sports acts as a leveler, with music and performance activities being more likely to differentiate middle- from working-class children.

22. Examples of such innovative visions and policies can be found in US Department of Education (2010), Thomas (2011), Facer (2012), Ito et al. (2013), and Aspen Institute (2014).

23. We note that research evaluating the provision of computers and internet access to poorer homes has recorded a range of benefits including improved engage-

ment with homework, more independent learning, and better ICT skills and confidence in the classroom. See Jewitt and Parashar (2011).

24. Grant (2011).

25. Bernstein (1990).

26. Despite much policy speculation about educational blogs adding a more creative, deep, or experimental dimension to the learning experience, those we checked out mainly provided revision materials, ways of uploading completed worksheets, or extra "fun facts." Such blogs will possibly take a more innovative direction in the future. See, for example, Ozcinar and Ekizoglu (2013). Also optimistic in their conclusions are McLeod and Vasinda (2009), whose evaluation of digital portfolios found that teachers gained insights into each child as a learner while parents gained a window into their child's classroom experience. See also Selwyn (2009) for an analysis of the disjunction between formal education and everyday uses of digital media.

27. Writing in the early days of the internet, Hallgarten (2000) calls for a future for the home-school relationship in which, rather than expecting parents to adapt to the institutional demands of school, schools put effort into adapting to parents. He argues further that this would require a fundamental shift on the part of the school from a command-and-control to a relational norm, one that treats parents as citizens who, along with the school, are surely committed to the best interests of their child.

28. European Schoolnet (2013, p. 10). Similar conclusions are reached by Selwyn et al. (2011). Passey (2014) reviews recent research showing how parents can support their children's school learning if they, themselves, are also supported by the school, regretting that this too rarely occurs in a constructive manner.

29. Grant (2011, p. 297).

30. As Rideout (2014) has showed in the US, parents reach varying conclusions about which media are educational for their children and why.

Chapter 9. Learning to Play Music

1. We drew particularly on Wortham (2005) for the notion of learning identity to capture the often-intangible mix of personal, social, academic, and nonacademic influences that combine to create a particular sense of oneself as a learner at any moment in time.

2. Scholars have examined the value of participating in sporting activities both intrinsically and in comparison with arts activities (for an overview, see Catterall, 2009). Participation in sports (mainly football) was important for a few boys in the class, but in a British context, sports do not offer the same range of institutions, practices, and domains as music did for the class. Music not only offered a way to explore tensions between academic and popular culture but, even more than sports, raises questions about equity and access by families.

3. See Bennett et al. (2009) for an analysis of the relationship between economic, social, and cultural capital.

4. As Kassabian says (2013), the experience of "ubiquitous music" is how we feel connection with others in the abstract, and that, over and above forms of direct engagement with particular others, is important to people. Finney (2011) takes the case of music as a paramount instance of the incompatibility between the standardized, top-down, assessment-led approach to teaching typical of English schools in the early 21st century and the progressive, child-centered tradition that can—although does not always—characterize out-of-school experiences of musical pleasures and music learning.

5. It may be noted that these groupings by music taste map partially onto the network diagram shown in chapter 3.

6. On a grade scale from 1 to 8, Grade 5 is taken to be equivalent to GCSE level (i.e., the level of attainment expected of 16-year-olds), and Grade 8 is recognized as a qualification in the university entrance procedures. See Green (2002) for an extended study of the relationships between informal music learning/playing and attainment of formal qualifications. Green argues that informal music leaning is based on different traditions of musicianship that may be as valuable and inspiring as more traditional ways of teaching music.

7. The Connected Learning Research Network, which funded the research on which this book is based, makes the case that interest-driven learning lies at the heart of connected learning, that finding ways to engage learners in authentic and "deep" ways and to build learning on the basis of their interests wherever these might lie is central to developing an a better education system. See Ito et al. (2013). Azevedo (2013) distinguishes between personal interest, as a way of describing a person's long-term disposition to engage in practices, and interest-based participation in activities that make up these larger practices. This distinction points to the ways that individuals learn to participate in what he calls "lines of practice" and hints at the ways that engaging in short-term activities do and do not build into longer, deeper, and wider practices.

8. See Lareau's notion of "concerted cultivation" (2011).

9. For reasons of space, we do not tell the stories of Alice, Sara, or Sebastian but note here that Alice's and Sara's experiences of music learning most closely resemble those of Max, while Sebastian's pleasure in improvisational work in his drama/singing group bears similarities with Giselle's experience. There is also a story to be told about the young people who began but then gave up learning music; Abby's is perhaps the most interesting case, and we briefly discuss her experiences in chapter 10. For Sara, learning the clarinet proved one of the domains in which she realized her limitations (as discussed in chapter 8), but she was now enjoying singing in the school choir.

10. As any learning theorist or teacher knows, learning progresses through hills and plateaus; what these parents are finding hard is how to sustain their children's motivation through the plateaus. Yet as the research on sustaining children's interests makes clear, this is what makes the difference between taking up an interest and really developing it. See Barron (2006) and Renninger and Hidi (2011).

11. Green (2008) takes on this challenge directly in her analysis of building informal music learning into the curriculum. In fairness to the school, we did not set out to investigate this systematically, and so our observations must remain tentative.

12. Such a disinterested approach is very much the bourgeois paradigm of "distanciation" as described by Bourdieu (1984). For a contrasting analysis of constructive links between youth-led fan interests and educational opportunity, see Jenkins et al. (2007).

13. See Green (2008).

14. For instance, she wanted to move to a well-known music school elsewhere in London, because of its reputation for artiness, as opposed to VFS's Science and Maths designation. For a further discussion of Giselle's and Fesse's artiness, see Sefton-Green (2015).

15. See Green (2008). For an extended analysis of building on informal learning processes within the school curriculum of learning, see also the work of Musical Futures, at www.musicalfutures.org, as an attempt to formalize such approaches.

16. This orientation is in line with the artistic critique of capitalism outlined in Boltanski and Chiapello (2007).

17. Mans (2009).

18. Finnegan (2007), Green (2002, 2008); see also www.musicalfutures.org/resources/c/informallearning.

19. For use of YouTube in informal learning and culture, see Burgess et al. (2009) and K. Miller (2012).

20. Other fields of interest (e.g., sports) might also represent fruitful domains for observing similar processes of informal learning, although music, we suggest, provides a particularly insightful route into analyzing the reproduction of cultural and social capital because musical taste cultures are strongly stratified by social class in ways that are widely recognized and institutionally valued. See note 2 above.

21. What appears to make the difference between these girls and the others in this chapter is what McPherson (2005) calls "thinking musically," the mix of musical imagination, listening practices, and task-oriented strategies that enable sustained progression in music learning and that bear little relation to measures of time spent practicing or external rewards offered for achievement.

22. Hull and Schultz (2002).

23. Alternative domains could have been that of sports or computer gaming, bringing different young people to the fore but, we suggest, resulting in similar arguments, although see Catterall (2009) for an argument that arts activities outperform all others.

24. See the approach to learning in, across, and between contexts in Erstad et al. (2016).

25. Relatedly, the after-school play rehearsals in which Max was involved supported an atmosphere of relaxed and irreverent fun overlaying an intense pedagogy based on clear direction, focused practice, extensive repetition, and yet no language of discipline or levels. Although his piano lesson lacked the relaxed

atmosphere, the sense of purpose in practicing the next steps in a clearly laid-out set of tasks was similar, as was his determination to succeed.

26. Bourdieu (1984), Bennett et al. (2009).

27. The distinction between avant-garde and bohemian is a difficult one to draw, given that both "depend on a stance of separation from the putative mainstream of culture, . . . both seek programmatically to break down barriers between art and life and to fuse them in a integral aestheticisation of everyday life, . . . [and] both are marked by ambiguous ties to popular culture" (T. Miller, 2005, p. 100). See also Nicholson (2003).

28. Bennett et al. (2009, p. 93) suggest the label "subcultural capital," which they define as "a matter of showing enthusiasm, allegiance and discriminating taste through a relationship to contemporary forms." While noting that Sedat's *saz* community is hardly "contemporary," given its lengthy tradition in his country and culture of origin, this label is helpful for their further observation that this capital is not convertible, into other domains of knowledge and recognition or other forms of capital.

Chapter 10. Life Trajectories, Social Mobility, and Cultural Capital

1. Lemke (2000). For an extended discussion, see Adam (2004).

2. The exceptions included those who were withdrawn from some lessons for support with their English, Sara's selection for an additional astronomy GCSE, and Adam, who had taken a German GCSE.

3. A smattering of vocational courses was also on offer, allowing a practically oriented engagement: for example, music BTEC was a more technologically oriented course including aspects of business, while music GCSE was more theoretical, requiring the ability to read music. As should be clear, British education tends to prioritize academic selection and stratification, offering fewer of the second chances that lie at the heart of the US education system. See Goldin and Katz (2008) and M. Rose (2009).

4. See studies deriving from Maurice Merleau-Ponty, for example, Merleau-Ponty (1979).

5. Facer (2011).

6. Thomson describes this process as part of the challenges of researching "identity in process" (2009, p. 15). In reviewing how the young people had changed over the year, in how they talked to us and how they talked about themselves, it seemed to us that such reflexivity emerges particularly during the early teenage years.

7. For the classic study of how young teenage girls "lose their voice," symbolically, psychologically, and sociologically, see Gilligan (1993). For more recent work, see Walkerdine et al. (2001). On how boys' masculinity is constructed as problematic within the education system, see Willis (1978). For more recent work, see Haywood and Mac an Ghaill (2013).

8. See, for instance, Brah and Phoenix (2004).

9. See Hodkinson and Sparkes (1997) for a discussion of how such language relies on metaphors that are problematically teleological in nature.

10. Bernstein (1970). A good example of the effort to make educational reform the crucible for any and all kinds of change that might lead to greater social mobility is the research and advocacy offered by the Sutton Trust (see www.suttontrust. com/research).

11. For worried parents, the fact that many teenagers spend so much time on computers is particularly ambiguous: is it a sign of a marketable interest and expertise developing or quite the opposite?

12. Indeed, recent studies of social development agree that interest-driven learning (or finding one's "spark") is effective. See Barron (2006), Csikszentmihalyi et al. (1997), Renninger and Hidi (2011), Peppler (2013), and Ben-Eliyahu et al. (2014).

13. All of the details in Sara's learning identity clearly show the impact of the "concerted cultivation" (Lareau, 2011) that her parents have invested in her.

14. In the UK system, it is common to change school for the last two years, 12 and 13 (known as Sixth Form, in which A-levels are taken), with young people often seeking a change of scene or educational level or specialism.

15. As we saw in chapter 9, the class position of Fesse, as the child of migrants, was difficult to describe. Although not well-off economically, his siblings who lived in the family home were educated and working in arts fields, so the suggestion that it is more likely middle-class families who consider working in the arts, and that he might not appear to come from such a background, cannot be taken at face value.

16. It is notable that these are mainly middle-class young people exploring values captured by Boltanski and Chiapello's (2007) artistic critique of the constraints of capitalism.

17. It may be that social networking will not retain its present hold over young people's attention, but as Horst (2010b, p. 92) has put it, for this generation, joining Facebook represents a "coming of age in networked public culture."

18. See our account of method and transcription conventions in chapter 2.

19. Relatedly, we discussed in chapter 9 how Giselle positioned her music lessons as part of the work she was engaged in to become an artist, building a plan that integrates artistic desires with a realistic appraisal of what it means to succeed as an artist and make a living. Both Giselle and Megan had fathers working at home as self-employed artists/designers offering a model of some security, although in Giselle's case, income seemed to be more precarious. In chapters 8 and 9, too, we theorized this life choice in terms of bohemian cultural capital.

20. We could perhaps continue through the rest of the class in this way; see, for instance, our description in chapters 7 and 9 of the considerable cultural and economic investments that Dom's and Sedat's families were making to ensure, for Dom, a competitive middle-class future and, for Sedat, a securely embedded member of his community.

21. For an extended discussion of this phenomenon, see Kehily (2002).

22. See, for example, Weis (2004), Williamson (2004), MacLeod (2009), Lareau (2011), and Heath (2012). These studies question whether people end up living predestined lives—following the paths that could have been predicted for them—or whether and in what ways individuals have exercised their own capabilities to follow different trajectories to be explored. The time scale of some of these books is generational, thus allowing the classic measures of social reproduction—the life chances of the child to be set against those of the parent—to be explored and explained. The challenge in these accounts is to show how predictable and predicted the lives of the younger generation are and how individuals are swept away by larger forces over which they have little control, despite the attention to exceptional cases.

23. As MacLeod puts it, the "white trash kids" (whom he calls "The Hallway Hangers") saw a ladder of opportunity but no rungs on it for them. Meanwhile, the black kids ("The Brothers"), who internalized their failure, were less angry at the world but ultimately more hurt. So when he returned after eight years, he found these young men still living out their problems. The white men were variously in jail, on drugs, or in low-paid work, while the black men were in even less secure jobs and often badly treated, and yet they picked themselves up and were ready to try again, less angry than disappointed. As MacLeod wittily summarizes, they were all "outclassed and outcaste," for society is structured so that some must lose. A further 15 years on, when these men had reached 40, MacLeod's colleagues revisited them, finding that, for all the complexities of particular lives lived in particular circumstances in a particular time, "the bottom line is that social reproduction marches on" (2009, p. 410). See also Sennett and Cobb (1972) and McClelland and Karen (2009).

24. Lareau (2011, p. 264).

25. Thomson et al. (2002); see also Thomson (2009).

26. See Bennett et al. (2009).

Conclusion

1. See Outhwaite (1994, writing about the work of Jürgen Habermas).

2. See www.world-challenge.co.uk (quoted from www.world-challenge.co.uk/pages /benefits-students.asp). World Challenge is one of the brands owned by a FTSE 100 leisure company: www.tuitravelplc.com/brand-experience/explore-all-our -brands/2/484/#.U6LpKxa2vxc. Its website linked to various forms of accreditation, offering clear advice about how the experience would help build a portfolio of valued skills and so contribute to participants' CVs and university applications. While this discourse was broadly accepted by the school, it may well have functioned more as a pretext than as a sincerely meant educational ideology. What matters is that we heard no alternative discourse for those who were involved—or those who were not involved—to frame their activities; perhaps for this reason, talk about the World Challenge centered on practical arrangements, sums raised, and hopes for the holiday.

3. Here, as elsewhere in this book, we saw how differences in economic and cultural capital worked to perpetuate social inequality—in this instance, excluding, for example, Abby, who we saw try valiantly with her application, only for it to be rejected, while giving Gideon a second chance.

4. Our interviews with teachers revealed this concern with the school's authority, which had the effect of disempowering the young people. For instance, in one after-school meeting we observed, this top-down stance was illustrated by Julie sitting behind her computer, talking authoritatively over the young people's variously tentative or silly suggestions. While she retained her authority, the young people felt free to be childish, unburdened by the commitment that a more equal interaction would have required of them. See also Crook (2011), Grant (2011), Player-Koro (2013), Vickery (2014).

5. This is partly because participatory websites are often poorly thought through, even patronizing, in their efforts to appeal to children (Banaji and Buckingham, 2013; Livingstone, 2007).

6. For a thorough discussion of the processes of re-mediation, see Bolter and Grusin (1999).

7. These are most evident in the school's emphasis on standardization and individual achievement (chapter 6), the school itself being in competition with other schools in the borough and even the country. Paralleling many critiques of the school, Webb (2011, p. 97) argues that "over the last century, dominant conceptions of family have transformed; from a site of affect to be protected from the vagaries of the outside world, the family has become a modern, transactional institution," subject to political, policy, and educational expectations and anxieties.

8. See Bennett et al. (2009), Biressi and Nunn (2013), Skeggs (2013), and Social Attitudes of Young People Community of Interest (2014).

9. Even though they regard the very idea of "the child" as a means by which parents might reenchant their lives in disillusioned times (Beck and Beck-Gernsheim, 2002). For a critique, see Vincent and Ball (2007) on middle-class families and the child as "project." We note that others have, however, sought to apply the idea of later modernity to the ways in which children and young people find opportunities for agency in a world largely structured for them by adults. See Staksrud (2013), Fornäs and Bolin (1995), Corsaro (1997), James et al. (1998), Furlong and Cartmel (2006), and France (2007). For a recent analysis that transcends the individual/society opposition by reading agency in relational terms, see Oswell (2012).

10. Giddens (1993).

11. Giddens (1991), Beck and Beck-Gernsheim (2002), Bauman (2005). As Brannen and Nilsen (2005) observe, while the notion of a pressured and uncertain choice biography finds some resonance in empirical research, that same research reveals a diversity of strategies by which young people meet this challenge, with varying outcomes that themselves continue to be shaped by gender and social class.

12. Social Attitudes of Young People Community of Interest (2014).

13. This flexibility meant that we could not simply map wealthier and poorer families onto competitive or conservative approaches, respectively, as discussed in chapters 8 and 9 in relation to multiple forms of cultural capital.

14. Amin (2012).

15. This shift might well form part of the analysis of "the quantified self." Lupton (2014) explicitly links self-tracking systems to the attempt to assert a reflexive sense of control over the self when faced with the uncertainties and pressures on individuals living in the risk society.

16. Ladwig (2010), Sefton-Green (2013).

17. Only for Yusuf did we see equally stringent pressures applied at school, home, and online, with his learning "leveled" in all places; but he was the exception that pointed to the rule.

18. So Jenna enjoyed a friendship with Max and Alice, and Shane with some of the more middle-class boys like Dominic. But these might be only the weak and bridging ties identified by social network theorists (Granovetter, 1983), in contrast to what appeared to be deeper ties between Sedat and the local Turkish community, and a deeper disconnect between Mark or Yusuf, for example, and the middle-class boys in the class.

19. Hills et al. (2010), Corak (2013), Cribb et al. (2013). Families draw on a range of economic, cultural, and subcultural resources, and while these seem likely to result in social reproduction of status from parents to children, we cannot predict this categorically from our year with the class. We saw some signs of "downward mobility" and some of upward mobility; across the range of backgrounds, we saw efforts to recuperate children who were struggling; we also saw interests go unsupported and pathways become blocked.

20. See the collection edited by Giroux (1983) for a discussion of the hidden curriculum and Willis (1978) on "learning to labor." Nayak (2003, p. 169) draws similar conclusions regarding the increasingly placeless and destabilized traditions of youth cultures in a globalizing world. Indeed, he concludes, perhaps provocatively, "for many young people, inhabiting the de-industrial landscapes where my research was undertaken, life-long labour and community ties to the mill or colliery would now appear to offer welcome respite against unemployment, insecurity and a sense of dislocation."

21. Dorling (2011).

22. See Arnett (2011) and Cunningham (1995).

23. Morley (2000), Pink and Mackley (2013).

24. Giddens (1993).

25. Intensification is not to be underestimated as a form of social change. As "daily life becomes increasingly saturated in communicational practices and increasingly dependent on the ubiquitous presence-availability, via electronic media, of information and human resources . . . this density of communicational connectedness promotes a new kind of intensity in everyday experience, mixing pace and vibrancy" (Tomlinson, 1999, p. 87).

26. Or, in the language of social network analysis, the metaphor is limited in its focus on links over nodes, thereby prioritizing extended social relations over grounded groupings; further, by tending to treat all links as equivalent, it seems to prioritize weak ties over strong ties.

27. Constructive examples included Giselle's music making (along with her game playing and other creative digital activities), which connected learning activities at home and outside, alone and with family or peers, offline and online, although recognition in the school was only partial (chapter 9). Examples of disconnection included the ways that the black boys in chapter 5 were encouraged to leave their cultural identity outside the history classroom or how definitions of learning and progression in Yusuf's home were designed to dovetail with school learning but did not (chapter 8).

28. The young people's civility online was discussed in chapters 3 and 4. It may be that the very extensiveness of Facebook networks among this cohort—taking in nearly the whole class and, indeed, much of the year group as well as peers beyond the school—meant that it functioned as a kind of digital extension of school life. Not to be civil on Facebook to people in the class or to people you do not know very well would cause difficulties the next day at school. Most of the young people (although not all and not always) were keen to avoid the eruption of such difficulties within the closely managed, largely civil sphere of the school.

29. Arguably, it would have been more disheartening to find evidence of young people's active embrace of competitive individualism, which for the most part we did not.

30. As noted in chapter 4, Strathern (1996) analyzes the necessity of "cutting the network" so that connections are limited and can, thereby, be deepened (rather than weak ties forever multiplied). In finding a balance between fewer deep or strong ties and more weak ties, the simple notion of connection becomes unhelpful. For instance, Smart (2007) frames connectedness not in terms of ever-extending networked individualism (Wellman and Rainie, 2012) but in terms of fewer deep relationships, prioritizing the same sense of local and familial embeddedness that we found to be important.

31. See, among others, Davies and Good (2009), US Department of Education (2010), OECD (2012), European Schoolnet (2013), White House (2013). For more critical approaches, see Buckingham (2007), Livingstone (2012), and Selwyn (2014).

32. Ofcom (2014).

33. Bruns (2008); see also Jenkins (2006) and Ito et al. (2013).

34. Jenkins (2006, 2012), Ito et al. (2013), Warschauer and Matuchniak (2010).

35. Buckingham et al. (2001) discuss families' probably misplaced investment in all kinds of homework materials, home tutors, and "edutainment" technologies. Gutiérrez et al. (2010) examine middle-class families' beliefs in the value of a busy schedule of enrichment activities. Lareau (2011) shows how middle-class families inculcate a sense of entitlement in their children along with the communicative skills to ensure they get what is on offer. See also Brantlinger's (2003) account

of how middle-class parents justify their strategies to get ahead. Relatedly, Threadgold and Nilan (2009, p. 48) argue that privileged youths' advantage is reproduced partly by their developing reflexivity, since "being reflexive, and successfully negotiating future risks, both real and perceived, constitutes privileged cultural capital."

36. Such inequalities were echoed in our class. For some of the higher-achieving individuals, continuities across home and school appeared advantageous (Sara and Dom). Others introduced a degree of disconnection in order to retain their own vision of pedagogy and learning identity (Giselle, Megan, Max). Meanwhile, for some of the lower-achieving individuals, continuities across sites may have compounded disadvantage (Lydia, Shane), making sense of their parents' efforts to keep home separate (Abby, Sedat).

37. Loveless and Williamson (2013); see also Cuban (1986), Buckingham et al. (2001), Monahan (2005), Selwyn (2010, 2013, 2014), and Bandy (2012).

38. As Loveless and Williamson (2013, p. 25) put it, in popular visions of connected learning and connected communities, "the potential for creative autonomy is shaped, controlled, and curtailed by a concentration of interlocking corporate multimedia, financial trade, and government strategies which have permitted the expansion of for-profit entertainment and the commodification of personal freedom." Bakan (2012, pp. 173–174) is yet more pessimistic, asserting that "a larger and more ominous threat is big business's ongoing campaign to co-opt the idealism of youth for its own self-interested purposes. . . . As a result, corporations have begun creating, sponsoring, and infiltrating youth-driven environmental and social justice campaigns as central parts of their marketing strategies."

39. Appealing both to the educational and domestic market, a host of technology and educational providers are developing and promoting ever more narrow, individualistic, instrumental, and competitive tools to teachers and parents. These, too, undercut the promise of connected learning, as witnessed in the class.

40. While we have not pursued studies of educational innovation in this book, it may be intriguing for advocates of connected or seamless or blended learning to note that Akkerman and Bakker (2011) identify that potential learning mechanisms that occur at boundaries are precisely stimulated rather than undermined by disconnections.

41. Digital affordances are discussed in chapter 4 as primarily persistence, scalability, asynchronicity, replicability, and searchability (boyd, 2014).

42. Lupton (2014). For critical reflections on the logics of digitally networked systems, see van Dijck (2013a).

Appendix

1. On the validity of such indicators, see Hills et al. (2010).

2. See Bennett et al. (2009).

3. This was partly a matter of ethnicity and partly also of family composition: many of the poorer families were, as noted here, from ethnic minority backgrounds

(and some were well educated, such as the families of Mark, Sergei, and Fesse), while some were poorer than might be expected from their education or employment because they were single-parent families (such as the families of Dilruba and Nick).

4. In this, they illustrate the phenomenon of "model minorities"; see Kao (1995).

5. DfE (2013b).

6. Such methods have been variously used by social researchers to map the home; we were especially influenced by Csikszentmihalyi and Rochberg-Halton (1990) and by Silverstone et al. (1992).

7. By "digital footprints," we simply mean whatever could be found online when searching using the young people's names or nicknames.

8. The examples that we learned most from were Lareau (2011) and MacLeod (2009). See chapter 10.

9. Monge and Contractor (2003).

References

Adam, B., 2004. *Time*. Cambridge, UK: Polity.

Akkerman, S.F., and Bakker, A., 2011. Boundary crossing and boundary objects. *Review of Educational Research* 81, no. 2: 132–169.

Albright, J., and Luke, A., eds. 2008. *Pierre Bourdieu and literacy education*. London: Routledge.

Alexander, R., 2001. *Culture and pedagogy*. Oxford, UK: Blackwell.

Alexander, R., 2009. *Children, their world, their education: Final report and recommendations of the Cambridge Primary Review*. London: Routledge.

Alvermann, D.E., 2012. Is there a place for popular culture in curriculum and classroom instruction? In A.J. Eakle, ed., *Curriculum and instruction* (pp. 214–220). Thousand Oaks, CA: Sage.

Amin, A., 2012. *Land of strangers*. Cambridge, UK: Polity.

Anthias, F., 2002. Where do I belong? Narrating collective identity and translocational positionality. *Ethnicities* 2, no. 4: 491–514.

Archer, L., Hollingworth, S., and Mendick, H., 2010. *Urban youth and schooling*. Milton Keynes, UK: Open University Press.

Arnett, J.J., 1995. Adolescents' uses of media for self-socialization. *Journal of Youth and Adolescence* 24, no. 5: 519–533.

Arnett, J.J., 2011. Emerging adulthoods: The cultural psychology of a new life stage. In L.A. Jensen, ed., *Bridging cultural and developmental approaches to psychology: New syntheses in theory, research, and policy* (pp. 255–275). Oxford: Oxford University Press.

Aspen Institute, 2014. *Learner at the center of a networked world*. www.aspeninstitute. org/publications/learner-center-networked-world.

Atkinson, W. (2007). Beck, individualization and the death of class: A critique. *British Journal of Sociology* 58, no. 3: 349–366.

Attewell, J., Savill-Smith, C., and Douch, R., 2009. *The impact of mobile learning: Examining what it means for teaching and learning*. London: Learning and Skills Network.

Azevedo, F., 2013. The tailored practice of hobbies and its implication for the design of interest-driven learning environments. *Journal of the Learning Sciences* 22, no. 3: 46–510.

Back, L., 1996. *New ethnicities and urban culture: Racisms and multiculture in young lives*. London: Routledge.

Backett-Milburn, K., Harden, J., Maclean, A., Cunningham-Burley, S., and Jamieson, L. 2011. *Work and family lives: The changing experiences of "young" families*. Timescapes Final Report Project 5. Leeds, UK: University of Leeds.

Bakan, J. 2012. *Childhood under siege: How big business ruthlessly targets children.* London: Vintage.

Bakardjieva, M., 2005. *Internet society: The internet in everyday life.* London: Sage.

Baker, B.M., and Heyning, K.E., eds. 2004. *Dangerous coagulations? The use of Foucault in the study of education.* New York: Peter Lang.

Balkam, S., 2014. Learning the lessons of the InBloom failure. *Huffington Post,* April 24. www.huffingtonpost.com/stephen-balkam/learning-the-lessons-of-t_b_5208724.html,

Ball, S.J., 1981. *Beachside Comprehensive: A case-study of secondary schooling.* Cambridge: Cambridge University Press.

Ball, S.J., 2007. *Education plc: Understanding private sector participation in public sector education.* London: Routledge.

Ball, S.J., ed., 2013. *Foucault, power, and education.* Routledge Key Ideas in Education. London and New York: Routledge.

Banaji, S., and Buckingham, D. 2013. *The civic web: Young people, the internet, and civic participation.* Cambridge, MA: MIT Press.

Bandy, E.A., 2012. The DML's terrible twos. *Journal of Children and Media* 6, no. 3: 408–411.

Barron, B., 2006. Interest and self-sustained learning as catalyst of development: A learning ecology perspective. *Human Development* 49: 193–224.

Bauman, Z., 2002. Foreword. In U. Beck and E. Beck-Gernsheim, *Individualization* (pp. xiv–xix). London: Sage.

Bauman, Z., 2005. Education in liquid modernity. *Review of Education, Pedagogy, and Cultural Studies* 27, no. 4: 303–317.

Baym, N.K., 2015. *Personal connections in the digital age: Digital media and society series.* 2nd ed. Cambridge, UK: Polity.

Baym, N.K., and boyd, d., 2012. Socially mediated publicness: An introduction. *Journal of Broadcasting and Electronic Media* 56, no. 3: 320–329.

Beaumont, J., and Lofts, H., 2013. *Measuring national well-being: Health, 2013.* Newport, UK: Office for National Statistics. www.ons.gov.uk/ons/dcp171766_310300.pdf.

Beck, U., (1986) 2005. *Risk society: Towards a new modernity.* Trans. M. Ritter. London: Sage.

Beck, U., and Beck-Gernsheim, E. 2002. *Individualization.* Trans. Patrick Camiller. London: Sage.

Beck, U., and Beck-Gernsheim, E., 2014. *Distant love: Personal life in the global age.* Trans. Rodney Livingstone. Cambridge, UK: Polity.

Beck, U., Giddens, A., and Lash, S., 1995. *Reflexive modernization: Politics, tradition and aesthetics in the modern social order.* Cambridge, UK: Polity.

Becker, H., 1972. Why school is a lousy place to learn anything in. *American Behavioural Scientist* 16: 85–105.

Becta, 2009. *An exploration of parents' engagement with their children's learning involving technologies and the impact of this on their family learning experience.* Coventry, UK: Becta.

Belfiore, E. 2012. "Defensive instrumentalism" and the legacy of New Labour's cultural policies. *Cultural Trends* 21, no. 2: 103–111.

Belle, D., ed., 1989. *Children's social networks and social supports*. New York: Wiley.

Ben-Eliyahu, A., Rhodes, J.E., and Scales, P., 2014. The interest-driven pursuits of 15 year olds: "Sparks" and their association with caring relationships and developmental outcomes. *Applied Developmental Science* 18, no. 2: 76–89.

Bennett, T., Savage, M., Silva, E., Warde, A., Gayo-Cal, M., and Wright, D., 2009. *Culture, class, distinction*. Abingdon, UK: Routledge.

Benwell, B., and Stokoe, E., 2006. *Discourse and identity*. Edinburgh: Edinburgh University Press.

Berker, T., Hartmann, M., Punie, Y., and Ward, K.J., eds., 2006. *The domestication of media and technology*. Maidenhead, UK: Open University Press.

Berlin, I., 1978. *Concepts and categories: Philosophical essays*. Ed. Henry Hardy. London: Hogarth.

Bernstein, B., 1970. Education cannot compensate for society. *New Society* 15, no. 387: 344–347.

Bernstein, B., 1973. *Class, codes and control: Theoretical studies towards a sociology of language*. London: HarperCollins.

Bernstein, B., 1990. *The structuring of pedagogic discourse. Class, codes and control*. Vol. 4. London: Routledge.

Bettie, J., 2003. *Women without class: Girls, race, and identity*. Berkeley: University of California Press.

Biesta, G.J.J., 2011. *Good education in an age of measurement: Ethics, politics, democracy*. Boulder, CO: Paradigm.

Bijker, W.E., Hughes, T.P., and Pinch, T., eds., 1987. *The social construction of technological systems*. Cambridge, MA: MIT Press.

Biressi, A., and Nunn, H., 2013. *Class and contemporary British culture*. New York: Palgrave Macmillan.

Blumer, H. 1954. What is wrong with social theory. *American Sociological Review* 18: 3–10.

Bohanek, J.G., Marin, K.A., Fivush, R., and Duke, M.P., 2006. Family narrative interaction and children's sense of self. *Family Process* 45, no. 1: 39–54.

Bohman, J., 1991. *New philosophy of social science: Problems of indeterminacy*. Cambridge, UK: Polity.

Boltanski, L., and Chiapello, E., 2007. *The new spirit of capitalism*. London: Verso.

Bolter, J.D., and Grusin, R., 1999. *Remediation: Understanding new media*. Cambridge, MA: MIT Press.

Bonal, X., and Rambla, X., 2003. Captured by the totally pedagogised society: Teachers and teaching in the knowledge economy. *Globalisation, Societies and Education* 1, no. 2: 169–184.

Boneva, B.S., Quinn, A., Kraut, R., Kiesler, S., and Shklovski, I. (2006). Teenage communication in the instant messaging era. In R. Kraut, M. Brynin, and S. Kiesler, eds., *Computers, phones, and the internet* (pp. 201–218). Oxford: Oxford University Press.

Bourdieu, P., 1984. *Distinction: A social critique of the judgement of taste.* Trans. Richard Nice. London: Routledge and Kegan Paul.

Bourdieu, P., 1990. *The logic of practice.* Cambridge, UK: Polity.

Bourdieu, P., and Passeron, J.-C., 1990. *Reproduction in education, society and culture.* Trans. Richard Nice. London: Sage.

Bovill, M., and Livingstone, S., 2001. Bedroom culture and the privatization of media use. In S. Livingstone and M. Bovill, eds., *Children and their changing media environment: A European comparative study* (pp. 179–200). Mahwah, NJ: Lawrence Erlbaum.

Bowles, S., and Gintis, H., 1976. *Schooling in capitalist America: Educational reform and the contradictions of economic life.* New York: Basic Books.

boyd, d., 2008. Why youth ♥ social network sites: The role of networked publics in teenage social life. In D. Buckingham, ed., *Youth, identity, and digital media* (pp. 119–142). Cambridge, MA: MIT Press.

boyd, d., 2014. *It's complicated: The social lives of networked teens.* New Haven, CT: Yale University Press.

Boyd, R., 2006. The value of civility. *Urban Studies* 43, nos. 5–6: 863–878.

Bradbrook, G., Alvi, I., Fisher, J., Lloyd, H., Moore, R., Thompson, V., and Livingstone, S., 2008. *Meeting their potential: The role of education and technology in overcoming disadvantage and disaffection in young people.* Becta Research Report. Coventry, UK: Becta.

Bradshaw, J., Martorano, B., Natali, L., and de Neubourg, C., 2013. *Children's subjective well-being in rich countries.* Working Paper 2013-03. Florence, Italy: UNICEF Office of Research.

Brah, A., and Phoenix, A., 2004. Ain't I a woman? Revisiting intersectionality. *Journal of International Women's Studies* 5, no. 3: 75–86.

Brannen, J., 2005. Time and the negotiation of work-family boundaries: Autonomy or illusion? *Time & Society* 14, no. 1: 113–131.

Brannen, J., and Nilsen, A., 2005. Individualisation, choice and structure: A discussion of current trends in sociological analysis. *Sociological Review* 53, no. 3: 412–428.

Brantlinger, E., 2003. *Dividing classes: How the middle class negotiates and rationalizes school advantage.* New York: Routledge.

Breiter, A., and Light, D., 2006. Data for school improvement: Factors for designing effective information systems to support decision-making in schools. *Educational Technology & Society* 9, no. 3: 206–217.

Brooks, G., 2011. *The idea of home.* Boyar Lectures 2011. Sydney, Australia: ABC Books.

Brown, P., Lauder, H., and Ashton, D., 2011. *The global auction: The broken promises of education, jobs, and incomes.* New York: Oxford University Press.

Bruner, J., 1991. Self-making and world-making. *Journal of Aesthetic Education* 25, no. 1: 67–78.

Bruner, J., 1996. *The culture of education.* Cambridge, MA: Harvard University Press.

Bruns, A. 2008. *Blogs, Wikipedia, Second Life, and beyond: From production to produsage.* Digital Formations. New York: Peter Lang.

Buchner, P., 1990. Growing up in the eighties: Changes in the social biography of childhood in the FRG. In L. Chisholm, P. Buchner, H.H. Kruger, and P. Brown, eds., *Childhood, youth and social change: A comparative perspective* (pp. 71–84). London: Falmer.

Buckingham, D., 2000. *After the death of childhood: Growing up in the age of electronic media.* Cambridge, UK: Polity.

Buckingham, D., 2004. *Media education: Literacy, learning and contemporary culture.* Cambridge, UK: Polity.

Buckingham, D., 2007. *Beyond technology: Children's learning in the age of digital culture.* Cambridge, UK: Polity.

Buckingham, D., Scanlon, M., and Sefton-Green, J., 2001. Selling the digital dream: Marketing educational technology to teachers and parents. In A. Loveless and V. Ellis, eds., *Subject to change: Literacy and digital technology* (pp. 20–40). London: Routledge.

Buckingham, D., and Sefton-Green, J., 2004. Structure, agency and pedagogy in children's media culture. In J. Tobin, ed., *Pikachu's global adventure: The rise and fall of Pokémon.* Durham, NC: Duke University Press.

Burawoy, M., 1998. The extended case method. *Sociological Theory* 16, no. 1: 4–33.

Burgess, J., Green, J., Jenkins, H., and Hartley, J., 2009. *YouTube: Online video and participatory culture.* Cambridge, UK: Polity.

Cahill, S.E., 1987. Children and civility: Ceremonial deviance and the acquisition of ritual competence. *Social Psychology Quarterly* 50, no. 4: 312–321.

Calhoun, C., 2000. The virtue of civility. *Philosophy & Public Affairs* 29, no. 3: 251–275.

Carrington, V., 2006. *Rethinking middle years: Early adolescents, schooling and digital culture.* Sydney, Australia: Allen & Unwin.

Castells, M., 1996. *The rise of the network society.* Oxford, UK: Blackwell.

Catterall, J.S., 2009. *Doing well and doing good by doing art: The effects of education in the visual and performing arts on the achievements and values of young adults.* Los Angeles: Imagination Group.

Chamberlain, T., George, N., Golden, S., Walker, F., and Benton, T. 2010. *Tellus4 National Report.* Slough National Foundation for Education Research. https://www.gov.uk/government/uploads/system/uploads/attachment_data/file/221932/DCSF-RR218.pdf.

Chambers, D., 2012. *A sociology of family life: Change and diversity in intimate relations.* Cambridge, UK: Polity.

Chambers, D., 2013. *Social media and personal relationships: Online intimacies and networked friendships.* Basingstoke, UK: Palgrave Macmillan.

Children's Society, 2012. *The good childhood report 2012.* London: Children's Society.

Children's Society, 2013. *The good childhood report 2013.* London: Children's Society.

Chin, T., and Phillips, M., 2004. Social reproductivity and child-rearing practices: Social class, children's agency, and the summer activity gap. *Sociology of Education* 77, no. 3: 185–210.

Chisholm, L., 2008. Re-contextualising learning in second modernity. In R. Bendit and M. Hahn-Bleibtreu, eds., *Youth transitions: Processes of social inclusion and patterns of vulnerability in a globalised world* (pp. 135–150). Leverkusen, Germany: Barbara Budrich.

Chisholm, L., Buchner, P., Kruger, H.H., and Bois-Reymond, M., eds., 1995. *Growing up in Europe: Contemporary horizons in childhood and youth studies*. Berlin and New York: de Gruyter.

Chouliaraki, L., 1998. Regulation in "progressivist" pedagogic discourse: Individualized teacher-pupil talk. *Discourse & Society* 9, no. 1: 5–32.

Clark, L.S., 2005. The constant contact generation: Exploring teen friendship networks online. In S. Mazzarella, ed., *Girl wide web* (pp. 203–222). New York: Peter Lang.

Clark, L.S., 2013. *The parent app: Understanding families in the digital age*. Oxford: Oxford University Press.

Clark, L.S., Demont-Heinrich, C., and Webber, S., 2005. Parents, ICTs, and children's prospects for success: Interviews along the digital "access rainbow." *Critical Studies in Media Communication* 22, no. 5: 409–426.

Clifford, J., 1983. On ethnographic authority. *Representations* 2: 118–146.

Coleman, J., and Hagell, A., eds., 2007. *Adolescence, risk and resilience: Against the odds*. Chichester, UK: Wiley.

Collishaw, S. 2012. Time trends in young people's emotional and behavioural problems, 1975–2005. In A. Hagell, ed., *Changing adolescence: Social trends and mental health* (pp. 9–26). Bristol, UK: Policy.

Commission on Assessment without Levels. 2015. *Final report of the Commission on Assessment without Levels*. https://www.gov.uk/government/uploads/system/uploads/attachment_data/file/461534/Commission_report_.pdf.

Common Sense Media, 2012. *Children, teens, and entertainment media: The view from the classroom*. San Francisco: Common Sense Media.

Contini, R. M., and Maturo, A. 2010. Multi-ethnic society and cross-cultural perspectives in the school. *Procedia: Social and Behavioral Sciences* 5, no. 1: 1537–1545.

Coontz, S., 1997. *The way we really are: Coming to terms with America's changing families*. New York: Basic Books.

Corak, M. 2013. Income inequality, equality of opportunity, and intergenerational mobility. *Journal of Economic Perspectives* 27, no. 3: 79–102.

Corsaro, W.A., 1997. *The sociology of childhood*. Thousand Oaks, CA: Pine Forge.

Cote, J.E., and Levine, C.G., 2002. *Identity formation, agency, and culture: A social psychological synthesis*. Mahwah, NJ: Lawrence Erlbaum.

Couldry, N., 2010. *Why voice matters: Culture and politics after neoliberalism*. London: Sage.

Couldry, N., Livingstone, S., and Markham, T., 2010. *Media consumption and public engagement: Beyond the presumption of attention*. 2nd ed. Basingstoke, UK: Palgrave Macmillan.

Cramer, M., and Hayes, G.R., 2010. Acceptable use of technology in schools: Risks, policies, and promises. *Pervasive computing, IEEE* 9, no. 3: 37–44.

Cribb, J., Hood, A., Joyce, R., and Phillips, D. 2013. *Living standards, poverty and inequality in the UK: 2013*. London: Institute for Fiscal Studies.

Crook, C., 2011. The "digital native" in context: Tensions associated with importing Web 2.0 practices into the school setting. *Oxford Review of Education* 38, no. 1: 63–80.

Csikszentmihalyi, M., Rathunde, K., and Whalen, S., 1997. *Talented teenagers: The roots of success and failure*. Cambridge: Cambridge University Press.

Csikszentmihalyi, M., and Rochberg-Halton, C., 1990. *The meaning of things*. Chicago: University of Chicago Press.

Cuban, L., 1986. *Teachers and machines: Classroom use of technology since 1920*. New York: Teachers College Press.

Cunningham, H., 1995. *Children and childhood in Western society since 1500*. London: Longman.

Cunningham, H., 2006. *The invention of childhood*. London: BBC Books.

Currie, C., Gabhainn, S, N., Godeau, E., Roberts, C., Smith, R., Currie, D., Picket, W., Richter, M., Morgan, A., and Barnekow, V., eds., 2008. *Inequalities in young people's health: Health Behaviour in School-aged Children (HBSC) international report from the 2005/2006 survey*. Copenhagen, Denmark: WHO Regional Office for Europe.

Davidson, E., 2011. *The burdens of aspiration: Schools, youth, and success in the divided social worlds of Silicon Valley*. New York: NYU Press.

Davies, C., and Eynon, R., 2013. *Teenagers and technology*. New York: Routledge.

Davies, C., and Good, J., 2009. *Harnessing technology: The learner and their context—Choosing to use technology: How learners construct their learning lives in their own contexts*. Oxford, UK: Becta.

Davies, W., 2014. Commentary: A bibliographical review of neoliberalism. *Theory, Culture & Society*, 7 March. http://theoryculturesociety.org/william-davies-a-bibliographic-review-of-neoliberalism.

de Certeau, M.D., 1984. *The practice of everyday life*. Trans. Steven F. Rendall. Berkeley: University of California Press.

Demerath, P., 2009. *Producing success: The culture of personal advancement in an American high school*. Chicago: University of Chicago Press.

DfE (Department for Education), 2008. *Young people, their social networks and school support: Exploratory analyses of friendships, well-being and multi-agency working in two secondary schools*. London: DfE.

DfE, 2013a. *Assessing without levels*. London: DfE. www.education.gov.uk/schools/teachingandlearning/curriculum/nationalcurriculum2014/a00225864/assessing-without-levels.

DfE, 2013b. *GSCE and equivalent attainment by pupil characteristics in England, 2011/12*. www.education.gov.uk/rsgateway/DB/SFR/s001111/index.shtml.

Dorling, D., 2011. *Injustice: Why social inequality persists*. Bristol, UK: Policy.

Dover, C., 2007. Everyday talk: Investigating media consumption and identity amongst school children. *Participations* 4, no. 1. www.participations.org/Volume%204/Issue%201/4_01_dover.htm.

Drotner, K., 1994. Ethnographic enigmas: "The everyday" in recent media studies. *Cultural Studies* 8, no. 2: 341–357.

Duneier, M., Kazinitz, P., and Murphy, A., eds., 2014. *The urban ethnography reader*. Oxford: Oxford University Press.

Ecclestone, K., and Hayes, D., 2008. *The dangerous rise of therapeutic education*. London: Routledge.

Eckert, P., 1989. *Jocks and burnouts: Social categories and identity in the high school*. New York: Teachers College Press.

Edwards, R., 1997. *Changing places? Flexibility, lifelong learning and a learning society*. London: Routledge.

Edwards, R., and Weller, S., 2011. *Your space! Siblings and friends: The changing nature of children's lateral relationship*. Timescapes Final Report Project 1. Leeds, UK: University of Leeds.

Eisner, E.W., 2004. *The arts and the creation of mind*. New Haven, CT: Yale University Press.

Elias, N., 2000. *The civilizing process*. 2nd ed. Oxford, UK: Wiley-Blackwell.

Elliott, A. 2002. Beck's sociology of risk: A critical assessment. *Sociology* 36, no. 2: 293–315.

Elliott, A., and du Gay, P., 2009. *Identity in question*. London: Sage.

Erickson, F., 1984. School literacy, reasoning, and civility: An anthropologist's perspective. *Review of Educational Research* 54, no. 4: 525–546.

Erstad, O., Gilje, O., Arnseth, H-C., and Sefton-Green, J., 2016. *Identity, community and learning lives in the digital age*. Cambridge: Cambridge University Press.

European Schoolnet, 2013. *Survey of schools: ICT in education: Benchmarking access, use and attitudes to technology in Europe's schools*. Brussels, Belgium: European Commission DG Communications Networks, Content & Technology.

Facer, K., 2011. *Learning futures: Education, technology and social change*. London: Routledge.

Facer, K., 2012. Taking the 21st century seriously: Young people, education and socio-technical futures. *Oxford Review of Education* 38, no. 1: 97–113.

Facer, K., Furlong, J., Furlong, R., and Sutherland, R., 2003. *ScreenPlay: Children and computing in the home*. London: RoutledgeFalmer.

Feldmann, L.J., 2001. Classroom civility is another of our instructor responsibilities. *College Teaching* 49, no. 4: 137–140.

Fiese, B.H., and Sameroff, A.J., 1999. I. The family narrative consortium: A multi-dimensional approach to narratives. *Monographs of the Society for Research in Child Development* 64, no. 2: 1–3.

Fine, B., 2000. *Social capital versus social theory: Political economy and social science at the turn of the millennium*. London: Routledge.

Finnegan, R., 2007. *The hidden musicians: Music-making in an English town*. Music Culture. Middletown, CT: Wesleyan University Press.

Finney, J., 2011. *Music education in England, 1950–2010: The child-centred progressive tradition*. Farnham, UK: Ashgate.

Fischer, C.S., 1981. What do we mean by "friend"? An inductive study. *Social Network* 3: 287–306.

Fishman, R.L., 1987. American suburbs / English suburbs: A transatlantic comparison. *Journal of Urban History* 13, no. 3: 237–251.

Flichy, P., 1995. *Dynamics of modern communication: The shaping and impact of new communication technologies.* London: Sage.

Flick, U., ed., 2014. *Sage handbook of qualitative data analysis.* London: Sage.

Fornäs, J., and Bolin, G., eds., 1995. *Youth culture in late modernity.* London: Sage.

France, A., 2007. *Understanding youth in late modernity.* Maidenhead, UK: Open University Press.

Foucault, M., 1988. *The history of sexuality, vol. 3: The care of the self.* Trans. Robert Hurley. New York: Vintage Books.

Furlong, A., and Cartmel, F., 2006. *Young people and social change: New perspectives,* 2nd ed. Milton Keynes, UK: Open University Press.

Gardner, F., Collishaw, S., Maughan, B., Scott, J., Schepman, K., and Hagell, A. 2012. Trends in parenting: Can they help explain time trends in problem behaviour? In A. Hagell, ed., *Changing adolescence: Social trends and mental health* (pp. 75–92). Bristol, UK: Policy.

Gee, J.P., 2004a. *Situated language and learning: A critique of traditional schooling.* London: Routledge.

Gee, J.P., 2004b. *What video games have to teach us about learning and literacy.* London: Palgrave Macmillan.

George, R., 2007. Urban girls' "race" friendship and school choice: Changing schools, changing friendships. *Race, Ethnicity and Education* 10, no. 2: 115–129.

George, R., and Clay, J., 2013. Challenging pedagogy: Emotional disruptions, young girls, parents and schools. *Sociological Research Online* 18, no. 2: 5.

Gergen, K.J. 2002. The challenge of absent presence. In J.E. Katz and M. Aakhus, eds., *Perpetual contact: Mobile communication, private talk, public performance* (pp. 227–241). Cambridge: Cambridge University Press.

Gergen, K.J., 2009. *Relational being: Beyond self and community.* Oxford: Oxford University Press.

Giddens, A., 1991. *Modernity and self-identity: Self and society in the late modern age.* Cambridge, UK: Polity.

Giddens, A., 1993. *The transformation of intimacy: Sexuality, love and eroticism in modern societies.* Cambridge, UK: Polity.

Giddens, A., 1995. Living in a post-traditional society. In U. Beck, A. Giddens, and S. Lash, eds., *Reflexive modernization: Politics, tradition and aesthetics in the modern social order* (pp. 56–109). Cambridge, UK: Polity.

Gill, T., 2007. *No fear: Growing up in a risk averse society.* London: Calouste Gulbenkian Foundation.

Gilligan, C., 1993. *In a different voice: Psychological theory and women's development.* 2nd ed. Cambridge, MA: Harvard University Press.

Giroux, H.A., ed. 1983. *Hidden curriculum and moral education: Deception of discovery.* San Pablo, CA: McCutchan.

Goetz, M., Lemish, D., Aidman, A., and Moon, H., 2005. *Media and the make-believe worlds of children: When Harry Potter meets Pokémon in Disneyland.* Mahwah, NJ: Lawrence Erlbaum.

Goffman, E., 1959. *The presentation of self in everyday life.* Harmondsworth, UK: Penguin.

Goffman, E., 1966. *Behavior in public places: Notes on the social organization of gatherings.* New York: Free Press.

Goldin, C., and Katz, L., 2008. *Race between education and technology.* Cambridge, MA: Harvard University Press.

Granovetter, M., 1983. The strength of weak ties: A network theory revisited. *Sociological Theory* 1: 201–233.

Grant, L., 2011. "I'm a completely different person at home": Using digital technologies to connect learning between home and school. *Journal of Computer Assisted Learning* 27, no. 4: 292–302.

Graue, M.E., and Walsh, D.J., 1998. *Studying children in context: Theories, methods and ethics.* Thousand Oaks, CA: Sage.

Green, J., and Luke, A., eds. 2006. *Rethinking learning: What counts as learning and what learning counts.* Review of Research in Education 30. Washington, DC: AERA.

Green, L., 2002. *How popular musicians learn: A way ahead for music education.* Aldershot, UK: Ashgate.

Green, L., 2008. *Music, informal learning and the school: A new classroom pedagogy.* Aldershot, UK: Ashgate.

Greig, A., and Taylor, J., 1999. *Doing research with children.* London: Sage.

Gutiérrez, K.D., 2005–2006. White innocence: A framework and methodology for rethinking educational discourse and inquiry. *International Journal of Learning* 12, no. 10: 223–230.

Gutiérrez, K.D. 2008. Developing a sociocritical literacy in the third space. *Reading Research Quarterly* 43, no. 2: 148–164. doi: 10.1598/RRQ.43.2.3.

Gutiérrez, K.D., Izquierdo, C., and Kremer-Sadlik, T., 2010. Middle class working families' beliefs and engagement in children's extra-curricular activities: The social organization of children's futures. *International Journal of Learning* 17, no. 3: 633–656.

Hagell, A., ed., 2012. *Changing adolescence: Social trends and mental health.* Bristol, UK: Policy.

Hagell, A., Coleman, J., and Brooks, F., 2013. *Key data on adolescence 2013: The latest information and statistics about young people today.* London: Association for Young People's Health.

Hagell, A., Peck, S. C., Zarrett, N., Gimenez-Nadal, J. I., and Symonds, J. 2012. Trends in adolescent time use in the United Kingdom. In A. Hagell, ed., *Changing adolescence: Social trends and mental health* (pp. 47–74). Bristol, UK: Policy.

Hagell, A., Sandberg, S., and MacDonald, R., 2012. Stress and mental health in adolescence: Interrelationship and time trends. In A. Hagell, ed., *Changing adolescence: Social trends and mental health*. Bristol, UK: Policy.

Hagell, A., and Witherspoon, S., 2012. Reflections and implications. In A. Hagell, ed., *Changing adolescence: Social trends and mental health* (pp. 165–178). Bristol, UK: Policy.

Halford, S., and Savage, M., 2010. Reconceptualizing digital social inequality. *Information, Communication & Society* 13, no. 7: 937–955.

Hall, L.A., 2012. How popular culture texts inform and shape students' discussions of social studies texts. *Journal of Adolescent & Adult Literacy* 55, no. 4: 296–305.

Hall, S., 1996. Introduction: Who needs identity? In S. Hall and P. du Gay, eds., *Questions of cultural identity* (pp. 1–17). London: Sage.

Hallgarten, J., 2000. *Parents exist, OK!? Issues and visions for parent-school relationships*. London: Institute for Public Policy Research.

Hammerberg, D.D., 2004. Technologies of the self in classrooms designed as "learning environments." In B.M. Baker and K.E. Heyning, eds., *Dangerous coagulations? The use of Foucault in the study of education* (pp. 359–383). New York: Peter Lang.

Hammersley, M., and Woods, P., eds., 1984. *Life in school: The sociology of pupil culture*. Milton Keynes, UK: Open University Press.

Hampton, K.N., Lee, C.-J., and Her, E.J., 2011. How new media affords network diversity: Direct and mediated access to social capital through participation in local social settings. *New Media & Society* 13, no. 7: 1031–1049.

Hampton, K.N., and Wellman, B., 2003. Neighboring in Netville: How the internet supports community and social capital in a wired suburb. *City & Community* 2, no. 4: 277–311.

Hargittai, E., and Litt, E., 2011. The tweet smell of celebrity success: Explaining variation in Twitter adoption among a diverse group of young adults. *New Media & Society* 13, no. 5: 824–842.

Hargreaves, D.H., 1967. *Social relations in a secondary school*. Abingdon, UK: Routledge.

Haywood, C., and Mac an Ghaill, M., 2013. *Education and masculinities: Social, cultural and global transformations*. Abingdon, UK: Routledge.

Heath, S.B., 2012. *Words at work and play: Three decades in family and community life*. New York: Cambridge University Press.

Heath, S.B., Brooks, R., Cleaver, E., and Ireland, E., 2009. *Researching young people's lives*. London: Sage.

Heil, T., 2014. Are neighbours alike? Practices of conviviality in Catalonia and Casamance. *European Journal of Cultural Studies* 17, no. 4: 452–470.

Henderson, S., Holland, J., McGrellis, S., Sharpe, S., and Thompson, R., 2012. *Inventing adulthoods: A biographical approach to youth transitions*. London: Sage.

Herold, B., 2014. inBloom to shut down amid growing data-privacy concerns. *Digital Education* (blog), *Education Week*, April 21. blogs.edweek.org/edweek/DigitalEducation/2014/04/inbloom_to_shut_down_amid_growing_data_privacy_concerns.html.

Hey, V., 2005. The contrasting social logics of sociality and survival: Cultures of classed be/longing in late modernity. *Sociology* 39, no. 5: 855–872.

Heywood, C., 2004. *A history of childhood*. Cambridge, UK: Polity.

Hidi, S., and Renninger, K.A., 2006. The four-phase model of interest development. *Educational Psychologist* 41, no. 2: 111–127.

Hill, M., and Tisdall, K., 1997. *Children and society*. London: Longman.

Hills, J., Brewer, M., Jenkins, S., Lister, R., Lupton, R., Machin, S., Mills, C., Modood, T., Rees, T., and Riddell, S., 2010. *An Anatomy of Economic Inequality in the UK: Report of the National Equality Panel*. London: Government Equalities Office.

Hochschild, A.R., 1979. Emotion work, feeling rules, and social structure. *American Journal of Sociology* 85, no. 3: 551–575.

Hodkinson, P., and Sparkes, A.C., 1997. Careership: A sociological theory of career decision making. *British Journal of Sociology of Education* 18, no. 1: 29–44.

Hogan, B., and Wellman, B., 2011. The immanent internet redux. In P.H. Cheong, P. Fischer-Nielsen, S. Gelfgren, and C. Ess, eds., *Digital religion, social media and culture: Perspectives, Practices and Futures* (pp. 43–62). New York: Peter Lang.

Hoggart, R., 1969. *The uses of literacy*. London: Penguin Books.

Holloway, S.L., and Pimlott-Wilson, H., 2014. Enriching children, institutionalizing childhood? Geographies of play, extracurricular activities, and parenting in England. *Annals of the Association of American Geographers* 104, no. 3: 613–627.

Holloway, S.L., and Valentine, G., 2000. Spatiality and the new social studies of childhood. *Sociology* 34, no. 4: 763–783.

Hoover, S.M., Clark, L.S., and Alters, D.F., 2004. *Media, home, and family*. New York: Routledge.

Horst, H., 2010a. Families. In M. Ito, S. Baumer, M. Bittanti, d. boyd, R. Cody, B. Herr-Stephenson, and L. Tripp, eds., *Hanging out, messing around, geeking out: Kids living and learning with new media* (pp. 149–194). Cambridge, MA: MIT Press.

Horst, H., 2010b. From MySpace to Facebook: Coming of age in networked public culture. In M. Ito, S. Baumer, M. Bittanti, d. boyd, R. Cody, B. Herr-Stephenson, and L. Tripp, eds., *Hanging out, messing around, geeking out: Kids living and learning with new media* (pp. 92–93). Cambridge, MA: MIT Press.

Horst, H.A., and Miller, D., 2012. The digital and the human: A prospectus for digital anthropology. In H.A. Horst and D. Miller, eds., *Digital anthropology* (pp. 3–36). London: Berg.

Hull, G., and Schultz, K., 2002. *School's out! Bridging out-of-school literacies with classroom practice*. New York: Teachers College Press.

Hunter, I., 1994. *Rethinking the school: Subjectivity, bureaucracy, criticism*. London: Allen & Unwin.

Hutchby, I., 2001. Technologies, texts and affordances. *Sociology* 35, no. 2: 441–456.

Ito, M., 2008. Introduction. In K. Varnelis, ed., *Networked publics* (pp. 1–14). Cambridge, MA: MIT Press.

Ito, M., Baumer, S., Bittanti, M., boyd, d., Cody, R., Herr-Stephenson, B., Horst, H.A., Lange, P.G., Mahendran, D., Martínez, K.Z., Pascoe, C.J., Perkel, D., Robinson, L., Sims, C., and Tripp, L., 2010. *Hanging out, messing around, geeking out: Kids living and learning with new media.* Cambridge, MA: MIT Press.

Ito, M., Gutiérrez, K., Livingstone, S., Penuel, B., Rhodes, J., Salen, K., Schor, J., Sefton-Green, J., and Watkins, C., 2013. *Connected learning: An agenda for research and design.* Irvine, CA: Digital Media and Learning Research Hub.

James, A., ed., 2013. *Socialising children.* Basingstoke, UK: Palgrave Macmillan.

James, A., and James, A.L., eds., 2008. *European childhoods: Cultures, politics and childhoods in Europe.* Basingstoke, UK: Palgrave Macmillan.

James, A., Jenks, C., and Prout, A., 1998. *Theorizing childhood.* Cambridge: Cambridge University Press.

Jenkins, H., 2006. *Fans, bloggers and gamers: Exploring participatory culture.* New York: NYU Press.

Jenkins, H., 2012. "Cultural acupuncture": Fan activism and the Harry Potter Alliance. *Transformative Works & Cultures* 10: 2–21.

Jenkins, H., Clinton, K., Purushotma, R., Robinson, A., and Weigel, M., 2007. *Confronting the challenges of participatory culture: Media education for the 21st century.* Chicago: MacArthur Foundation. https://mitpress.mit.edu/sites/default/files/titles/free_download/9780262513623_Confronting_the_Challenges.pdf.

Jenkins, H., and Kelley, W., 2013. *Reading in a participatory culture: Remixing "Moby-Dick" in the English classroom.* New York: Teachers College Press.

Jenks, C., 1996. The postmodern child. In J. Brannen and M. O'Brien, eds., *Children in families: Research and policy* (pp. 13–25). London: Falmer.

Jessop, B., 2002. *The future of the capitalist state.* Cambridge, UK: Polity.

Jewitt, C., and Parashar, U., 2011. Technology and learning at home: Findings from the evaluation of the Home Access Programme pilot. *Journal of Computer Assisted Learning* 27, no. 4: 303–313.

Jivraj, S., and Khan, O., 2013. *Ethnicity and deprivation in England: How likely are ethnic minorities to live in deprived neighbourhoods?* Manchester: ESRC Centre on Dynamics of Ethnicity, University of Manchester.

Jones, K., 2009. *Culture and creative learning: A literature review.* London: Creativity, Culture and Education.

Jones, O., 2012. *Chavs: The demonization of the working class.* London: Verso.

JWT, 2012. *Gen Z: Digital in their DNA.* New York: JWT. www.jwtintelligence.com/wp-content/uploads/2012/04/F_INTERNAL_Gen_Z_0418122.pdf.

Kao, G., 1995. Asian Americans as model minorities? A look at their academic performance. *American Journal of Education* 103, no. 2: 121–159.

Kassabian, A., 2013. *Ubiquitous listening: Affect, attention, and distributed subjectivity.* Berkeley: University of California Press.

Katz, V.S., 2010. How children of immigrants use media to connect their families to the community. *Journal of Children and Media* 4, no. 3: 298–315.

Kehily, M.J., 2002. *Sexuality, gender and schooling: Shifting agendas in social learning*. London: Routledge.

Kennedy, S., 2010. *Social mobility: Missing an opportunity?* Key Issues for the New Parliament. London: House of Commons Library Research. www.parliament.uk/documents/commons/lib/research/key_issues/Key-Issues-Social-mobility-missing-an-opportunity.pdf.

Kraidy, M., and Murphy, P., 2008. Shifting Geertz: Towards a theory of translocalism in global communication studies. *Communication Theory* 18: 335–355.

Kremer-Sadlik, T., Fatigante, M., and Fasulo, A., 2008. Discourses on family time: The cultural interpretation of family togetherness in Los Angeles and Rome. *Ethos* 36, no. 3: 283–309.

Kremer-Sadlik, T., Izquierdo, C., and Fatigante, M., 2010. Making meaning of everyday practices: Parents' attitudes toward children's extracurricular activities in the United States and in Italy. *Anthropology of Education Quarterly* 4, no. 1: 35–54.

Krotz, F., 2007. The meta-process of "mediatization" as a conceptual frame. *Global Media and Communication* 3, no. 3: 256–260.

Kupiainen, R., 2013. Young people's creative online practices in the context of school community. *Cyberpsychology: Journal of Psychosocial Research on Cyberspace* 7, no. 1: article 8.

Ladson-Billings, G., 1995. But that's just good teaching! The case for culturally relevant pedagogy. *Theory into Practice* 34, no. 3: 159–165.

Ladwig, J., 2010. Beyond academic outcomes. *Review of Research in Education* 34: 113–143.

Lareau, A., 2011. *Unequal childhoods: Class, race, and family life*. 2nd ed. Berkeley: University of California Press.

Lash, S., 2002. Foreword: Individualization in a non-linear mode. In U. Beck and E. Beck-Gernsheim, *Individualization* (pp. vii–xiii). London: Sage.

Leander, K.M., and McKim, K., 2003. Tracing the everyday "sitings" of adolescents on the Internet: A strategic adaptation of ethnography across online spaces. *Education, Communication and Information* 3, no. 2: 211–224.

Leander, K.M., Phillips, N.C., and Taylor, K.H., 2010. The changing social spaces of learning: Mapping new mobilities. *Review of Research in Education* 34, no. 1: 329–394.

Leander, K.M., and Sheehy, M., 2004. *Spatializing literacy research and practice*. New literacies and digital epistemologies 15. New York: Peter Lang.

Lee, N., 2001. *Childhood and society: Growing up in an age of uncertainty*. Milton Keynes, UK: Open University Press.

Lefstein, A., and Snell, J., 2011. Promises and problems of teaching with popular culture: A linguistic ethnographic analysis of discourse genre mixing in a literacy lesson. *Reading Research Quarterly* 46, no. 1: 40–69.

Lemke, J., 2000. Across the scales of time: Artefacts, activities, and meanings in eco-social systems. *Mind, Culture and Activity* 7, no. 4: 273–290.

Lenhart, A., 2015. *Teen, social media and technology overview 2015*. Washington, DC: Pew Research Center. April 9. www.pewinternet.org/2015/04/09/teens-social-media-technology-2015/.

Leurs, K., 2014. Digital throwntogetherness: Young Londoners negotiating otherness on Facebook. *Popular Communication* 12, no. 4: 251–265.

Levinson, B., Foley, D., and Holland, D., eds., 1996. *The cultural production of the educated person: Critical ethnographies of schooling and local practice*. Albany: SUNY Press.

Licoppe, C., 2004. Connected presence: The emergence of a new repertoire for managing social relationships in a changing communications technoscape. *Environment and Planning D: Society and Space* 22: 135–156.

Lievrouw, L., 2004. What's changed about new media? Introduction to the fifth anniversary issue of *New Media & Society*. *New Media & Society* 6, no. 1: 9–15.

Lievrouw, L., and Livingstone, S., 2006. Introduction: The social shaping and consequences of ICTs. In L. Lievrouw and S. Livingstone, eds., *Handbook of new media: Social shaping and social consequences* (pp. 1–15). London: Sage.

Lilley, C., and Ball, R., 2013. *Younger children and social networking sites: A blind spot*. London: National Society for the Prevention of Cruelty to Children.

Ling, R., 2008. *New tech, new ties: How mobile communication is reshaping social cohesion*. Cambridge, MA: MIT Press.

Livingstone, S., 2002. *Young people and new media: Childhood and the changing media environment*. London: Sage.

Livingstone, S., 2005. In defence of privacy: Mediating the public/private boundary at home. In S. Livingstone, ed., *Audiences and publics: When cultural engagement matters for the public sphere* (pp. 163–185). Bristol, UK: Intellect.

Livingstone, S. 2007. The challenge of engaging youth online: Contrasting producers' and teenagers' interpretations of websites. *European Journal of Communication* 22, no. 2: 165–184.

Livingstone, S., 2008. Taking risky opportunities in youthful content creation: Teenagers' use of social networking sites for intimacy, privacy and self-expression. *New Media & Society* 10, no. 3: 393–411.

Livingstone, S., 2009a. *Children and the internet: Great expectations, challenging realities*. Cambridge, UK: Polity.

Livingstone, S., 2009b. Half a century of television in the lives of our children and families. In E. Katz and P. Scannell, eds., *The end of television? Its impact so far*. *Annals of the American Academy of Political and Social Science* 625: 151–163.

Livingstone, S., 2012. Critical reflections on the prospects for ICT in education. *Oxford Review of Education* 38, no. 1: 9–24.

Livingstone, S., and Helsper, E.J., 2008. Parental mediation of children's internet use. *Journal of Broadcasting & Electronic Media* 52, no. 4: 581–599.

Loveless, A., and Williamson, B., 2013. *Learning identities in a digital age: Rethinking creativity, education and technology*. London: Routledge.

Luckin, R., Bligh, B., Manches, A., Ainsworth, S., Crook, C., and Noss, R., 2012. *Decoding learning: The proof, promise and potential of digital education.* London: National Endowment for Science, Technology and the Arts (Nesta).

Luckmann, B., 1970. The small life-worlds of modern man. *Social Research* 37, no. 4: 580–596.

Luke, C., 1989. *Pedagogy, printing and Protestantism: The discourse of childhood.* Albany: SUNY Press.

Lukes, S., 1971. The meanings of "individualism." *Journal of the History of Ideas* 32, no. 1: 45–66.

Lundby, K., ed., 2014. *The handbook on mediatization.* Berlin: Mouton de Gruyter.

Lupton, D., 2014. Self-tracking cultures: Towards a sociology of personal informatics. *OzCHI '14: Proceedings of the 26th Australian Computer-Human Interaction Conference: Designing Futures, the Future of Design.* December 2–5, University of Technology, Sydney, Australia.

MacKenzie, D., and Wajcman, J., eds. 1999. *The social shaping of technology.* 2nd ed. Buckingham, UK: Open University Press.

MacLeod, J., 2009. *Ain't no makin' it: Aspirations and attainment in a low-income neighborhood.* 3rd ed. Boulder, CO: Westview.

Madianou, M., and Miller, D., 2012. *Migration and new media: Transnational families and polymedia.* Abingdon, UK: Routledge.

Mans, M., 2009. *Living in worlds of music: A view of education and values.* Rotterdam, Netherlands: Springer.

Mansell, R., 2012. *Imagining the internet: Communication, innovation, and governance.* Oxford: Oxford University Press.

Mansell, R., and Silverstone, R., eds., 1996. *Communication by design: The politics of information and communication technologies.* New York: Oxford University Press.

Marcus, G., Neumark, T., and Broome, S., 2011. *Power lines.* London: RSA.

Marcus, G.E., 1995. Ethnography in/of the world system: The emergence of multi-sited ethnography. *Annual Review of Anthropology* 24: 95–117.

Martorano, B., de Neubourg, C., Natali, L., and Bradshaw, J., 2013. *Child well-being in economically rich countries: Changes in the first decade of the 21st century.* Working Paper 2013-02. Florence, Italy: UNICEF Office of Research.

Marwick, A., and boyd, d., 2014. "It's just drama": Teen perspectives on conflict and aggression in a networked era. *Journal of Youth Studies* 17, no. 9: 1187–1204.

Mascheroni, G., and Olafsson, K., 2014. *Net children go mobile: Risks and opportunities.* Milan, Italy: Educatt.

Massey, D.B., 2005. *For space.* London: Sage.

McClelland, K., and Karen, D., 2009. Analysis. In J. MacLeod, *Ain't no makin' it: Aspirations and attainment in a low-income neighborhood* (pp. 409–463). Boulder, CO: Westview.

McLaughlin, T. 1996. *Street smarts and critical theory: Listening to the vernacular.* Madison: University of Wisconsin Press.

McLeod, J.K., and Vasinda, S., 2009. Electronic portfolios: Perspectives of students, teachers and parents. *Education and Information Technologies* 14, no. 1: 29–38.

McPherson, G.E., 2005. From child to musician: Skill development during the beginning stages of learning an instrument. *Psychology of Music* 33, no. 1: 5–35.

McRobbie, A., and Garber, J., 1976. Girls and subcultures. In S. Hall and P. Jefferson, eds., *Resistance through ritual: Youth cultures in the post-war Britain* (pp. 209–222). London: Hutchinson University Library.

Merleau-Ponty, M., 1979. *Consciousness and the acquisition of language*. Evanston, IL: Northwestern University Press.

Miller, D., and Slater, D., 2000. *The internet: An ethnographic approach*. London: Berg.

Miller, K., 2012. *Playing along: Digital games, YouTube, and virtual performance*. New York: Oxford University Press.

Miller, T., 2005. The avant-garde, bohemia and mainstream culture. In L. Marcus and P. Nicholls, eds., *The Cambridge history of twentieth-century English literature* (pp. 100–116). Cambridge: Cambridge University Press.

Mitchell, W.J.T., 1995. Translator translated: Interview with cultural theorist Homi Bhabha. *Artforum* 33, no. 7: 80–84.

Moje, E., 2000. Critical issues: Circles of kinship, position, and power: Examining the community in community-based research. *Journal of Literacy Research* 32, no. 1: 77–112.

Monahan, T., 2005. *Globalization, technological change, and public education*. New York: Routledge.

Monge, P.R., and Contractor, N.S., 2003. *Theories of communication networks*. Oxford: Oxford University Press.

Morley, D., 2000. *Home territories: Media, mobility and identity*. London: Routledge.

Morley, D., and Silverstone, R., 1990. Domestic communications: Technologies and meanings. *Media, Culture & Society* 12, no. 1: 31–55.

Murray, M., 2004. *Freaks, geeks, and cool kids: American teenagers, schools, and the culture of consumption*. New York: Routledge.

National School Boards Association, 2007. *Creating and connecting: Research and guidelines on online social—and educational—networking*. Alexandria, VA: National School Boards Association.

Nayak, A., 2003. *Race, place and globalization: Youth cultures in a changing world*. Oxford, UK: Berg.

Neale, B., and Flowerdew, J., 2003. Time, texture and childhood: The contours of longitudinal qualitative research. *International Journal of Social Research Methodology* 6, no. 3: 189–199.

Nicholson, V., 2003. *Among the Bohemians: Experiments in living 1900–1939*. London: Penguin.

Nissenbaum, H., 2010. *Privacy in context: Technology, policy, and the internet of social life*. Stanford, CA: Stanford University Press.

Nocon, H., and Cole, M., 2006. School's invasion of "after-school": Colonization, rationalization, or expansion of access? In Z. Bekerman, N.C. Burbules, and

D. Silberman-Keller, eds., *Learning in places: The informal education reader* (pp. 99–121). New York: Peter Lang.

Nuffield Foundation, 2012. *Social trends and mental health: Introducing the main findings.* London: Nuffield Foundation.

Nussbaum, M.C. 2012. *Not for profit: Why democracy needs the humanities.* Princeton, NJ: Princeton University Press.

Ochs, E., and Kemer-Sadlik, T., eds., 2013. *Fast-forward family: Home, work, and relationships in middle-class America.* Berkeley: University of California Press.

OECD (Organisation for Economic Co-operation and Development), 2012. *Connected minds: Technology and today's learners.* Paris: OECD.

Ofcom, 2014. *Children and parents: Media use and attitudes report 2014.* London: Ofcom.

O'Hear, S., and Sefton-Green, J., 2004. Creative "communities": How social and technological worlds collaborate? In D. Miell and K. Littleton, eds., *Collaborative creativity: Contemporary Perspectives* (pp. 113–125). New Haven, CT: Free Association Books.

Olwig, K.F., and Gullov, E., eds., 2003. *Children's places: Cross-cultural perspectives.* London: Routledge.

Osgerby, B., 1998. *Youth in Britain since 1945.* Oxford, UK: Blackwell.

Oswell, D., 2002. *Television, childhood and the home: A history of the making of the child television audience in Britain.* Oxford: Oxford University Press.

Oswell, D., 2012. *The agency of children: From family to global human rights.* Cambridge: Cambridge University Press.

Outhwaite, W. 1994. *Habermas: A critical introduction.* Cambridge, UK: Polity.

Ozcinar, Z., and Ekizoglu, N., 2013. Evaluation of a blog based parent involvement approach by parents. *Computers & Education* 66: 1–10.

Pahl, R., 2000. *On friendship.* Cambridge, UK: Polity.

Park, A., Bryson, C., Clery, E., Curtice, J. and Phillips, M., eds., 2013. *British social attitudes: The 30th report.* London: NatCen Social Research.

Passey, D., 2014. *Inclusive technology enhanced learning: Overcoming cognitive, physical, emotional and geographic challenges.* New York: Routledge.

Paus-Hasebrink, I., Ponte, C., Dürager, A., and Bauwens, J., 2012. Understanding digital inequality: The interplay between parental socialisation and children's development. In S. Livingstone, L. Haddon, and A. Görzig, eds., *Children, risk and safety on the internet: Research and policy challenges in comparative perspective* (pp. 257–272). Bristol, UK: Policy.

Peppler, K., 2013. *New opportunities for interest-driven arts learning in a digital age.* New York: Wallace Foundation.

Perrotta, C., 2013. Assessment, technology and democratic education in the age of data. *Learning, Media and Technology* 38, no, 1: 116–122.

Piketty, T., 2014. *Capital in the twenty-first century.* Trans. Arthur Goldhammer. Cambridge, MA: Harvard University Press.

Pink, S., and Mackley, K.L, 2013. Saturated and situated: Expanding the meaning of media in the routines of everyday life. *Media, Culture & Society* 35, no. 6: 677–691.

Player-Koro, C., 2013. Hype, hope and ICT in teacher education: A Bernsteinian perspective. *Learning, Media and Technology* 38, no. 1: 26–40.

Pollard, A., and Filer, A., 1999. *The social world of pupil career: Strategic biographies through primary school.* London: Continuum.

Pope, D., 2003. *Doing school: How we are creating a generation of stressed out, materialistic, and miseducated students.* New Haven, CT: Yale University Press.

Predelli, L.N., and Cebulla, A., 2011. Perceptions of labour market risks: Shifts and continuities across generations. *Current Sociology* 59, no. 1: 24–41.

Pugh, A.J., 2009. *Longing and belonging: Parents, children, and consumer culture.* Berkeley: University of California Press.

Putnam, R.D., 2015. *Our kids: The American dream in crisis.* New York: Simon & Schuster.

Qvortrup, J., 1995. Childhood and modern society: A paradoxical relationship. In J. Brannen and M. O'Brien, eds., *Childhood and parenthood* (pp. 189–198). London: Institute of Education, University of London.

Radway, J., 1988. Reception study: Ethnography and the problems of dispersed audiences and nomadic subjects. *Cultural Studies* 2, no. 3: 359–376.

Rampton, B., 2006. *Language in late modernity: Interaction in an urban school.* Cambridge: Cambridge University Press.

Rawolle, S., and Lingard, B., 2014. Mediatization and education: A sociological account. In K. Lundby, ed., *Mediatization of Communication (pp. 595–614).* Berlin: De Gruyter Mouton.

Reay, D., 2006. The zombie stalking English schools: Social class and educational inequality. *British Journal of Educational Studies* 54, no. 3: 288–307.

Reich, S.M., Subrahmanyam, K., and Espinoza, G., 2012. Friending, IMing, and hanging out face-to-face: Overlap in adolescents' online and offline social networks. *Developmental Psychology* 48, no. 2: 356–368.

Renninger, K.A., and Hidi, S., 2011. Revisiting the conceptualization, measurement, and generation of interest. *Educational Psychologist* 46, no. 3: 168–184.

Rideout, V., 2014. *Learning at home: Families' educational media use in America.* Families and Media Project. New York: Joan Ganz Cooney Center.

Robinson, L., and Schulz, J., 2013. Net time negotiations within the family. *Information, Communication & Society* 16, no. 4: 542–560.

Rose, J., 2001. *The intellectual life of the British working classes.* New Haven, CT: Yale University Press.

Rose, M., 2009. *Why school? Reclaiming education for all of us.* New York: New Press.

Rose, N., 1999. *Governing the soul: Shaping of the private self.* Sidmouth, UK: Free Association Books.

Rutter, M., Maughan, B., Mortimore, P., Ouston, J., and Smith, A., 1979. *Fifteen thousand hours: Secondary schools and their effects on children.* London and Cambridge, MA: Open Books and Harvard University Press.

Rye, S.A., 2013. Connected youth: Young students' extensibility and use of the internet to search for information. *Nordicom Review* 34, no. 1: 33–48.

Salen, K., ed., 2008. *The ecology of games: Connecting youth, games, and learning.* Cambridge, MA: MIT Press.

Savage, M., 2010. *Identities and social change in Britain since 1940: The politics of method.* Oxford: Oxford University Press.

Scannell, P., 1988. Radio times: The temporal arrangements of broadcasting in the modern world. In P. Drummond and R. Paterson, eds., *Television and its audience: International research perspectives* (pp. 15–31). London: British Film Institute.

Schuller, T., and Desjardins, R., 2007. *Understanding the social outcomes of learning.* Paris: OECD.

Schuller, T., Hammond, C., Bassett-Grundy, A., Preston, J., and Bynner, J., 2004. *The benefits of learning: The impact of education on health, family life and social capital.* London: Routledge Falmer.

Schwartz, D., and Arena, D., 2013. *Measuring what matters most: Choice-based assessments for the digital age.* Cambridge, MA: MIT Press.

Scollon, R., and Scollon, S.W., 2003. *Discourses in place: Language in the material world.* New York: Routledge.

Scott, J., and Carrington, P.J., eds., 2011. *The Sage handbook of social network analysis.* London: Sage.

Scribner, S., and Cole, M., 1981. *The psychology of literacy.* Cambridge, MA: Harvard University Press.

Sefton-Green, J., 2013. *Learning at not-school: A review of study, theory, and advocacy for education in non-formal settings.* Cambridge, MA: MIT Press.

Sefton-Green, J., 2015. Negotiating the pedagogicization of everyday life: The art of learning. In M. Watkins, G. Noble, and C. Driscoll, eds., *Cultural pedagogies and human conduct* (pp. 45–59). New York: Routledge.

Seiter, E., 2005. *The internet playground: Children's access, entertainment, and mis-education.* New York: Peter Lang.

Selwyn, N., 2009. The digital native: Myth and reality. *Aslib Proceedings* 61, no. 4: 364–379.

Selwyn, N., 2010. *Schools and schooling in the digital age: A critical analysis.* London: Routledge.

Selwyn, N., 2013. *Education in a digital world: Global perspectives on a technology and education.* New York: Routledge.

Selwyn, N., 2014. *Distrusting educational technology: Critical questions for changing times.* New York: Routledge.

Selwyn, N., Banaji, S., Hadjithoma-Garstka, C., and Clark, W., 2011. Providing a platform for parents? Exploring the nature of parental engagement with school learning platforms. *Journal of Computer Assisted Learning* 27, no. 4: 314–323.

Sennett, R., 2008. *The craftsman.* New Haven, CT: Yale University Press.

Sennett, R., 2012. *Together.* London: Penguin.

Sennett, R., and Cobb, J. 1972. *The hidden injuries of class.* Cambridge: Cambridge University Press.

Shaw, B., Watson, B., Frauendienst, B., Redecker, A., Jones, T., and Hillman, M., 2013. *Children's independent mobility: A comparative study in England and Germany (1971–2010)*. London: Policy Studies Institute.

Shotter, J., and Gergen, K.J., 1988. *Texts of identity*. London: Sage.

Siapera, E., 2014. Review essay: Diasporas and new media: Connections, identities, politics and affect. *Crossings: Journal of Migration & Culture* 5, no. 1: 173–179.

Silverstone, R., 2005. *Media, technology and everyday life in Europe: From information to communication*. Aldershot, UK: Ashgate.

Silverstone, R., 2006. Domesticating domestication: Reflections on the life of a concept. In T. Berker, M. Hartmann, Y. Punie, and K.J. Ward, eds., *The domestication of media and technology* (pp. 229–248). Maidenhead, UK: Open University Press.

Silverstone, R., Hirsch, E., and Morley, D., 1992. Information and communication technologies and the moral economy of the household. In R. Silverstone and E. Hirsch, eds., *Consuming technologies: Media and information in domestic spaces (pp. 9–17)*. London: Routledge.

Sims, C. 2012. The cutting edge of fun: Making work play at the New American School. PhD dissertation, University of California, Berkeley.

Skeggs, B., 2013. *Class, self, culture*. London: Routledge.

Skelton, C., and Francis, B., 2012. The "renaissance child": High achievement and gender in late modernity. *International Journal of Inclusive Education* 16, no. 4: 441–459.

Smart, C., 2007. *Personal life*. Malden, MA: Polity.

SMCP (Social Mobility and Child Poverty) Commission, 2013. *State of the nation 2013: Social mobility and child poverty in Great Britain*. London: SMCP Commission.

Social Attitudes of Young People Community of Interest. 2014. Social attitudes of young people. In HM Government, ed., *Horizon Scanning Programme*. London: HM Government.

Somekh, B., 2000. New technology and learning: Policy and practice in the UK, 1980–2010. *Education and Information Technologies* 5, no. 1: 19–37.

Somerville, K. 2008. Transnational belonging among second generation youth: Identity in a globalized world. In "Youth and migration," special issue, *Journal of Social Sciences* 10: 23–33.

Spencer, L., and Pahl, R., 2006. *Rethinking friendship: Hidden solidarities today*. Princeton, NJ: Princeton University Press.

Spigel, L., 1992. *Make room for TV: Television and the family ideal in postwar America*. Chicago: University of Chicago Press.

Staksrud, E., 2013. *Children in the online world: Risk, regulation, rights*. Aldershot, UK: Ashgate.

Star, L., and Bowker, G., 2006. How to infrastructure. In L. Lievrouw and S. Livingstone, eds., *The handbook of new media* (updated student ed.; pp. 230–245). London: Sage.

Steele, J.R., and Brown, J.D., 1994. Studying media in the context of everyday life. *Journal of Youth Adolescence* 24, no. 5: 551–576.

Steiner-Adair, C. 2013. *The big disconnect: Protecting childhood and family relationships in the digital age.* London: HarperCollins.

Steinfeld, C., Ellison, N., and Lampe, C. 2008. Social capital, self-esteem, and use of online social network sites: A longitudinal analysis. *Journal of Applied Developmental Psychology* 29: 434–445.

Stevens, P., Lupton, R., Mujtaba, T., and Feinstein, L., 2007. *The development and impact of young people's social capital in secondary schools.* Wider Benefits of Learning Research Report 24. London: Centre for Research on the Wider Benefits of Learning, Institute of Education.

Strand, S., de Coulon, A., Meschi, E., Vorhaus, J., Frumkin, L., Ivins, C., Small, L., Sood, A., Gervais, M.-C., and Rehman, H., 2010. *Drivers and challenges in raising the achievement of pupils from Bangladeshi, Somali and Turkish backgrounds.* London: Department for Children, Schools and Families. www.gov.uk/government /uploads/system/uploads/attachment_data/file/221943/DCSF-RR226.pdf.

Strathern, M., 1996. Cutting the network. *Journal of the Royal Anthropological Institute* 2, no. 3: 517–535.

Sullivan, W.M., 1994. *Education as care of the self: Identity and meaning in the global era.* Bloomington: Poynter Center, Indiana University.

Sundén, J. 2003. *Material virtualities: Approaching online textual embodiment.* New York: Peter Lang.

Taylor, A.S., and Harper, R., 2002. Age-old practices in the "new world": A study of gift-giving between teenage mobile phone users. CHI 2002, April 20–25, Minneapolis, MN.

Thomas, D., and Brown, J.S., 2011. *A new culture of learning.* North Charleston, SC: CreateSpace.

Thomas, M., ed., 2011. *Digital education: Opportunities for social collaboration.* New York: Palgrave Macmillan.

Thompson, A., 1998. Not the color purple: Black feminist lessons for educational caring. *Harvard Educational Review* 68, no. 4: 522–554.

Thompson, J.B., 2011. Shifting boundaries of public and private life. *Theory, Culture & Society* 28, no. 4: 49–70.

Thomson, R., 2009. *Unfolding lives.* Bristol, UK: Policy.

Thomson, R., Bell, R., Holland, J., Henderson, S., McGrellis, S., and Sharpe, S., 2002. Critical moments: Choice, chance and opportunity in young people's narratives of transition. *Sociology* 36, no. 2: 335–354.

Thorne, B., 1994. *Gender play: Girls and boys in school.* New Brunswick, NJ: Rutgers University Press.

Thornham, H., and Myers, C.A., 2012. Architectures of youth: Visibility, agency and the technological imaginings of young people. *Social & Cultural Geography* 13, no. 7: 783–800.

Threadgold, S., and Nilan, P., 2009. Reflexivity of contemporary youth, risk and cultural capital. *Current Sociology* 57, no. 1: 47–68.

Tomlinson, J., 1999. *Globalization and culture.* Chicago: University of Chicago Press.

Turkle, S., 1984. *The second self: Computers and the human spirit.* New York: Simon & Schuster.

Turkle, S., 2011. *Alone together: Why we expect more from technology and less from each other.* New York: Basic Books.

Turkle, S., 2015. *Reclaiming conversation: The power of talk in a digital age.* New York: Penguin.

UNICEF Office of Research, 2013. *Child well-being in rich countries: A comparative overview.* Innocenti Report Card 11. Florence, Italy: UNICEF Office of Research. www.unicef-irc.org/publications/pdf/rc11_eng.pdf.

US Department of Education (Office of Educational Technology), 2010. *Learning: Powered by technology; National Education Technology Plan 2010.* Alexandria, VA: US Department of Education.

van Cleemput, K., 2011. Friendship type, clique formation and the everyday use of communication technologies in a peer group. *Information, Communication & Society* 15, no. 8: 1258–1277.

van Dijck, J., 2013a. *The culture of connectivity: A critical history of social media.* Oxford: Oxford University Press.

van Dijck, J., 2013b. "You have one identity": Performing the self on Facebook and LinkedIn. *Media, Culture & Society* 35, no. 2: 199–215.

van Dijk, J., 2012. *The network society.* 3rd ed. London: Sage.

van Zoonen, L. 2013. From identity to identification: Fixating the fragmented self. *Media, Culture & Society* 35, no. 1: 44–51.

Varnelis, K., 2008. Conclusion: The meaning of network culture. In K. Varnelis, ed., *Networked publics* (pp. 145–163). Cambridge, MA: MIT Press.

Vertovec, S., 2007. Super-diversity and its implications. *Ethnic and Racial Studies* 29, no. 6: 1024–1054.

Vickery, J.R., 2014. The role of after-school digital media clubs in closing participation gaps and expanding social networks. *Equity & Excellence in Education* 47, no. 1: 78–95.

Vincent, C., and Ball, S.J., 2007. "Making up" the middle class child: Families, activities and class dispositions. *Sociology* 41: 1061–1077.

Visscher, A., Wild, P., Smith, D., and Len, N., 2003. Evaluation of the implementation, use and effects of a computerised management information system in English secondary schools. *British Journal of Educational Technology* 34, no. 3: 357–366.

Walkerdine, V., Lucey, H., and Melody, J., 2001. *Growing up girl.* Basingstoke, UK: Palgrave.

Warschauer, M., 2006. *Laptops and literacy: Learning in the wireless classroom.* New York: Teachers College Press.

Warschauer, M., and Matuchniak, T., 2010. New technology and digital worlds: Analyzing evidence of equity in access, use, and outcomes. *Review of Research in Education* 34, no. 1: 179–225.

Watkins, M., 2011. *Discipline and learn: Bodies, pedagogy and writing.* Amsterdam: Sense.

Watson, S., and Saha, A., 2013. Suburban drifts: Mundane multiculturalism in outer London. *Ethnic and Racial Studies* 36, no. 12: 2016–2034.

Webb, P., 2011. Family values, social capital and contradictions of American modernity. *Theory, Culture & Society* 28, no. 4: 96–123.

Weis, L., 2004. *Class reunion: The remaking of the American white working class.* London: Routledge.

Wellman, B., and Rainie, L., 2012. *Networked: The new social operating system.* Cambridge, MA: MIT Press.

Wessendorf, S., 2014. "Being open but sometimes closed": Conviviality in a super-diverse London neighbourhood. *European Journal of Cultural Studies* 17, no. 4: 392–405.

White House, 2013. President Obama unveils ConnectED initiative to bring America's students into the digital age. 6 June. Washington, DC: Office of the Press Secretary.

Whitty, G., 2010. Revisiting school knowledge: Some sociological perspectives on new school curricula. *European Journal of Education* 45, no. 1: 28–45.

Wilkinson, R., and Pickett, K., 2010. *The spirit level: Why equality is better for everyone.* London: Penguin.

Willett, D.R., Richards, D.C., Marsh, P.J., Burn, P.A., and Bishop, D.J.C., 2013. *Children, media and playground cultures: Ethnographic studies of school playtimes.* London: Palgrave Macmillan.

Williams, R., 1961a. *Culture and society.* London: Fontana.

Williams, R., 1961b. *The long revolution.* London: Chatto and Windus.

Williamson, H., 2004. *The Milltown boys revisited.* Oxford, UK: Berg.

Willis, P.E., 1978. *Learning to labour: How working class kids get working class jobs.* Aldershot, UK: Ashgate.

Wingard, L., and Forsberg, L., 2009. Parent involvement in children's homework in American and Swedish dual-earner families. *Journal of Pragmatics* 41, no. 8: 1576–1595.

Witteborn, S., 2012. Forced migrants, new media practices, and the creation of locality. In I. Volkmer, ed., *The handbook of global media research* (pp. 313–329). Chichester, UK: Wiley-Blackwell.

Woodman, D. 2009. The mysterious case of the pervasive choice biography: Ulrich Beck, structure/agency, and the middling state of theory in the sociology of youth. *Journal of Youth Studies* 12, no. 3: 243–256.

Wortham, S., 2005. *Learning identity: The joint emergence of social identification and academic learning.* Cambridge: Cambridge University Press.

Yin, R.K., 2014. *Case study research: Design and methods.* London: Sage.

Ziehe, T., 1994. From living standard to life style. *Young: Nordic Journal of Youth Research* 2, no. 2: 2–16.

Index

Abby (class member), 2, 52, 214, 256, 299n12, 309n3; bullied at VFS, 153; family's emotional support, 154, 166; father on communication media, 169; gendering exception, 56; music appreciation, 54, 153, 304n9; parents' description, 43, 153; on teachers' relationship with, 118

academic direction decisions, 57

Adam (class member), 3, 77, 166, 256, 282n33; anger and school refusal, 162; bilingualism, 43; the class relationships, 63; computer gaming levels, 71, 138, 173, 175, 224; end of project involvement in schoolwork, 175; learning integration, 180, 184; learning space, *174*; *A Life in the Day of VFS* participation, 57; mother's and father's computer gaming thoughts, 161–63, 173, 299n21

Adriana (class member), 1, 55, 77, 166, 256, 282n33; bilingualism, 43; the class relationship, 63, 225; digital media restrictions, 299n19; family's television watching, 159–60; father, on SIMS, 145; father's acceptance of levels, 134–35; home for, 149; homework and, 54; multiple media devices, 157–58; reluctant piano learning, 192, 193, 194–95, 208; on resistance in classroom, 120, 124, 293n30; show-off strategy, 122

Aiden (class member), 2, 256; black London English use, 100; disruptive exclusion, 214; expulsions of, 98; Facebook communications, 98–99; on peer interactions separate from school, 99,

100; transgressive networking and, 98–101

Alice (class member), 2, 74, 113, 256; bohemian cultural capital, 65, 151; in clique, 72, 105, 227; on designated seating, 112; domestic media of, 160; dyslexia, 43; home and, 151–52; mother's confusion over levels, 134; music learning experiences, 304n9

Alone Together (Turkle), 165

alternative visions of learning, 180–82, 184, 251–52; music, 199–201, 208

Alvermann, D. E., 293n21

Amin, A., 110–11

anger management techniques, 87–88, 112–13, 162, 226

Arnett, J., 34

arrival at school, 49, 280n13, 281n20

arts learning, 110, 139, 151, 181–82, 199–200, 205, 303n2

assessment, 130, 296n23

attainment: criteria defining, 295n5; culture of anxiety over, 168; at different levels, 132, 302n20; music level, 132–33, 137; standardized level of, 133

avant-garde cultural capital, 210, 306n27

Bauman, Z., 24, 34, 272n17

Baym, N., 269n6

BBM (Blackberry Messenger), 68, 89, 90, 122, 267, 293n28

Beck, U., 23, 26, 278n103, 280n14; choice biography, 36; on individualization, 277n88; on social inequality, 37; on social reproduction, 273n34

About the Authors

Sonia Livingstone is Professor in the Department of Media and Communications at the London School of Economics and Political Science. She is the author or editor of nineteen books, including *Media Regulation: Governance and the Interests of Citizens and Consumers* (with Peter Lunt, 2012) and *Digital Technologies in the Lives of Young People* (edited with Chris Davies and John Coleman, 2014). She leads the research projects "Parenting for a Digital Future" and "Global Kids Online."

Julian Sefton-Green is Principal Research Fellow at the Department of Media and Communications at the London School of Economics and Political Science and Associate Professor at the University of Oslo. He is the author or editor of eleven books including *Learning at Not-School* (2013) and *Identity, Community and Learning Lives in the Digital Age* (edited with Ola Erstad 2013). He is the series editor for the Connected Youth and Digital Futures series.

Lightning Source UK Ltd.
Milton Keynes UK
UKOW02f2124070716

277867UK00003B/76/P